On the Way to the Future

HANS SCHWARZ

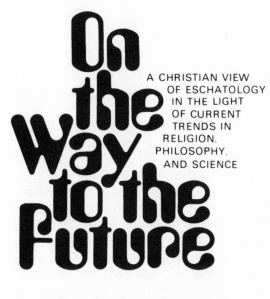

On the Way to the Future

A CHRISTIAN VIEW
OF ESCHATOLOGY
IN THE LIGHT
OF CURRENT
TRENDS IN
RELIGION,
PHILOSOPHY,
AND SCIENCE

REVISED EDITION

AUGSBURG Publishing House • Minneapolis

MANUFACTURED IN THE UNITED STATES OF AMERICA

Contents

PART II
VIEWS AND ISSUES TO CONSIDER

PART III
WHAT CAN WE HOPE FOR?

b. Creative newness of Christ's resurrection
c. Christ's resurrection as the presupposition of our own resurrection
d. Resurrection of the body
e. "Between" death and resurrection
   Time as a this-worldly entity
   The eternity of God as fulfillment of time
   Death as finality and transition

Preface

Speak out, O saints of God!
Despair engulfs earth's frame;
As heirs of God's baptismal grace,
His word of hope proclaim.
(Lutheran Book of Worship 383)

WHEN I MENTIONED TO COLLEAGUES that I planned to revise *On the Way to the Future*, the immediate reaction usually was: Does this mean that you have changed your view on eschatology? Or is your revision connected with the delay of the parousia? With a qualified "no" I attempted to assure the inquirers that neither was the case. My fundamental convictions about eschatology have not changed and neither have the intervening years necessitated a revision with regard to Christ's second coming. Yet I hope that I have not ceased learning in these years; certainly the world around us has not stopped changing. Therefore, this revised edition provides me with the opportunity to add discussions of some views and issues that did not exist—at least I did not see them—when the book first appeared in 1972, and delete some sections that now appear less important. I also coveted the opportunity to formulate some sections more precisely and to learn from the suggestions of others and from the reviews. Thus the whole book has been thoroughly updated with regard to language, style, issues, and argumentation.

Again, I would like to express my gratitude to the various publishers for their generous consent to allow reprint of the passages quoted. The material contained in this book has been presented many times in lectures and discussions with colleagues, students, pastors, and laity. If someone finds this or that phrase familiar, it may show how much I owe to the questions, criticisms, and suggestions I have encountered. My special thanks to my colleague, Jim Schaaf, who again undertook the arduous task of improving my style. His wife, Phyllis, must be thanked again for typing the final draft of the manuscript with both speed and accuracy. Larry Hamilton deserves thanks for checking out the references, helping with the bibliography, and improving the. coherence of the manuscript. Ron Grissom again did an excellent job with proofreading and compiling the indices with help from Gary Rawson. Finally, I want to mention our growing children, Hans and Krista, who did not see me much during the final stages of this revision, but who are always anxious for at least a quick hug and an occasional evening hour in my study. However, I would like to dedicate this revised edition to my patient and enduring wife, May, who always breathes a justified sigh of relief when one literary venture is finished and hopes that there is at least a little break before the next deadline arrives.

Hans Schwarz

Columbus, Ohio

Introduction: Eschatology and the Race for Survival

DURING THE LAST 35 YEARS we have grown accustomed to the permanent threat of global extinction through nuclear warfare. While this threat has made the future more uncertain, it has not demanded that we change our way of life. This situation has changed radically, however, with the increasing dominance of oil-producing countries over industrialized economies, the Arab oil embargo of 1973, the dismal prognoses of the Club of Rome, and a growing awareness of the finitude of our planet and the limitedness of its resources.

Granted, some older people in our society may still feel that there are enough resources available to allow them to live their lives without any drastic changes. But younger people cannot evade the issue. The question for them is no longer, "How much better will we live than our parents?" but instead, "Will we be able to survive the continuously increasing strain on the earth's resources with dignity?" And even the generation that is in the prime of its life can ask no longer, "How can we best reap the fruits of our labor once we retire?" but rather, "Is there anything left to reap once we retire?" All of us, in one way or another, are haunted by the issue of our personal and corporate survival. The big question for us is no longer simply how to shape the future; the future has become less predictable than ever in regard to natural resources, political alliances, population expansion, and employment security. The fundamental question for us today is how to live with meaning and confidence in the present if the future is becoming more and more uncertain.

Of course, we could simply close our eyes to the future and devote our energy to attempting to solve the urgent issues of the present. Yet it is precisely this myopic vision in which only the present really matters that, pursued individually and corporately, has brought us to our current dilemma. If we want to survive at all, let alone in dignity, on this globe, we cannot just blindly stumble along the road toward the future. We must recognize that every one of our present decisions deeply shapes and informs our future and the future of others. Thus the biblical admonition that sooner or later we will reap what we have sown (Gal. 6:7) will prove to be truer than we ever imagined.

When we consult Scripture with this in mind, we notice that it tells us not only that our present attitude affects our future and the future of others but also that our understanding of the future fundamentally affects our approach to present issues. Since Albert Schweitzer's seminal work at the beginning of this century, theologians have continuously reminded us that eschatology, or the doctrine of the last things, has informed the whole message of the New Testament. At the same time, theologians have failed to relate this eschatological outlook convincingly to our own situation. The reason for this is evident. Our everyday life reflects an emphasis on the present, or at most the immediate future, and a disinterest in the final end of all history. We have become so much children of the world we have shaped that we feel uneasy if we are not in control of affairs. And, of course, we consider ourselves to be more in control of that which is close at hand than of the distant future or end of history. Accordingly, we become children of the present, setting our minds on instant results.

Biblical eschatology runs counter to our attempt to control the present. We try to do everything to eliminate the impact of the last things in our everyday life. Even if we are still exposed to the doctrine of the last things in the traditional teachings of our church, it does not appeal to us any longer.

Our attempt to forget the last things is shown best in our attitude toward death. Prospects such as the threat of a global, push-button war, frequent gun fights in metropolitan areas and an inescapable death toll in daily traffic make us accept a sudden death as a by-product of modern life. The term "traffic victim" makes us believe that death on the road is not the fault of a careless driver or of a careless pedestrian, but the result of our modern traffic conditions. We are used to these daily death reports, and unless a whole busload of people is killed in one accident it hardly makes the front page of the newspapers. Sudden death is an undesirable but inescapable by-product of modern living, and is hardly understood as leading up to the last things.

Even when death hits us personally, for instance when one of our loved ones dies, our feelings are only slightly different. We are embarrassed with this occasion and a little helpless. But soon we regain our composure and try our best to belittle and forget death. Evelyn Waugh's "Death in Hollywood" gives a shockingly vivid description of our attempts to do away with the embarrassing fact that everyone has to die.[1] First, we try to counteract the basic law of nature that everything in our world is doomed to decay. Cosmetologists are employed to restore the life-likeness of the corpse, because we do not want to admit that death has interfered with our artificial environment.

Second, we do not want to admit in our vocabulary that someone has died. Death is an impolite word.

> Undertaker has been supplanted by "funeral director" or "mortician." (Even the classified section of the telephone directory gives recognition to this; in its pages you will find "Undertakers—see Funeral Directors.") Coffins are "caskets"; hearses are "coaches," or "professional cars"; flowers are "floral tributes"; corpses are "loved ones," but mortuary etiquette dictates that a specific corpse be referred to by name only—as, "Mr. Jones"; cremated ashes are "remains." Euphemisms such as "slumber room," "reposing room," and "calcination—the *kindlier heat*" abound in the funeral business.[2]

Finally, we have also done away with a special mourning color. In most other countries, whether pagan or Christian, the immediate relatives of the dead dress in a special mourning color, mostly white or black, for a certain period of time. With this, affection to the dead is indicated and other people are encouraged to shield the mourners from the ensuing hardship. Often the mourning colors are at the same time colors of joy, to express that the dead have reached their destiny and are now in union with their god(s).

During the Middle Ages life was centered much more around death. The allegorical concept of the Dance of Death expressed the all-conquering power of death and influenced the thinking of many generations. Its impact can be seen in most countries of Western Europe in poetry, music and visual arts which depicted and dramatized processions of the living and the dead. Through the encounter with the Black Death in the mid-14th century it gained momentum and was soon popularized by the belief in the nocturnal dances of the dead as part of their purgatory punishment. Paintings of that time show us people of all classes dancing to the tune of death. This motive with half-decayed corpses was used by the church to lead people to repentance. The quest of Martin Luther: "How do I find a gracious God?" is certainly not unrelated to the theme of the Dance of Death and to other topics such as the *dies irae* (day of wrath), *memento mori* (a reminder of death), and *ars moriendi* (art of dying). Though Luther discovered that the Judgment Day need not be conceived as a day of wrath *(dies irae),* but a day of joy, he did not take it less seriously. In reading the letters of his later years one gets the impression that his outlook is more determined by longing for death than by craving for life.[3]

We are now more than ever aware of the sudden possibility of death in knowing that a heart attack can terminate our life in the blink of an eye, and in being constantly threatened with an "all-out" atomic war. But our life outlook is in neither a positive nor a negative way determined by the uncontrollable fact of death. We do not want to admit that death is the final incalculable end of our life. This became evident in the enthusiastic response to the first heart transplants. The possibility of removing the death barrier seemed to emerge, and we were again hoping for eternal life here on earth. Medical doctors are already doing their best to prolong life and they would rather "pull the plug" too late than too soon. Many people sacrifice the pleasures of gourmet cooking and try through dietary asceticism to escape from threatening heart attacks, while politicians spend a million dollars a day to save us from the attacks of other people.

But why do books abound that describe the end times in vivid colors? Why do doomsday prophets, both secular and religious, get a mass following? For instance, Hal Lindsey's book, *The Late Great Planet Earth,* has sold in the millions and has even been made into a movie. Robert Heilbroner's book, *An Inquiry into the Human Prospect,* was the focus of a special symposium of the Institute of Religion in an Age of Science. Elisabeth Kübler-Ross started a movement that no longer considers "death" and "dying" unspeakable words, but investigates the very stages of death. As one result many states are considering or have enacted legislation on death with dignity, i.e., without unnecessary and prolonged human suffering in cases of terminal disease. Courses on death and dying have been introduced in many college and high school curricula and have become amazingly attractive. Even more attractive have become courses on the occult and attempts to prove scientifically that there is indeed life beyond our present life on earth. How shall we interpret this resurgent interest in "the end"?

The areas dealing with human extremity have been shrouded in mystery for so long that people rightly want to know what is going on behind the taboo curtains of the funeral homes and hospital wards. Thus funeral homes are conducting tours for the public, and funeral directors are giving lectures on the various aspects of their profession. This emerging openness concerning death is certainly a healthy sign. But present preoccupation with the end and the beyond involves more than mere curiosity.

Ernest Becker in his award-winning book, *The Denial of Death,* gave us a clue to the larger context of our question when we claimed that our basic life attitude is death-denying. We do not want to admit that we are mortal. Thus our interest in the future, death, and the last things, as stimulated by people such as Robert Heilbroner, Elizabeth Kübler-Ross, Hal Lindsey, Raymond A. Moody *(Life Beyond Life),* and many others, is not to learn how to live as if each day were our last. The opposite is true. If we can avert threatening doom, if we can decipher the stages of death and the timetable for the coming of the eschaton, and if we find the way to life beyond life, we have beaten the surprise moment that Jesus spoke of when he cautioned: "But of that day and hour no one knows . . ." (Matt. 24:36). We can relax, since we presume that we finally know how things work. We may consider our end as inevitable, but we know the details of its final stage and therefore we will be in charge, even of our own doom. Evangelistic preachers, such as Billy Graham, still get immense applause when they proclaim:

> That's the way a Christian should live his life, in constant anticipation of the return of Jesus Christ! If we could live every day as though it might be the very last one before the final judgment, what a difference it would make here on earth!
>
> But we don't like to think that way! We don't like to think that our carefully made plans, our long-range schemes may be interrupted by the trumpets of God! We're so engrossed in our own little activities that we can't bear the thought of having anything spoil them! Too many people would rather say, "Oh well, the end of the world hasn't come yet, so why think about it—it's probably a thousand years away!" [4]

But who really cares about such a message? Does it ever penetrate beneath our skin? Hardly, because the style of our life is so different from the time of Jesus or even from that of the Middle Ages.

We sing from our hymnals, "Refresh your people on their toilsome way; lead us from night to never-ending day," [5] but leaving the church service, we attempt to grab all the gusto we can get. Life is not supposed to be a vale of toil and tears. Emotional upsets are cured through psychiatric treatment, through pills, or in a less expensive way through our pastor. Life must be thrilling and exciting and we are usually too busy to be bothered with any last things. While people of past generations had to hope for a life beyond, because life here was short and filled with drudgery, for the majority of us there is no such need. The claim of Karl Marx that "religion is only the illusory sun which revolves round man as long as he does not revolve round himself" and that *"the task of history,* therefore, once the *world beyond the truth* has disappeared, is to establish the *truth of this world"* is already a historical fact for us when applied to eschatology.[6] We have almost succeeded in forgetting the last things and instead devote exclusive attention to life here on earth.

The last things are no longer appealing. The picturesque language of a celestial banquet with which the Bible frequently describes eternal life and heaven is out of place for people who have to watch their diet. And the prospect of golden streets, gates of pearls, and celestial choirs does not mean much in an affluent society. They would be interesting museum pieces or something you could visit while touring Disneyland or other amusement parks, but to live there would be a different matter. Our present life is in constant opposition to any life beyond. While the life beyond should be devoted to eternal worship and service of God, we find enjoyment in busy streets, and even good church members hardly find time for their daily devotions. We read in the New Testament that in heaven there will be no male nor female, while our life here is centered around sex, and we are "out" if we are not informed about the latest sex techniques. In heaven, we are told, we will mostly sing hymns and adore God, while here it is one of the most frustrating jobs to recruit new choir members. Above that, Sunday school attendance is declining and atheism is increasing all over the world. We could continue to list the characteristics of our attitude here on earth which are clearly opposite to those which are expected from us in heaven.

We can only conclude that our life here on earth is in no way determined by God's eternity. While access to life beyond death depends on God's grace, access to life here on earth depends on our own success; and while forgiveness of sins is the essential prerequisite of heavenly

bliss, earthly blessing is determined by our own efficiency. We have become mature, we have taken the future in our own hands and do not
rely any longer on vague promises of a life hereafter.

Secular progress founded in Christian eschatology: The amazing fact
remains, however, that modern life, with its confidence in humanity and
its ability to determine the future, is a result of the Judeo-Christian
environment out of which modernity originated. Secular progress presupposes a linear concept of time, a time arrow that has a definite starting point and a definite goal. This linear understanding of time originated in the Judeo-Christian religion. As far as we know, all other world-
views and religions are confined to a cyclical understanding of time.[7]

For instance, in the Canaanite religion of the neighbors of Israel the
two seasonal gods Baal and Mot determined the religious life of the
people.[8] In the beginning of summer the people lamented the death of
Baal and the triumph of the death god Mot, because in the summer
drought all vegetation dried out and perished through the merciless rays
of the sun and the glowing winds of the desert. Half a year later the
people rejoiced and celebrated the death of Mot and the "resurrection"
of the fertility god Baal when the winter rain drenched the dry ground
and promised a good crop.

Such a seasonal rhythm between "life and death" does not provide
much incentive for any long-range planning, because humanity feels
itself subjected to the power of nature. The Indian religions of Buddhism
and Hinduism provide even less stimulus to engage in any intensive
planning for the future. They advocate as one of the main goals of this
life the negation of all craving for life, in order to break out of the fatal
samsara of birth, death, and reincarnation. Any interest in the future
and any appreciation of the life here on earth would contradict the
dominant cyclical understanding of time.

One might argue that the Greeks are an exception, because they
reached a very high cultural level without a linear concept of time. There
certainly is some truth in this argument. But when we penetrate the
cultural facade, we realize very quickly that the Greek view of life was
utterly pessimistic. During the classical period of Greek history the gods
of Homer looked like deified people and were themselves subject to the
destiny of the world.[9] In later Hellenism, the mystery religions indicate
an unfulfilled yearning for immortality in which the Christian hope of
resurrection of the dead easily found open ears. Friedrich Nietzsche in

his *Philosophy in the Tragic Age of the Greek* advocated the basic understanding of time as "an eternal recurrence of the same."

The British historian Arnold Toynbee, who was largely influenced by
Greek philosophy, wanted to understand all history as a rhythmic pattern of challenge and response.[10] One civilization emerges, attains its
height, and provokes another civilization to originate. The latter conflicts
with the former, gains strength while fighting the other, and finally
prevails until a third emerges. Like the waves of the sea crashing against
the shore and receding, one civilization after the other is doomed to
death without any evident progress.

Why is the Judeo-Christian religion so different that it can provide
the ground for the modern emphasis on this world and a concern for
the future? The reason for this can be found in two basic convictions:
the belief in one God and the identifying of this one God as the creator
and redeemer of everything that is. Often the people of Israel were attracted to the polytheism of their neighbors, but their religious leaders
always brought them back to Yahweh, the only God. Though Yahweh
was in a special sense regarded as the divine head of the Hebrew community, this theocracy tended to be universalistic.[11] Especially under the
influence of the prophetic movement, that is, from about the middle of
the eighth century B.C. onward, the Israelites thought of Yahweh more and
more as the divine head of all humanity, while the neighboring nations
still worshiped their respective particularistic gods.

How decisive this monotheistic and universalistic view of God is can
be shown by comparing the Judeo-Christian religion with Zoroastrianism.
Both conceive history as a forward movement, but the strict dualism
between the two main gods Ormuzd and Ahriman, while finally resolved
in the eschaton, prevented Zoroastrianism from pursuing the idea of
progress.[12] The Judeo-Christian belief in historic progression is largely
due to the understanding of history as salvation history *(Heilsgeschichte)*.
The God of Israel is not a God of the past but of the future. This is
already indicated in the Old Testament covenant concept and is even
more emphasized through apocalyptic periodization of history in the
intertestamental period.

Greco-Roman thinking was past-oriented and mainly interested in the
eternal laws beyond and above history out of which historical events
flowed in eternal occurrence and recurrence.[13] Thus the Greeks were not
concerned about the Lord of history, but about the regularity and steadi-
ness of the cosmos which they first perceived in the movements of the

heavenly bodies.[14] In the Judeo-Christian religion God was conceived as the agent of history, who works in and with history. Though the God of Israel undoubtedly was first understood as the redeemer of Israel, the consequent development of the universalistic view of God led to the understanding of God as the creator of everything that is. One should realize, however, that the gradual understanding of Yahweh as the creator of the world did not evolve to replace other creation stories that might have been prevalent within the Israelite community. As soon as the concept of creation emerged, the Israelites assumed Yahweh as the creator.

It is vital for the Judeo-Christian faith that the understanding of Yahweh as creator did not develop as a separate belief system parallel to the notion of Yahweh as the redeemer. The belief in God the creator was conceived in a strictly soteriological way [15] to assert that the God who will provide the redemption of the world *did* also create it. Yahweh provided the origin of the world, he is active in the world, and he will provide the redemption of the world. This latter part came to its fulfillment in the Christian faith when the history of Jesus of Nazareth was understood as the redemptive act of God. Thus history had a definite beginning (its creation), a definite course (the present acts of God), and a definite goal (redemption in and through Christ). History had a goal worth living for, and the present gained its well-deserved recognition too because it was the arena in which the faithful could prove themselves to be eligible for that final goal.

There was no emphasis on humanity though. In the Judeo-Christian tradition it was clearly understood that humanity could never reach the final goal without the saving grace of God. This emphasis on the grace of God is already expressed in the covenant concept. According to Jewish thinking a covenant is always offered by a stronger power (Yahweh) to a weaker power (the Israelite community) and not vice versa. When the Christian church saw itself in continuance with the Old Testament community the church found it impossible to accept the prevailing humanistic anthropology of the Greco-Roman world. In the Greco-Roman world, history was seen as a record of human deeds, purposes, successes and failures. "The gods have no plan of their own for the development of human affairs; they only grant success or decree failure for the plans of men.[16] Christianity, however, rejected such optimistic ideas of human nature. The inability to achieve clearly planned goals was no longer understood as accidental but as a permanent element in human nature,[17] arising out of the condition of humanity as a fallen creature. Especially Augustine with his concept of a corrupt humanity influenced the thinking of the Western world for at least a thousand years.[18]

But, at the same time, this did not indicate a rejection of humanity. Admittedly, the historical process is not the working-out of humanity's purposes, but of God's, because it is basically salvation history. We do not control the goal of history; God does. But God's purpose is not self-gratifying. It is a purpose intended for us, embodied in human life, and achieved through the activity of human wills. God predetermines the final goal, and he sees to it that everything will eventually move in this direction. But each human being is a historically important and responsible agent. We know what we want and pursue it, though often we do not know why we want it and therefore might stand in the way of obtaining what we want.

But God still works through us, even when we resist his purpose. We receive ultimate dignity and importance only as vehicles of God's redemptive purpose. All hope is founded and centered in God and not in the belief in progress or in humanity. The acting and active God who provided the beginning, who controls the present, and who will provide the future is the decisive center of all Christian and Jewish hope. Even now Christian churches still emphasize human unworthiness, though sometimes this is done more out of tradition than out of conviction, and it is questionable whether the hope in an active and gracious God still determines the life-orientation of most church members.

Estrangement between secular progress and Christian hope: Throughout the Middle Ages God-confidence prevailed over self-confidence. The pope ranked higher than the emperor, and everything was done to the glory of God and through God's grace. Gradually, however, humanity became more confident in itself.

One of the first documents in which self-confidence prevailed over God-confidence was René Descartes' *Discourse on Method* (1637). It is probably not just coincidence that this treatise was written during the devastating and bewildering time of the Thirty Years' War.[19] Descartes introduced radical doubt into modern philosophy and into Western thought; he stated that it is possible to doubt everything.[20] But still the "I" is there even in the midst of all doubt. *Someone* has to doubt. Otherwise there could be nothing. Consequently, the "I" of the solitary human being became the foundation of all reality. Though Descartes still needed God to guarantee for him the reality of the world outside him, the decisive point was made. Humanity is the center of everything; it is more reliable to trust in humanity than anything or anyone else.

One hundred fifty years later Immanuel Kant went a decisive step further in his essay "Answer to the Question: What Is Enlightenment?" (1783) in saying:

> Enlightenment is man's release from his self-incurred tutelage. Tutelage is man's inability to make use of his understanding without direction from another. Self-inflicted is this tutelage when its cause lies not in lack of reason but in lack of resolution and courage to use it without direction from another. *Sapere aude!* "Have courage, to use your own reason!"—that is the motto of enlightenment.[21]

Kant is here advocating human freedom in political and religious matters and the dominance of human intellect and reason over any outside force. Humanity should no longer be dependent on someone or something else, and Kant calls such dependence immaturity. We have become mature and are capable of determining our own destiny. This optimistic attitude prevailed throughout the enlightenment era.

Gottfried Ephraim Lessing in *The Education of the Human Race* (1780) draws an important analogy between education and revelation. Education is revelation made to the individual, while revelation is an education which has come and still continues to come to the whole human race. Nevertheless, education does not give a person anything one might not have derived from "within oneself," but one merely obtains it more quickly and easily. By the same token, revelation gives to the race nothing that human reason, left to itself, might not also have attained, although it has given, and significantly continues to give, the most important of these things more quickly.[22] This would mean that according to Lessing the goal of human progress is no longer found beyond humanity, but in humanity itself. But Lessing did not yet realize that his insistence on the rediscovery of "innate ideas" as the goal of progress must necessarily exclude true progress in the sense of creative novelty. Still the optimistic trust in the newly established self-confidence continued.

Charles Darwin's theory of evolution in the 19th century made humanity even more optimistic, because now the door seemed to be open for new and unprecedented human progress. If we had evolved so high above the animal world, we could evolve much higher. While Kant emphasized human autonomy, that we should have enough self-confidence to determine our own views, here the next step was taken with the implicit hope that we are able to evolve beyond our present state.

Herbert Spencer shaped the outlook of North America in the second half of the 19th century unlike any other writer by converting the theory of evolution into "an instrument of unbridled optimism."[23] Development for him is a cosmic principle that pertains especially to the human species. The universal development has to be made fruitful for humanity to drive it to further progress. Nothing can be excluded from this progress, no knowledge, no value systems, and no feelings. Humanity is in control of its future; it can determine its own progress and need no longer rely on an active God.

Along with the change from God-confidence to self-confidence, another important shift emerged which contributed to the belief in progress induced by humanity, the secularization of the kingdom of God. The root for this shift lies in the Calvinistic theory of double predestination. We are predestined by birth either to be received into heaven after life on earth or to be condemned to eternal damnation. Of course, we want to find out as early as possible what our destiny is. In popular understanding the fact of election could be seen in earthly success. Thus Calvinists worked tirelessly in an ascetic manner to prove to themselves and to others that they were on the right side. The results of this work, of course, could not be enjoyed but had to be added to the constant increase of the employed capital. Max Weber and Ernst Troeltsch rightly called Calvinism the forerunner of modern capitalism.[24]

Surprisingly, pietism played a similar role with its radical orientation toward the other world. This other-worldliness, by necessity, led pietists to responsible use of the time here on earth. Time was not to be spent in worldly joy and amusement but in self-crucifying work. The father who presided over hours of devotions is at the same time the ancestor of many industrial endeavors. In the 19th century the centers of the pietistic movement in Germany, Rhineland-Westphalia and Württemberg, became the centers of industrial development. The religious convictions of the ancestors led to the splendid industrial success of the grandchildren, most of whom have long ago discarded the religious premises of their forefathers.

In America the development was similar, partly in direct connection with the immigration of German pietists. One of the biggest American steel companies, the Bethlehem Steel Company in Bethlehem, Pennsylvania, was begun by a blacksmith who had immigrated from Herrnhut,

Germany, at the beginning of the 18th century.[25] He settled in Bethlehem, a Moravian missionary settlement in the forests of Pennsylvania, and started a small blacksmith shop there. Quality and industriousness helped to develop his workshop into a huge enterprise. Though the name Bethlehem still points to the pietistic and pacifist origin of one of the largest steel companies in the United States, it has turned into a huge armament enterprise without regard to its religious premise.

In his book, *The Kingdom of God in America,* H. Richard Niebuhr pointed to an important factor that caused this loss of the religious premise. He claimed that the spiritualistic and Calvinistic groups favored a heaven of their own design. They considered humanity to be virtuous enough to acquire such a heaven. Also, the radical transformation of life on earth eventually undermined the expectation of heavenly bliss. Through hard work, conditions on earth became attractive enough to cause them to forget life in heaven, especially when they felt that humanity was on its way to bringing about the kingdom on earth.[26]

Necessity for re-integrating secular progress into an eschatological context: Hope is as necessary for human life as oxygen. When we have no hope, we have no incentive to live and we might as well die. Even the rate of mental illness is higher in periods of uncertainty or economic and social depression than in periods of economic growth. But religious hope is cyclical, the recurrence of the same, and secular hope is necessarily finite. The self-perpetuating progress of the Eastern Marxist or the Western capitalist stands on rather shaky ground. Marxists must design one five-year plan after another to keep progress progressing, while the West promises larger and larger pieces of a pie that is continuously shrinking. Humanity is no longer the beneficiary of progress, but has become subservient to it in order to sustain its momentum. Ceaseless division of labor and automation in modern hospitals or huge corporations give us some taste of how inhuman and dissatisfying progress can be. It also can become quite totalitarian as electronic surveillance systems and endless automated "red tape" indicate, and it does not bring about just earthly blessings as we had naively hoped.

Since we are finite creatures in need of the infinite, progress emerges as a new god whom we must worship and who demands our life. We have abandoned God-confidence to gain self-confidence. However, this could only be a transitory state. Human imperfection demands our surrender to forces which we then endow with perfection and ultimate significance. Being derived from our finite world, they are finite too and cannot grant us freedom and ultimate meaning. Since they do not allow us to be related to God, the truly ultimate, they will at best provide us with a truncated future and a dehumanized humanity. Emil Brunner was right when he called the belief in progress and the hope for the better future an "illegitimate child of Christianity." [27]

The loss of a meaningful goal in our uncertain situation causes an even more severe threat to the modern belief in progress and the interest in the immediate future. To what end are we progressing? Is there anything worthwhile to hope for except uncertainty? As long as God provides the goal as the end of history and beyond history, progress has a definite goal. This goal determines the destiny of our life but cannot be reached within our own life. Once this God-provided destiny is denied, the goal must be found within time. However, it can never be reached, because then there would be nothing left to hope for. Thus it has to recede within the farther and farther progressing horizons of history, and the speed of its recession must be at least equivalent to the speed of our own progress. The idea of never-ending progress is already indicated in Lessing's remark that, if God offered him a choice between the possession of truth and the quest of it, he would unhesitatingly prefer the latter.[28] Kant went along similar lines in interpreting life immortal as endless advance towards a perfection that can never actually be attained.

But what happens when the god of progress falters? What happens when the clouds on the horizon of history darken more and more the bright prospects of the future? It should at least arouse our suspicion when we notice the increasing number of people of all ages that resort to alcohol and to drugs, whether illegal narcotics or prescribed tranquilizers, to escape from an uncertain and progress-demanding future. Perhaps we have created a world of standards without meaning and goals without ultimate direction. Though we are transitory beings, we do not receive our identity from transitoriness and steady change, even if this process might allure us to an ever better future, but from something beyond change and transitoriness. Humanists readily admit this too when they refer to the infinite, and this means unchangeable, value of a human being. But what are we doing? Are we trying to catch our own shadow that the idea of progress is projecting in front of us? It might even be that we shall some day discover that there is no ultimate hope for us as long as we try to provide it (penultimately) for ourselves, because it is constantly superseded by our own steps into the future.

At this point Christian eschatology gains new significance. (1) It shows us that the modern idea of progress alienated itself from its Christian foundation. Though maintaining a linear view of history, it deprived history of its God-promised goal. Consequently, the progressiveness of history became an end in itself. At the same time, we promoted ourselves from the position of God-alienated and God-endowed actors *in* history to the position of deified agents *of* history. Then we slipped into the dilemma of how convincingly to assert a linear progressiveness of history while still denying the metaphysical origin and goal of this progressiveness.[29] Our present situation of environment exploitation, human deprivation, and threatening meaninglessness of life seems to indicate that we are unable to achieve self-redemption, a goal that the pursuit of steady progress demands.

(2) At this point Christian eschatology provides a hope and a promise that we are unable to attain through our own efforts. Eschatology is not obsolete, nor can it be replaced by any secular or religiously colored idea of progress or self-fulfillment. But it endows our life and even the idea of progress with new meaning. Secular endeavors for progress have to be related and must be based on Christian eschatology. On the basis of the Christ-event they can be understood as proleptic anticipation of the God-promised eschaton which at the same time is their incentive, their directive, and their judgment. Secular endeavors for progress and a social and ethical transformation of the world are legitimate and necessary, but they are preliminary and inadequate, and they yearn for their final completion through God's redemptive power. Apart from Christian eschatology, they miss not only God, but humanity too. Instead of leading to freedom and new humanity, they lead to new slavery and potential self-destruction. This is the reason eschatology is so crucial in our time.

NOTES

1. Evelyn Waugh, "Death in Hollywood," *Life* (Sept. 29, 1947) 73-84. See also Jessica Mitford, *The American Way of Death* (New York: Simon and Schuster, 1963) 148-160, in her vivid description of Forest Lawn Memorial Park in Southern California.
2. Mitford, *The American Way of Death*, 18f.
3. Paul Althaus, *The Theology of Martin Luther*, trans. by R. C. Schultz (Philadelphia: Fortress, 1966) 409ff.
4. Billy Graham, *Peace with God* (Westwood, N.J.,: Revell, 1968) 229.
5. *Lutheran Book of Worship*, Hymn 567, stanza 4.

6. Karl Marx, "Contribution to the Critique of Hegel's Philosophy of Right," *On Religion,* intr. by R. Niebuhr (New York: Schocken, 1964) 42.

7. Karl Löwith, *Meaning in History* (Chicago: University of Chicago Press, 1957), p. 19, expresses this very well when he says: "It seems as if the two great conceptions of antiquity and Christianity, cyclic motion and eschatological direction, have exhausted the basic approaches to the understanding of history. Even most recent attempts at an interpretation of history are nothing else but variations of these two principles or a mixture of both of them."

8. Hans-Joachim Kraus, *Worship in Israel; A Cultic History of the Old Testament,* trans. by G. Bushwell (Richmond, Va.: John Knox, 1966) 38ff.

9. Friedrich Heiler, *Die Religionen der Menschheit in Vergangenheit und Gegenwart* (Stuttgart: Reclam, 1959) 464f.

10. Arnold Toynbee, *Civilization on Trial* (London: Oxford University, 1953) 14f. However, he concedes the possibility that our present civilization may survive because this cyclic movement is no inescapable fate and leaves room for the freedom of choice to give history "some new and unprecedented turn" (pp. 38f.).

11. R. G. Collingwood, *The Idea of History* (London: Oxford University, 1967) 17.

12. Morris Ginsberg, *Essays in Sociology and Social Philosophy,* Vol. 3: *Evolution and Progress* (New York: Macmillan, 1961) 6. It seems strange that Ginsberg does not point to this evident difference between the two religions but only shows the similarity in their understanding of history as a "forward movement."

13. Collingwood, *The Idea of History,* 42f., rightly speaks of a "substantialism" which is incompatible with a due recognition of history.

14. Löwith, *Meaning in History,* 4f.

15. Gerhard von Rad, "The Theological Problem of the Old Testament Doctrine of Creation" (1936), *The Problem of the Hexateuch and Other Essays,* trans. by E. W. Trucman Dicken (Edinburgh: Oliver & Boyd, 1966), 138.

16. Collingwood, *The Idea of History,* 41.

17. *Ibid.,* 46.

18. John Baillie, *The Belief in Progress* (New York: Scribner, 1951) 20ff.

19. Descartes himself refers to the wartime in which his Discourse was written. Cf. *Discourse on Method,* in *Descartes; Philosophical Writings,* sel. and trans. by N. K. Smith (New York: Modern Library, 1958) 101.

20. Cf. for the following, *Ibid.,* 118-123.

21. Immanuel Kant, "What Is Enlightenment?" in *Foundations of the Metaphysics of Morals and What Is Enlightenment?,* trans. and intr. by L. W. Beck (Indianapolis: Bobbs-Merrill, 1959) 85.

22. Cf. Henry E. Allison, *Lessing and the Enlightenment* (Ann Arbor: University of Michigan Press, 1966) 151f.

23. Baillie, *The Belief in Progress,* 144f.

24. Ernst Troeltsch, *Protestantism and Progress; A Historical Study of the Relation of Protestantism to the Modern World,* trans. by W. Montgomery (Boston: Beacon, 1958) 131ff. Whereas Max Weber sees at this point a close affinity between Calvinism and Judaism, Troeltsch rejects this idea, since the Calvinistic use of Jewish ethical teaching cannot sufficiently explain the phenomenon of modern capitalism (Max Weber, *The Protestant Ethic and the Spirit of Capitalism,* trans. by T. Parsons, with a foreword by R. H. Tawney [London: Allen & Unwin, 1948]). Though Max Weber's thesis certainly needs modification (cf. Robert W. Green, ed., *Protestantism and Capitalism; The Weber Thesis and Its Critics* [Boston: Heath, 1959]), the stimulus that pietism and Calvinism provided for the development of modern capitalism and industrialization is undeniable (cf. Ernst Benz, *Evolution and Christian Hope; Man's Concept of the Fu-*

ture from the Early Fathers to Teilhard de Chardin, trans. by H. G. Frank [Garden City, N.Y.: Doubleday, Anchor, 1968], esp. pp. 129ff.).

25. Benz, *Evolution and Christian Hope,* p. 130, quotes this striking example.
26. H. Richard Niebuhr, *The Kingdom of God in America* (New York: Harper Torchbooks, 1959) 150ff.
27. Emil Brunner, *Eternal Hope,* trans. by H. Knight (London: Lutterworth, 1954) 25.
28. Baillie, *The Idea of Progress,* p. 182.
29. Löwith, *Meaning in History,* pp. 205ff., observes that modern trust in the continuity of history is irreconcilable with a linear view of history and is actually much closer to the classic theory of a cyclic movement. Thus the modern view of history is an eclectic and inconsistent combination of the Greco-Roman and the Judeo-Christian views of history.

Part I

HOW
WE DISCOVERED
THE FUTURE

1. Eschatology as a religious phenomenon

IN ITS BROADEST SENSE the term eschatology includes all concepts of life beyond death and everything connected with it—heaven and hell, paradise and immortality, resurrection and transmigration of the soul, rebirth and reincarnation, last judgment and doomsday, and many other concepts. Eschatology also is determined by and determines our understanding of humanity, of body and soul, and of value systems and world views. A naturalistic concept of the human species will result in a different concept of eschatology than a spiritualistic one, and a dualistic concept of body and soul will result in yet a different outlook on eschatology. Eschatology is also correlated with funeral, burial, and mourning customs. When the Egyptians left certain presents in the tombs of the dead, it showed their understanding of the life beyond, e.g., that the dead need food on their journey and servants to serve them. Or let us remember that our Christian custom of burying the dead emphasizes in a symbolic way the unity of the person in expectation of a "bodily" resurrection. Hindu mourners, however, burn the dead and strew the ashes into the holy Ganges River, since they do not believe in a resurrection of the body, but that only the *spirit* of the cremated person will be wafted to higher worlds.

Eschatology always influences and determines the conduct of life. In an individual eschatology the conduct of this life will determine the destiny of the individual after death, whereas in a collective eschatology the destiny of all humanity is taken into consideration. A cosmic eschatology even goes beyond the scope of humanity and includes the destiny of this earth or of the whole cosmos. Cosmic eschatology often reckons with recurrent world periods, first a Golden Age, then a decline in a period of crises, and finally a return to the conditions of the Golden Age in the period of cleansing or renewal. Of course, this is based on a cyclical concept of time. In Jewish apocalyptic a different periodization was reached. Here the distinction was made between the present *aeon* of turmoil and anxiety and the future *aeon* of the final end of all history and the coming of the Savior. Resistance against political and religious oppression contributed to an intensified expectation of the end which provided the best possible context for the proclamation of Jesus of Nazareth.

Historical catastrophes and crises often influence eschatological expectations. For instance, the catastrophe of World War II in Europe brought many estranged people back to the churches, and the proclamation of the Word of God gained renewed attention. In a similar way the rise of dialectical theology which pronounced the immediacy of God cannot be properly understood without considering the political and economic turmoil after World War I. The present interest in eschatological realism, not to say heavenly eschatology, by many members of society is also related to the mood of uncertainty and despair to which many people are subjected. Even disasters, such as the earthquake in Lisbon (1755), can cause a reorientation in eschatological thinking. But the eschatological time is not only a time of crisis. It is also a time of salvation. The coming of the redeemer and of the Messiah is expected and celebrated. The cargo cult in New Guinea and the messianic movements in Africa both expect a time of redemption, though in a mostly secularized, political and economic manner. Lumumba in Africa and Castro in Latin America are regarded as messianic leaders who initiate the era of secular salvation. Similarly, in the United States we experience in increasing number of saints and pseudo-saints who promise their devout followers new spiritual insights and often also redemption from anxieties and physical ailments.

The eschaton is often regarded as a repetition of the primeval time. For instance, in Paul's letters in the New Testament, Christ is seen as the new Adam, and the new creation is understood in contrast to the first creation. For Paul, however, there is a progressive movement from the first creation to the new creation, while in most religions the movement is not conceived as linear and singular, but as cyclical and periodic. Very often the seasonal rhythm influences the cultic calendar, and the seasonal changes provide the pattern for the cultic periods of expectation and fulfillment. Sigmund Mowinckel and later S. H. Hooke attempted to understand primitive Old Testament eschatology in a similar rhythmic pattern.[1]

The enthronement of Yahweh was considered the central festival in Israel at which Yahweh came and occupied his throne in Jerusalem. Psalms 47, 93, 96, and others that use the term "Yahweh has become king" allude to this occasion. The festival of the enthronement of Yahweh was at the same time the New Year's festival and was celebrated in the fall prior to the beginning of the rainy season which "created anew the earth." [2] Since Yahweh promised the advent of the rainy season, this was a time of expectation. It was also a time of remembrance, because Yahweh, who had once conquered the powers of chaos, would now conquer all evil powers and all enemies of Israel and secure his kingship. "At this festival the congregation has most vividly experienced the personal coming of the Lord to save his people—his epiphany. In the cultic festival, past, present and future are welded into one." [3] This idea of Yahweh's final victory outlived the destruction of the Israelite nation and laid the ground for the new cosmic enthronement of Yahweh when he will establish his kingdom at his "day." "The eschatology of Judaism drew its ideas from the experience and the thoughts that were connected with the festival of the enthronement of Yahweh." [4]

We agree with Mowinckel that the harvest festival as an agricultural feast may have been taken over from the Canaanites after settlement, along with the conception of their deity as a king, and the annual celebration of his ascension and enthronement.[5] Yet there are decisive differences. While in the Canaanite religion the god Baal gained his final victory and ascension after defeat, death, and resurrection, this was an impossible thought for the Israelites. Yahweh the Lord has always lived and always lives; he is the holy God who does not die (Hab. 1:12). This means that the basic rhythmic and thus cyclic pattern had to be abandoned in favor of the God who everlastingly creates and sustains life. Of course, in many places the worship of the vegetational god did make its way into Israel without these fundamental modifications, as we can see from finds of figurines connected with the worship of Baal. But whenever the Old Testament, the official document of the Israelite religion, refers to this worship, it is in order to condemn it as paganism. In the Israelite faith the enthronement festival was removed from the pattern of cyclic vegetational religion to the world of historical reality. It served to emphasize the coming presence of Yahweh who is active and discloses himself in living history.

This brief survey shows that single motifs (enthronement of god, dying and rising of god) never exist independently. Although there is a basic structure of eschatology, there is always a complexity of motifs imbedded in the whole religious and cultic life of the people.

2. Eschatology and the idea of an afterlife

Eschatology in Israelite religion did not just emerge all of a sudden through the events of the Babylonian exile when Israel was exposed to the influence of the Iranian religion (Parsiism) and the Babylonian religion. Yet "anyone who has even a superficial knowledge of the Iranian religion cannot but be struck by the parallels that may be drawn between it on the one hand and Judaism and Christianity on the other. The ideas of God, angels and archangels, of Devil, demons and archfiends, as found in both, present so great a similarity that comparisons between the angelology and demonology of the two types of religion become inevitable." [6] Some resemblances in their cosmological systems might likewise tempt one to seek a common source of both systems in Babylonia. We could continue to list more resemblances, but to determine any possible dependence we have to outline the origin and the basic characteristics of the Iranian religion.

As far as we know, the Iranian religion goes back to the priest and prophet Zarathustra (Zoroaster according to the Greek transcription). He seems to have lived in Eastern Iran, but the dates of his life are uncertain. While Greek writers date him 6000 years before Plato, the Parsees themselves date him 258 years prior to Alexander the Great. It is the opinion of most scholars that this latter date holds more truth, and that he probably lived in the sixth century before Christ. [7] In the center of his proclamation was the god Ahura Mazda or Ormuzd. He was the creator of heaven and earth, without image, and the lawgiver of the whole cosmos. Loyalty to Ahura Mazda excluded the worship of any other old Iranian gods.

This strict monotheism resembles that of the Israelite religion. However, Zoroaster emphasized the insurmountable opposition between almighty Ahura Mazda and Angra Mainyu, or Ahriman, the manifestation of everything evil. This cleavage seems to result in a dualism of an ethical and metaphysical nature, though Zoroaster deliberately refrains from attributing both spirits, Ahura Mazda and Angra Mainyu, to the same source or origin. Once these "gods" made their initial ethical choice they separated themselves and the world into a sphere of light and a sphere of darkness.[8]

The incompatibility of both gods is for Zarathustra the basis for his ethical demands. Though the ethical demands remain mostly in the realm of social ethics, to liberate the suppressed peasants and herdsmen, the actual goal of ethical realization lies in the eschaton. There will be a pleasant dwelling in green pastures for those who adhere to the good.[9] Characteristic for Zoroaster's doctrine is a twofold outcome of history; an eternity of bliss and an eternity of woe allotted respectively to good and evil people in another life beyond the grave. After death the soul of the deceased has to cross the Chinvat bridge which stretches over hell, an abyss of molten metal and fire. For the good the bridge grows broader and broader for easier transit and subsequent ascent into heaven, where the pious soul will live in eternal joy. But for the wicked the bridge grows narrower until it is like the blade of a razor-sharp sword and the soul falls into the abyss of hell, where there will be eternal torment and suffering. There is also some kind of intermediate state for those whose good and bad deeds are in strict balance.

Zoroastrian religion also knows of a judgment and completion of the whole world. Three thousand years after Zarathustra the Saoshyans or savior will come and bring the present world to its end. The dead will be resurrected, and both wicked and good will have to pass through a flood of molten metal. The good will pass without harm and enter the new world. The wicked will either be purified or burned; the evil spirits will be burned. After this worldwide purification in the last days of the present crisis, Ahura Mazda's sovereignty will be complete, and together with him the good will enjoy a new heaven and a new earth. Of course, not all ideas that we know from the Iranian religion go back to Zoroaster. Some are later developments, but most have their roots in his teachings.

If we want to sum up the possible influence of Zoroaster's doctrines on the Judeo-Christian religion, we can conclude the following:

(1) There are evident analogies between the relationship of good and evil in the Israelite religion and the relationship of good and evil in Zoroaster's system. This becomes especially clear in Qumran.[10] The sons of light and the sons of darkness, the realm of truth and the realm of lies, are important in the Qumran theology. This seems to point to a direct borrowing on the Jewish side. However, the Qumran scrolls never found their way into the Old Testament corpus. Even the terminological

dualism in the New Testament, as in the Gospel of John, bears only a very limited resemblance to Parsiistic dualism.

(2) The dramatic salvation-historical periodization of history as found in the idea of the four empires in Daniel 2:1-47 and 7:1-28 comes close to the periodization of Parsiism.

(3) The expectation of the heavenly savior in the last time as seen in Enoch resembles the Zoroastrian idea of a Saoshyans, especially since he could be understood as a descendant of Zarathustra. It is difficult, however, to decide to whom we should attribute chronological priority because for Zoroaster, unlike later Zoroastrianism, the Saoshyans is not yet an eschatological figure and a final *new* existence is only vaguely indicated.

(4) We are in a similar dilemma with the Zoroastrian idea of punishment of the ungodly through fire. Though there might be an influence on the development of these ideas in the later writings of Judaism (Dan. 7:10f. and Eth. Enoch 67:4-7), the motif of a cosmic fire is also a well-known Greek and Stoic feature of eschatology.

(5) The case of rewards and punishments, heaven and hell, is different, however.[11] The assumption of a direct Zoroastrian influence on postexilic Judaism makes it easy to understand why the Jews suddenly abandoned the idea of sheol, as a shadowy and depersonalized existence which is the lot of people irrespective of what they had done on earth, and why they advanced, at exactly the time when they had made contact in exile with the Medes and Persians, an understanding of afterlife which paralleled that in Zoroaster's teachings.[12] For instance Daniel, the alleged minister of Darius the Mede, distinctly mentions everlasting life and eternal punishment in saying: "And many of those who sleep in the dust of the earth shall awake, some to everlasting life, and some to shame and everlasting contempt" (Dan. 12:2).[13]

It is remarkable that once the Jews had made contact with the Iranians they took over the typical Zoroastrian doctrine of an individual afterlife in which rewards are to be enjoyed and punishments endured. Contrary to other "syncretistic" attempts, there seem to have been no objections made by the prophets.[14] Would this indicate that in Israel the time was ripe for such beliefs?

Moreover, the whole Near East seemed to wrestle during the fifth or sixth century before Christ with the destiny of the individual and of the world at large. This would cover the second half of what Jaspers termed the "pivotal age of world history."[15] Soteriological and eschatological systems were developed in Hellenistic Gnosticism, apocalyptic Judaism, and finally in Christianity.

To understand why it was so easy for the Jewish people to adopt Zoroaster's doctrine of the afterlife, we have to inquire more deeply into the Old Testament understanding of human destiny.

NOTES

1. Sigmund Mowinckel, *Psalmstudien; II Das Thronbesteigungsfest Jahwäs und der Ursprung der Eschatologie* (Amsterdam: Schippers, 1961; reprint of Oslo, 1921); and S. H. Hooke, ed., *Myth and Ritual; Essays on the Myth and Ritual of the Hebrews in Relation to the Culture Pattern of the Ancient East* (London: Oxford University 1933). While Mowinckel attempts to show how Israel adopted the cultic pattern of the vegetational Canaanite religion to the point where the cyclical pattern was historicized in view of the salvational activity of Yahweh, Hooke is more interested in trying to show the similarity between the Israelite religion and the vegetational religions of its environment. According to Hooke there was never a "pure" Israelite religion that did not share much in common with the religions of its neighbors. On the contrary, the cultic pattern of the divine kingship, an essential part of Israelite worship, was prevalent throughout the ancient Near East (cf. S. Mowinckel, *The Psalms in Israel's Worship*, trans. by D. R. Ap-Thomas [New York: Abingdon, 1962], 1:130-40; and S. H. Hooke, "Myth and Ritual: Past and Present," in S. H. Hooke, ed., *Myth, Ritual, and Kingship; Essays on the Theory and Practice of Kingship in the Ancient Near East and in Israel* [Oxford: Clarendon, 1958] 13-20).

   Ivan Engnell must at least be mentioned here as one of the most fervent advocates of the idea of an enthronement festival of Yahweh. In his doctoral dissertation *Studies in Divine Kingship in the Ancient Near East* (Oxford: Blackwell [1943], 1967) he confines himself to establishing the theory of a divine kingship prevalent throughout the ancient Near East. In later writings, however, he suggests that the enthronement festival in its Canaanite version lays the groundwork for the Israelite understanding of Passover, the Feast of Booths, the belief in the resurrection, messianism, and even essential features of the idea of God (cf. his essay "Old Testament Religion," in *Critical Essays on the Old Testament*, trans. and ed. by J. T. Willis with the collab. of H. Ringgren [London: SPCK, 1970] 35-49). It seems that the history of Israelite religion is more complicated and many-faceted than Engnell suggests.
2. Sigmund Mowinckel, *Religion and Kultus* (Göttingen: Vandenhoeck & Ruprecht, 1953) 79.
3. Cf. Mowinckel, Psalms 1:112f.
4. Mowinckel, *Religion und Kultus,* 80.
5. It has to be mentioned here that many scholars deny that such a festival of enthronement of Yahweh ever existed. For instance Georg Fohrer, *History of Israelite Religion,* trans. by D. E. Green (Nashville: Abingdon, 1972) 143f., rejects the idea of such a festival, and also points out that an identification of God and king, which such a festival presupposes, is an unacceptable thought for Israel. Th. C. Vriezen, *An Outline of Old Testament Theology* (Newton, Mass.: Bradford, 1958) 183, says that "the so-called feast of the ascension of Yahweh to the throne is an unfounded modern hypothetical construction which is confusing rather than clarifying. Yahweh's life is not

renewed, neither is His Kingship." For Vriezen the New Year's day which, according to the advocates of this idea, is supposed to be identical with the enthronement festival of Yahweh, is the occasion on which Yahweh is *glorified* as Creator and King (285). Cf. also the excellent study of Hans-Joachim Kraus, *Worship in Israel,* 18f. and 39f., who concurs with Martin Noth's position advanced in his essay "God, King, and Nation in the Old Testament," in *The Law in the Pentateuch and Other Studies,* trans. by D. R. Ap-Thomas, intr. by N. W. Porteous (Philadelphia: Fortress, 1967) 145-78, in saying that the historical foundations of Israelite kingship rule out such a "mythical interpretation."

6. A. V. Williams Jackson, *Zoroastrian Studies; The Iranian Religion and Various Monographs* (New York: AMS, 1965) 205.

7. Friedrich Heiler, *Die Religionen der Menschheit in Vergangenheit und Gegenwart,* 423.

8. *Ibid.,* 428.

9. Cf. for instance Yasna 48, 11f., as trans. from the Avesta by D. F. A. Bode and P. Nanavutty in *Songs of Zarathustra; The Gates,* foreword by Radhakrishnan (London: Allen & Unwin, 1952) 92.

10. Cf. the lucid comments by Raymond E. Brown, *New Testament Essays* (Milwaukee: Bruce, 1965) 105ff., in his comments on the relationship between Zoroastrianism, Old and New Testament Scriptures and Qumran.

11. Cf. R. C. Zaehner in his excellent study, *The Dawn and Twilight of Zoroastrianism* (London: Weidenfeld and Nicolson, 1961) 57f.

12. Geo Widengren, *Die Religionen Irans* (Stuttgart: Kohlhammer, 1965) 355, shows in his careful study that eschatology and apocalyptic have received their decisive impulses from Iran. The periodization of history and the resurrection of the body are specific Iranian doctrines that gained great significance. He also mentions the interesting fact that in pre-Islamic times there are only a few Semitic words found in the Iranian languages, while the Iranian influence on the Hebrew, Aramaic, and Syriac languages is truly impressive. A similar relationship can be established for the Iranian and the Greek languages (357). This seems to indicate in which direction the influence was exerted.

13. Although the Book of Daniel is postexilic (ca. 150 B.C.), this passage seems to individualize the metaphoric imagery of Ezek. 37 and expands it into a twofold outcome (for Israel). (cf. Otto Plöger, *Das Buch Daniel* [Gütersloh: Gerd Mohn, 1965] 171f. to this passage.) This means that the material used in this passage is certainly older than the Book of Daniel and thus the reference to Darius the Mede and his time is not totally unjustified.

14. Of course, we should not forget that at the time of Jesus the resurrection of the body was still a controversial subject in the eyes of the Sadducees.

15. Karl Jaspers, *Origin and Goal of History,* trans. by M. Bullock (New Haven: Yale University, 1953) 24.

1
The Old Testament View of Eschatology

THE OLD TESTAMENT IS NOT a book that fell straight down from heaven. The Old Testament has a story behind it and was written by various people who reflected on God's self-disclosure that they had encountered or that they had heard about through other people. The oldest traceable historical events to which the Old Testament refers go back beyond 1000 B.C., while the most recent occurred barely before 150 B.C. This is the approximate time-span we have to cover when we talk about eschatological awareness as encountered in the Old Testament. There are three main areas which are decisive for eschatological thinking in the Old Testament: the human destiny, the last judgment, and the promise of and hope for a Messiah. This also indicates a historical progression. The promise of and hope for a Messiah emerged fairly late while the human destiny is one of the earliest topics in the Old Testament.

1. The human destiny

While the writings of the Old Testament which reflect on the beginning of the Israelite nation are not oblivious to the destiny of the individual, they show almost no concern about a life or destiny after death. During the nomadic period of the Israelite tribes the dead were either left behind in a foreign environment (Gen. 23:19f.) or they were carried with the tribes (Gen. 50:5f.). When the Israelites settled down in the promised land, they could no longer leave their dead behind, but encountered their corpses whenever they had to bury someone else. They had to open the stone-hewn family tombs and make room for the newly deceased. The expression "gathered to his people" (Gen. 25:8) refers to the custom of using a tomb over again after a certain time.[1] In contradistinction to the elaborate conceptions of other peoples, the Israelites did not often reflect on a life beyond. Of course, the Israelites knew that death was not the end of human existence. But death was not understood as the transition to a better hereafter. It was at best a shadowy existence that they envisioned. Therefore the dead had no power over the living and no cult of the dead developed. In contrast to other Near Eastern religions the resting places of the dead were forbidden ground for the Israelites. If one encountered a death in the family or had touched a dead person one was considered unclean and was excluded from the worship of Yahweh. The Lord is a God of life and the emphasis was upon life here on earth.

a. Emphasis on the this-worldly aspect of life

The emphasis lies clearly on the this-worldly aspect of life.[2] Their almost exclusively corporate thinking seemed to make it unnecessary for the Israelites to reflect on individual "survival." Man continued to live on in his sons and through them in his community. It was one of the most devastating fates to die without a male heir. Then there was no hope. The end that the Israelites desired was a death in old age with their sons assembled around them (Gen. 49:33). The Bible says of Abraham that he died as an old man and full of years (Gen. 25:8); of Job that he died as an old man and full of days, and in similar fashion of many of the other great figures of the Old Testament. To die at a ripe old age is understood as a blessing, and the Proverbs pronounce this very definitely: "The fear of the Lord prolongs life, but the years of the wicked will be short" (Prov. 10:27). An early death is understood as punishment for godlessness (1 Sam. 2:32). This is why even a king may pray to Yahweh and ask him in fervent words for temporary deliverance from death (Isa. 38:3). When later the Israelites wrestled with the concept of salvation, again this was initially understood in strictly this-worldly terms. Life will then be prolonged to an amazing degree "for the child shall die a hundred years old" (Isa. 65:20).

This does not mean that the Israelites accepted death as a natural phenomenon. Life and death were understood as ordered and destined by Yahweh. He provides both life and death. But death was not yet conceived as the transitional stage which leads to life eternal. Hezekiah expresses very well why he wants to be saved from the pit, the place in the tomb where the remains of the decayed corpse are preserved, "for Sheol cannot thank thee, death cannot praise thee; those who go down to the pit cannot hope for thy faithfulness" (Isa. 38:18). God is a God of

the living, but not of the dead. That Hezekiah's sickness can be connected with death and sheol shows that both terms are also used in a
metaphoric sense. They can denote hostile and threatening powers and
the anxiety they produce.

The cultic laws express clearly that the dead are "off limits" for the
living.[3] Saul's attempt to communicate with the dead does not end in
failure but in personal catastrophe. He is finally rejected by Yahweh
(1 Sam. 28). This also shows that from their earliest days onward the
Israelites knew that death was not the final end. The dead existed beyond
death in the shadowy sphere of sheol (Isa. 14:10). Such an existence
beyond death is also indicated by the gifts, such as lamps, pots with food,
and water which were put into the tomb.[4] Later these gifts were only of
symbolic nature, as can be seen from the use of broken pottery.[5]

b. Translation and resurrection

Parallel to the emphasis on the undesirability of death are some exceptions mentioned in the Old Testament. There is first the exceptional
occurrence of translation. Enoch was faithful to God, and thus he received him into his immediate presence (Gen. 5:24). A chariot of fire and
horses separated Elijah from Elisha, and Elijah was taken up into heaven
by a whirlwind (2 Kings 2:11). But these are the only two instances in
the Old Testament of a translation from life here on earth to a life beyond. Even a person like Moses had to die, although God himself buried
him so that nobody could find his tomb (Deut. 34:5f.).

Death, though, is not the all-decisive event. In different parts of the
Old Testament there is also the expectation of a kind of resurrection.
Traditionally quoted passages, such as Job 19:25f. ("I know that my
Redeemer lives . . ."), or Psalm 73:24 ("Thou dost guide me with thy
counsel, and afterward thou wilt receive me to glory") hardly fit here.[6]
They either point to an expectancy that lies strictly within the realm of
life here on earth, or rely on an ambiguous Hebrew text. But then we
read in Isaiah 26:14, "They are dead, they will not live; they are shades,
they will not arise," and later in the same chapter, "The dead shall live,
their bodies shall rise. O dwellers in the dust, awake and sing for joy!"
(v. 19). Similarly we hear: "But God will ransom my soul from the
power of Sheol, for he will receive me" (Ps. 49:15).[7] In later parts of the
Old Testament we even hear about resurrection with a twofold outcome:
"And many of those who sleep in the dust of the earth shall awake, some

to everlasting life, and some to shame and everlasting contempt" (Dan. 12:2).[8]

Can we discard these passages as indicating a personal pagan piety that is alien to corporate trust in Yahweh? Or shall we try to harmonize these passages with those that seem to know nothing about a *life* after death? Both solutions seem to do injustice to the fact that most passages that indicate such a hope are of later date. It seems to be a gross over-simplification to say that in the Old Testament death is the end of humanity according to God's order so that only this world is open to the faithful.[9]

To read the whole New Testament understanding of an individual and a universal resurrection back into the Old Testament would be equally unjustified. Though the Old Testament understanding of human destiny had not yet risen to the clarity of New Testament perceptions, for the Israelites death was not the end. But God's revelation does not occur in a single day. It occurs according to the human needs and questions that have to be met and answered. When Israel's corporate existence collapsed and most of the people were led into the Babylonian exile, the almost exclusive focus on corporate fulfillment no longer sufficed. That there is outside help to clarify burning issues, as the Canaanite and Parsiistic influences indicate (Dan. 12:2), shows that non-Israelite terms and concepts were not despised in explaining and clarifying Yahweh's plan of salvation for his people.

2. The last judgment

In analogy to the Israelite's emphasis on life here on earth, God's judgment was first conceived as a judgment here on earth and during our lifetime. God judges all misdeeds here on earth, because "vengeance is mine, and recompense, for the time when their foot shall slip" (Deut. 32:35). He is the protector of his law.

a. God as the protector of his law

God is not understood as a capricious power who plays dice with the world. He is a faithful God who sticks to his orders and promises and who in turn wants us to be like-minded. The whole Old Testament cult is grounded in the knowledge that God is trustworthy and reliable. Yahweh is the God who brought the Israelites from Egypt into the promised land. He is holy, and therefore Israel should be holy too (Exod.

19:6; Lev. 11:44). He has given his law to Israel and as a righteous God he is always connected with law. This law expresses God's gracious ordering of and caring for life and as such is unquestionable, unchangeable, and reliable. The delight of the good is in the law of the Lord (Ps. 1:2) and he is pleased with the law (Ps. 119:13f.). Such a positive understanding of the law expresses the response of the Israelites to the covenant God made with Israel, and it corresponds with the faithfulness and trustworthiness of Yahweh expressed in the covenant.[10]

God judges those who do not adequately respond to his gracious care and therefore ignore his law. Nathan and Elijah have to remind their kings of the law of the Lord, and beginning with Amos the prophets frequently remind the whole Israelite nation of its obligation to the Lord and his law. Of course, this is not a unilateral process. Especially the Psalms show us that, knowing about God's covenant with Israel and knowing about God's past history with Israel, individuals could also remind God of his obligations. But the Old Testament usually shows that God observes his part of the covenant, so that Israel could address him in the polarity of praise and expectation.[11] Yet most stories of the Old Testament show the people of Israel in a different light. While Yahweh keeps his obligations and his promises, the people do not live up to theirs. Then Yahweh becomes the judge of his people.

Not only Israel is included in the judgment of God. Already Amos announces that other nations are included also. Often the judgment occurs because these nations have offended Israel (Isa. 34:8) and sometimes Yahweh gives them directly into the hands of Israel. Arrogance, pride (Isa. 16:6f.), or disobedience (Mic. 5:15) is the cause for God's judgment. Not even the mightiest powers at that time, Egypt and Assyria, are excluded from the rule of God. Finally, toward the close of the Old Testament, the empires are compared with wild and ferocious animals that have to accede to the final victory of God when he will erect his kingdom.

b. God as the God of judgment day

God is not just a God of promise and threat. He brings his promises and threats into reality. They can often be seen as occurring within history. The exodus from Egypt and the occupation of the promised land (Palestine) were crucial fulfillments of God's promises. In a similar way the coming of judgment was initially conceived as an event within history. The destruction of Jerusalem was still understood as judgment over Israel (Lam. 1:4f.). But similar to the promises of God that, though being fulfilled, were always modified and expanded, the day of judgment too was eventually understood to include more than the immediate historical event.[12]

Already the royal psalms (2, 20, 21, et al.) expressed a hope in the Lord who will destroy all enemies of Israel. Yet they did not speak of a future, eschatological judgment, but of an earthly king like David, who has just been enthroned and whom Yahweh will assist.[13]

As early as the eighth century, however, the day of the Lord, the judgment day, seemed to have been a familiar object of expectation in Israel.[14] This day was thought to be a day of light and the great day of salvation. Popular expectations also went in the direction of historical, political and cosmic changes. Sometimes the expectation of catastrophes in nature was part of this idea of the judgment on all nations and the salvation of Israel (Zech. 14:5ff.). But the prophets turned these nationalistic eschatological expectations into a pronouncement of calamity and disaster. Especially Amos emphasized the day of the Lord as a day of darkness and not of light, as a day of gloom with no brightness in it (Amos 5:19f.). It would be a day of sword, hunger and pestilence, a day of great slaughter (Isa. 30:25), a day of fright and anxiety. God would destroy the whole world (Isa. 13:5), and great changes would occur in nature, such as earthquakes, darkness, drought and fire (Mal. 4:1). The judgment that the Lord executes when his great and fearful day comes is one of the main themes of the prophetic proclamation.[15]

But God's judgment is not his last word. The terms "the end of the days," "in the latter days," "in those days," "in this time" (Isa. 2:2; Jer. 23:20; 30:24; 48:47; Ezek. 38:16; Hos. 3:5 and many others) are a common vocabulary for most prophets and point to the day of the Lord, to the coming of his kingdom. Yet the prophets did not share the naive and popular hope that "Israel as a state and a people would always and in all respects be victorious without more ado."[16] They eventually realized that a new creation and a full salvation could only be reached through defeat and absolute destruction. This did not impair their confidence in the dominance and kingship of Yahweh over all nations. But they were less confident than their audience in the dignity and power of their own nation. For instance, in the context of announcing the day of the Lord, Amos pronounces total destruction over Israel unless they immediately return to Yahweh. And even if they would return, Yahweh is free to grant them forgiveness or to withhold it (Amos 5:14f.).[17]

c. Universal scope of salvation

Judgment does not result in the ultimate destruction of Israel and the other nations. There is a redirection to something new that it is hoped will come. Even in the Book of Amos, after long and serious threats of impending judgment, all of a sudden we find the affirmation of salvation (Amos 9:11ff.). Of course, one can suggest that these are additions to Amos by a later editor, but already in Amos' own announcement of judgment we find the possibility of a new future (Amos 5:4b). With Isaiah, then, the hope for a new future is so intensified and expanded that we can call him *"the first preacher of the eschatological expectation."*[18] Isaiah expects complete destruction and afterwards universal salvation. Salvation is no longer confined to Israel, but is open for the whole world. In picturesque language this is expressed in Isaiah 2:2-4; Mount Zion will tower over all other mountains, and all nations and tribes shall flock to it to hear the ordinances of God. When Isaiah here employs mythical imagery, this shows that the expected new order of salvation reaches out beyond historical reality. God will also be judge between all nations; all wars will cease and there will be everlasting peace. This peace will affect the realm of nature. Everybody will have plenty of food and will enjoy a long life (cf. Isa. 7:21-25 and 11:6-9). Salvation in the picture of Isaiah still comes via Israel, and even Jesus did not change this. But this understanding is not one of nationalistic prejudice, because the "house of the Lord" is in the center, and the destruction of Israel is the beginning of the kingdom of God.

The prophets after Isaiah stand in continuity with this picture. Yet the immense and hopeless struggle of the Israelite nation for survival lets them express the hopes of salvation in a more spiritualistic and individualistic way. God will create something new in forgiving the sins of the past and burying them in the depths of the sea (Jer. 31:34; Ezek. 16:63; Mic. 7:18f.). He will take out of his people the old heart of stone and will give them a new heart of flesh so that they can keep his will and be his people (Ezek. 11:19f.). In contrast to Isaiah, a hope for all nations is missing here. This is not surprising when we remember that Ezekiel spoke to Israel in a time of the collapse of the nation. Still, the theocentric emphasis is maintained: They shall be my people and I will be their God (Ezek. 11:20b). It may be noteworthy to mention that Ezekiel uses the metaphor of the resurrection of the dead to stress the miraculous aspect of God's restitutive action (Ezek. 37:1-14).[19]

With Deutero-Isaiah the picture changes, since the destruction of Jerusalem is already past history. The prophet has experienced the judgment to which Isaiah still pointed, and now he proclaims the immediate future as the time of salvation. He even draws a parallel between the impending time of salvation, the creation in the beginning, and the exodus from Egypt (Isa. 51:9f.). God had created the earth, he had provided a land for Israel, and now the time of salvation will be like a new creation. In describing salvation Deutero-Isaiah uses the same term *bara'* (to create) that is used in the creation stories in Genesis. In so doing he indicates that salvation is a creative act of God in the same sense as the creation in the beginning.[20]

The time of salvation also causes a change in nature. In paradisiac fertility the land will yield good crops (Isa. 41:18f.), and everything and everybody will praise the Lord (Isa. 43:21). The Lord will now make an everlasting covenant with Israel that will fulfill God's gracious faithfulness once promised to David (Isa. 55:3). Israel has the missionary task to be the light to all nations and to serve as a covenant with the people (Isa. 42:6f.). God will create a new heaven and a new earth; he will rejoice in Jerusalem and be glad in his people. After the exile a later writer even adds that now the former things will be forgotten and there will be no sorrow and distress as in bygone days (Isa. 65:17ff.).

If one were to elaborate only the positive eschatological side of Deutero-Isaiah's message, one might classify him as a universalistic utopian with a strong nationalistic tinge. But he knows that the message of impending salvation is preached to almost deaf ears. The Israelites in Babylon complain that their way is hidden from the Lord (Isa. 40:27), that the Lord has forsaken and forgotten them (Isa. 49:14). They hear the message but reject the content. And yet the prophet does not give in; he knows that the Israelites have always had a rebellious character (Isa. 48:8) and do not hesitate to resort to physical resistance in rejecting the word of salvation (Isa. 50:4ff.). Finally, he understands that merely proclaiming the salvation of Israel does not change anybody. The only access to salvation for his people and for the whole world is through the substitutionary suffering of the innocent Servant of Yahweh (Isa. 42:1-4; 49:1-6; 50:4-11a; 52:13—53:12). But who is that Servant of Yahweh whom Deutero-Isaiah introduced? It is difficult to prove convincingly that he symbolizes Israel in a collective way because Israel was never the innocent, willing, and faithfully suffering servant.[21] It must rather be a person with a universal, prophetic mission. Deutero-Isaiah was such a man and re-flections of his personal encounter with Israel may have colored the sec-tions about the Servant of Yahweh. But would he describe his own future death? Perhaps we come closer to an answer when we associate the figure of the Servant of the Lord with the figure we meet in the last part of our survey of Old Testament eschatology.

3. The coming Messiah

Christos, the Greek equivalent for Hebrew Messiah, is the title that is most frequently applied to Jesus of Nazareth in the New Testament. Most Christians therefore understand Jesus of Nazareth to be the Mes-siah and assume that title to have originated from promises contained in the Old Testament. But in looking for explicit references in the Old Testament we discover that there are hardly any messianic references that have eschatological significance.[22]

a. The significance of the term Messiah

The term Messiah, or anointed one, can refer to the high priest (Lev. 4:5), but usually it denotes the king of Israel (2 Sam. 1:16), who was anointed when he was designated king of Israel. Yet the expected king of the final time, the *eschaton,* is never called the Messiah.[23] The only exception is Isaiah 45:1, where a foreigner, the Persian king Cyrus, is called the Messiah to whom God speaks. This reference demonstrates the high expectations that had been connected with the Edict of Cyrus which permitted the exiles to return to Jerusalem. But the Old Testament writers are not aware of a person, called the Messiah, who is to bring the eschatological salvation. The eschatological fulfillment is too closely connected with God as the actor in history to be mediated by a messianic figure. This is different from the New Testament, in which Jesus is primarily understood as the Messiah, because he was believed to be re-turning to fulfill the eschatological expectations once pronounced to Israel. Though the title Messiah is not used in the Old Testament in an eschatological context, the hope for a God-provided figure who will usher in the eschaton is already present. We will see later that this figure seems to have originated from a retrospective glorification of David and from the promise that was given to him through Nathan (2 Sam. 7:12-15).

b. Main sources for the concept of a Messiah

From the very beginning Israelite history is seen as a promissory history (Gen. 12:2f.). The messianic figure in this history who is expected to bring about eschatological salvation is usually associated with the house of David. The blessing of Jacob over Judah (Gen. 49:8-12) can be considered as the oldest of these "messianic" expectations. The one who is supposed to come is described as one who will bring about and live in an age of paradisiac fruitfulness.[24] He will bind his foal to the vine and he will wash his garments in wine. The oracle, of Balaam (Num. 24:15-19) talks with a nationalistic and political tinge about the star that shall come forth out of Jacob and that shall have dominion over the neighboring nations. The restoration of the fallen "booth of David," as indicated in the Book of Amos, goes almost along similar lines (Amos 9:11-15). This restoration is expected as a dominion of Israel over all the nations. In recapitulating an idealized past as the "days of old" (Amos 9:11) the messianic time is described as a time of prosperity and peace ("The mountains shall drip sweet wine . . . and my people Israel . . . shall rebuild the ruined cities and inhabit them" [Amos 9:13ff.]).

In Isaiah's proclamation the messianic references are expanded beyond the scope of the immediate national and historical reality (Isa. 7:10-17; 9:1-7; 11:1-8). Many exegetes hesitate to consider Isaiah 7:10-17 as a messianic reference, since the birth of a child with the name Immanuel by a young woman could easily refer to Isaiah's own wife.[25] But the other two announcements, Isaiah 9:1-6 and 11:1-8, have clearly messianic character. In the midst of the darkness of destruction a light is emerging (Isa. 9:1-6). The Lord has broken the yoke that Assyria had imposed on Israel and now his anointed will be enthroned. The child who was conceived and the son who was given is not a child in the physical sense but the anointed one who becomes the son of Yahweh through his enthronement (Cf. Ps. 2:7). His names "Wonderful Counselor, Mighty God, Everlasting Father, Prince of Peace" indicate that his reign will be a reign of justice and of peace. In Isaiah 11:1-8 the messianic peace is emphasized even more in stating that the "Spirit of the Lord" will rest on the Messiah, and his reign now encompasses all of nature. Finally Micah proclaims that from Bethlehem, the village of David, the messianic ruler will come forth whose origin is from of old (Mic. 5:1ff.). The return of the Israelites to their homes is presupposed and the messianic peace and the magnitude of the kingdom are stressed.[26]

Toward the end of the Old Testament era, Haggai and Zechariah appear. For them the destruction of the Israelite nation and the return from exile are past events. They are aware that these events did not usher in the messianic kingdom. But God once was present in his temple in Jerusalem. So they emphasize the importance of rebuilding the temple as the prerequisite for the coming of Yahweh and of his kingdom (Hag. 1:7f.; Zech. 4:9). It is not enough to reoccupy the promised land, but it is necessary to reinstitute the place of worship as the cultic center of Israel and to be ready for the eschatological advent of Yahweh. Both prophets see themselves at the beginning of the time of salvation. The building of the temple initiates the time of salvation, the messianic prosperity starts (Hag. 2:19), and everybody will live in messianic peace (Zech. 8:12). Both see in Zerubbabel the anointed of the Lord, the coming Messiah (Hag. 2:20-23; Zech. 4:6-10).

But their high expectations end in disappointment. Zerubbabel is never enthroned and the hope for the fulfillment of the Davidic promise has to be revised again. The exulting words: "Lo, your king comes to you; triumphant and victorious is he, humble and riding on an ass, on a colt the foal of an ass" (Zech. 9:9) are too early. One generation before Zechariah, Deutero-Isaiah judged the situation much more realistically in the songs of the Servant of Yahweh. Confronted with the stubbornness and unbelief of his people he realized that true deliverance and fulfillment of salvation could only be brought about through the vicarious suffering of the true Servant of Yahweh. "We have turned every one to his own way; and the Lord has laid on him the iniquity of us all" (Isa. 53:6). Though the messianic element of the victorious king is not lacking in Deutero-Isaiah's description of the suffering servant, he ultimately did not dare to identify him with a historic figure. The understanding that the bringer of salvation could not be identified with a figure of present or past history, but will be a figure acting in and through history was more clearly conceived in the time of apocalyptic.

c. Expansion of the messianic hopes in the period of apocalyptic

Two important changes occurred in eschatological thought during the time of apocalyptic. A different role was attributed to the Messiah and a new understanding of history was gained. In the apocalyptic visions of Daniel God is still the ruler of the world. God brings about the cosmic and political changes and causes the eschatological time of salvation. In the apocalyptic books of 1 Enoch, 2 Ezra and 2 Baruch, the Messiah enjoys a more independent position. He himself destroys the enemies and brings about the salvation of Israel. Together with his independence goes an increasing emphasis on his pre-existence. He who existed before all worlds comes in the last time from heaven to initiate the time of salvation. To some degree this is already prefigured in the "son of man" imagery of Daniel 7. There the son of man (be he a corporate or an individual figure) signifies the final victory of God's power and greatness over the anti-Godly powers.[27] As a messianic figure he ushers in the final triumph of God's people in God's kingdom in God's appointed time.[28]

While the prophets conceived of the enemies of Israel as also God's enemies who will either be converted or destroyed in the last time, in apocalyptic all anti-Godly powers were included in this picture. If God shall have dominion over the world, all powers have to succumb. For instance, according to 1 Enoch, God smites the Gentiles in their final assault against Israel. Thereafter he sets up his throne, and the coming of the messianic kingdom is preceded by "the day of the great judgment" in which not only wicked people but also Azazel, demons and fallen angels will be punished or destroyed.[29] All the Gentiles will become righteous and worship God, and Jerusalem with its holy temple will be the center of the kingdom. While in 1 Enoch the kingdom is established on this earth, the tendency is to idealize this kingdom. Thus Jerusalem as its center is not the old Jerusalem, but a new Jerusalem which is either conceived as a purification of the old (1 Enoch 6-36) or as a replacement of it (1 Enoch 83-90).[30]

In the Similitudes of Enoch this view is expanded. The kingdom is now seen to be established not only on a transformed earth but also in a transformed heaven. In the Assumption of Moses, a book which probably originated when Jesus was still in his teens, this tendency goes even further. We are told that God's kingdom "will appear throughout all his creation." The whole conception of the coming events of the end is no longer confined within nationalistic or this-worldly expectations. It is supramundane and the kingdom is viewed as a kingdom of heaven.

The supra-nationalistic and supra-worldly view of God's reign was only possible because the apocalyptists could view history as a unity. The unity of history, however, presupposed a monotheistic faith in the one God who shaped and destined the world to his purpose.[31] This was already part of the Israelite heritage when the intertestamental period began. But the apocalyptists believed that they stood so close to the end of the world that they were able to take in the whole history at one glance and declare its meaning in terms of the divine purpose. "Within this purpose the people of Israel had a very high destiny which they dared not evade." [32] God is the Lord of the whole earth, Judaism is the embodiment of religion for all humanity, and Israel is the instrument for the establishment of God's world-wide rule. From their vantage point the apocalyptists assumed they could see past, present, and future in one continuous progression preordained by God. In this age all evil tendencies will grow until they culminate in the dominion of the political powers of this world. Then the end of this age will be near. The visible symptoms of the coming end are: utmost evil, unrest and wars, disturbance in nature and especially in the stellar courses. These are at the same time the travails that indicate the birth of the new aeon. The new aeon will be the complete opposite of the old. It will be the unlimited dominion of the kingdom of God.

This theocentrically developed, systematic, and highly deterministic concept of history culminates in the promised reign of the kingdom of God. "This historifying of the world in the category of the universal eschatological future is of tremendous importance for theology, for indeed it makes eschatology the universal horizon of all theology as such. Without apocalyptic a theological eschatology remains bogged down in the ethnic history of men or the existential history of the individual." [33] Apocalyptic, by including all powers and all nations, transcends the nationalistic eschatological expectations of Israel and opens the dimension of a new hope for the whole universe. H. H. Rowley captures this important deed of apocalyptic thinking very clearly when he says:

> They did not believe that God was indifferent to the world He had made; nor did they think He was impotent to take a hand in its course. They would have smiled at the idea so widespread in our day that God is of all beings the most helpless. . . . The apocalyptists believed in God, and believed that He had some purpose for the world He had made, and that His power was equal to its achievement. Their faith goes beyond the faith in divine control of history, indeed. It is a faith in the divine initiative in history for the attainment of its final goal. Such a belief is fundamental to the Christian view of God and the world. . . . Unless we believe in the eternity of human history in our world, we must expect that somehow, somewhere, the course of

history will come to an end. We can look for it to peter out, or we can look for the world to be snuffed out ignominiously. But if we believe that it is God's world, and that He created it with some purpose, we must find some way of translating the faith of the apocalyptists that that purpose will be achieved.[34]

Gerhard von Rad, to quote just one prominent representative of a very different evaluation of the apocalyptic movement, states that though apocalyptic cannot deny its relationship to prophecy, it exposed itself to the danger of teaching "a great cosmological gnosis."[35] Although in the fourth edition of his *Old Testament Theology* von Rad rewrote the whole chapter on "Daniel and Apocalyptic," his tone was not much more positive. The concept of salvation history that had prevailed in the prophetic view of history is now abandoned in the period of apocalyptic, according to von Rad, and history is conceived of in strictly deterministic terms.[36] (Such a view is, of course, clearly rejected by Rowley.) But even von Rad leaves open the question whether the apocalyptic view of history is a detrimental alienation from the belief in Yahweh or "a breakthrough to new theological horizons."[37] This breakthrough, we must assert, has occurred in Jesus of Nazareth. For him the apocalyptic dimension of the kingdom of God has become the center of his eschatological message.

NOTES

1. Walther Eichrodt, *Theology of the Old Testament*, trans. by J. A. Baker, 2 vols. (Philadelphia: Westminster, 1961-67) 2:213, states rightly that the concern to be united with one's father and the other members of the family is clearly derived from a belief that the dead still survive in some way or other in the grave. "This is, in fact, the oldest form of belief in survival." Eichrodt, however, does not admit a development from the belief of a survival in the grave to the belief of a survival in sheol, since the custom of giving food to the dead continued in Israel up to the very latest period.

   Though it is likely that both forms of conceptualization (survival in the grave and survival in sheol) co-existed for some time, the spiritualization (survival in sheol) seems to have prevailed in the long run. This would also be analogous to the changing conceptualization of God (from picturesque anthropomorphism [Gen. 3] to a more spiritualized and transcendent understanding [Isa. 6 or Ezek. 1]). We also must remember that the younger parts of the Old Testament are undeniably more interested in the final destiny of the dead than the older parts; a fact which seems to indicate a development.

2. Georg Fohrer, *History of Israelite Religion*, 215.

3. Th. C. Vriezen, *An Outline of Old Testament Theology,* 204, mentions that this attitude may be due to the fact that the belief in Yahweh as the giver of life always had to combat the ancient Eastern beliefs in spirits, the worship of the dead, and the rising of the spirits. According to Vriezen this conflict also accounts for the fact that the Old Testament speaks very little about life after death.

4. Cf. Leonhard Rost "Grab," in *Biblisch-Historisches Handwörterbuch,* ed. by B. Reicke and L. Rost, 3 vols. (Göttingen: Vandenhoeck & Ruprecht, 1962-66) 1:605f.

5. Kurt Galling, *Biblisches Reallexikon* (Tübingen, Mohr, 1937) 239.

6. Christoph Barth in his instructive book, *Die Errettung vom Tode in den individuellen Klage- und Danlkliedern des Alten Testamentes* (Zollikon: Evangelischer Verlag, 1947) 163, mentions: "So far nobody has convincingly stated that Psalm 73 contains a proof passage for the idea of an eternal life after death. Such a proof cannot be built on verse 24, since the text seems to be ambiguous." He also asserts that according to the psalms salvation from death is not conceived of as a bodily resurrection of the decayed corpse or as a continuation of life beyond death. The realm of the dead is "a land of no return" (165). Salvation from death means salvation from a hostile, threatening, and judging death. God will take the bitterness of death from the pious and let them die in peace.

7. The argument of Hans-Joachim Kraus, *Psalmen,* 2 vols. (Neukirchen, Kreis Moers: Neukirchner Verlag, 1958-60) 1:367f., to understand Ps. 49:15 as testimony to the belief in the resurrection, seems to be convincing.

8. Fohrer, *History of Israelite Religion,* 389f., claims that Dan. 12:2 is the only Old Testament passage that supports the hope for a resurrection. At the beginning of the end time Yahweh's power will extend over the living *and* the dead, so that the dead will no longer be excluded forever from the reign of God. Fohrer leaves no doubt that he appreciates a different train of thought much more: to find fulfillment of life in the reign of God and communion with God in this life so that the hereafter becomes irrelevant. According to Fohrer this view is dominant throughout the Old Testament.

   Other scholars think differently. Vriezen, *An Outline of Old Testament Theology,* 204, for instance, claims that faith in God as the Lord of life who performs miracles and who rules everywhere, even in sheol, "was the root from which afterwards the belief in the resurrection of man could spring." This seems to indicate that the hope for the resurrection is a consequent conclusion from the emerging belief in Yahweh's dominion over all the world, Israelite and non-Israelite, and visible and invisible. And if Eichrodt, *Theology of the Old Testament,* 2:512, is right in claiming that the belief in the resurrection attested by the book of Daniel is "clearly both much more strongly developed and indeed already a fixed dogma," this again suggests that such belief did not just originate around 200 B.C., but had its roots much earlier in history.

9. Cf. Ludwig Köhler, *Old Testament Theology,* trans. by A. S. Todd (Philadelphia: Westminster, 1957) 150. The German original says it even more drastically: "Nach Gottes Ordnung is der Tod das Ende. Es gibt nur ein Diesseits." (*Theologie des Alten Testaments* [3rd ed., Tübingen: J. C. B. Mohr, 1953] 137). But even Köhler concedes that the belief in the resurrection is at least "vaguely hinted at in the Old Testament" (ibid.).

10. Cf. Eichrodt, *Theology of the Old Testament,* 1:255. He also mentions that from Deuteronomy onward the word *berit* (covenant) was almost regularly used in the sense of the law to designate the content of the duties of the pious (2:345).

11. Claus Westermann, *The Praise of God in the Psalms,* trans. by K. R. Crim (Richmond, Va.: John Knox, 1965) 153f.

12. Cf. Fohrer, *History of Israelite Religion,* 269ff., in his treatment of the concepts of the day of the Lord and the remnant; and Jürgen Moltmann, *Theology of Hope; On*

the Ground and the Implications of a Christian Eschatology, trans. by J. W. Leitch (New York: Harper & Row, 1967), 104f., who convincingly demonstrates how God's promises were constantly being modified and expanded. Cf. also to the whole issue of faith in Yahweh and the prospect of the future the excellent study by Horst Dietrich Preuss, *Jahweglaube und Zukunftserwartung* (Stuttgart: W. Kohlhammer, 1968).

13. Sigmund Mowinckel, *He That Cometh*, trans. by G. W. Anderson (New York: Abingdon, 1954) 11.

14. Köhler, *Old Testament Theology*, 219f. Th. C. Vriezen, "Prophecy and Eschatology," in *Supplements to Vetus Testamentum*, vol. 1: *Congress Volume; Copenhagen 1953* (Leiden: E. J. Brill, 1953), 199-229, advocates a very interesting development of Israel's understanding of eschatology which seems to have some merit (225ff.): 1. Pre-eschatological period (before the classical prophets): There the future is seen to a great extent in the light of the past, the idealized age of David. Israel's hopes are mainly political-national. 2. Proto-eschatological period (Isaiah and his contemporaries): This is the period in which the vision of a new people and a new kingdom is beginning to play a part, a kingdom that will embrace the whole world and that rests on the spiritual forces that spring from God. 3. Actual-eschatological (Deutero-Isaiah and his contemporaries): The kingdom of God is not only seen as coming in *visions* but it is *experienced* as coming, and the world is going to be changed. 4. Transcendental-eschatological period of apocalyptic: Salvation is not expected to come in this world, but either spiritually in heaven or after a cosmic catastrophe in a new world.

    Of course, Vriezen is aware of the danger of such a periodization and he states that many of these lines run parallel to each other and extend their influence for centuries afterwards in various movements (e.g., the pre-eschatological period and the development of the concept of the Messiah).

15. Köhler, *Old Testament Theology*, 220f.

16. Vriezen, *An Outline of Old Testament Theology*, 351.

17. Fohrer, *History of Israelite Religion*, 246.

18. Vriezen, *An Outline of Old Testament Theology*, 360.

19. Though the vision in Ezekiel 37 concerns a picture of the people's restoration after the return from exile, the elements of this symbolism leave it to be understood that the resurrection of the dead is envisaged as a possibility (cf. Edmond Jacob, *Theology of the Old Testament*, trans. by A. W. Heathcote and Ph. J. Allcock [London: Hodder & Stoughton, 1958] 310).

20. Vriezen, *An Outline of Old Testament Theology*, 361f., mentions that Deutero-Isaiah uses the term *bara'* sixteen times. In Genesis, where the term is used with second highest frequency, we find it nine times.

21. Cf. Gerhard von Rad, *Old Testament Theology*, vol. 2: *The Theology of Israel's Prophetic Traditions*, trans. by D. M. G. Stalker (New York: Harper & Row, 1965) 259f. Von Rad in his careful, yet brief discussion of the problem of who the servant of Yahweh is supposed to be, comes to the conclusion that Deutero-Isaiah points to a prophetic figure of the future, "a prophet like Moses" (262).

22. Hans-Peter Müller, *Ursprünge und Strukturen alttestamentlicher Eschatologie* (Berlin: Töpelmann, 1969) 212, points out very convincingly that in the total context of Old Testament eschatology the hope for a Messiah plays only an unimportant role. The Messiah belongs mostly on the side of the people who are redeemed by Yahweh and only seldom is he conceived of as the actual bringer of salvation or even its mediator.

    In coming from the New Testament, however, we notice that there the Messiah is usually understood as an eschatological figure, as a redeemer sent by and representing God and as one who initiates the end time and brings salvation to the people.

23. Cf. A. S. van der Woude, "Messias," in *Biblisch-Historisches Handwörterbuch*, ed. by B. Reicke and L. Rost, 2:1197. For the following cf. also Hugo Gressmann, *Der*

Messias (Göttingen: Vandenhoeck & Ruprecht, 1929) 1. Though the king was understood as viceroy and mandatory of Yahweh himself, as expressed in the royal psalms, the office of the king did not seem to exert much influence on the development of the idea of the Messiah. Cf. Gerhard von Rad, *Old Testament Theology*, vol. 1: *The Theology of Israel's Historical Traditions*, trans. by D. M. G. Stalker (Edinburgh: Oliver & Boyd, 1962) 318ff.

24. Gerhard von Rad, *Genesis: A Commentary*, trans. by J. H. Marks (Philadelphia: Westminster, 1961) 419f.

25. Cf. Georg Fohrer, *Messiasfrage und Bibelverständnis* (Tübingen: Mohr, 1957) 11f., who treats there all pertinent messianic references. Cf. also von Rad, *Old Testament Theology*, 2:173f., who gives a good survey of the discussion on Isa. 7:10-17. Edward J. Young, *The Book of Isaiah*, 3 vols. (Grand Rapids, MI: Eerdmans, 1965-72) 1:289, is somewhat too confident when he comments on this passage: "There can be only one of whom this can be predicated, namely, Mary, the mother of the Lord."

26. We certainly agree with Georg Fohrer, "Die Strukturen der alttestamentlichen Eschatologie," in *Studien zur alttestamentlichen Prophetie (1949-1965)* (Berlin Töpelmann, 1967) 45f., when he says that the eschatological prophecy of the Old Testament usually does not refer to the end of the world or of history. It views the eschatological events as taking place within the framework of the nations, where political events or other historical incidents provide the starting point. But Fohrer also points out that nature and the cosmos are often included in these views. Especially toward the later parts of the Old Testament, the tendency is clearly universalistic in comprising the totality of world and history.

27. Cf. D. S. Russell, *The Method and Message of Jewish Apocalyptic; 200 BC-AD 100* London: SCM, 1964) 327.

28. H. H. Rowley, *The Relevance of Apocalyptic; A Study of Jewish and Christian Apocalypses from Daniel to the Revelation* (New York: Harper, 1955) 28f., mentions that no member of the Davidic house led the rising against Antiochus Epiphanes, so that it would have been a sheer lack of realism to import a Davidic Messiah into the visions. On the other hand, the thought of a Levitic Messiah had not yet arisen. Rowley also gives a good treatment of the question whether the son of man in Daniel can be interpreted as the Messiah and comes to the conclusion that "there is no evidence that the Son of Man was identified with the Messiah until the time of Jesus" (30). Though literally speaking Rowley is right, the son of man figure in Dan. 7 certainly cannot be regarded as totally unmessianic. We rather follow here von Rad, *Old Testament Theology*, 2:312, who says that there can be no doubt "that the son of man described in Dan. VII. 13 is initially presented as a Messianic figure in the wider sense of the term."

29. Russell, *The Method and Message of Jewish Apocalyptic*, 287.

30. Cf. for the following, Russell, 290f.

31. Ibid., 218ff.

32. Ibid., 221.

33. Moltmann, *Theology of Hope*, 137f.

34. Rowley, *The Relevance of Apocalyptic*, 152 and 155.

35. Von Rad, *Old Testament Theology*, 2:308.

36. Von Rad, *Theologie des Alten Testaments*, 4th ed. (Munich: Kaiser, 1965) 2:321.

37. Ibid., 322.

2
The Eschatological Proclamation of the New Testament

T
HE OLD TESTAMENT PROVIDES the historical background
for the eschatological proclamation of Jesus of Nazareth and of the New Testament. Although the New
Testament in its eschatological outlook cannot be adequately explained
without reference to the Old Testament, it is not simply a continuation
of the Old Testament. Yet the continuity between the two must be
affirmed in a twofold way: (1) Yahweh, the God of Abraham, Isaac
and Jacob, the God of the Old Testament, is the father of Jesus of Nazareth; and (2) Jesus was a Jew. The New Testament is still concerned
with the promises that are given by the same God to the same ethnic
community in the same geographical area of our earth. But the New
Testament shows that only the sameness of the God is decisive, while
the ethnic and geographical limits are no longer valid. Everyone and
everything will participate in the new future.

Though there is a very legitimate interest in the "theologies" of the
composers of the different parts of the New Testament, the decisive figure is still Jesus of Nazareth. We agree with Rudolf Bultmann that we
are not interested in Jesus' personality.[1] But we cannot agree with him
when he regards the proclamation of Jesus as just a presupposition of
New Testament theology and not as a part of it.[2] The eschatological
proclamation of Jesus is an integral part of the New Testament. And
an attempt to understand the New Testament meaning of eschatology
without considering Jesus' own proclamation is a contradiction in itself.

1. The eschatological figure of Jesus

The relationship between Jesus and eschatology is significant in three
areas: in his proclamation, in his own self-understanding, and in his
attitude towards the future. As far as we know, Jesus had a definite

53

proclamation, he had a definite understanding of himself that is reflected in his conduct,[3] and he was not oblivious to the future.

New Testament research has shown us how difficult it is to penetrate beyond the reflections of the first Christian community and the writers of the New Testament texts to the historical Jesus. But the new quest and the continued quest have also shown us that such a task is not impossible. Yet the historical Jesus alone is not what matters. If it were, the New Testament would have missed its point, since it neither provides us nor wants to provide us with a biography of Jesus of Nazareth. But it is of fundamental theological relevance how the historical Jesus is reflected in the New Testament.[4] He is the starting point and the focus of the New Testament proclamation, and without an adequate understanding of him we cannot arrive at an adequate interpretation of the New Testament *kerygma*. Without a basic knowledge of Jesus and his message we would be unable to determine whether the New Testament proclamation is in continuity or in discontinuity with Jesus' own teaching. This is one of the reasons why a strictly kerygmatic theology always seems somewhat abstract, lacking the dynamic power exhibited by Jesus.[5]

a. Jesus' eschatological message of the kingdom of God

Jesus' proclamation was a totally eschatological proclamation.[6] Jesus did not give his listeners a timetable and inform them in detail about the things that are going to happen at some future point, but he addressed his audience in such a way that his address implied an immediate decision.[7] He did not spell out certain eschatological doctrines, but he confronted the people with a radical decision for or against God. This demand for a decision became at the same time a decision for or against Jesus and his actions. His proclamation, his own person, and his own actions form a unity that provoked and called for a decision. "Follow me, and leave the dead to bury their own dead" (Matt. 8:22); "No one who puts his hand to the plow and looks back is fit for the kingdom of God" (Luke 9:62); "And blessed is he who takes no offense at me" (Matt. 11:6); these are only a few passages that show the urgency of an immediate decision here and now. The now is the decisive point of history and no longer the future as in apocalyptic or in the promissory history of the Old Testament. This decisiveness of the present that Jesus proclaimed is enlightened through his own actions.

When John the Baptist sent two of his disciples to ask Jesus whether he was the promised one or whether they should wait for someone else, Jesus referred them to his actions. He did not refer to any titles that were conferred on him, but to his actions.[8] "The blind receive their sight, the lame walk, lepers are cleansed, and the deaf hear, the dead are raised up, the poor have good news preached to them" (Luke 7:22), was his answer. With this remark he applied to himself the Old Testament imagery which was connected with the time of salvation (Isa. 35:5f.). When at the wedding in Cana he turned water into wine (John 2:11), this epiphanic miracle[9] referred to the Old Testament understanding of wine as the symbol of the time of salvation. Jesus introduced himself here as the one in whom this salvation had become manifest. Jesus also talked about the new wine that should not be poured into old wineskins (Matt. 9:17). The old time is past; the time of salvation has been initiated. At one point Jesus stated it even more clearly: "But if it is by the finger of God that I cast out demons, then the kingdom of God has come upon you" (Luke 11:20). With Jesus of Nazareth the kingdom of God has already started. What had been expected for centuries, what had been projected into the future or into the present for so long, has started now. The kingdom of God is in the midst of you, said Jesus. Not because he was such an important preacher, or because he had such an important message, did he call for an immediate decision. The kingdom of God has come with his appearance and thus it is time, decisive time. The today of Jesus is the goal of history.

Although Jesus emphasized the decisiveness of his own person and of the present time, he did not point to an impending or immediately coming end of the world, except to reinforce the urgency of an immediate decision for or against God.[10] As far as we know, the oral tradition of the sayings of Jesus, sometimes called "Q," contains no indication that Jesus was a "doomsday prophet" of the immediately approaching end of the world. If there are any authentic words of Jesus about such matters, they should be found in the Q source. But there is no evidence in Q. This coincides with another finding: neither the Jewish contemporaries of Jesus nor the Jewish polemics after Jesus accused him of announcing an immediate end of the world that did not come. We cannot imagine that they would not have exploited such false prophecy. Evidently Jesus was not interested in such prophecies. The gospels tell us that he showed John the Baptist, who fervently proclaimed the immediate coming of the end, a cold shoulder. Why was Jesus not interested in the immediate future and in prophecies of the immediate end of the world? Perhaps we may get a better understanding of this phenomenon if we investigate Jesus' self-understanding.

b. Jesus' self-understanding

It was neither the task nor the intention of Jesus to proclaim a doctrine of the last things or a flawless doctrine of Christ. Nevertheless, if we correlate his assertions about the eschaton and especially about the kingdom of God with his person, we cannot but ask what kind of person he was. We get some clues about his self-understanding from the way he related himself to his message and from the few instances when he talked about himself. While Jesus did not make himself the focus of his teachings, it would be unrealistic to assume that he never said a word about himself. But can we distinguish clearly enough between the way people experienced him and reflected upon him and the way he actually talked about himself? The dilemma is most evident when we consider the titles of Jesus.

Most Christians would state without hesitation that Jesus was the Christ and that he called himself the Messiah. However, a careful analysis of the New Testament shows us that the title Messiah, or *Christos* in Greek, is used only 53 times in the gospels, but 280 times outside the gospels. It is entirely missing in the oldest source, Q, and so are the titles Son of David, King of Israel, and King of the Jews.[11] Mark, the oldest gospel, does not give us clear evidence that Jesus used the term Messiah either. The Gospel of John, which uses the term quite frequently, never does it in such a way as to indicate that Jesus himself had used it. This shows that the term Messiah could not have played an important role in the life of Jesus.

Jesus probably refused the title Messiah whenever it was conferred on him.[12] He was not interested in the political and nationalistic aspirations connected with the coming of the Messiah and he did not want to be taken for a political liberator. Never do we hear that he conspired against the Roman occupation army or that he wanted to revolt against them. Though the charges against him were finally of political nature, he clearly denied them. He did not want to be a Judas Maccabaeus or a Bar Kochba or any of the many other political and religious Messiahs that emerged in Israel before or after him.

There was, however, another less politically and nationalistically colored title Jesus seemingly used, the title "Son of man." This title occurs about 80 times in the gospels and only four times outside of them. It occurs in all four gospels, including Q. But it is almost exclusively used in sayings of Jesus and hardly ever by people addressing Jesus. As an indirect support for the thesis that Jesus could have used the title, we may note that it was never used in the Jewish apocalyptic literature after Christ. Only 2 Ezra uses the term and Rabbi Abbahu (ca. 300) says in the Jerusalem Talmud: "If a man says to you: 'I am God,' then he lies; if 'I am the son of man,' he will finally regret it" (J. Taan 2:1).[13]

Jesus and the first Christian community certainly did not invent the term Son of man. Already in Judaism it has a definite connotation in its apocalyptic context.[14] In later Judaism the main eschatological function of the Son of man was one of judging.[15] Jesus, however, expanded and modified this picture of the Son of man who is coming to judge all nations. For him this title is not just one of exultation but of humiliation and he connects it with the title of the suffering servant. Thus he who judges the world in the name of the Lord also suffers vicariously for it and reconciles it with God. In an almost classic way this is expressed in Mark 10:45 where Jesus says: "For the Son of man also came not to be served but to serve, and to give his life as a ransom for many."

With this word we have already touched the first group of Son of man sayings that speak about the Son of man who is going to die and then will be resurrected. The second group deals with sayings of the Son of man who has come to judge and to save. The third deals with the Son of man who has power to forgive sins. All three have eminent eschatological significance but are not colored by popular nationalistic overtones. Jesus is the Son of man who lives unknown among the people. But in the end of time he will appear openly to judge and to redeem. Though he does not live as the Son of man in glory, his actions already show who he is. He is the master of the law, he can judge and forgive sins (Mark 2:10, 28), he can condemn and provide salvation. According to the Gospel of John he even permits someone to fall down before him and adore him (John 9:35ff.). This kind of adoration was strictly reserved for God, but Jesus as the Son of man, the representative of God, is eligible for such cultic devotion.[16] The attitude toward him decides the future of the individual. Thus the present is decisive; it is the time of the Son of man.

The deepest self-understanding of Jesus, however, cannot be coined into a title. It is a strictly singular phenomenon, namely that Jesus is the final self-disclosure of God. In Jesus there occurred the final self-disclosure of God and thus the end of all history in anticipation.[17] Jesus' confession that he was this direct and final self-disclosure of God led to his being convicted as a heretic. But how did he express this self-understanding? We remember that in the trial of Jesus, the High Priest concluded from the answer that Jesus had given to the question: Are you the Christ, the Son of the Blessed? (Mark 14:61) that Jesus had committed blasphemy. But what is contained in Jesus' answer that would lead to such a devastating reaction? Jesus seemingly recited only Jewish eschatological expectations when he said: "I am; and you will see the Son of man sitting at the right hand of Power, and coming with the clouds of heaven" (Mark 14:62).

The issue becomes clear when we consider the Old Testament use of the phrase *ego eimi* (I am). In the Septuagint we find this phrase several times, especially prominently in Deutero-Isaiah, rendering the Hebrew *ani hu,* meaning "I [am] He" into Greek.[18] In Deutero-Isaiah the phrase *ani hu* is a solemn statement or assertion that is always attributed to Yahweh (cf. Isa. 41:4; 43:10; 46:4). Over against claims made by other gods this phrase asserts polemically that only Yahweh is the Lord of history. It also seems to be a concise abbreviation of the longer form of divine self-predication, especially of "I am Yahweh." While the *ani hu* formula as divine self-predication of Yahweh occurs outside Deutero-Isaiah only in Deuteronomy 32:39, the self-predication "I am Yahweh" is rather widespread in the Old Testament. As Ethelbert Stauffer has pointed out, there is also some evidence that the *ani hu* was used liturgically in the worship of the Jerusalem temple, since the Levites presumably sang the Song of Moses, containing Deuteronomy 32:39 on the Sabbath of the Feast of Tabernacles.[19] The use of *ani hu* lived on in the worship service of the temple and of the synagogues and was known even to the Qumran community.[20]

At a few decisive places in the gospels Jesus uses the term *ego eimi* in a way analogous to the Old Testament theophany formula. For instance, according to Mark 13:6 Jesus says: "Many will come in my name, saying, 'I am he!' and they will lead many astray." [21] In Matthew this theophanic self-predication is expanded into an explicitly christological statement which reads: "and say I am the Christ" (Matt. 24:5).

Returning to the answer that Jesus gave the high priest in Mark 14:62, we must admit that it could be interpreted without reference to the Old Testament revelational formula *ani hu* or to any of its variations. It could simply have been a solemn way of saying "yes," as for instance Matthew interprets it in 26:64. Philip B. Harner, for instance, arrives at the notion that "it is not likely that we can understand the *ego eimi* of Mark 14:62 and Luke 14:70 in an absolute sense." [22] This conclusion is surprising, however, considering that the corollary evidence seems to lead in the opposite direction, namely that the *ego eimi* in Mark 14:62 is indeed used in an absolute sense as a divine self-predication. The matter becomes clearer if we look at the usage of *ego eimi* in other passages in Mark. The phrase appears first in Mark 6:50 at the conclusion of the miracle of the walking on water, where Jesus tells his disciples: "Take heart, it is I; have no fear." Here the phrase functions almost in a titular sense and as a revelational formula. In Mark 13:6 we have heard that Jesus warns his disciples that: "Many will come in my name, saying, 'I am he!' and they will lead many astray." Again *ego eimi* is used as a formula of revelation or identification, since its misappropriation leads the believer astray.

We may conclude that Jesus' use of the *ego eimi* in Mark 14:62 is more than a simple affirmation. He uses a revelational formula to disclose himself and identify himself with God. As the words following the *ego eimi* show, the messianic secret is lifted and Jesus unashamedly admits his messianic sonship. "In Mark 14:62, therefore, Jesus is making an explicit Messianic claim, the Messianic Secret is being formally disclosed." [23] Since the messianic secret was carefully hidden in Mark, we may wonder whether Jesus' response does not reflect the theology of the evangelist more than Jesus' own words. We might be overestimating the historical value of this passage if we would not concede the possibility that this passage has been carefully edited to reflect the eschatological hopes of the nascent church. But there is another way of determining the historical probability of the *ego eimi* response of Jesus.

As Ernst Fuchs has pointed out, Jesus emphasized in his proclamation the will of God in such a way as only someone could do who stood in God's place.[24] For instance, in his parables Jesus did not simply tell us how God acts, but he told us that God acts the way Jesus acts. We see this especially well in the parable of the lost sheep (Luke 15:3-7). Luke tells us that when the Pharisees and scribes remarked, "This man receives sinners and eats with them" (Luke 16:2), Jesus told them parables of God's concern for the lost and sinful, implying that God acts like Jesus. Mark 14:62 would then indicate that at the end of his career Jesus not only acted as if he stood in God's place but evidently even told his audience that he stood in God's place and did so by using the revelational formula *ego eimi*. In all likelihood *ego eimi* was Jesus' own response to the high priest. Since Jesus did not conform to the prevalent messianic expectations but nevertheless made claims that could only be understood in messianic terms, the high priest and most other people at that time concluded that Jesus had committed blasphemy.

Another similarly misunderstood theophanic self-predication occurs in Jesus' reply to the Samaritan woman. When she said to him in the traditional messianic expectation, "I know that Messiah is coming; when he comes, he will show us all things" Jesus corrected her by saying, "I who speak to you am he" (John 4:25f.). He revealed himself herewith as the full self-disclosure of God. But the woman did not understand him. She was too much entangled in the traditional pattern of messianic thinking.

This is the overall impression that Jesus of Nazareth left: he emphasized his presence as the decisive hour, he emphasized himself as the full self-disclosure of God, and he emphasized that with him the kingdom of God had come.[25] Nobody really believed him until Easter. They were all caught up in the traditional thinking that the Messiah and the eschaton were close at hand. They shut their eyes to the present and expected everything in the near future. But what does Jesus' emphasis on the present mean? Is there no future to come? Did everything already happen in the life and death of Jesus of Nazareth?

c. Jesus and the question of the future

Jesus rejected any predictions of when the end of the world would occur. About that day nobody knows except God himself (Mark 13:32). Since God has entered this world in Jesus, we cannot postpone preparing for our encounter with God until we assume that this world will soon come to an end. We must always be ready.

Jesus is the decisive point in history. He did not comfort the one criminal on the cross with some future expectation, but assured him that today he would be with him in paradise (Luke 23:43). Jesus' person, his proclamation, and his action demanded an immediate decision, and this decision implied an immediate reward. This does not mean that the future will be insignificant. Quite the opposite! Only because of Jesus' presence will our future make any sense.

Jesus and his destiny are, symbolically speaking, the lens through which the rays of all history since the creation of the world are focused and projected into the future.[26] The future is predictable solely because it receives its future-directedness from Jesus Christ. In this way Jesus determined the future. He told his followers not to be worried about the future, because in him and in the attitude toward him the future was already irreversibly decided. Of course, this was contrary to most of the popular messianic hopes and expectations. People expected total fulfill-ment of history in the present. They saw in Jesus the political messianic leader who should once and for all redeem Israel from all its enemies. Even some of the disciples confessed after Jesus' death with bitter resig-nation: "But we had hoped that he was the one to redeem Israel" (Luke 24:21).

When Jesus was finally resurrected the question had to be decided again: should the resurrection be interpreted in the strictly apocalyptic context as the first act of the final eschatological drama, or was it the ultimate event of the proleptic anticipatory history of Jesus? Many seem to have interpreted it as the first act of the eschatological drama after which the other acts were to follow in rapid succession.[27] The hope that the end should come soon is traceable in many places in the New Testa-ment. Most of the books of the New Testament reflect this situation.

2. The eschatological proclamation of the gospel writers

The evangelists faced the all-decisive question of how they should re-spond to the person and destiny of Jesus. Should they interpret his resur-rection as the first act of the final eschatological drama and intensify the eschatological fever of an end of the world near at hand? Or should they admit that the end did not come as soon as most of them had hoped and concentrate on a biographical report? Or should they try to interpret the future history in the light of the final self-disclosure of God as it had occurred in and with Jesus of Nazareth? Regardless of their individual emphases and predilections the gospel writers seemed to work along one and the same line: in the life, destiny, and resurrection of Jesus there had occurred the final self-disclosure of God.[28] We live in an interim between this self-disclosure and the universal transformation of the world. But exegetical research shows more and more clearly that the gospels considerably differed from each other in interpreting this interim period.

a. The interim in the view of the synoptics

The synoptic writers seek to counter the eschatological fever of the impending end of the world and the resulting disenchantment when the final events did not occur by emphasizing the length of the interim be-fore the final eschaton.[29] Statements that suggest an immediately ap-proaching eschaton are balanced by passages that speak of it in the most distant future. The statement for example that "there are some standing here who will not taste death before they see the kingdom of God come with power" (Mark 9:1) is countered with assurance that before Christ will finally return the gospel must be preached to all nations (Mark 13:10). Or in a similar way the words "Truly, I say to you, this generation will not pass away, before all these things take place," are immediately followed by the assertion "heaven and earth will pass away, but my words will not pass away" (Mark 13:30; Matt. 24:34f.; Luke 21:32f.). The first part of the verse seems to point clearly to the eschaton at hand, while the next sentence in pointing to the trustworthiness of Jesus' word seems to counteract any possible disappointment.[30]

Mark, as the oldest gospel, stands closer than the other gospel writers to the disturbing situation caused by Jesus' death and resurrection. He sees one way of combating all vain hopes in the impending end by asserting that Jesus wanted no outsider to understand fully the secret of the kingdom of God. Only his disciples, in coming from the Easter event, have the privilege to understand completely the life, destiny, and proclamation of Jesus (Mark 4:11f.).[31] Before Easter even the disciples could not really understand him (Mark 6:52; 9:32). Through the Easter experience the interim period is no longer a time of frustrated waiting, but of intense activity. The period between the resurrection of Jesus Christ and his final coming is the time of the world mission. However, unlike Matthew and Luke, Mark does not yet reflect on the activities of the exalted Christ during this time, and he mentions the emerging church only implicitly in connection with the task of world mission.

When we look at the approach of the Gospel of Matthew we see a much more elaborate and clarified understanding of the interim period. This gospel wants to show that the Old Testament promises have found their fulfillment in Jesus.[32] He did not come to abolish the law and the prophets, but to fulfill them (Matt. 5:17f.). He fulfilled the Immanuel promise (Isa. 7:14; Matt. 1:22f.), the Galilee promise (Isa. 9:1; Matt. 4:12-15), the Bethlehem promise (Mic. 5:2; Matt. 2:5f.), the servant of the Lord promise (Isa. 53:4; Matt. 8:17), and many others. Consequently a multitude of Old Testament eschatological titles are bestowed upon him. He is the Messiah, the Son of David, the King of Israel, the Son of God, and the Son of man, to name just a few. This intends to show not so much that Jesus is the bringer of the eschaton, but that he stands in true continuity with the Old Testament.

This continuity is crucial for the interpretation of the interim period, because the church that Jesus founded is through his authority the true Israel (Matt. 16:18). The historical nation of Israel has neglected and lost its commission to be the light of the nations. Thus the church replaces it and steps into continuity with the Israel of promise. Though there are specific orders and structures in the church (Matt. 18:15ff.), the church is not here to stay. It is only an interim community. It is also far from being a pure community of true believers. Not until the final judgment will the just be separated from the unjust (Matt. 13). Yet the church is already on its way towards this final judgment when Christ will appear and select the chosen ones.[33] The theme of the coming judgment is consistent throughout the gospel. The Sermon on the Mount (5-7), the sending out of the Twelve (10), and the Apocalypse (24), all indicate the judgment as *the* coming event.

Luke finally moved beyond the notion of a strict interim period by introducing a salvation-historical understanding of history. Already in the opening chapters of his gospel he placed Jesus in the context of world history (Luke 2:1-4 and 1:5f.). But the evangelist does not want to convey the idea that the life and destiny of Jesus are subject to the course of history. Jesus is the focal point of history through whom all history receives its significance and proper valuation. Luke distinguishes three main epochs of history: (1) the time of Israel; (2) the time of Jesus as the center of history; and (3) the time of the church. John the Baptist is depicted as the last prophet and not as the forerunner of Jesus (Luke 16:16), since Jesus is without forerunner and without precedent.[34] The whole epoch of the law and the prophets leads up to Jesus and then, all of a sudden, Jesus appears as the center of time.

Luke does not seem to encounter the issue of impending eschatology, nor is he bothered with any other exuberant eschatological expectations. "When you hear of wars and tumults, do not be terrified; for this must first take place, but the end will not be at once" (Luke 21:9) seems to be his dominant theme. The decisive event has happened. Jesus has come, and some day, he will usher in the final end of all history and judge the living and the dead. But the end will bring nothing essentially new concerning salvation. In analogy to his ascension Christ will only return as the exalted Lord.[35]

This view of history and of eschatology is by no means one of resignation or pessimism. God has provided the interim as the time of the church. Since the Gospel is spread to ever new shores and since the Christians are given God's Holy Spirit, it is of no interest how long the

church will last and when the end will come. In viewing the life and
destiny of Jesus we realize that he has announced the end and the coming of his kingdom. The truth of what he stood for and the truth of his
proclamation are guaranteed through his miracles, his resurrection, and
his ascension.[36] The Christians are not even alone in the world. The exalted Christ in heaven is active in his word which is proclaimed in history. His people work in "his name" and in "his spirit." The Christians
live in this world without fear and without wild expectations, but with
hope. To incorporate the Christian existence into the world, yet to keep
it open for the final end of all history, is the main concern of Luke both
in his gospel and in the Acts of the Apostles.

b. The emphasis on the present in the Gospel of John

For Martin Luther the Gospel of John was the main gospel, because
it proclaimed Christ so clearly. In recent times, however, the Gospel of
John has become more and more "the puzzle of the NT, both historically and literally, in theology and in the history of religion." [37] This is
also true for its eschatological outlook. It replaces the eschatological
terms of the synoptics with its own terminology. The standard synoptic
term "the kingdom of God" is only used twice in John, and the term
"this aeon" is replaced by "this cosmos," "the future aeon" by "the eternal
life," and "the end of the aeon" by "in the last day" to list just a few
changes. It is also the only gospel that talks about the "ruler of this
cosmos," and it has no specific apocalyptic passages in contrast to the
synoptic gospels (Mark 13; Matt. 24; Luke 17; 21).

In the Gospel of John, Jesus talks about "his Father's house" instead
of about "heaven" (John 14:2), and he says he "will come again" (John
14:3), a phrase not used in the synoptic gospels. On the other hand he
assures those who believe in him who sent him that they already have
eternal life (John 5:24). They will not even come into judgment, but
have passed from death to life. When Martha tells Jesus about her dead
brother, "I know that he will rise again in the resurrection at the last
day," he replies in a similar way, "I am the resurrection and the life;
he who believes in me, though he die, yet shall he live, and whoever
lives and believes in me shall never die" (John 11:24ff.). Does this mean
that the now is so decisive as to devaluate the future? Or do we already
have eternal life now and is nothing else to come?

It would be a serious misunderstanding to assume that John eliminated all future eschatology and concentrated strictly on the present

as the time of salvation. It is true that according to John salvation is a present reality for the believer.[38] But the true future is not eliminated, it is rather actualized.[39] John wants to demonstrate that in Jesus Christ the exclusive opposition between God and the world is bridged. Jesus is the incarnate word of God (John 1:14). One can see through the authority that Jesus claims and through the actions that he performs that God himself speaks and acts in and through him (John 14:9ff.). In Jesus the opposition is bridged between the present life and the life beyond. Therefore the opposition between life and death, between time and eternity, and between present, past, and future is only a relative one.[40] Even the law of gravity is suspended when confronted with Jesus Christ (John 6:19). Through the coming of the Godly into the sphere of the created, the boundaries of this world have only relative, but not ir-relevant, character. The main task is accomplished, the ruler of this world is already judged (John 16:11).

While in Jesus Christ the opposition between this life and the future life is bridged, for the believer a new dichotomy emerges. Jesus was not the Messiah everybody expected. He came to his own, but his people received him not (John 1:11).[41] The Gospel of John is the gospel of the great misunderstandings. In fascinating style the gospel writer managed to point out that the unbelievers are confronted with Jesus like a color-blind person with traffic lights. One may know everything about it, but in the decisive moment one cannot grasp the exact meaning. The unbe-lievers constantly miss Jesus. They exclude themselves from participation in the real future, because only the believers can discern that Jesus opens for us the real future. The believers have the promise of the comforter or the Holy Spirit (John 14:15ff., 25f.; 16:4b-11, 12-15) whom Jesus Christ will send to guide them into all truth. The comforter bridges the gulf between the historical Jesus who is no longer among them and the proclamation of the gospel. He legitimizes the existence of the believers as a waiting existence, an existence of participation in a salvation which has been brought about through Jesus but which is not commonly ac-cessible.

The eschatological aspect of the Gospel of John shows less missionary character than that of the synoptics.[42] This is not surprising because by now the Jews had evicted the Christians from the synagogues (John 16:2). Thus the liberating and encouraging power of Jesus' coming gains renewed significance. The Gospel of John encourages a faithful eschato-logical existence of proleptic fulfillment and yet of expectation. "But these are written that you may believe that Jesus is the Christ, the Son of God, and that believing you may have life in his name" (John 20:31). This characterizes the intention of the gospel: to give witness to the eschatological significance of Jesus, and to bridge the gulf between Jesus' redemptive act and his second coming. Though the Gospel of John does not proclaim a dynamic message that incites to action, but a comforting message that invites to contemplation, its basic description of the Christian existence is very close to that of Paul.

3. The eschatological message of Paul

It is not for chronological reasons that we introduce Paul as the last important representative of New Testament eschatology. Paul's writings are the earliest we have in the New Testament. Thus he should be listed first. But of the writers mentioned so far, he is the only one who was no disciple or follower of Jesus during Jesus' life on earth. Once a persecutor of the early Christian community, he became one of their most fervent advocates. He came in late, as he himself admits (1 Cor. 15:9). Though it is safe to assume that he had some knowledge of Jesus and the Christian faith before he was converted, his knowledge was not extensive.[43] Soon after his conversion, however, he became one of the most influential Christians, and in considering his eschatological outlook we will notice that he probably comes closest to the eschatological message of Jesus of Nazareth. He also understood best how to incorporate the life, destiny, and resurrection of Jesus Christ into his eschatological picture. As Paul represents, so to speak, the most influential and the most reflected eschatological perspective within the New Testament, it is proper to present him as the conclusion of the New Testament.

a. Paul's eschatological call

The key to understanding Paul's eschatological message is his call. When Paul introduces himself to the Roman congregation he says:

> Paul, a servant of Jesus Christ, called to be an apostle, set apart for the gospel of God which he promised beforehand through his prophets in the holy scriptures, the gospel concerning his Son, who was descended from David according to the flesh and designated Son of God in power according to the Spirit of holiness by his resurrection from the dead, Jesus Christ our Lord, through whom we have received grace and apostleship to bring about the obedience of faith for the

sake of his name among all the nations, including yourselves who were
called to belong to Jesus Christ (Rom. 1:1-6).

Paul does not introduce himself as a free-style, self-made missionary, but
as one called to serve as apostle. "He is a man who has been appointed
to a proper place and a peculiar task in the series of events to be accomplished in the final days of this world." [44] Those events have as their
central figure the Messiah, the Christ Jesus, crucified, risen, and returning to judgment and salvation. It is important for Paul that Jesus Christ
is the fulfillment of the Old Testament prophecies and that he lived here
on earth as a descendant of David. [45] This establishes the continuity between Paul's proclamation and the Old Testament faith. On the other
hand it is also important that through his resurrection Jesus of Nazareth
was exalted as our Lord Jesus Christ and designated Son of God. This
establishes and emphasizes the continuity between the Old Testament
promises and the resurrection of Jesus Christ. According to the Old
Testament expectations and promises the series of final events had started with Jesus' coming and his death and resurrection.

Through his death and resurrection as the Messiah, Jesus had taken
his place at the right hand of his father in heaven. "What remained was
his *parousia* and the coming of the kingdom of heaven in power and
glory." [46] The ethnic particularity of salvation had become obsolete since
Jesus, formerly the Messiah of the Jews, had been enthroned as Lord
and Savior of the whole world. Our Savior is at the same time the Lord
of the universe (Phil. 2:9ff.): All humankind, all cosmic powers, the
whole universe belong to him. Through his enthronement all people
have access through faith to his kingdom and to salvation. This fact
constitutes the gospel for the non-Jewish people. Paul was chosen to proclaim this gospel in the interval between the resurrection of Jesus Christ
and his coming in power. The conviction that the gospel must be spread
so that people can accept Christ and be saved gave Paul the drive to
proclaim the gospel in an unknown and pagan environment. Paul did
not want to deprive them of their choice just because he had not fully
responded to his call in the eschatological time.

b. Our life as a life between the aeons

Paul also sees the life of the Christians as a life between the aeons.
He was convinced that we live in the final era. [47] The old aeon has
passed away and the Messiah has come. But the new aeon is not fully

here, because the Messiah has not yet returned in power. This "not yet" is no reason for bewilderment. The events of the final era will occur successively according to the preordained plan of God and will lead up to the definite goal, the destruction of the old world, and the creation of the new and eternal aeon. The decisive events in this apocalyptic picture are the resurrection of the dead which was made possible and initiated by Christ's resurrection (1 Cor. 15) and the surprising coming of the day of the Lord (1 Thess. 5:2).

Christ is the end of the law (Rom. 10:4) and the end of history. The old covenant no longer applies to us since a new covenant has been established (2 Cor. 3:6). But we still live in a transitional period, in a time of faith (2 Cor. 5:7) and of waiting (Rom. 8:23ff.). This does not mean that the coming eschaton is totally outstanding. Our interim existence is determined by the future, because salvation is already active in us. We participate in the gifts of grace: in faith, love, and hope (1 Cor. 13). We are not like those who have no hope. We have died with Christ in our baptism and we live in Christ and Christ lives in us (Gal. 2:20). This means that the Christian existence is a dialectical existence. It is lived in the world, but not from this world.[48] The power of existence is given us from beyond, the beyond which will come to us in the eschaton.

The future was certainly important for Paul and cannot be eliminated from his expectations.[49] Though Paul actualized the future by saying that we already live with Christ, he was looking forward to being resurrected with him and living with him in a manifest way (2 Cor. 4:14; 1 Thess. 4:14). This expectation is both being actualized in the present and still to be fulfilled in the future. The final eschatological events and the fulfillment of our eschatological existence lie in the future. In spite of his emphasis on the dialectical character of existence between actualization in anticipation and the still outstanding fulfillment, he occasionally succumbed to the eschatological fever of impending eschatology. For instance, he was convinced that since his conversion the coming of the eschaton had already made progress (Rom. 13:11); he was sure that the Lord was close at hand (Phil. 4:5); and he assured the people in Thessalonica that the Lord would return in his lifetime (1 Thess. 4:15). But advocating an impending eschatology was only a sideline in his faith. His hope was not bound to a fixed date only to falter with the resulting delay, but it was grounded in the gospel that pronounced the fulfillment of the Old Testament promises and that asked at the same time for a faithful existence. Moreover, Paul knew that salvation is realized in us today in a paradoxical way (2 Cor. 4:7-12). While Jesus emphasized the present as the time of decision, Paul emphasized it as the time of faithful and active waiting to enter into the fulfillment of the new creation. Paul included the Christ event in the kerygma and proclaimed it in a "Christian" time. For him the decisive turning point of history was already past.[50]

c. Eschatology beyond spiritualism and disappointment

Paul, the most influential writer of the New Testament, saved Christian eschatology from two blind alleys, from unhistorical spiritualism and from overanxious disappointment.[51] Especially in his firm discussions with a Gnostic group in Corinth he emphasized the proleptic and preliminary eschatological character of Christian existence. The interim is not yet the time of fulfillment. The eschaton is still to come and a faithful existence is the only way to be prepared for it. The interim is the time of the proclamation of the gospel and the time where we can and shall realize the (ethical) teachings of Christ. In our new allegiance to Christ we enjoy an existence of freedom from law but without libertinism. On the other hand, Paul emphasizes for those who are about to be disappointed because the eschaton has not yet arrived that the eschatological fulfillment will not tarry. It is a future event affecting us, our earth, and the whole creation. Christ's resurrection was the first part of it, and, since we know that the resurrection of the dead is part of the eschatological events, the end cannot wait indefinitely.[52] Jesus' resurrection has validated for us the apocalyptic idea of the resurrection of the dead. By anticipating it as the Christ through his own resurrection, he has provided us with a foundation for hope.

NOTES

1. Cf. Rudolf Bultmann, "On the Question of Christology" (1927), in *Faith and Understanding,* vol. 1, ed. with an intr. by R. W. Funk, trans. by L. P. Smith (London: SCM, 1969) 132, in his discussion with Emanuel Hirsch.
2. So Rudolf Bultmann, *Theology of the New Testament,* vol. 1, trans. by K. Grobel (New York: Scribner's, 1951) 3.
3. Ernst Fuchs, "The Quest of the Historical Jesus" (1956), in *Studies of the Historical Jesus,* trans. by A. Scobie (Naperville, Ill.: Allenson, 1964) 21f.
4. It is not only the great enigma of New Testament theology, *"how the proclaimer became the proclaimed,"* as Bultmann had thought (cf. "The Christology of the New Testament," in *Faith and Understanding* 1:283). It is of decisive theological relevance whether and to what degree there is a continuity between Jesus and the New Testament kerygma in the midst of all discontinuity (cf. James M. Robinson, *A New Quest of the Historical Jesus* [Naperville, Ill.: Allenson, 1959] 90f.).

5. Cf. Karl Heim, *Ich gedenke der vorigen Zeiten: Erinnerungen aus acht Jahrzehnten* (Hamburg: Furche, 1960) 316ff., where he claims that the extreme dialectic of Bultmann dissolves the historic basis in which the kerygma is grounded.

6. A total eschatological understanding was first advocated by Albert Schweitzer. Dialectic theology, with its most prominent representatives in Karl Barth and Rudolf Bultmann, picked up this idea.

   When Hans Conzelmann, *An Outline of the Theology of the New Testament*, trans. by J. Bowden (New York: Harper & Row, 1969) 99, suggests that Jesus' idea of God can only in a qualified sense be called eschatological, he does have a point. Jesus certainly said many things that have no eschatological significance. The synoptic tradition has even preserved for us sayings that clearly go in a non-eschatological direction. Still, the main and overwhelming intention of his proclamation is undeniably eschatological.

7. Bultmann, *Theology of the New Testament*, 1:9ff.

8. Many exegetes who are concerned about the historical Jesus emphasize too that only Jesus' actions can illuminate the significance of his person and his call for a decision. Ernst Fuchs, for instance, advocated this method in his programmatic essay "The Quest of the Historical Jesus," in *Studies of the Historical Jesus*, 11-31. This method seems to have been picked up by other students of Bultmann. But even Joachim Jeremias, coming from an entirely different direction, did extensive studies of the parables of Jesus in his quest for the *ipsissima vox Jesu* (original sayings of Jesus). Cf. Joachim Jeremias, *The Parables of Jesus*, trans. by S. H. Hooke (New York: Scribner's, 1963).

9. Rudolf Bultmann, *The Gospel of John: A Commentary*, trans. by G. R. Beasley-Murray et al. (Philadelphia: Westminster, 1971) 118f. Though Bultmann recognizes this miracle as an epiphanic miracle, he wants to connect it with a Hellenistic environment Dionysius cult) instead of with the Old Testament.

10. Cf. for the following Ethelbert Stauffer, *Jesus and His Story*, trans. by R. and C. Winston (New York: Knopf, 1960) 155f. Bultmann, *Theology of the New Testament;* 1:29, mentions too that the synoptic tradition contains no sayings in which Jesus says that he will sometime (or soon) return.

11. Cf. Stauffer, *Jesus and His Story*, 160f.; and Vincent Taylor, *The Names of Jesus* (New York: St. Martin's, 1953) 19, 24, 77.

12. So Ferdinand Hahn, *The Titles of Jesus in Christology: Their History in Early Christianity*, trans. by H. Knight and G. Ogg (London: Lutterworth, 1969) 161. Hahn connects this possible repudiation of the messianic title with the fact that in Jesus' life any indication of a zealotic tendency in thought or action is entirely lacking. Taylor, *The Names of Jesus*, 20, states too that Jesus' unwillingness "to use the title must mean that He repudiated the current nationalistic expectations associated with it." Since this seems a commonly accepted position among exegetes, advocates of a "theology of rebellion" or of revolution will find it difficult to base their ideas on sound exegetical ground.

    A very exceptional position is taken by S. G. F. Brandon, *Jesus and the Zealots: A Study of the Political Factor in Primitive Christianity* (New York: Scribner's, 1969), who advocates the idea that Jesus sympathized with the Zealot movement, whereas the apostles wanted to present a pacifist Christ. For an evaluation of Brandon's ideas cf. the review of *Jesus and the Zealots* by John T. Townsend in *Journal of Biblical Literature*, 89 (June 1970) 246f. Cf. also Oscar Cullmann, *Jesus and the Revolutionaries*, trans. by G. Putnam (New York: Harper & Row, 1970), who states that Jesus' attitude was one of radical obedience to the will of God, anchored in the most intimate communion with God and in the expectation of his kingdom and his prevailing justice (viif.). This led Jesus on the one side to an unreserved criticism of the existing order, but "on the other side also to a rejection of resistance movements, since these divert one's attention from the kingdom of God with their setting of goals, and violate by their use of violence the command of absolute justice and absolute love" (51f.).

13. Hermann L. Strack and Paul Billerbeck, *Kommentar zum Neuen Testament aus Talmud und Midrasch*, vol. 1: *Das Evangelium nach Matthäus* (Munich: Beck, 1922) 486f. Cf. also Stauffer, *Jesus and His Story*, 163f.

14. Cf. Hahn, *The Titles of Jesus in Christology*, 20.

15. Cf. for the following Oscar Cullmann, *The Christology of the New Testament*, rev. ed., trans. by S. C. Guthrie and Ch. A. M. Hall (Philadelphia: Westminster, 1963) 157ff.

16. Cf. Bultmann, *The Gospel of John*, 339n.3.

17. Cf. Wolfhart Pannenberg, "Dogmatic Theses on the Doctrine of Revelation," in *Revelation as History*, ed. by Wolfhart Pannenberg, trans. by D. Granskou (New York: Macmillan, 1968) 134. The reader of this translation of Pannenberg's Theses is well advised to check the German original over against the often very "free" translation.

18. Cf. for the following the valuable comments by Philip B. Harner, *The "I am" of the Fourth Gospel: A Study in Johannine Usage and Thought* (Philadelphia: Fortress, 1970) esp. 6-26. The absolute use of the *ego eimi*, i.e., with no object following, should not be confused with the *ego eimi* sayings that necessitate an object (e.g., I am the bread of life). For the latter cf. Eduard Schweizer, *Ego eimi: Die religionsgeschichtliche Herkunft und theologische Bedeutung der johanneischen Bildreden, zugleich ein Beitrag zur Quellenfrage des vierten Evangeliums* (Göttingen: Vandenhoeck & Ruprecht, 1965).

19. Stauffer, *Jesus and His Story*, 179.

20. So Harner, *The "I am" of the Fourth Gospel*, 23.

21. Cf. Ernst Lohmeyer, *Das Evangelium des Markus* (Göttingen: Vandenhoeck & Ruprecht, 1954) 270f.; and W. Manson, "Ego eimi of the Messianic Presence in the New Testament," in *Journal of Theological Studies*, 48(1947):137ff. Cf. also Vincent Taylor, *The Gospel according to St. Mark* (London: Macmillan, 1957) 503f., who is hesitant to see a theophanic formula contained in this passage.

22. Harner, *The "I am" of the Fourth Gospel*, 33f., in his careful analysis of the *ego eimi* formula. Cf. also Ernst Haenchen, *Der Weg Jesu; Eine Erklärung des Markus-Evangeliums und der kanonischen Parallelen* (Berlin: Töpelmann, 1966) 511f., who in his discussion with Stauffer rejects the thesis that this passage dates back to Jesus. According to Haenchen it simply reflects the expectation of the first Christian community. Since this expectation (the return of Christ before the death of the members of the Sanhedrin) was not fulfilled, the passage was changed in Matthew and Luke. Taylor, *The Gospel according to St. Luke*, 568f., also admits that this passage reflects the apocalyptic hopes of the church, but comes to the conclusion that it is in every way probable that it is actually the reply of Jesus to the challenge of the high priest. Its emphasis lies on the enthronement, and on the enthronement as the symbol of triumph.

For the following cf. the careful study by John Donahue, *Are You The Christ? The Trial Narrative in the Gospel of Mark* (Missoula, Montana: Society of Biblical Literature, 1973) 91ff., that arrives at similar conclusions to ours.

23. So rightly Norman Perrin in his careful study, "The High Priest's Question and Jesus' Answer (Mark 14:61-62)," in Werner H. Kelber, *The Passion in Mark. Studies on Mark 14-16* (Philadelphia: Fortress, 1976) 82.

24. Fuchs, *Studies of the Historical Jesus*, 154f., cf. also Joachim Jeremias, *New Testament Theology*, vol. 1: *The Proclamation of Jesus*, trans. by J. Bowden (London: SCM, 1971) 251ff., who makes the connection between the emphatic use of the word *ego* and Jesus' own conduct.

25. Of course, the singular character of Jesus can be advocated with other arguments.

Rudolf Bultmann, for instance, who disclaims that Jesus' life had any messianic characteristics, asserts that for Jesus God again became a God at hand. This closeness finds its expression when Jesus addressed God simply as "Father" *(Theology of the New Testament,* 1:23). While Bultmann mentions the phrase "Father" only in passing, Joachim Jeremias has recognized the decisive character of this phrase when he says: "His Father has given him the revelation of himself in such a total way as only a father can disclose himself to a son. Therefore only he, Jesus, can disclose to others the real knowledge of God" *(New Testament Theology,* 1:61). Though we cannot doubt that the address "Father" in the mouth of Jesus means something special, it emphasizes more the difference between God and Jesus, while the theophany formula *ego eimi* emphasizes more the unity.

26. This is especially well-captured in the Gospel according to Luke. Cf. Hans Conzelmann, *The Theology of St. Luke,* trans. by G. Buswell (London: Faber & Faber, 1960) 16f.

27. Wolfhart Pannenberg, *Jesus—God and Man,* trans. by L. L. Wilkins and D. A. Priebe (Philadelphia: Westminster, 1968) 66f., has characterized this situation very appropriately. However, we wonder if the occurrence of the resurrection was so self-evident for Jesus' Jewish contemporaries that they knew exactly what it meant, even if they shared the common apocalyptic expectation.

28. Cf. Thesis 4 in Pannenberg's *Revelation as History,* 139.

29. For the view of the synoptics cf. Hans Conzelmann, "Eschatologie IV. Im Urchristentum," in *Religion in Geschichte und Gegenwart,* 3rd ed., 2:671f. For a good survey for the different positions in *redaktion* history (the different approaches to the kerygma by the composers of the gospels) cf. Joachim Rohde, *Rediscovering the Teaching of the Evangelists,* trans. by D. M. Barton (London: SCM, 1968).

30. Erich Grässer, *Das Problem der Parusieverzögerung in den synoptischen Evangelien und in der Apostelgeschichte* (Berlin: Töpelmann, 1960) 199f. However, we wonder if Grässer is right in pointing already to Mark 3:30 and similarly to Mark 9:1 as words of comfort because of the delayed parousia. While most exegetes, Grässer included, admit a gradual weakening of impending eschatology, many do not check whether the idea of the impending eschaton is in continuity or in discontinuity with Jesus' own proclamation. It is interesting that Grässer, for instance, does not reach his conclusion that Jesus' expectation of the imminent eschaton was his only eschatological hope after a careful exegesis of pertinent New Testament passages, but after a review of positions that differ from his own view (16).

31. Cf. for the following Conzelmann, *An Outline of the Theology of the New Testament,* 141f. Conzelmann also advances an interesting interpretation of the "parable theory" (Mark 4:10ff.). He claims that it means that Jesus' work can be understood only from after Easter, i.e., through faith (139). Though there is certainly some validity in this statement, we wonder if this explains the "parable theory" sufficiently.

32. Cf. for the following, Ibid., 145f.

33. Günther Bornkamm, "Matthäus als Interpret der Herrenworte," *Theologische Literaturzeitung,* 79 (June 1954): 341ff.

34. Cf. Conzelmann, *The Theology of St. Luke,* p. 101.

35. Cf. Ulrich Wilkens, "The Understanding of Revelation within the History of Primitive Christianity," in Pannenberg, *Revelation as History,* 97, in his review of the understanding of revelation in Luke.

36. For the following cf. Conzelmann, *An Outline of the Theology of the New Testament,* 150f. It should become evident through our quoted references that Conzelmann provides by far the most enlightening view of eschatology during the decisive period of the formation of the synoptic gospels.

37. Stauffer, *New Testament Theology,* trans. by J. Marsh (New York: Macmillan, 1959) 39.

38. Cf. C. H. Dodd, *The Interpretation of the Fourth Gospel* (Cambridge: Cambridge University Press, 1958) 147f., who rightly mentions that the miracle of Lazarus' bodily resurrection anticipates the final resurrection.

39. Cf. Conzelmann, *An Outline of the Theology of the New Testament*, 356, who opposes here Bultmann's rather one-sided interpretation of a "present eschatology." Cf. also L. van Hartingsveld, *Die Eschatologie des Johannes-Evangeliums; Eine Auseinandersetzung mit Rudolf Bultmann* (Assen: Van Gorcum, 1962).

40. Ethelbert Stauffer, "Agnostos Christos: Joh. XI. 24 und die Eschatologie des vierten Evangeliums," in *The Background of the New Testament and Its Eschatology*, ed. by W. D. Davies and D. Daube (Cambridge: Cambridge University Press, 1956) 299.

41. Dodd, *The Interpretation of the Fourth Gospel*, 228f. suggests that, unlike any other New Testament writer, the writer of the Fourth Gospel is fully aware of the Jewish ideas associated with the title "Messiah" but puts Jesus' messiahship, in part, in clear opposition to such ideas.

42. Cf. Conzelmann, *An Outline of the Theology of the New Testament*, 332. It may be an overstatement to say with Conzelmann that the Gospel of John has no missionary character. When Bultmann, *The Gospel of John*, 698, mentions that the gospel wants to "awaken the faith that Jesus is the Messiah, the Son of God," he seems to be closer to the truth.

43. Bultmann, "The Significance of the Historical Jesus for the Theology of Paul" (1929), in *Faith and Understanding*, 1:221f.; and Conzelmann, *An Outline of the Theology of the New Testament*, 163.

44. Anton Fridrichsen, in his short but excellent study *The Apostle and His Message; Uppsala Universitets Årsskrift, 1947:3* (Uppsala: Lundequistska Bokhandeln, 1947) 3.

45. Cf. for the following also C. H. Dodd, *The Epistle of Paul to the Romans* (New York: Harper, 1932) 4f.

46. Fridrichsen, *The Apostle and His Message*, 4.

47. Martin Dibelius, *Paul*, ed. and completed by W. G. Kümmel, trans. by F. Clarke (Philadelphia: Westminster, 1953) 62, emphasizes that for Paul the "whole life was regarded from the point of view of the end: this life was only an intermediate state."

48. Cf. Bultmann, *Theology of the New Testament*, 1:308, where he explains this dialectic in pointing to the situation of the church. On the one hand the church belongs to the new aeon and is no longer a phenomenon of this world, but on the other hand it manifests itself in individual congregations which exist in this world.

49. Cf. the excellent exposition by Conzelmann, *An Outline of the Theology of the New Testament*, 184ff. Bultmann, *Theology of the New Testament*, 1:306f., emphasizes that such a cosmic drama can only be the completion and confirmation of the eschatological occurrence that has already now begun.

50. Cf. Günther Bornkamm, *Paul*, trans. by D. M. G. Stalker (New York: Harper & Row, 1971) 232ff., in his discussion with Ernst Bloch who depicts Jesus as the rebel and arch-heretic, while claiming that Paul brought Jesus' gospel of the kingdom to nothing and robbed it of its power. Bornkamm, however, affirms rightly that to a greater extent than any of his predecessors or successors in the primitive church Paul thought out and developed the implications of the change brought about by Jesus' death on the cross and the presence in the Spirit of the living Lord (236).

51. Cf. Conzelmann, *An Outline of the Theology of the New Testament*, 185. Ulrich Luz, *Das Geschichtsverständnis des Paulus* (Munich: Kaiser, 1968) 396, claims that Paul used future eschatological assertions primarily in his proclamation to those in temptation, but usually did not use them directly to combat enthusiastic anticipation of the future. We wonder if such a distinction is possible. The arguments cited by Luz are not very convincing.

52. Cf. Pannenberg, *Jesus—God and Man*, 106ff., in his enlightening treatment of the "delay of the parousia and the meaning of Jesus' resurrection."

Part II

VIEWS AND ISSUES TO CONSIDER

3
Present Discussion
of Eschatology

IN OUR ATTEMPT TO OUTLINE the biblical scope of eschatology we were, of course, aware that there are many other approaches to New Testament and Old Testament eschatology.[1] Indeed, the quest for a proper understanding of New Testament eschatology has dominated 20th century theology more than any other item. At first glance the still on-going debate might appear confusing. Except for a common agreement that the New Testament has a basically eschatological outlook there is hardly any conceivable standpoint or opinion concerning New Testament eschatology which has not been advocated by some respectable scholar during the last 80 years. But amid all diversity and even controversy four major trends are discernible. These four trends followed one another in a more or less temporal sequence, although in some instances they even ran parallel.

(1) The first and oldest approach has often been called consistent or consequent eschatology and has been advocated by theologians such as Albert Schweitzer, Fritz Buri, and Martin Werner, who see Jesus in the strict context of the Jewish apocalyptic world view. His message was centered on the announcement of the impending eschaton. He expected his own parousia as the Son of man, first during his lifetime and then in connection with his death. Since the end did not come as he or his disciples had expected, the New Testament proclamation must now be de-eschatologized or even de-kerygmatized.

(2) The next approach emphasizes the existential character of Jesus' proclamation and, at the same time, tends to consider the teachings of Jesus about the future eschaton as of lesser or no importance. Scholars such as C. H. Dodd, Rudolf Bultmann, and Amos N. Wilder have pursued this approach. Future eschatology was never an essential part of Jesus' message. In part the emergence of future eschatology was due to the first Christians, who rephrased the original kerygma according

to popular eschatological trends, such as Jewish apocalyptic. And in part it was also due to Jesus' own primitive first-century world view.

(3) The third approach tries to maintain the future-directedness of eschatology. More conservative scholars such as Ethelbert Stauffer, Werner Georg Kümmel, and Oscar Cullmann advocate this trend. Either impending eschatology never played a role in Jesus' proclamation, because he emphasized the all-decisive now, or he was never concerned with the categories of time.

(4) Finally, some scholars emphasize the revolutionary power of eschatology. Theologians like Jürgen Moltmann, Johann Baptist Metz, Carl E. Braaten, Wolfhart Pannenberg, and Gustavo Gutiérrez claim that eschatology cannot be confined to the so-called last things. Biblical eschatology has a transformative power so that it pervades all phases of Christian life. Since our eschatological existence is a present reality, it will and must change our society as well as our attitude toward nature, and it will lead us to a new creation.

We have attempted to learn from these different emphases and theologians, including those to whom we could not devote a special paragraph. How valid these approaches are should become evident from the following presentations.

1. The rediscovery of the eschatological proclamation of Jesus

The rediscovery of the eschatological proclamation of Jesus marks the beginning of modern, biblically-oriented theology and is largely connected with the name of Albert Schweitzer.

a. Albert Schweitzer and the rediscovery of eschatology

In 1901 Albert Schweitzer published a small booklet with the title: *The Mystery of the Kingdom of God: The Secret of Jesus' Messiahship and Passion.*[2] Here Schweitzer posed the alternative that Jesus was to be understood either in eschatological terms or in non-eschatological terms, but not in both. With this alternative he attacked traditional liberalism which had praised Jesus as a moral teacher and pitied him as a victim of popular apocalyptic thinking. For instance, just the year before Adolf von Harnack in his famous lectures, *What Is Christianity?* (1899/1900), had told his audience that Jesus simply shared with his contemporaries the idea of the coming of the kingdom with outward signs. But actually he meant that it is "a still and mighty power in the hearts of men." Thus he proclaimed God the Father and the infinite value of the human soul and called for the higher righteousness and the practice of the commandment of love.[3]

In contrast Schweitzer proposed a consistent eschatological understanding. He affirmed that we do not know anything about Jesus' earlier development. But "at his baptism the secret of his existence was disclosed to him, namely, that he was the one whom God had destined to be the Messiah. With this revelation he was complete, and underwent no further development."[4] From that time on he was sure that he had to work as the unknown and hidden Messiah until the messianic age appeared. He and his followers had to purify themselves in the final affliction. Thus the idea of suffering was present for him from the very beginning. His message was similar to that of John the Baptist: Repent and attain righteousness, because the kingdom of God is close at hand. But, in contrast to John, Jesus performed miracles. These gave John the idea that Jesus could be the Messiah, and he sent disciples to him to inquire about him. Jesus' preaching did not yield much success, though he tried hard. This resulted in the first disappointment for Jesus. Then the coming of the kingdom was delayed, though all the necessary signs were present. As one of these significant signs of the coming kingdom, Jesus had discovered that John the Baptist was Elijah reincarnate. When John was beheaded and the kingdom still did not come, Jesus realized that he had to suffer death too. Thus he turned with his disciples to Jerusalem and was determined to bring the kingdom of God about. He entered Jerusalem and claimed to be the Messiah. The Jewish authorities, who had always been suspicious of him, accused him of blasphemy and put him to death. He died, but nothing happened.

Schweitzer concludes his book with the hope that his critics will find no fault with his aim: *"to depict the figure of Jesus in its overwhelming heroic greatness and to impress it upon the modern age and upon the modern theology."* [5] This was the first significant attempt to explain Jesus' mission as completely eschatological. But it saw that mission as founded on an idea that had proved to be wrong. This booklet contained enough dynamite both for conservatives and liberals to shatter many of their cherished thoughts. Yet it received hardly any attention.

A different reception greeted Schweitzer's next book in 1906. *The Quest of the Historical Jesus* opened with a study of the rationalistic sceptic Reimarus, who had been the first to grasp the eschatological world-view of Jesus. It concluded with William Wrede, one of Schweitzer's contemporaries, who had proved the non-eschatological picture of Jesus to be untenable. Schweitzer again posed the alternative:

> There is, on the one hand, the eschatological solution, which at one stroke raises the Marcan account as it stands, with all its disconnectedness and inconsistencies, into genuine history; and there is, on the other hand, the literary solution, which regards the incongruous dogmatic element as interpolated by the earlier Evangelist into the tradition and therefore strikes out the Messianic claim altogether from the historical life of Jesus. *Tertium non datur.*[6]

Again Schweitzer took a clear stand for a thoroughgoing eschatological interpretation of Jesus. He declared that Jesus' ethics were interim ethics which aimed at the preparation for the kingdom of God. Since the kingdom had not come when Jesus expected it, our ethics cannot be derived from Jesus' ethics. But his demand of world denial and perfection of personality is still valid for us, though it is in contrast to our ethics of reason.[7] We need more persons like Jesus. His enthusiasm and heroism are important for us, because they were derived from choosing the kingdom of God and from faith in this kingdom which was only strengthened by his encounter with obstacles.

> In the knowledge that He is the coming Son of Man [Jesus] lays hold of the wheel of the world to set it moving on that last revolution which is to bring all ordinary history to a close. It refuses to turn, and He throws Himself upon it. Then it does turn; and crushes Him. Instead of bringing in the eschatological conditions, He has destroyed them. The wheel rolls onward, and the mangled body of the one immeasurably great Man, who was strong enough to think of Himself as the spiritual ruler of mankind and to bend history to His purpose, is hanging upon it still. That is His victory and His reign.[8]

It is relatively unimportant for Schweitzer that Jesus was actually deceived in his eschatological expectations. All-decisive is his attitude toward history and toward the obstacles he had to overcome in accomplishing his goal.

b. The impact of the consistent or consequent eschatological approach

With his *Quest of the Historical Jesus* Schweitzer started an immense uproar. The liberals could tolerate Schweitzer's portrayal of Jesus as a kind of religious fanatic who was deceived by his own ideas. But they rebuked him because he had declared Jesus' ethics to be mere interim ethics.[9] Regardless of how critical liberalism had been toward the Jesus of the New Testament, it cherished his ethical ideals. Now Schweitzer had declared quite rightly that it is impossible to separate Jesus' ethics from his eschatological proclamation. This meant that the attempt of liberal theology to eliminate the eschatological dimension of Jesus' proclamation and to confine itself to the "timeless" validity of his ethical teachings could no longer be founded in the historical Jesus.

Conservative scholars applied to Schweitzer's own position his claim that each scholar had projected his own image of Jesus back into the New Testament in trying to write a life of Jesus. They concluded that the true historical Jesus could not be found by strictly historical investigation, but only through faith.[10] In England, however, Schweitzer's position found more approval. F. C. Burkitt, a leading New Testament scholar, immediately translated the *Quest of the Historical Jesus* and wrote a preface to it. William Sanday, another prominent figure in British New Testament scholarship, initially praised Schweitzer's books, but after having actually read Schweitzer's first study he realized the radical attitude behind it and quickly changed his mind.[11] Twenty years later Schweitzer published *The Mysticism of Paul the Apostle*[12] and received an entirely different response in Germany. He described the eschatological teaching of Paul as an eschatological mysticism that should lead to Christ. But now the time was ripe for an eschatological understanding of the New Testament and Schweitzer's book was hailed as the concept of a genius.[13]

Today there are very few serious representatives of consistent or consequent eschatology—mainly among Swiss liberal theologians. Martin Werner, for instance, tries to explain the whole development of the Christian dogma from the fact that the eschaton and the parousia did not come as expected.[14] The delay of the parousia was *the* problem in early Christianity and could only be bridged through the reinterpretation of the kerygma and the emergence of the church. Fritz Buri claims that the Christian proclamation should be de-kerygmatized and de-eschatologized, because we no longer wait for the coming eschaton. Our eschatological possibility consists of being freed from the anxiety of the world and being devoted to a reverence for life.[15]

The theologians following the path of consistent or consequent eschatology have never had many followers. One reason might be that their approach to eschatology is not close enough to the biblical witnesses to please a conservative, while for a liberal, secular philosophies prove more satisfying. Nevertheless, Schweitzer and his disciples made one point unmistakably clear: The New Testament provides in all its diversity a homogeneous outlook that is totally eschatological. But they failed in providing an adequate interpretation of this eschatological perspective. The interpretation they proposed seems to be inconsistent and unrealistic. They failed to show convincingly how Christianity could have survived and grown so rapidly if it originated and developed only through constant disappointments. And they could not explain what it was that gave the Christians of the first centuries the strength to maintain their faith in the face of persecutions.

2. Present-oriented approaches to eschatology

Much more popular and convincing were approaches of scholars who followed Albert Schweitzer in emphasizing the all-pervading eschatological perspective of the New Testament, but unlike him sought the solution not in disappointment but in the existential impact of eschatology. Most of the scholars who went in this direction emphasized the present as the decisive point in history. One attempt to accomplish this was to consider the present of the individual as the decisive moment in which one is encountered by the eschaton. This approach finds expression in the existential interpretation of New Testament eschatology and is mainly pursued by Rudolf Bultmann and his school. Another variation of the present-oriented approach assumes that the decisive event has already happened. The kingdom has already come with Jesus of Nazareth and thus it is unnecessary to wait for any future eschatology. C. H. Dodd, who is the main representative of this trend, has coined the phrase "realized eschatology" for this approach.

a. Existential and ethical approaches (Rudolf Bultmann and Amos N. Wilder)

Characteristic of Rudolf Bultmann and his school is a critical skepticism about the historical reliability of the New Testament documents. The criterion of Ernst Troeltsch, that all phenomena in the history of religions have to be subjected to the principles of analogy and correlation,[16] is generally accepted by the Bultmann school. Whatever can be historically ascertained about Jesus' own proclamation can be traced to the influence of Judaism and Near Eastern mystery religions. But contrary to liberal theology, Bultmann is not much interested in the historical Jesus. He asserts: "How things looked in the heart of Jesus I do not know and I do not want to know." [17] It is not surprising, therefore, that Bultmann is skeptical concerning Jesus' messianic self-understanding.

Though Jesus is presented in the New Testament as the Messiah and the Son of man, both terms have very different backgrounds and are used differently. The term Messiah is always used by others in speaking about Jesus—never by Jesus himself—whereas Jesus often used the term Son of man.

There are three different ways in which the term Son of man is used by Jesus in the New Testament.[18] The first class are scriptural references that describe the coming of the Son of man as in apocalyptic expectation. The Son of man comes from heaven as judge and Savior; he will come unexpectedly like a flash of lightning (cf. Mark 8:38; 13:26). These Son of man sayings are the oldest, since they are used primarily in Mark and in Q.

However, all these sayings talk about the Son of man in the third person (he will . . .) and nothing is mentioned in them about his identity with Jesus, though this identity was taken for granted by the first Christian community.[19] Bultmann, Günther Bornkamm, Heinz Eduard Tödt, and others contend that some of these references to the Son of man were used by Jesus.[20] In using them he did not refer to himself, but to someone else. However, to introduce such a distinction between Jesus and the Son of man seems to pose more problems than it solves.[21] Therefore other scholars are more critical and suggest that none of these sayings is authentic.[22] They were all introduced by the first Christians and attributed to Jesus. Thus they would rule out any investigation of Jesus' self-understanding.

The next group of sayings talks about the suffering, death, and resurrection of the Son of man. While Schweitzer was convinced that Jesus knew about his suffering and death and the subsequent coming of the eschaton, such a knowledge is commonly doubted by Bultmann and his followers. Jesus may have known that he would die a violent death. The sayings of the suffering, death, and resurrection of the Son of man, however, presuppose the passion and Easter stories in detail. Furthermore these sayings are mainly found in the tradition of Mark and have no connection to the sayings of the Son of man who will come in power. Bultmann therefore suggests that these sayings are "probably later products of the Hellenistic church."[23] This means that none of these sayings goes back to the historical Jesus.

The third group of sayings refers to the present activity of the Son of man. He has power to forgive sins (Mark 2:10); he is the Lord of the Sabbath (Mark 2:28). While Bultmann, in following an early thesis of Hans Lietzmann, assumed that the Son of man reference in these sayings results from a mistranslation and meant originally "man" or "I,"[24] most scholars today admit that it is an actual title. But again its authenticity is disallowed.[25] This group of sayings was used by the first Christians to endow the historical Jesus with the authority of the exalted one. Endowed with this authority, Jesus is shown as having the power to forgive sins and to free his disciples from keeping the Sabbath. In his succession the first Christians exercised the same authority.[26]

Günther Bornkamm asks the question why Jesus should have used such an ambiguous title as Son of man, since it could designate either the Messiah or just mean "man." He argues that the Palestinian Christians used this title first and conferred it on Jesus. It expressed the essence of their faith and had an eschatological connotation.[27] Philipp Vielhauer brings this argument to its logical conclusion in contending that neither the Son of man title nor the title Messiah were fitting for Jesus.[28] None of the Son of man sayings mentions the kingdom of God.[29] The kingdom of God and the Son of man title are of different origin and have nothing in common. The Son of man title is not an essential part of the hope for the eschatological kingdom of God. But Jesus' message had the eschatological kingdom of God as its center. Thus Jesus could not have thought of himself as the Son of man. Vielhauer's argument seems to be logically conclusive and convincing. But is it impossible to assume that Jesus combined two concepts that according to Vielhauer were not previously connected, though they seem to point in a similar direction? If the first Christians did not hesitate to do it, why was it impossible for Jesus?

At least parenthetically it should be mentioned here that many scholars outside the Bultmann school are much more reluctant to abandon the idea that Jesus called himself the Son of man. Most arguments for an authenticity of the Son of man sayings presuppose a messianic consciousness of Jesus. Knowing about himself as the Son of man, Jesus must have realized from the common messianic expectations that after his suffering and death he was to be exalted.[30] It has also been argued that as a faithful Jew Jesus must have known that his actions would bring upon him persecution and death through the Jewish authorities.[31] A man who deliberately breaks the law and incites others to do the same will be summoned to death.

That the sayings of Jesus concerning the suffering of the Son of man correspond very closely to the passion story has already been observed by Bultmann. However, Vincent Taylor objects to Bultmann that to assign the passion sayings to the creativity of the first Christian community is a suggestion far less convincing "than the view that Jesus Himself creatively reinterpreted the idea of the Son of Man in terms of the Servant conception."[32] Similarly T. W. Manson reverses Bultmann's argument that these sayings presuppose the passion story in detail. Manson argues that the sayings of Jesus "concerning the suffering of the Son of Man correspond so closely with what is recorded in the Gospels concerning his own Passion that it was the most natural thing in the world to regard them simply as prediction of the Passion. And so, in a sense, they are."[33] Confronted with these conflicting assertions we wonder if at this point the presuppositions do not determine the outcome of the investigation.

We have noticed that Bultmann and his followers are extremely hesitant to concede the authenticity of any Son of man titles. Yet it soon became obvious that this did not eliminate the importance of the historical Jesus. Biblical eschatology after all is grounded in Jesus. Bultmann had already claimed that "Jesus' call to decision" implied a Christology.[34] This means that the proclamation of Jesus, which is essentially eschatological, expresses a certain self-understanding of Jesus. Ernst Fuchs develops Bultmann's idea further in also considering Jesus' actions. Fuchs asserts that Jesus' conduct was the actual framework of his proclamation and both word and conduct (action) point in the same direction.[35] The remaining question, however, is how we are to understand the eschatological vision of Jesus that originated out of a certain self-understanding on his part and was transformed in the gospels through the impact of his life, death, and resurrection.

At first glance the answer seems simple for Bultmann. *"The mythical eschatology* is untenable for the simple reason that the parousia of Christ never took place as the New Testament expected. History did not come to an end, and, as every schoolboy knows, it will continue to run its course."[36] Bultmann is convinced that we cannot reiterate the New Testament eschatology, because it is expressed in a mythical framework and it is part of a past mythical world view. This does not mean that we can simply discard it. Bultmann insists that the mythical world view of a future eschaton does not even lend itself to a strictly cosmological interpretation, as one might assume, but to an anthropological or existential one.[37] Instead of taking the apocalyptic imagery literally, we have to ask for its existential meaning.

Bultmann is convinced that Jesus and the New Testament writers believed in a future eschaton.[38] They thought that the end of history had come and the end of the world was close at hand. Since the announced parousia did not occur, the Christians eventually doubted the immediate coming of the end of the world. The early church still kept the hope for a future eschaton, though it increasingly expected the end of the world in a distant and unknown future. The Christians did not abandon the belief in a future eschaton altogether because they thought that God determined the course of the world. The end of the world coincided for them with the end and the goal of history that God had provided.

For Bultmann it is not necessary to understand the expected end as the goal of history. He finds that two important New Testament writers, Paul and John, distinguish between the expected end and the goal of history. While in Jewish apocalyptic, history is interpreted from the standpoint of eschatology, for Paul history is dissolved into eschatology. Eschatology has lost its meaning as the goal of history and is understood as the goal of the individual human being.[39] World history is no longer decisive, having been replaced in importance by the history of the individual. The encounter with Christ is the most important event for this history, because confrontation with this eschatological event enables the individual to exist truly historically. The individual encounters the eschaton in the now, and history becomes dissolved into eschatology. This permits the believer to exist truly eschatologically in radical openness for the future and without being tied to the past.

Bultmann relies here on Paul, for whom the turn of the aeons has already come. In Christ the appearance of the future has become a present possibility. Judgment and resurrection are happening now. We die and rise with Christ in our baptism, and salvation is present for the believer who is in Christ. Our existence is not tied to the past. The future is open to us in the present as a dialectic existence of indicative and imperative, an existence according to flesh or to spirit. Bultmann admits that Paul still described the eschatological judgment in apocalyptic terms as some future event. He even points out that throughout his lifetime Paul expected the great drama of the eschatological events. Yet he feels that this is an unimportant sideline in Paul's actual eschatological outlook. It is only the "now" of one's own existence which bears eschatological significance.[40]

The Gospel of John and the Johannine Letters are interpreted by Bultmann as substantiating this emphasis on the existential impact of eschatology. For both Paul and John the eschatological events start with the coming of Jesus and continue into the present. While Paul is indebted to Jewish apocalyptic terminology, John uses Gnostic terms. In Gnosticism the dualism between light and darkness, truth and falsehood, above and below, and freedom and bondage is usually understood in cosmological terms in referring to certain "places" in the Gnostic world view. Bultmann, however, affirms that John changed this cosmological dualism into *"a dualism of decision."*[41] Being confronted with Jesus, one has to decide for or against God. This decision is inevitable because Jesus is the revelation of God. Thus the coming of the revealer is the judgment, and the reaction to revelation is decisive. Salvation becomes a radical present act and all who accept Jesus as the revelation of God already have eternal life; they have passed through judgment.

Bultmann understands the Gospel of John as a protest against the traditional, dramatic, popular, national, and primitive eschatology. Of course, he also recognizes passages in John that point to a future eschaton (John 6:44; 6:54). But he concludes that a later editor introduced these passages, which also indicate a cultic sacramental piety.[42]

Although the existence of such a later editor is not unquestioned by other scholars, one might wonder whether it is not an implicit admission that in the long run Christian theology cannot exist without a future goal of history. If the original writer of the Gospel of John seemingly omitted the announcement of a future eschaton, a later generation found it necessary to re-introduce the future dimension of history into John's original interpretation of Jesus' proclamation.[43]

Far from being a student of Bultmann, Amos N. Wilder also emphasizes the present impact of eschatology. He agrees with Bultmann that one can no longer take the future-directed mythological imagery of the New Testament literally. "Eschatology is that form of myth which represents the unknown future."[44] But he questions the "individualistic character" of Bultmann's interpretation,[45] since non-historical individualistic interpretations reflect the mood of pessimism induced by our present situation. They refuse to take into account a realistic modern view of the social process and of social progress as measured by the whole human story.[46] "Jesus anticipated a new and revolutionary this-worldly order." "Jesus felt himself the prophet and instrument of the coming of this new order and conducted himself with a fully realistic understanding of the circumstances involved." [47]

Of course, Wilder rejects Schweitzer's insistence that Jesus' ethics are purely for an interim.[48] Wilder observes that Jewish ethics were still ethics for an interim, primarily designed to prepare for the coming of salvation. But the character of ethics changed radically with the coming of Jesus. There was no longer an interim, since through God's redemptive action Jesus signified the presence of the time of salvation and the days of the new covenant. The transition from the old era to the new accounts for the urgency of Jesus' ethics which commonly assumes the form of a summons to Jesus and confession of him. This urgency, however, cannot be expressed by an "anachronistic and literal Second Coming or forensic Judgment viewed as impending in our day." [49] The dynamic vision of God in his historical activity is the compelling force that continually redirects and animates us along the line of his purpose. Still, Wilder does not want to abandon the rich symbolic expression of New Testament mythological eschatology, because he is convinced that only by retaining it can the fullness and wholeness of the message be conveyed and safeguarded.[50]

Evaluating Bultmann's and Wilder's approach we must note that they emphasize rightly the present-oriented aspect of eschatology. Eschatology is not just something that has to do with the so-called last things, but it is also essentially connected with the present. Yet, both seem to neglect the fact that eschatology determines the present because it has determined the future. The future element in the New Testament, which in its ultimate sense speaks of the end of our particularistic and corporate history here on earth, cannot be fully expressed in strictly non-historical and existential categories or by taking it as a symbolic expression. Wilder modifies the highly individualistic approach of Bultmann by relating it to the ethical and social issues of our time.[51] In so doing he opens the future dimension of eschatology. But his symbolic interpretation does not give a strong enough incentive to wrestle successfully with our present social and ethical issues. Jesus' call for a decision cannot be replaced by symbols or by a mystical kingdom of God.

However, both Bultmann and Wilder pose a more serious question to which we too must give careful attention (cf. Chapter 4): How can we in the 20th century still accept a future eschaton in the sense of the coming of a new world or of a total transformation of this present world? Our secular world in which we extend our dominion over more and more facets of life does not seem to allow for any God-provided novelty. It seems to run its own course according to its own scientifically predictable laws.

b. Transcendentalistic approaches
(C. H. Dodd and John A. T. Robinson)

C. H. Dodd is another influential theologian who emphasizes the existential impact of eschatology. But it is not the dichotomy between the world view of antiquity and that of modern science that leads him to a non-historical interpretation of the future-oriented eschatological imagery of the New Testament. Dodd starts with the unsolved question of the consistent eschatology of Albert Schweitzer: How is it possible that the false hope for an early return of Christ in glory could not touch the substance of the Christian hope? [52]

The first Christians expected the last judgment and the coming of Christ almost any day. "During the first century events occurred from time to time which raised hopes that it was at hand; but they were always disappointed, as similar hopes have been disappointed many times since." [53] Though their hopes for an early return of Jesus Christ proved to be an illusion, the center of their hope did not change. Gradually they realized that the decisive event had already happened; Christ had come. All these years when they were hoping for a second coming they derived the strength to continue their hope in the face of disappointment from the fact that he had come and not, as they had thought, from the "prospect of his second coming." God had confronted the Jewish people in his kingdom, power, and glory. This world had become the scene of the divine drama, in which the eternal issues were laid bare. It was the hour of decision. It was realized eschatology,[54] because in Jesus the eternal entered decisively into history. The eschaton was realized in the coming of the kingdom of God. This means that while Jesus used the traditional apocalyptic symbolism to indicate the "other-worldly" or absolute character of the kingdom of God, he used parables to enforce and illustrate the idea that the kingdom of God had come upon people then and there. The coming of the kingdom of God even implied a judgment because those who censured Jesus for his work and teaching pronounced judgment upon themselves. They excluded themselves from the kingdom.

"The act of acceptance or rejection determines the whole direction of a man's life, and so of his destiny." [55]

Finally, the first Christians realized that God's victory was won, that Christ had won it, and that they already shared in it. This discovery allowed them to make the necessary readjustments in their thinking without a disastrous disappointment. They did not, however, discard the hope for another coming of Christ. They knew about the tensions between realization and expectation: God's victory was won, yet there were many difficulties to overcome. But how was the victory won? Dodd points here to the characteristic signs of the day of the Lord.[56] Jesus, as presented by the gospel writers, had announced threatening catastrophes which were more than mere personal disasters. And he proclaimed a final triumph. He would rise from the dead, the kingdom of God would come with power, and the Son of man would come with the clouds of heaven. All this points to the same thing: "Immediate victory out of apparent defeat." He returned to life after his death, gathered his disturbed followers, empowered them with his Holy Spirit, and sent them out into the world.[57] So a new era started with the kingdom of Christ on earth. Through his resurrection Christ was invested with power and glory and became the invisible king of all people. This source of power kept the church alive throughout the centuries.

> The Church prays, "Thy Kingdom come;" "Come, Lord Jesus." As it prays, it remembers that the Lord did come, and with Him came the Kingdom of God. Uniting memory with aspiration, it discovers that He comes. He comes in His Cross and Passion; He comes in the glory of His Father with the holy angels. Each Communion is not a stage in process by which His coming draws gradually nearer, or a milestone on the road by which we slowly approach the distant goal of the Kingdom of God on earth. It is a re-living of the decisive moment at which He came.
>
> The preaching of the Church is directed towards reconstituting in the experience of individuals the hour of decision which Jesus brought. . . . It assumes that history in the individual life is of the same stuff as history at large; that is, it is significant so far as it serves to bring men face to face with God in His Kingdom, power and glory.[58]

Dodd's magnificent interpretation of the existential impact of eschatology has to wrestle with another line of thought in the New Testament. Dodd realizes that some passages in the New Testament mention a breakdown of the physical universe before Christ's coming. Though he does not want to take the imagery of falling stars and darkening sun literally, he knows that the most elegant symbolic interpretation cannot do justice to the reality behind it. Thus he asserts that the final coming of Christ will not be a coming in history, because the coming of Christ in history has already been fulfilled in his resurrection. The final coming will not be an event *in* history, but *beyond* history.[59] In hoping for it as an event *in* history we might also be tempted to see it in close parallel to the restoration of the kingdom of David, which was the utopia of popular Jewish hopes in the time of Jesus. But Jesus expressly rejected such thought and no alternative utopia is suggested. "There is no hint that the Kingdom of God is Utopia." [60]

The attempt to escape both from an antiquated cosmology and from seeking the coming of the kingdom in earthly utopia leads Dodd to a transcendentalistic approach, that asserts the eschaton in the future but beyond history. Yet Dodd does not absolutize this approach but tries to balance it with an equal emphasis on the existential now of the aspired eschaton. He concludes that when John emphasized in his Gospel that *now* the judgment of this world had come, he was not mistaken, and whenever people believed that the Lord was near and the judgment was to come, they were not mistaken, because Christ comes beyond space and time. Although the blessedness of God's kingdom may be enjoyed here and now, "it is never exhausted in any experience that falls within the bounds of space and time." [61] But when all history is taken up into the larger whole of God's eternal purpose, Christ will come the last time, everything will reach its fulfillment, and we will see our lives the way God sees them.

We must admit that Dodd presents an impressive interpretation of eschatology which does justice to its emphasis on the present. He also seems to provide a convincing and scriptural approach to the future-oriented aspect of eschatology.[62] But we cannot fully agree with him when he asserts that Christ comes whenever we firmly believe in his coming, and that *all* history will eventually be taken up into God. A twofold outcome of history is so firmly imbedded in the New Testament that it cannot be changed to a universal homecoming as Dodd suggests, which indeed does not even coincide with the end of all history. Of course, it is always tempting to envision the final goal of history as an earthly utopia. Dodd rightly warns us against this fallacy. But his alternative of a spiritualization of the future eschaton is too high a price to pay.

John A. T. Robinson presented a very fascinating thesis in his book *Jesus and His Coming: The Emergence of a Doctrine* that sounds much like Dodd's conviction: The oldest synoptic traditions know nothing of a second coming. The idea of a second coming emerged shortly before Paul as a result of uncertainty as to whether or not the earthly life of Jesus was already messianic. The primitive tradition believed the climax of Jesus' ministry was his being received up into "the presence and triumph of God, from which, already glorified, he shows himself to the disciples, and from which henceforth he pours out his Spirit on the Church and comes to his world in judgment and power." [63] The future belongs to Christ until the final consummation of this age. The catastrophic climax is seen and interpreted as an integral part of the coming of the Son of man which has already started in the ministry of Jesus.

Robinson sees no evidence in the teaching of Jesus, or in the earliest preaching and creeds of the church, that there should be a second eschatological moment, a second advent of Christ after a certain time has elapsed. In the Gospels the application of the teaching of Jesus to a parousia after an interval is "a purely editorial feature." [64] Of course, Jesus talked about the coming of the Son of man. However, with this he did not refer to his second coming but the "visitation of God to his people focused in the challenge and climax of his own ministry." [65] Why then did the church reinterpret these sayings as applying to a second coming? Similar to Dodd, Robinson finds the reason in an unresolved crisis in the christology of the primitive church caused by the doubt whether or not the messianic event had taken place and whether or not the Christ had come. The result was a compromise: "part of it had taken place and part of it had not, the Christ had come and yet would come." [66] Thus the messianic drama had two main parts, separated by an interval. The Gospel of John represents the original teaching of Jesus best, since it was not so much exposed to and distorted by apocalyptic thoughts as most other New Testament writings. We notice in John a gradual change from a primitive non-apocalyptic eschatology to a subsequent and more apocalyptic way of thinking. [67]

Robinson rightly reminds us that Christ's first coming at "Christmas" and his last coming in the final parousia form a unity and must be equally emphasized. But, contrary to Robinson's assumption, they are not one and the same parousia. The sameness of Christ in both events does not mean that they should be merged into one single event. They mark the starting point of God's redemptive action in Jesus Christ on the one hand and his final mission on the other hand and are thus to be distinguished as two different events.

With Dodd, Robinson does not conceive of the end of history as co-inciding with Christ's final coming.[68] The encounter with God does not change the confines of space and time, because it occurs beyond them. Again we notice that the twofold outcome of history is dismissed in favor of a universalistic approach when Robinson says:

> Christ, in Origen's old words, remains on the Cross so long as one sinner remains in hell. That is not speculation; it is a statement grounded in the very necessity of God's nature. In a universe of love there can be no heaven which tolerates a chamber of horrors, no hell for any which does not at the same time make it hell for God. He cannot endure that, for *that* would be the final mockery of his nature. And he will not.[69]

In other words, God's omnipotent love excludes the possibility of hell and will not allow for anyone to be condemned.

3. The future-directedness of eschatology

a. Impending eschatology as rejudaization (Ethelbert Stauffer)

The New Testament scholar Ethelbert Stauffer acknowledges a common tendency in New Testament studies to see Jesus in close connection with the immediate coming of the kingdom of God. But he wonders whether this must imply that Jesus was an apocalypticist who proclaimed the immediate coming of the eschaton. Perhaps only his contemporaries understood him in this way, and words of the impending eschaton which some scholars now regard as the most authentic words of Jesus were only attributed to him after Easter by the first Christian community.[70] Two observations seem to sustain this thesis: (1) Jesus consistently rejected the title Messiah. He never used it for himself nor did he approve the title when it was conferred upon him. (2) The Gospel of John is seen as a protest of the last apostle against the misinterpretation of Jesus prevalent in the time of apocalyptic enthusiasm. The Gospel of John seems, he claims, to know the history of Jesus better than the synoptics, and thus we have to admit the possibility that it represents the eschatology of Jesus better than its synoptic predecessors.[71]

In pre-Christian Palestinian Judaism the idea was developed of a Messiah who lived unknown among people until he was recognized as the reincarnate Elijah and made known to the people.[72] John attributed this idea of the Messiah incognito to Jesus. Jesus begins to make himself known, he performs signs and miracles, but he does not entrust himself to everybody. This incognito of Jesus never totally disappears. He is constantly misunderstood in his acting and talking, and he dies because the Jews do not realize that he is the Messiah. The disciples and followers of Jesus, however, know that according to Jewish beliefs once the Messiah has appeared unknown, he will soon be revealed. In thinking that Jesus is the Messiah incognito they wait already during his lifetime for the hour of revelation and enthronement in power and for the beginning of the final events. Especially the Easter events encourage their hopes for a revelation of this hitherto unknown Messiah.

At Easter the first act of the eschatological drama, the resurrection of the dead, has started. The end of all things is approaching. All the apostles are fascinated by the idea of the immediately coming eschaton, and at that time many words about the coming end are accepted into the authoritative tradition of Jesus.[73] But all these hopes are disappointed. The followers and disciples of Jesus die and the end does not come. During this big disappointment John leads back in his gospel to the unknown glory of Jesus. This does not mean that Jesus or John did not expect an end of the world. But the future John expected is only the visible development of the hidden glory that appeared in the historical Jesus.[74]

For Jesus the "now" was much more important than the impending eschaton, and Stauffer emphasizes very convincingly that the time of Jesus is the time of the *kairos* (decisive moment) against which the future is of lesser interest. It also seems likely that the sayings that are connected with an impending eschatology are closer to the apocalyptic environment of Jesus than to Jesus himself. Though Stauffer seems to be right in recognizing in the Gospel of John a corrective to the synoptic approach, most New Testament writers, John *and* the synoptics included, are almost consistently opposed to any kind of apocalyptic enthusiasm and the subsequent threat of disappointment. Yet this does not mean, Stauffer realizes, that Jesus and his mission could be sufficiently explained in a context other than that of apocalyptic. This is especially true for the resurrection,[75] because here the future-directed emphasis of Jesus as the Christ becomes unmistakably clear.

Stauffer, however, does not seem to take sufficiently into account the fact that John and the synoptics did not intend to write a biography of

Jesus, in which, of course, it would have to be mentioned that Jesus did not proclaim the immediate coming of the eschaton. They wrote about Jesus under the impression of the resurrected Christ. From this perspective, then, any confrontation with Jesus as the Christ cannot remain in the present, but has to point to the future.

b. Eschatology as fulfillment and promise (Oscar Cullmann and Werner Georg Kümmel)

Others have been more successful in emphasizing the future-directedness of eschatology by pointing to the necessary tension between the already occurred fulfillment and the still outstanding future. Oscar Cullmann, for instance, recognizes that Jesus expected the coming of the eschaton in the near future, but he distinguishes between the future dimension in Jesus' expectation and the setting of a date.

Cullmann admits that the end was first expected within the lifetime of the present generation, while later this assumption was corrected without affecting the future dimension of Jesus' expectation.[76] Consistent in this expectation, however, was the future dimension which remained unchanged even though the parousia did not occur as expected. Jesus, too, was aware of an interim period which was to elapse between his ministry and his final parousia. Of course, he reckoned with a very short time span before this parousia would occur. In principle, however, this is not different from Luke's concept of the interim period as the time of the church. According to Cullmann the idea of an *immediately* coming eschaton resulted from immediate confrontation with the tension between the already occurred salvation in Jesus Christ and the not yet occurred final realization of this salvific act. Since salvation is *already* actually present, it guarantees that the *not yet* of its final realization will soon be changed, and thus the hope for an immediately coming eschaton can emerge.

Notwithstanding the emergence of this hope, the already present salvation strengthens the conviction that the coming of the end cannot be postponed indefinitely. When later the unknown duration of the interim is more strongly emphasized, the idea that we live in the last time is nevertheless not abandoned. The death of Jesus, together with the resurrection which followed, was conceived as the decisive event. The historical work of Jesus is concluded, and the mid-point of time is passed.[77] Though we cannot emphasize either the *already* occurred salvation or the *not yet* occurred final realization of salvation in an exclusive way, the two are not in opposition. The decisive act has already taken place in the Christ-event. That the expectation of the future eschatological events is grounded in the *already* shows that the already prevails over the not yet.[78] Jesus proclaimed the coming of the kingdom of God as a future event and anticipated it in his person in a proleptic way. But this caused the tension between the already fulfilled eschaton and the not yet completed eschatological events.[79] The combination of the parallelism and mutual dependence of the already and the not yet is the actual essence of Jesus' eschatological outlook. The already and the not yet depend on each other and presuppose each other: the present assertions point toward the coming fulfillment, while the futurist assertions are grounded in the present anticipation and initiation.

Cullmann's approach seems to be very close to the New Testament and he asserts emphatically the present and future dimension of eschatology. However, can one really refute so easily the advocates of consistent eschatology in saying that essentially it does not matter whether the coming of the eschaton was expected during the next two years or during the next 2,000 years? [80] Was Bultmann right after all when he pointed out that the early expectation of the approaching end of the world was part of Jesus' out-dated world-view?

Although following an approach similar to Cullmann's, the Marburg New Testament scholar and successor of Bultmann, Werner Georg Kümmel, seems to find a better solution to this dilemma. He claims that the eschatological proclamation of Jesus can be regarded neither as a particular form of Jewish apocalyptic nor as a completely non-Jewish, non-apocalyptic, present eschatology.[81]

Kümmel rejects the idea of a rejudaization of eschatology after Jesus' death as well as the attempts of Robinson and Stauffer to play the priority of the Gospel of John against the synoptics.[82] Neither an exclusive orientation toward the present or the future, nor an elimination of the expectation of an immediately coming eschaton, does justice to Jesus and the New Testament tradition. After Easter, Jesus' disciples and followers did not change the present-oriented eschatological proclamation of Jesus to a future-directed eschatology in the fashion of Jewish apocalyptic. The opposite assumption, that the first Christians expected salvation in the near future and then under the impact of Easter realized gradually that the eschaton was already present, is equally unfounded.

From the very beginning Jesus and the first Christians expected the impending coming of God and his salvation and expected at the same time the appearance of his anointed one from heaven. The first Christians combined, as did Jesus, the expectation of salvation with the belief in the presence of salvation in Jesus and his actions. But already Jesus reckoned with an interval between his resurrection and the parousia. This interval gained importance in the thinking of the first Christians.[83] Kümmel does not regard the expectation of the soon-approaching eschaton merely as an emphasis on the certainty of the present beginning of the kingdom of God. Jesus talked in the imagery of his time about the nearness of the kingdom of God in order to actualize God's redemptive action directed toward the consummation.

This means that the expectation of the nearness of the eschaton need not be repeated nowadays. It is part of an out-dated imagery. However, the expectation of the future completion is essential and cannot be detached from Jesus' proclamation without distorting it. Through such an expectation we can talk about God's redemptive action as an action in history.[84] The future expectation must be seen in correlation with the fulfillment in Jesus Christ. The future promise and the past fulfillment depend on each other, because the promise receives its peculiar and reliable character through the past fulfillment, and the fulfillment is seen as partial and preliminary in the light of the still outstanding realization of the promise.[85]

Kümmel's approach seems to be very close to the scriptural basis and well balanced. We have only one reservation, and it is more in the form of a question: did Jesus really at any time advocate an impending eschatology?

4. The revolutionary and liberating aspects of eschatology

The positions so far reviewed were presented mainly by New Testament scholars who convinced us of the centrality of eschatology for the Christian faith. Yet these scholars have hardly moved beyond the limitations of their own field of biblical and exegetical theology. The case is different for the last group of scholars we want to review. Though they do not take lightly the biblical basis from which they argue, their field of competence as systematic theologians necessarily forces them to relate the biblical insights to the spiritual, social, political, and economic issues of today. But their main impetus for connecting the biblical horizon to life today seems to come from extra-biblical stimuli. For instance, Jürgen

Moltmann has been influenced by the Neo-Marxist philosopher Ernst Bloch, Wolfhart Pannenberg has been enriched by the thoughts of Georg Wilhelm Friedrich Hegel, and Gustavo Gutiérrez has been shaped in his outlook by Marxist sources. As we will see later, these outside influences are not totally discontinuous with the biblical message. While Marxists and Neo-Marxists have largely abandoned the metaphysical dimension of eschatology, they have preserved its revolutionary and liberating force. It may be one of the ironies of history that from a trend of thought which is so inimical to Christian faith, this very faith should be persuaded to recapture the revolutionary and liberating power that it once possessed and with which it conquered the entire Roman Empire.

a. The prolepsis of eschatology (Wolfhart Pannenberg)

Had it not been for his own experience as a "liberated" refugee from Stettin (formerly part of Pomerania and now part of Poland), Wolfhart Pannenberg might have become the leader of the liberating and revolutionary aspect of eschatology. Certainly his system of thought, as far as it has been developed, emphasizes very strongly that eschatology does not simply pertain to the future, but is already proleptically anticipated within the Christian community. Pannenberg's understanding of eschatology is intimately connected with his perception of Jesus of Nazareth and the God-disclosive history of Israel. In his widely discussed "Dogmatic Theses on the Doctrine of Revelation" (1961), Pannenberg claims that God's self-disclosure, as reflected in the biblical documents, does not occur in a direct way as a theophany, but indirectly through the acts of God in history. Furthermore, Pannenberg observes that "revelation is not comprehended completely in the beginning, but at the end of the revealing history.[86] History discloses its full meaning as God's history only at the end. This is due to the fact that the individual historical acts are transparent for God not in themselves but only if perceived in the universal historical context. This can be seen especially well in the Old Testament when, in the course of history, the content of revelation ascribed to various historical events had to be revised and expanded according to the historical progression.

But Pannenberg rejects the historical relativism that might result from the simple progression of history and the necessary revisions of our perception of God's self-disclosure derived from history when he states: "The universal revelation of the deity of God is not yet realized in the history of Israel, but first in the destiny of Jesus of Nazareth, insofar as the end of all events is anticipated in his destiny." [87] The destiny of Jesus does not have a universal character just because the end of all history was *envisioned* in that destiny. The assertion taken by itself would only be a repetition of the claim of Albert Schweitzer that Jesus believed that with his life, or at least with his death, the end of the world would come, a belief that was never fulfilled. But Pannenberg goes a decisive step further, claiming that in Jesus the end of the world has indeed occurred in proleptic anticipation. This means that that which had been anticipated as the end and fulfillment of history, the resurrection of the dead, in fact *happened* in a proleptic way in and with Jesus. Since history comes to its conclusion in the destiny of Jesus, this destiny is the key to our understanding of God's self-disclosure. The Christ-event has truly eschatological character, since there is no self-disclosure of God necessary beyond this event. At the end of the world there will only occur on a cosmic scale what happened in and with Jesus on an individual scale.

One might question why Pannenberg attributes so much significance to the resurrection of Jesus, since up to now it has been an exceptional event without any precedent or consequence in other resurrections. But Pannenberg counters that one must perceive it in its proper context, the time of apocalyptic and the expectation of the resurrection of the dead prevalent during that time. If we consider Jesus' resurrection in the apocalyptic context in which Jesus lived, it becomes clear that the resurrection must bear the significance of foreshadowing the eschaton. It is on the one hand the validation of the claim of Jesus made before Easter that he represents and carries the authority of God. But it also means that in his destiny the end has started and God is revealed in him. Jesus therefore becomes the focal point for our understanding of eschatology.

Jesus is the paradigm and the anticipation of our own future and at the same time the inspiration and possibility of living toward that future. In Jesus, God's love was announced to us before his kingdom had fully come. Thus the coming of the kingdom should not cause surprise or terror. Since Jesus announced it, we are able to open ourselves to God's future. We can find communion with him who decides the future of all things and can anticipate the final significance and essence of all things. Of course, the communion with God possible through Christ necessitates our active participation in his creative love which supports all creatures, grants them their limited duration, and brings them to fulfillment of life by relating them to one another. Immediately we notice the individual and social ethical implications of Pannenberg's approach to eschatology.

Since we are able to participate proleptically in the promised future, we are encouraged to anticipate this future proleptically.

Yet Pannenberg cautions that Jesus was only the forerunner and herald of the still imminent kingdom. Thus we should not destroy and disdain the values of the past and present in the name of the future. Pannenberg reminds us: "The history of modern revolutions illustrates the fatal flaw in living so exclusively for the future that all cherishing and celebrating of the present are precluded."[88] Pannenberg cautions us not to pursue such unrealistic futurism, since the ultimate fulfillment of the coming kingdom is beyond our human power to effect. But he also reminds us that we are far from being relegated to inactivity. On the contrary, we are inspired to prepare the present for the future to come. Such preparation is the work of hope carried out by love and will make our present conditions more attuned to the promised future. Together with the world we live in, we must be open beyond ourselves to the future of God's kingdom.

Wolfhart Pannenberg was one of the first systematic theologians in this century to succeed in showing that the eschatology of Jesus had significance beyond our existential now. He directed our attention again to the relation of eschatology and time and to the necessity of integrating nature and existence. We know God's kingdom will find its fulfillment in the future, since it can be proleptically anticipated in the present, and we know that this proleptic anticipation has implications beyond my own existence. Yet once Pannenberg had succeeded in making eschatology acceptable again in the sense of a new historical creation of the kingdom of God, his suggestion was picked up by many other theologians.

b. Theology of hope (Jürgen Moltmann)

Unlike Pannenberg, Jürgen Moltmann's main emphasis is on the implications of eschatology. In his seminal book, *Theology of Hope: On the Ground and the Implications of a Christian Eschatology* (1967), Moltmann makes it clear from the first page on that he does not want to confine himself to a strictly theological treatise. He is much more interested in showing the practical consequences of a biblical eschatological perspective as they inform church life and the burning political issues, such as social justice, world peace, and personal freedom. Eschatology is for Moltmann the doctrine of Christian hope that embraces both the object hoped for and also the hope inspired by it.[89] He no longer wants to confine eschatology to discourse about the so-called last things which will happen in the end, but to consider the whole cause which drives towards this end. Backed by the earlier thesis of Ernst Käsemann that "apocalyptic was the mother of all Christian theology," [90] Moltmann claims that Christianity in its totality is eschatological, and nothing that pertains to it is exempt from this.

Moltmann distinguishes between the Israelite religion of promise and the static epiphanic religions in the environment of Israel.[91] After the Israelites' conquest of Palestine, Yahweh still appeared as the promising God who pointed to a new future. This meant that the Old Testament promises were never superseded by historic events, but were constantly modified and expanded. Of course, some were realized in history. These "fulfilled" promises to which Israel owed its existence (exodus, promised land, David's kingship) proved amid all the upheavals of history to be a *continuum* in which Israel was able to recognize the faithfulness of its God. Yet, the promises were not completely resolved in any event, but there remained an overspill that pointed to the future. The tension between promise and fulfillment was not superseded by the simple progression of Israel's history, but was much more strongly creative of Israel's historic progress.

Moltmann sees the same feature in the New Testament, because the revelation in Christ is at the same time good news and promise. This revelation presupposes the law and promise of the Old Testament, since Yahweh (the God of Abraham, Isaac and Jacob, the God of promise) resurrected Jesus, and Jesus was a Jew. This means that Jesus is not to be understood as a particular case of human being in general, but rather from the perspective of the Old Testament history of promise and in conflict with it. Jesus is not a *theos aner* (divine man) who descended from heaven and whose life on earth is only a temporary episode. On the contrary, Jesus' life, work, death, and resurrection have utmost significance and are described in the categories of expectation appropriate to the God of promise.

The Old Testament history of promise does not simply find its fulfillment in the gospel, but it finds its future in the gospel. Gospel is promise, and as promise it is a first installment on the promised future.[92] Here the centrality of Christ's resurrection for the Christian faith becomes evident. The resurrection of Christ is a "history-making event" from which all other history is enlightened, questioned, and transformed.[93] The stories of the resurrection stand in the line of prophetic and apocalyptic expectations, hopes, and questions about what is bound to come according to the promises of God. Cross and resurrection point toward the future in promising the righteousness of God, the new life as a result of the resurrection from the dead, and the kingdom of God in a new totality of being.[94]

Moltmann understands the Easter appearances as call appearances in which recognition of Christ coincides with recognition of his mission and his future. Again the forward thrust becomes noticeable. Moltmann concludes that for theology the reality of the world becomes historic inasmuch as in its mission the world is seen to be the field of the missionary charge and is examined in a search for real possibilities for the world-transforming missionary hope. "The call to obedient moulding of the world would have no object, if this world were immutable." [95] The world must be open toward the future for good or ill. Secularization has realized these Christian expectations in the field of world history and has outstripped the Christian hope in a chiliastic way. Thus we cannot reject the revolutionary progressiveness of the modern age; we must incorporate the open horizons of modern history into the true eschatological horizon of the resurrection and thereby "disclose to modern history its true historic character." [96] The church cannot confine itself to serving individuals and acting as a conservative force as society might expect. The task and mission of the church is determined by its own peculiar horizon—the eschatological expectation of the coming kingdom of God, the coming righteousness and the coming peace, and the coming freedom and dignity of all humanity. This means "the realization of the eschatological *hope of justice,* the *humanizing* of man, the *socializing* of humanity, *peace* for all creation." [97]

Moltmann presents an impressive approach that makes eschatology meaningful for our present-day life. He goes beyond Albert Schweitzer in pointing out that not only the proclamation of Jesus but all of biblical religion is totally eschatological in outlook. He rightly accuses the church of the past of leaving the earthly-eschatological anticipation of the kingdom of God too readily in the hands of enthusiasts and utopianists.[98] In reacting against this evident neglect, however, Moltmann draws the future-directedness of eschatology so much into human reach that autonomous humanity will have trouble understanding that all its work is only of anticipatory character. That some accuse Moltmann of reintroducing a concept of the kingdom of God once advocated by liberal 19th century German Protestantism is indicative of this evident danger.[99] This coincides with another observation. Moltmann moves so far away from a one-sided emphasis on the so-called last things to a total eschatological outlook that he almost forgets to mention these last things. When he mentions them, however, they are mostly described as earthly, humanly-engendered goals, such as peace for all creation and socializing of humanity.

In more recent writings, Moltmann pursues the same topic from other angles. For instance, in *The Crucified God* (1972), he states at the outset: "The cross is not and cannot be loved. Yet only the crucified Christ can bring the freedom which changes the world because it is no longer afraid of death." [100] After developing a theology of the cross Moltmann then arrives at the conclusion that since the rejected Son of man was raised up in the freedom of God, "faith in the resurrection becomes faith that raises up, wherever it transforms psychological and social systems, so that instead of being oriented on death they are oriented on life." [101] Even the theology of the cross therefore urges the psychological and political liberation of humanity.

Similarly, we read in his ecclesiology, *The Church in the Power of the Spirit* (1975): "The Prayer for the Spirit makes people watchful and sensitive. It makes them vulnerable and stimulates all the powers of the imagination to perceive the coming of God in the liberation of man and to move in accord with it. This prayer therefore leads to political watchfulness, and political watchfulness leads to prayer." [102] Eschatology for Moltmann implies liberation in this world in terms of political and economic liberation, human solidarity, solidarity with nature, and the struggle for hope. Moltmann rightly reminds us that eschatology leads to action instead of other-worldly passivity or resignation. But his almost exclusively socio-political emphasis reminds us too much of the vain human endeavors to establish a theocracy or an earthly utopia, so that we dare not assent to it without expressing a strong eschatological proviso to all such human pursuits. The necessary balance between involvement and restraint is advocated remarkably well by Johannes Baptist Metz.

c. Theology of the world (Johannes Baptist Metz)

Similar to Moltmann the Roman Catholic scholar Johannes Baptist Metz affirms that "eschatology is not a discipline beside other disciplines, but that basic discipline which determines, forms, and shapes every theological statement." [103] Metz's point of direction is again politically and socially oriented. He understands the world in which Christian faith has to account for its hope as fundamentally future-oriented. This forward thrust of modern thinking, and the understanding of the world as history which results from it, are based on the biblical belief in the promises of God.[104] Thus the relationship between the Christian faith and the world can be interpreted theologically as creative and critical eschatology, since the hope of the Christian faith is oriented toward the future and cannot be realized by bypassing the world and the future of the world. The hope for a promised future is responsible for the *one* promised future and therefore also for the future of the world.[105] This means that transcendental, personalistic, or existential categories alone are not sufficient to provide a true theology of the world which at the same time is creatively and productively eschatological.[106]

Although Metz opts for a political eschatology, he knows that the creative and critical Christian hope is not just a militant optimism. A political eschatology, however, serves as a critical correction to the extreme privatization in present-day theology and as "a positive attempt to formulate the eschatological message under the conditions of our present society."[107] The church as an institution is not a reality above or besides this societal reality but *within* it, and it has a critical liberating task in regard to it.[108] This does not mean that it should act as a political pressure group to make its point.[109] On the contrary, the church has to mobilize the Christian love which plays such a central role in the Christian tradition. This love does not exhaust itself in the interpersonal sphere of the I-Thou or in charitable work within a neighborhood. It is the unconditional determination to bring justice, liberty, and peace to others.

The critical function of the church lies in its pronouncement of the eschatological proviso in the face of every abstract idea of progress and of humanity which regards the individual, living here and now, only as matter and means for the construction of a completely rationalized technological future.[110] The church must also announce to all present political systems that history as a whole stands under God's echatological proviso. Christians must take the initiative in reconciling opposing camps in society and the world, and must mobilize their social and political imagination in order to cooperate critically in the transformation of human conflict into a lasting world peace that effectively excludes war. Yet they must warn against any romanticism of peace and criticize "any idea of peace without conflict as an ideological utopia."[111]

Metz's good balance between the present-directed socio-political implications of eschatology and its future-directedness stands in sharp contrast to a more radical movement which opts for a theology of revolution.

d. Theology of revolution and liberation (Carl Braaten and Gustavo Gutiérrez)

The theology of revolution and liberation is a hotly debated topic of ecumenical importance. The decision of the World Council of Churches in 1978 to give aid for strictly humanitarian purposes from its fund to combat racism to certain liberation groups that operate in Rhodesia caused quite an uproar among many member churches. When Pope John Paul II in 1979 addressed the Third General Conference of the Latin-American Episcopate at Puebla, Mexico, again his speech caught the attention of millions of people. Pope John Paul II stated there that violence, of the left or of the right, is unChristian and must be condemned. He further stated that a theology of liberation that is based not on the gospel but on a Marxist analysis of reality is a false theology. But he affirmed that many liberation theologies incorporate Christian values without ideological overtones and are true theology.

The situation under many dictatorial regimes that brutally suppress any criticism of prevailing practices, while catering only to the rich at the expense of the poor, calls for liberation, redistribution of wealth, and perhaps even revolution. Even the modern technological structures in industrialized nations, that initially were embraced by virtually everyone because they brought widespread affluence in these countries, are more and more being considered a mixed blessing because they dehumanize the lives of people in industrialized nations and empty them of lasting values. There is also an increasing awareness that their opulent life-style can only be supported by people on alien shores who work for cheap wages and under less than desirable circumstances. Following the biblical admonition to side with the poor and powerless, theologians have become ever more sensitive to the needs of the exploited, the oppressed, and the underprivileged. Though Roman Catholic theologians, especially from Latin America, are in the forefront of this movement, we will mention first a Protestant North American theologian whose approach has decisive eschatological implications.

Carl E. Braaten, Professor of Systematic Theology at the Lutheran School of Theology in Chicago, wrestles with the socio-political implications of Christian eschatology from a Lutheran perspective. Braaten defines "a theology of revolution as the politics of eschatological hope in society." [112] He claims that the seeds of revolutionary dreams and hopes were scattered far and wide by the preaching of a gospel whose very essence is revolution. While the churches preached a gospel which pointed the way of hope for the future, they built institutions that impeded its coming. They secured alliances with the classes that possessed privileges of power, property, and position, and thus were indirectly responsible for the anti-Christian character of modern revolutionary movements.

Braaten finds fault especially with his own Lutheran heritage. Luther's two-kingdom doctrine, which separates the political kingdom to the left ruled by political powers through force from the spiritual kingdom to the right ruled by the means of grace, "leads to a conservative political ethic in which the question of revolution is invariably answered in the negative." [113] Braaten realizes that the stress on the *two* kingdoms has cautioned against two possible dangers, that of a "Christianization of society" by ecclesiastical heteronomy, remaking the world into the image of the church, or of a "secularization of the church," remaking the church into the image of the world. [114] But the Achilles' heel of this doctrine is found in its contrast between the two kingdoms, to the neglect of pressing for earthly signs which foreshadow its ultimate resolution in the common future of the church and the world in God's rule of glory.

> It may be useful to make such distinctions, but if they are separated, or united only in the *person* of the individual Christian, the results are catastrophic. It means, in short, that the eschatological dynamics of the gospel, the social and political features of the onrushing kingdom of God, are diverted from their aim to transform this world. When they are released into the world, they set in motion waves of revolutionary expectations that threaten structures of injustice and inequality. [115]

But if we abandon the dualism of the two kingdoms and reactivate the kingdom-of-God eschatology of the Bible, emphasizing not a spatial duality of spheres but a temporal difference between the "already now" and the "not yet," between the present and the future aspects of the power of God's rule, we not only recapture the dynamics of hope which the two-kingdom doctrine obliterated, but also avoid the dangers against which the two-kingdom doctrine protected us. [116]

The christocentric emphasis is evident when Braaten affirms that a theology of revolution must have as its primary paradigm the death and resurrection of Jesus Christ.[117] This protects him from opting for mere futurism. In pursuing the future the Christian will not lose the past, because it also belongs to the future summed up in Christ. The Christ reality that stretches backward and forward comprises the individual and the social and pulls the Christian revolutionary forward by the vision of the coming kingdom of God which Christ enabled. The kingdom of God in history is not achieved by a progressive development in a straight line or a smooth rhythm. Yet it triumphs whenever a revolution succeeds in creating new conditions of equality, justice, and freedom without sacrificing the richness of past expressions of creativity. It also scores a victory when community is built between nations and when the unity of humanity is advanced, when higher unities are built without war and when peace on earth makes mutual fulfillment of individuals and nations possible.[118] But Braaten cautions Christians who decide for revolutionary change not to become agents of a political party or social group whose success they pursue to the point of dominion. And he calls it a "stupid illusion" to strive for a total revolution that wipes the slate clean and leads to an absolutely new beginning. Instead of a *total* revolution Braaten opts for a *permanent* revolution.[119]

> Christians are to form peace corps of God's kingdom in the world, an army of salvation signaling "the way" to a future in which violence will be no more, and "there shall be an end to death, and to mourning and crying and pain." That is the final goal of the revolutionary existence of Christians in the world.[120]

Braaten reminds the church that it has abandoned its own eschatological heritage. The tranquility that set in with the Constaninian Era has always been a great temptation. But by the same token this tranquility enabled the church to permeate the state and to create a "Christian" Occident with all the cultural, political, and social benefits that we so readily take for granted. The Christian community must be reminded constantly that it does not only live in a transitory way in this world, but that the world is also of transitory nature.

In more recent writings Braaten notes, "The social idealism and revolutionary romanticism that we witnessed in the decades of the '60s have been shattered by profound disappointment."[121] Braaten realizes that one of the great Western fallacies was the notion that the idea of freedom could be divorced from the notion of God. But only the infinite God can serve as the ultimate ground and source of freedom and, as witnessed in God being with us in Jesus, freedom basically means the freedom to love. It is in following their master that Christians venture their life, "to participate in the liberation movements in the world." [122] Thus an eschatological vision is not just a fad that emerges from the optimism of its social and political environment. On the contrary, Braaten contends that political revolutions are only surface revolutions, since they lack the eschatological dimension.[123] But a biblical apocalyptic theology of revolution is "a visionary preconstruction of all things in the light of the eschatological future that irradiates from the Christ-event in history." [124] Biblical eschatology implies a total and all-encompassing change and it might well be that when things seem most hopeless, in actuality we are witnessing the growth pangs of the future. "So in spite of all, this is a time of hope." [125]

Braaten has well captured the eschatological message of the New Testament when he points out that both this world and Christianity are transitory phenomena. He also realizes that Jesus was a revolutionary of a unique kind—neither a social reformer nor a political revolutionary. Jesus told both earthly authorities and overanxious zealotic followers that his business was not that of the worldly authorities. Yet the same Jesus radicalized all individual and social ethics in an unprecedented way. But is it not too difficult a task and an impossible enterprise to hope with Braaten that the world and the objectives of the Christians are governed by the same principle? [126] While the coming of Jesus and the kingdom of God cannot be separated, human visionary preconstruction of all things in the light of the eschatological future can at best only be an inadequate prelude to the God-provided second coming of Christ and the new creation it entails.

Since Carl Braaten grew up in an overseas mission field, his interest in the revolutionary power of eschatology is certainly shaped by having lived among people of the Third World. When we come to the actual representatives of liberation theology, we are mainly confronted with theologians who still live in this context, that of the exploited, the underprivileged, and the poor. Yet liberation theology would be unthinkable without the encouragement from secular liberation movements and ideologies. Instead of doctrine and thought, its main emphasis is on strategy and action. This becomes obvious when we name a few of the book titles which reflect this emphasis on strategy and action: Hugo Assmann, *Theology for a Nomad Church* (1976); Denis Goulet, *A New*

Moral Order. Studies in Development Ethics and Liberation Theology (1974); José Miguez Bonino, *Doing Theology in a Revolutionary Situation* (1975); Juan Luis Segundo, *Liberation of Theology* (1976).

Liberation theology has been picked up in many Christian quarters and is no longer limited to a special segment of the underprivileged and exploited. As James H. Cone, *God of the Oppressed* (1975), indicates, its eschatological emphasis is valid for Blacks and Chicanos, for Whites and Native Americans, for people of the Third World and people of the First World. Yet the main representatives of liberation theology still come from Latin America. One of its most eloquent advocates is Gustavo Gutiérrez, professor of theology and social sciences at the University of Lima, Peru.

For Gutiérrez the theology of liberation is a theology of salvation incarnated in the concrete historical and political conditions of today. That theology is seen here under the aspect of salvation is understandable in light of the situation to which liberation theology primarily speaks. The situation of the oppressed calls for a revolutionary transformation of the very basis of a dehumanizing society. Though liberation theologians often employ Marxist terminology, there is no conceptual panacea that would safeguard such a revolutionary transformation. The Christians involved in the process of liberation proceed by trial and error in their attempt to build a different social order and to establish a new way of being human. While hope is central to a theology of liberation, one does not pursue its goal in euphoria. The joy of the resurrection first requires death on the cross.

But in his comprehensive *Theology of Liberation. History, Politics and Salvation* (1973), Gutiérrez makes it clear that "it is important to keep in mind that beyond—or rather, through—the struggle against misery, injustice, and exploitation the goal is the *creation of a new man*." [127] Gutiérrez learns from the Old Testament that God is a history-making God and that salvation is there spoken of in terms of a re-creation of history. The God who creates the cosmos out of chaos is the same God who leads Israel from alienation to liberation. Similarly, in the New Testament we hear of a new creation. Creation and salvation therefore belong together. By means of our labor we participate in the all-embracing salvific process, thereby engaging ourselves in the work of creation. By transforming this world we become human and build a human community. In our struggle against misery and exploitation and in our attempt to build a just society we become part of the saving action which is on its way toward complete fulfillment. Salvation is not a return to the days of old, but a striving forward toward something new and unprecedented. In talking about the new creation, Gutiérrez rightly emphasizes Christ as the center and goal of the new creation.

The vision of salvation and new creation would lose its driving force without the eschatological promises that permeate virtually the whole Bible. Gutiérrez appropriately distinguishes between the promises made by God throughout history and the Promise that unfolds and becomes richer and more definite in these individual promises. "The Promise is not exhausted by these promises nor by their fulfillment; it goes beyond them, explains them, and gives them their ultimate meaning. But at the same time, the Promise is announced and is partially and progressively fulfilled in them." [128] The promises replacing each other urge history on to new horizons and new possibilities. The Promise is gradually revealed in its fullness. Since it is already fulfilled in historical events, yet not completely, it incessantly projects itself into the future and creates a permanent historical mobility. Gutiérrez knows that both the present and the future aspects are indispensable for properly aligning the relationship between the Promise and history.

When one asks what this Promise might be, Gutiérrez points to the efficacious self-disclosure of God's love and God's consequent self-communication. This Promise, which is both revelation and good news, is at the heart of the Bible, and enters into a decisive stage in the incarnation of the Son and the sending of the Spirit. Since the Promise is intimately connected with salvation and with the time of fulfillment, it is clear for Gutiérrez that in the Bible eschatology is "the driving force of salvific history radically oriented toward the future. Eschatology is thus not just one more element of Christianity, but the very key to understanding the Christian faith." [129]

Gutiérrez is adamant in pointing out that the intrinsic eschatological structure of the Christian faith is not to be spiritualized. Neither its present nor its future aspects should be related merely to spiritual realities, since their origin and goal have definitely historical bearings. For instance, when the prophets announce the kingdom of peace this presupposes the establishment of justice on earth. Similarly, the coming of the kingdom and the expectation of the parousia necessarily imply historical, temporal, earthly, social, and material realities. A spiritualization, however, would tend to forget the human consequences of the eschatological promises and the power to transform the unjust social structures which they imply. Elimination of misery and exploitation therefore can be understood as signs of the coming kingdom.

Gutiérrez emphasizes that the eschatological promises are being fulfilled throughout history. And he cautions that they cannot be clearly and completely identified with a specific social reality. Yet we are somewhat bewildered when we hear him say: "The complete encounter with the Lord will mark an end to history, but it will take place in history." [130] Does this mean that we are evolving toward a state of eschatological fulfillment, a state that, because it is eschatological, will not be just another point on the map of history? If that be the case Gutiérrez would place on us the impossible task of demonstrating that we are evolving towards that state. Gutiérrez is right when he claims that the liberating action of Christ is not marginal to the real life of humanity but strikes at its very heart. The struggle for a just society can in its own right also be considered a part of salvation history. But Gutiérrez seems to neglect the fact that the immense depravity of humanity not only causes the conditions that cry out for liberation but also prevents liberation from becoming a historical event. That is why salvation is not simply perfection or fulfillment but implies a totally new creation.

NOTES

1. I have tried to take account of them within the presentation of my own position. But since most of these approaches deserve more extensive attention, a separate chapter will be devoted to them.
2. Albert Schweitzer, *The Mystery of the Kingdom of God: The Secret of Jesus' Messiahship and Passion*, trans. with an intr. by Walter Lowrie (New York: Macmillan, 1950). The extensive introduction by Lowrie provides a good acquaintance with the immediate reaction this book received and also gives the translator's own evaluation of the book.
3. Adolf von Harnack, *What Is Christianity?*, trans. by Th. B. Saunders, intr. by Rudolf Bultmann (New York: Harper, 1957) esp. 51 and 54.
4. Schweitzer, *The Mystery of the Kingdom of God*, 160.
5. Schweitzer, *The Mystery of the Kingdom of God*, 174.
6. Albert Schweitzer, *The Quest of the Historical Jesus; A Critical Study of Its Progress from Reimarus to Wrede*, with a preface by F. C. Burkitt, trans. from the first German ed. by W. Montgomery (New York: Macmillan, 1966) 337.
7. Cf. Albert Schweitzer, *The Quest of the Historical Jesus*, 402f.; and *The Mystery of the Kingdom of God*, 174.
8. Schweitzer, *The Quest of the Historical Jesus*, 370f.
9. Cf. Schweitzer, *The Mystery of the Kingdom of God*, 55, where he introduces the

term "interim-ethics." Cf. also E. N. Mozley, *The Theology of Albert Schweitzer for Christian Inquirers*, with an epilogue by Albert Schweitzer (London: Black, 1950) 50ff.; and Albert Schweitzer, *The Kingdom of God and Primitive Christianity*, ed. with an intr. by Ulrich Neuenschwander, trans. by L. A. Garrad (London: Black, 1968), in his section on "Jesus' Ethic of Preparation for the Kingdom," 81ff. Cf. also Albert Schweitzer, *The Philosophy of Civilization*, trans. by C. T. Campion (New York: Macmillan, 1949) 111, where he describes the world view of Jesus as being fundamentally optimistic. Biased by the expectation of the end of the world, however, it is indifferent to all attempts made to improve the temporal, natural world by a civilization of outward progress. Jesus' world view concerns itself only with the inward ethical perfecting of individuals.

In pointing to the eschatological dimension Schweitzer has certainly discovered the starting point and the direction of Jesus' ethics. But it seems almost artificial to assert that the inward perfection which Jesus advocated should have no implications for outward circumstances.

10. Cf. Werner Georg Kümmel's instructive essay "Die 'konsequente Eschatologie' Albert Schweitzers im Urteil der Zeitgenossen," in *Heilsgeschehen und Geschichte; Gesammelte Aufsätze 1933-1964*, ed. by E. Grässer et al. (Marburg: Elwert, 1965) 332.

11. Cf. Walter Lowrie in his introduction to Schweitzer, *The Mystery of the Kingdom*, 3f. Cf. also Schweitzer's own assessment in *Geschichte der Leben-Jesu-Forschung* (6th ed.: Tübingen: Mohr, 1951) 592.

12. Trans. by W. Montgomery with a prefatory note by F. C. Burkitt (New York: Macmillan, 1955).

13. Cf. Kümmel, "Die 'konsequente Eschatologie' Albert Schweitzers im Urteil der Zeitgenossen," 337.

14. Cf. Martin Werner, *The Formation of Christian Dogma; An Historical Study of Its Problem*, trans. with an intr. by S. G. F. Brandon (New York: Harper, 1957) 47, 71f., and other places. Werner attempts to describe the process of the formation of the Christian dogma as a process of de-eschatologizing the main apostolic doctrine caused by the crises that emerged when the parousia was more and more delayed.

15. Cf. Fritz Buri in his response to Rudolf Bultmann "Entmythologisierung oder Entkerygmatisierung der Theologie," in *Kerygma und Mythos*, vol. 2, ed. by Hans-Werner Bartsch (Hamburg-Volksdorf: Reich, 1952) 85-101; and Fritz Buri, *Christian Faith in Our Time*, trans. by E. A. Kent (New York: Macmillan, 1966) 124ff., where in relying on Albert Schweitzer and Karl Jaspers he advocates the concept of awe or reverence for life as the guiding ethical principle in our attitudes toward ourselves and our environment. Cf. also John Macquarrie, *The Scope of Demythologizing; Bultmann and His Critics* (New York: Harper Torchbooks, 1966) 129ff.

In recent years Buri seems to have modified his approach gently, perhaps adopting more features of classical liberalism. In *How Can We Still Speak Responsibly of God*, trans. by Ch. D. Hardwick (Philadelphia: Fortress, 1968) 40, he suggests that love constitutes the fulfillment of human existence. And in his book *Theology of Existence*, trans. by H. H. Oliver and G. Onder (Greenwood, S.C.: Attic, 1965) 110, he asserts that the general resurrection of the dead, the last judgment, Christ's victory over the powers, and the new heaven and the new earth represent symbols for the communal context of existence as it shall be realized in the church as Christian existence in community. Though he introduces thereby the term "universal *Heilsgeschichte*," he understands it as mythology that expresses this supra-individual character of existence.

16. For Troeltsch cf. Wilhelm Pauck, *Harnack and Troeltsch; Two Historical Theologians* (New York: Oxford University Press, 1968) 66f.

17. Bultmann, "On the Question of Christology," in *Faith and Understanding*, 1:132.

18. For the following cf. Ibid., 30f.; and Bultmann, *Jesus and the Word*, 9, where he says: "Considering that it was really no trifle to believe oneself Messiah, that, further, whoever so believed must have regulated his whole life in accordance with this belief, we must admit that if this point is obscure we can, strictly speaking, know nothing of the personality of Jesus. I am personally of the opinion that Jesus did not believe himself to be the Messiah, but I do not imagine that this opinion gives me a clearer picture of his personality."
19. Günther Bornkamm, *Jesus of Nazareth*, trans. by I. and F. McLuskey together with J. M. Robinson (London: Hodder and Stoughton, 1960) 228. A former student of Martin Dibelius, Bornkamm agrees with Bultmann in saying that in this first group of sayings nothing is mentioned about the identity of Jesus with the Son of man, though the believing community was certain of it.
20. Cf. Bultmann, *Theology of the New Testament*, 1:30; Bornkamm, *Jesus of Nazareth*, 228; and Heinz Eduard Tödt, *The Son of Man in the Synoptic Tradition*, trans. by D. M. Barton (London: SCM, 1965) 224f., where he gives a good summary of his careful exegesis.
21. Cf. the objections to Bultmann's position by Oscar Cullmann, *The Christology of the New Testament*, 156; and August Strobel, *Kerygma und Apokalyptik: Ein religionsgeschichtlicher und theologischer Beitrag zur Christusfrage* (Göttingen: Vandenhoeck & Ruprecht, 1967) 56f.
22. So Philipp Vielhauer, "Gottesreich und Menschensohn in der Verkündigung Jesu," in *Aufsätze zum Neuen Testament* (Munich: Kaiser, 1965) 80; cf. also his essay "Jesus und der Menschensohn: Zur Diskussion mit Heinz Eduard Tödt und Eduard Schweizer," in Ibid., 92-140, where he rejects the approach of Tödt.
23. Bultmann, *Theology of the New Testament*, 1:30.
24. Ibid. Cf. Hans Lietzmann, *Der Menschensohn: Ein Beitrag zur neutestamentlichen Theologie* (Berlin, 1896).
25. Vielhauer, "Gottesreich und Menschensohn in der Verkündigung Jesu," 61.
26. Cf. Bornkamm, *Jesus of Nazareth*, 229; and Strobel, *Kerygma und Apokalyptik*, 60, who allows for the possibility that some of these sayings date back to Jesus of Nazareth.
27. Bornkamm, 230f.
28. Vielhauer, "Gottesreich und Menschensohn in der Verkündigung Jesu," 78.
29. So Vielhauer, 80. Hahn, *The Titles of Jesus in Christology*, 28, however, objects that the origin of some of the words concerning the eschatological working of the Son of man on the lips of Jesus cannot be disputed. "Neither the relative lack of connection with sayings about the Kingdom of God nor the peculiar features of the teaching of Jesus furnish essential arguments against authenticity."
30. Cf. Strobel, *Kerygma und Apokalyptik*, 83f.; and C. F. D. Moule, *The Birth of the New Testament* (New York: Harper & Row, 1962) 63, who attempts to explain Jesus' use of the term Son of man as the use of a symbol from Daniel 7, "which is both historical and eschatological." He also quotes some other important literature to the highly technical discussion on the origin of the Son of man terminology.
31. So Stauffer, *Jesus and His Story*, 170ff.
32. Taylor, *The Names of Jesus*, 32; cf. also Maurice Goguel, *Jesus and the Origins of Christianity*, vol. 2: *The Life of Jesus*, trans. by O. Wyon (New York: Harper Torchbooks, 1960) 578.
33. T. W. Manson, *The Teaching of Jesus, Studies of Its Form and Content* (Cambridge: Cambridge University Press, 1948) 230.
34. Bultmann, *Theology of the New Testament*, 1:43. Hans Conzelmann, "Zur Methode der Leben-Jesu-Forschung," in *Zeitschrift für Theologie und Kirche*, 56, sup. 1 (1959) 6, calls this statement "perhaps the most important sentence in Bultmann's *Theology of the New Testament*."

35. Fuchs, "The Quest of the Historical Jesus," 21f.
36. Bultmann in his programmatic essay "New Testament and Mythology," in *Kerygma and Myth: A Theological Debate*, ed. by Hans Werner Bartsch, trans. by R. H. Fuller (London: SPCK, 1953) 1:5.
37. Ibid., 15f.
38. Bultmann, "History and Eschatology in the New Testament," in *New Testament Studies* (1954-1955) 1:9.
39. Ibid., 13.
40. Thus Bultmann can say that the process of demythologizing began partially already with Paul (cf. Bultmann, *Jesus Christ and Mythology* [New York: Scribner, 1958] 32). Very fittingly he entitles his Gifford lectures in which he addresses himself to the problem of history *History and Eschatology: The Presence of Eternity* (New York: Harper, 1957).
41. Bultmann, *Theology of the New Testament*, 2:21.
42. Bultmann, *The Gospel of John*, 220, 234ff., 472, and other places. Cf. also Bultmann, "Johannesevangelium," in *Religion in Geschichte und Gegenwart*, 3rd ed., 3:841.
43. This convincing argument is advanced by Wolfhart Pannenberg, "Redemptive Event and History" (1959), in *Basic Questions in Theology: Collected Essays*, trans. by G. H. Kehm (Philadelphia: Fortress, 1970) 1:25.
44. Amos N. Wilder, *Eschatology and Ethics in the Teaching of Jesus*, Revised Edition (New York: Harper, 1959) 21.
45. Wilder, 65. He also mentions that Bultmann's reinterpretation verges on Gnosticism and psychologism. In his essay "Kerygma, Eschatology, and Social Ethics," in *The Background of the New Testament and Its Eschatology*, 519, Wilder indicates that Bultmann's theology of the Word of God has a strange resemblance to an older individual pietism and he assumes that his individualistic interpretation of the kerygma is presumably connected with Bultmann's Lutheran background. Wilder's observation, however, could only be true if Bultmann represented an un-Lutheran view of Luther. Even explaining Bultmann's approach from an individualistic pietistic background would leave many questions open.

    Though Wilder is basically right in seeing Lutheran and pietistic influences in Bultmann's approach, we hope to make unmistakably clear throughout this book that a Lutheran understanding of New Testament eschatology, i.e., an eschatology founded on Luther's basic insights in the New Testament proclamation, is neither exclusively individualistic nor exclusively other-worldly in orientation. Only in continuous tension between concern for the individual and the community, and between concern for this world and the world to come, can we live truly eschatologically.
46. Wilder, *Eschatology and Ethics in the Teaching of Jesus*, 62.
47. Ibid., 59.
48. For the following cf. ibid., 176f.
49. Ibid., 193.
50. Ibid., 69f.
51. When Wilder talks about mythopoetic images (cf. his *Otherworldliness and the New Testament* [New York: Harper, 1954] 9), he does not talk about mythology in the same sense that Bultmann does. But do these images provide more than an incentive for immanent hope? While Bultmann attempts to merge the dichotomy between immanent and transcendent in his existential interpretation of the New Testament message, Wilder seems to leave the transcendent "up there" as a power to solve our problems here on earth (cf. 117ff.).
52. Cf. C. H. Dodd, *The Parables of the Kingdom* (New York: Scribners, 1961) vii.
53. Dodd, *The Coming of Christ: Four Broadcast Addresses for the Season of Advent* (Cambridge: Cambridge University Press, 1954) 6.

54. Cf. Dodd, *The Parables of the Kingdom*, 159.
55. Ibid., 162.
56. Cf. Dodd, *The Coming of Christ*, 12ff.
57. Cf. Dodd, *The Interpretation of the Fourth Gospel*, 405ff., where he emphasizes that already John (13:31—14:31) understood Christ's return in a sense different from that of popular Christian eschatology. After the death of Jesus, and because of it, Jesus' followers will enter into union with him as their living Lord. Thus death marks his departure from this earth, while resurrection stands for his enthronement in power and his return.
58. Dodd, *The Parables of the Kingdom*, 164f. Cf. also his *The Founder of Christianity* (New York: Macmillan, 1970) 172, where he again emphasizes the experience of a new corporate life, made possible because God himself had come to men in a way altogether new.
59. Cf. Dodd, *The Coming of Christ*, 15f.
60. Dodd, *The Parables of the Kingdom*, 166f.
61. Ibid., 169; and *The Coming of Christ*, 19-25.
62. We are inclined to agree with Dodd when he says *(The Interpretation of the Fourth Gospel*, 447) that the formula "the hour is coming, and now is" (cf. John 5:25) with the emphasis on the "and now is," without excluding the element of futurity, "probably represents the authentic teaching of Jesus as veraciously as any formula could."

   Without engaging in a discussion whether the priority belongs to the synoptics or to John, we must ask if such an *ipsissima vox* could substantiate Dodd's claim to give priority to present-oriented eschatology? Hardly, because we cannot proclaim like Jesus, but like Jesus of Nazareth *and* under the impression of the resurrected Jesus Christ. This shifts the emphasis from the present to a "progressive" balance between present and future.
63. John A. T. Robinson, *Jesus and His Coming: The Emergence of a Doctrine* (London: SCM, 1957) 136f.
64. Ibid., 137f.
65. Ibid., 141.
66. Ibid., 142.
67. Cf. Ibid., 163f.
68. Cf. Robinson, *In the End God* (New York: Harper & Row, 1968) 81.
69. Ibid., 133. At least parenthetically we must mention at the end of our brief survey of transcendentalist approaches the position of T. W. Manson, who, like John A. T. Robinson, is influenced by C. H. Dodd's concept of realized eschatology. In his book *The Teaching of Jesus*, for instance, in advocating a corporate understanding of the Son of man title Manson suggests: "The 'Son of Man' in the present is a name for Jesus plus any who take up the cross and follow him: the 'Son of Man' coming in glory and power is the same, Jesus and all who have faithfully followed him, Christ plus those that are Christ's, who suffer with him and are glorified with him" (269). However, the final victory of good over evil will not be delayed indefinitely, and the final consummation will come sooner or later, suddenly or gradually, otherwise the kingdom of God would become an empty dream (284). Again a universalistic tinge seems to come up when Manson asserts that every generation will be judged by its response to the manifestation of the sovereignty of God as available in its day (271).
70. Ethelbert Stauffer, "Agnostos Christos: Joh. XI. 24 und die Eschatologie des vierten Evangeliums," in *The Background of the New Testament and Its Eschatology*, 282.
71. Cf. ibid., 286. With these theses Stauffer shows more affinity to C. H. Dodd and other Anglo-Saxon New Testament scholars than to most of his German colleagues.
72. For the following cf. ibid., 292ff.

114   *Views and Issues*

73. Stauffer, *Jesus and His Story*, 158f.
74. Stauffer, "Agnostos Christos," 298.
75. Cf. Wolfhart Pannenberg, *Jesus—God and Man*, 82, who rightly mentions that if the apocalyptic expectations should be totally excluded from the realm of possibility for us, then the early Christian community's faith in Christ is also no longer possible for us.
76. Cf. for the following, Oscar Cullmann, *Salvation in History*, trans. by S. G. Sowers *et al.* (London: SCM, 1967) 179f.
77. Cullmann, *Christ and Time: The Primitive Christian Conception of Time and History*, trans. by F. V. Filson (London: SCM, 1962) 84f.
78. Cullmann, *Salvation in History*, 183f.
79. Ibid., 202f.
80. Cf. Cullmann, "Das wahre durch die ausgebliebene Parusie gestellte neutestamentliche Problem" (1947), in *Vorträge und Aufsätze; 1925-1962* (Tübingen: Mohr, 1966) 422. Cullmann's reference to the Hellenization of eschatology which was connected with the growth of the church does not solve the problem either (cf. also *Christ and Time*), because the question must be asked if the process of Hellenization was a necessity and whether it can ever be reversed. Thomas J. J. Altizer's attempt to reverse this process shows at what results one might arrive.
81. Cf. Werner Georg Kümmel, in his excellent study *Promise and Fulfillment: The Eschatological Message of Jesus*, trans. by D. M. Barton (Naperville, Ill.: Allenson, 1957) 141.
82. Cf. for the following Kümmel, "Futurische und Präsentische Eschatologie im ältesten Christentum," in *Heilsgeschehen und Geschichte*, 356ff.
83. Ibid., 360ff.
84. Kümmel, *Promise and Fulfilment*, 152f.
85. Ibid., 155.
86. Pannenberg, *Revelation as History*, 131 (thesis 2).
87. Ibid., 139 (thesis 4; my trans.). For the discussion of Pannenberg's concept of revelation in history cf. also Wolfhart Pannenberg, "Insight and Faith," in *Basic Questions in Theology. Collected Essays*, trans. by G. H. Kehm, 2 vols. (Philadelphia: Fortress, 1970-71), 2:28-45, in his discussion with Paul Althaus; and "Redemptive Event and History," ibid., 1:15-80.
88. Wolfhart Pannenberg, *Theology and the Kingdom of God*, ed. by Richard J. Neuhaus (Philadelphia: Westminster, 1969) 126.
89. Jürgen Moltmann, *Theology of Hope*, 16.
90. Ernst Käsemann, "The Beginnings of Christian Theology (1960), in *New Testament Questions of Today*, trans. by W. J. Montague (London: SCM, 1969) 102.
91. Cf. for the following Moltmann, *Theology of Hope*, 110ff.
92. Ibid., 148.
93. Ibid., 180.
94. Ibid., 203.
95. Ibid., 288.
96. Ibid., 303.
97. Ibid., 329.
98. Ibid.
99. Cf. Heinz Eduard Tödt, "Aus einem Brief an Jürgen Moltmann," in *Diskussion über die 'Theologie der Hoffnung' von Jürgen Moltmann*, ed. by Wolf-Dieter Marsch (Munich: Kaiser, 1967) 197.
100. Jürgen Moltmann, *The Crucified God. The Cross of Christ as the Foundation and Criticism of Christian Theology*, trans. by R. A. Wilson and J. Bowden (New York: Harper, 1974) 1.
101. Ibid., 294.

102. Jürgen Moltmann, *The Church in the Power of the Spirit. A Contribution to Messianic Ecclesiology*, trans. by M. Kohl (New York: Harper, 1977) 287.
103. Johannes B. Metz, *Theology of the World*, trans. by W. Glen-Doepel (New York: Herder, 1969) 90.
104. Cf. ibid., 87.
105. Cf. ibid., 91f. It must be mentioned here that the English translation varies considerably from the German original. For instance, while the German edition reads: "Das Verhältnis zwischen Glaube und Welt lässt sich theologisch bestimmen mit dem Begriff einer 'schöpferisch-kritischen Eschatologie'; eine solche Theologie der Welt muss gleichzeitig 'politische Theologie' sein" (*Zur Theologie der Welt* [Munich: Kaiser, 1968] 84) the English reads: "The relationship between the Christian faith and the world should be characterized from a theological viewpoint as a creative and militant eschatology" (91). Since I wonder if this radical translation would be acceptable to the author, I have always compared the English version with the German and given preference to the German except for direct quotations.
106. Metz, *Theology of the World*, 95f.
107. Ibid., 107.
108. Ibid., 115.
109. Ibid., 119.
110. Cf. for the following ibid., 117f.
111. Ibid., 139f.
112. Carl E. Braaten, *The Future of God; the Revolutionary Dynamics of Hope* (New York: Harper & Row, 1969) 142.
113. Ibid., 146.
114. Ibid., 152.
115. Ibid., 151.
116. In a more recent publication Carl Braaten distinguishes between the traditional-institutional type of theology, the trademarks of which are order and space, and the apocalyptic-revolutionary type, characterized by liberation and time. The former is disinterested in the plight of the poor and the oppressed, comforting them with the hope of life after death, while the latter provides a heavenly critique of earthly existence and has led the movement of protest in the revolutionary struggle against the established order. Cf. Carl Braaten, *Eschatology and Ethics: Essays on the Theology and Ethics of the Kingdom of God* (Minneapolis: Augsburg, 1974) esp. 129ff.
117. Braaten asserts that the resurrection of Jesus Christ serves as the key to a theology of the future, since Christian hope is based on the resurrection of Jesus of Nazareth, because through it God defined himself as the power of the living future beyond the finality of death (Carl E. Braaten, "God and the Idea of the Future," *Dialog*, 7 [1968]: 257f.).
118. Braaten, *The Future of God*, 158f.
119. Ibid., 164.
120. Ibid., 166.
121. Carl E. Braaten, *Eschatology and Ethics*, 7.
122. Carl E. Braaten, *Christ and Counter-Christ: Apocalyptic Themes in Theology and Culture* (Philadelphia: Fortress, 1972) 38.
123. Ibid., 111.
124. Ibid., 103.
125. Ibid., 113.
126. His attempt to combine Pannenberg's "theology of universal history" with Moltmann's "theology of hope" (cf. Carl E. Braaten, "Toward a Theology of Hope," in *Theology Today*, 24 [1967]: 218), cannot convince us that he can meaningfully maintain a theology of hope which does not result in mere rhetoric or a utopian

dream. When Braaten adopts as his theological slogan Ernst Bloch's assertion that the real genesis is not at the beginning but at the end (Braaten, *The Future of God*, 18), we wonder whether this does not inevitably result in a sanctification of the evolutionary or revolutionary process of history.

127. Gustavo Gutiérrez, *A Theology of Liberation. History, Politics and Salvation*, trans. and ed. by C. Inda and J. Eagleson (Maryknoll, New York: Orbis, 1973) 146.

128. Ibid., 161.

129. Ibid., 162.

130. Ibid., 168. While we cannot agree with the claim of Juan Gutierrez, *The New Libertarian Gospel: Pitfalls of the Theology of Liberation*, trans. by P. Burns (Chicago, Ill.: Franciscan Herald Press, 1977) 97, that Gustavo Gutiérrez has emptied theology of its content, we agree with Juan Gutierrez that in liberation theology evangelization in terms of conversion as the specific mission of the church certainly loses significance at the expense of socio-political reforms.

4
Eschatology and Science

MOST CONTEMPORARY DISCUSSION of eschatology, especially of its social and political implications, presupposes a steadily progressing line of history. Though we have seen that the modern concept of progress is undeniably related to the Judeo-Christian tradition out of which it originated, this does not automatically necessitate the realization of the future to which, they point. In an age which is dominated by science and technology we must also consider the scientific and technological aspect of such a future. We have to ask ourselves if a future is actually projectable as far as we and our universe are concerned. If this question is answered in the affirmative then we must ask the other decisive question whether such a predictable or conceivable future would allow for an eschaton provided by God *or* by us.[1] We remember the verdict of Rudolf Bultmann that the expected end of the world did not come, and that, as every schoolchild knows, world history will continue its course indefinitely. Two scholars devoted special attention to the scientific aspect of Christian eschatology, Teilhard de Chardin and Karl Heim.

1. The evolutionary approach of Teilhard de Chardin

The late French Jesuit paleontologist Pierre Teilhard de Chardin holds a unique position. In his writings and in his profession he combined profound scientific erudition with an incisive theological mind. At first glance his writings are bewildering, since he coined many new terms and frequently endowed scientific concepts with theological significance.[2]

a. Humanity in transition

Teilhard conceives of humanity as being part of the universal evolutionary process. The evolutionary process is moving from alpha to omega

117

(Rev. 1:8). Cosmosphere (the inanimate world), biosphere (the animate world), noosphere (the human world) and christosphere (the realm of Christ) are the main stages of the universal, upward-slanting evolutionary process. Through hominization, humanity became human and emerged from the animal world to the noosphere. Through christification the evolutionary process will come to its fulfillment and everything will be received into Christ. The universe, and within it humanity, has a definite destiny and a definite future.

Life is neither an absurdity as held by Jean-Paul Sartre,[3] nor is human existence a "being towards death" as projected by Martin Heidegger.[4] Even totalitarianism, as seen in modern technology or in bureaucratic government, is not the final word in evolution. It is only a temporary aberration in the movement toward unity.[5] There will be a further and consistent complexification of the noosphere. Our knowledge about the universe at large will increase, and so will the psycho-social pressure on the surface of the planet.[6] The condensation of human mass which we already face in modern technopolis will take place on a world-wide scale. We cannot withdraw from each other without stumbling over people while going backward.

But Teilhard does not despair just because our planet is becoming too small for our ever-growing population. On the contrary, Teilhard is convinced that the psycho-social pressure will unify humanity, its society, and its culture, and will lead toward personalization, increased differentiation and a richer fulfillment of the individual. Evolution is always an ascent to increased consciousness.

b. Synchronization between evolution and parousia

But what is the end of evolution? Teilhard does not conceive of it as an infinite process, but as having a definite goal in the paroxysm under the intense psycho-social pressure that will lead to christification. Everything will be received and end in Christ. This excludes any final catastrophe as the end of our present world, since such a sidereal disaster could lead only to the extinction of part of our universe, rather than to the fulfilling of the universe as a whole. Teilhard would not agree that he portrays an almost naive and blind trust in the future. On the contrary he assures us that "worldly faith is not enough in itself to move the earth forward."[7]

If we wish properly to understand Teilhard's confidence about the future, we must note three items:

(1) Teilhard identifies the center of humanity's present crisis as a real but unnecessary conflict between two major forces. One, operating on the horizontal plane, is the forward energy of faith in humanity, in the world, in human progress, moving toward the "ultra-human." The other is the traditional Christian faith, aspiring on a vertical plane in a personal transcendence and adoration toward God. The purely human drive, however, "can neither justify nor sustain its momentum to the end" because it discounts a center at its consummation and therefore needs to be centered in the Christian faith.[8] On the other hand, the purely upward drive is not the full story of the Christian faith either, since it is rooted in the incarnation and "has always based a large part of its tenets on the tangible values of the World and of Matter."[9] Teilhard wants to rectify and reconcile these two faiths into a mutually complementary, supportive, and fortifying synthesis.[10] He sees in the parousia the perfect example of this synthesis, a single case "which sums up everything."

(2) Teilhard sees humanity's complete evolution and Christ's second coming in analogy with the conditions of Christ's first appearance on earth: "The mystery of the first Christmas which (as everyone agrees) could only have happened between Heaven and an Earth which was *prepared,* socially, politically and psychologically, to receive Jesus."[11] Why, Teilhard asks, should we not also assume "that the parousiac spark can, of physical and organic necessity, only be kindled between Heaven and a Mankind which has biologically reached a certain critical evolutionary point of collective maturity?"[12] In other words, as Christ first came to us when the time was fulfilled, so he will come again when the conditions for the parousia are ripe.

(3) While Teilhard stipulates that humanity must reach maximum maturation, this alone is not a sufficient condition for Christ's second coming. The evolutionary climax is a necessary pre-condition for Christ's return, and is indeed assisted by Christ's presence presently veiled in all things. But it *cannot* itself cause the parousia to take place. The "supernatural" always predominates and makes the event more than the natural course of human evolution. Yet Teilhard insists that the parousia will not be an *arbitrary* event, independent of the progress of human evolution.[13] Just as the incarnation took place in "the fullness of time," so too will Christ's return take place in the ultimate and complete fullness of time.

A Christian understands, Teilhard says, that the process of hominization is only a preparation for the final parousia. Yet christogenesis, when everything will be received and end in Christ, is not a natural phenomenon or a product of evolution. There is an ascending anthropogenesis and a descending permeation of christogenesis. The natural evolution up to humanity and the "supernatural" descent in the incarnation have merged to form a unity in salvation history. The unifying movement of the human family (upward-slanting and forward-moving) and the activity of Christ in salvation history (from above and permeating the whole reality of humanity) are fused in the christogenesis. Thus hominization serves as a preparation for and a way toward the parousia.

The Christian community must remain faithful and keep alive the expectation of the return of Christ. Teilhard affirms that we cannot determine the hour or the mode of this event, but we *must* expect it. "Expectation—anxious, collective and operative expectation of an end of the world, that is to say of an issue for the world—that is perhaps the supreme Christian function and the most distinctive characteristic of our religion." [14]

We are to recognize that historically expectation has been the illumination of our faith. It has been the light at the end of the tunnel that offers us hope. Starting with the messianic hope of the prophets and culminating in the return of Christ so impatiently expected by many in the first Christian community, Christians have as their heritage the charge of "keeping the flame of desire ever alive in the world. . . . It is an accumulation of desires that should cause the Pleroma to burst upon us." [15]

Teilhard tempers this full expectation of Christ's return with the caution and encouragement to persist in this vigil, even in the seeming slowness of its advent. He cautions us not to follow the early Christians in their "childish haste" to expect an immediate return since such an attitude leads to pessimism, disillusionment, and suspicion. But we are to rekindle and renew in ourselves the hope and desire for Christ's return, even when we know neither the day nor the hour.

Once again we hear Teilhard's call to the reconciliation and the potential harmony between this world and our hope in Christ. "The expectation of heaven cannot remain alive unless it is incarnate." [16] The body of our hope lies in the progress of the world, not in contempt toward it.

The progress of the universe, and in particular of the human universe, does not take place in competition with God, nor does it squander energies that we rightly owe to Him. The greater man becomes, the more humanity becomes united, with consciousness of, and mastery of, its potentialities, the more beautiful creation will be, the more perfect adoration will become, and the more Christ will find, for mystical extensions, a body worthy of resurrection.[17]

While the genesis of humanity is constitutive for the genesis of Christ in the human family through his church, it is this descent of Christ that superanimates humanity. Not the crowding upon each other of the human family warms the human heart, but the union through and in love brings individuals together. In Christianity, Teilhard claims, we have witnessed the birth of love. He sees it as central to the Christian faith that the human individual cannot achieve self-perfection or exist in fullness except through organic unification of all people in God.

The universal movement, forward toward the future and upward in an evolutionary and metaphysical sense, does not express a neglect of the personal. The personal and universal at the summit of evolution rather endows our individual and corporeal existence with meaning and direction. Teilhard asserts that in Christianity alone the faith in a personal and personalizing center of the universe is alive and has a chance of surviving today. In Christianity the hope is kept alive, growing, and set to work that one day

the tension gradually accumulating between humanity and God will touch the limits prescribed by the possibilities of the world. And then will come the end. Then the presence of Christ, which has been silently accruing in things, will suddenly be revealed—like a flash of light from pole to pole. Breaking through all the barriers within which the veil of matter and the water-tightness of souls have seemingly kept it confined, it will invade the face of the earth. And, under the finally liberated action of the true affinities of being, the spiritual atoms of the world will be borne along by a force generated by the powers of cohesion proper to the universe itself and will occupy, whether within Christ or without Christ (but always under the influence of Christ), the place of happiness or pain designated for them by the living structure of the Pleroma.[18]

The whole evolutionary process is directed toward and finds its fulfillment in the parousia of Christ, in the creation of a new heaven and a new earth.

We could still question whether Teilhard does not view the evolutionary process as too unilinear when he judges, for instance, the notion of original sin to be primarily an intellectual and emotional straight-
jacket.[19] We might also wonder whether Teilhard does not perceive the
evolution of humanity and the kingdom of God or salvation in and
through Christ too much as two sides of the same homogeneous process. Lastly, we might ask whether Teilhard does not grossly underestimate the strain our growing population and our technological civilization put on the environment and its diminishing resources. Though we
dare not pass over these questions too lightly, we should not forget that
in an impressively christocentric manner Teilhard reminds us that the
eschatological goal is a gift provided by God's grace and not a human
attainment resulting from that grace. But his interest in a personal future
notwithstanding, Teilhard's basic concern is for humanity and not for
the individual person, for the cosmos and not for our earth. The individual does not matter much in the evolutionary process. The emphasis
of the New Testament, however, contradicts this: Christ did not open
the future to the world in general, but to individuals, to you and to
me. Our reservations are not intended to reject Teilhard's approach. They
only aim to point to his limitations, limitations which we all share in
some way or other.

2. The dimensional approach of Karl Heim

Karl Heim never gained the same worldwide recognition as did Teilhard de Chardin. He never fell into temporary disgrace with his church
superiors either. Liberals respected him more and more as his academic
career advanced, while conservatives always adored him, though they
did not always understand him. To rank him next to Teilhard de
Chardin is appropriate when we consider his immense knowledge of
modern science and technology. What other Protestant theologian could
expect anniversary eulogies in a journal of chemistry or of engineering?
Heim is the only Protestant theologian of stature who chose as his own
the task of bridging the chasm between theology and natural science.[20]

Being aware of the impact of modern science and technology on our
lives, Heim did not simply re-narrate the biblical views of eschatology
in modern language. He knew that two fundamental questions bother
our modern mind most: Do I have a future, and if so, what will this
future bring?

a. *Is a future-directed eschatology possible?*

Time is constantly elapsing and the future is constantly approaching and becoming present to us. The future becoming present and the present becoming past give the impression of a never-ending process. Time as the eternal flow is endowed with scientific sanctification. This view seems to be substantiated by the law of the conservation of energy, which was first introduced by J. Robert Mayer in 1842. It asserts that in an energetically closed system the quantity of energy remains constant, while the form of energy is changeable. Energy can only disappear to re-enter the scene in a different form. The energy of electricity, for instance, can be transformed into energy of light and of heat. Or the kinetic energy of flowing water can be transformed into electric energy. Energy can also be released by burning materials which disintegrate into charred substance and produce the energy of light and heat, or by nuclear fission through which the mass of the fission material decreases and the "lost" mass is converted into energy. The decisive question is whether our universe is such a closed system that can neither lose energy nor gain it from outside. As far as scientific investigation has revealed to us, it is unlikely that our universe will be subjected to forces from without. This would mean that our universe will always remain the same; it has no beginning and no end, and the future is only a modification of the past.

The law of the conservation of energy, however, was soon supplemented by the law of entropy. The German physicist Rudolf Julius Emanuel Clausius in 1850, and the British scientist William Thomson, the later Lord Kelvin, in 1851, discovered independently from each other that, though the quantity of energy in a closed system always remains the same, this cannot lead to perpetual motion. The entropy or non-convertibility of energy never decreases; it either remains constant or increases.[21] For instance, if we place a pot with boiling water in a cold room, the energy of the water disperses into the room and heats up the room a little, while the water cools down. Though it is theoretically comprehensible that the room could cool down again and the water be heated up by the energy released from the room, the law of entropy tells us that this is impossible. Although not lost, the energy is in a sense used up and is no longer convertible.

Similarly, we can run a movie backwards and get the effect of water running back into the pipe, or of a diver leaping back from the pool onto a platform, but the amusement of the onlookers already tells us that in reality these reversals do not occur. Every process in our universe is singular and not repetitive. Even the obviously eternal orbits of the stellar bodies are singular and never quite the same again. The inter-stellar gas dispersed throughout the universe is slowing them down, not noticeably, but enough eventually to use up their kinetic energy.

All processes will slow down and come to a standstill. Of course, we can tell ourselves that this will not happen to us or our children, since the state of heat death in which everything levels to the state of energetic equilibrium is still millions of years away. Einstein has taught us, however, that time is only a relative measure, and depending on our perspective, it elapses more slowly or more quickly. Furthermore, scientists have discovered that another fate is threatening us in the more "immediate" future. Within the next two to five billion years the surface temperature of our sun will increase by one hundredfold.[22] Through nuclear fusion, hydrogen is constantly being transformed into helium in the interior of the sun. Helium, however, is less heat permeable and encloses the sun like an insulating envelope. Thus the more helium is produced, the more the sun will heat up, until the heat pressure is high enough to counterbalance the helium pressure on the surface so as to establish a new equilibrium of pressure. The resultant heat increase will eventually cause all water on our earth to evaporate and will make the surface of our planet similar to that of Venus. Needless to say, this kind of heat death, followed by the final heat or ice death when all energy levels will have attained an equilibrium, will make life on our planet impossible.

At this point one might be tempted to follow Pierre Teilhard de Chardin, who claimed that while entropy is perhaps a sufficient theory for inanimate nature it does not pertain to life.[23] Life, he asserted, shows at every moment that it is progressing toward a greater complexity and diversity; by its very success it clearly counteracts all physical entropy. Thus, there cannot be a total death of the animate world, because in all adversity the stream of life is irreversible. This is certainly a persuasive argument against a final and total equilibrium at all energy levels. But we must remember the source of the building blocks of life. Only through exploitation of the inanimate world is life sustained. What happens when the natural resources are exhausted and the sun stops giving its life-nourishing light? We cannot exempt life from its context in the rest of nature. It may be uncomfortable or even offensive for us to face, but there is no eternal force within our world. The world in which we now live is doomed to death.

b. Is a future-directed eschatology necessary?

Heim points out with convincing clarity that by itself our universe implies no eternal concept of life. But is an indefinite continuation of life, even in a different and transformed way, at all desirable? [24] As we look around us we notice a universal and continuous struggle for existence in all phases and places of life. One person competes with another to survive in our competitive economic system. Animals mercilessly kill each other or devour plants merely to exist, and every neglected patch of soil shows us that even plants struggle with each other for the most favorable spot. The atomic realm is not much different; one molecular combination "strives" with another to maintain its own existence. Life can be preserved and developed only by destroying other life. Is this the essential state of our existence, or does not this almost demand a basic change? Will there never be an end to this universal struggle, or will there someday be a place where we can rest and simply enjoy nature around us?

Connected with the struggle for existence is the transitoriness of life. The essence of time is its passage and replacement. The future is constantly replaced by a new future and the present by a new present. But we desire more than continuous transitoriness. We realize that life is only an episode, and that it goes back to the spot from whence it came. The verse in Genesis, "You are dust and unto dust you shall return" (Gen. 3:19), is one of the most profound and devastating remarks in the whole Bible. We came out of nothingness and will go back into nothingness. As we confront this destiny there are only two possibilities open to us.

(1) There is really nothing of permanence in the world; we shall return to the nothingness from whence we came, and the world at large will face the same fate when the equilibrium of all energy levels brings life processes to a final stop. Knowing about this fate, our reaction can only be despair or resignation, and nihilism would be the appropriate philosophical position.

(2) The world as we perceive it really calls for redemption from this vicious circle, and there is indeed a power from beyond this world that leads to fulfillment and redemption beyond the limits of this world. If the hope for such a power is not just wishful thinking but a living reality, then in thankfulness we can see our present situation under an entirely different aspect. God's self-disclosure as it culminates in Jesus

Christ opens to us the reality of this hope. It shows us that life here on earth is a preparation for the life beyond granted to us through the power of God revealed in Jesus Christ.

c. A supra-polar eschatology

Heim finds the key to this eschatological hope in Christ's resurrection. Christ's resurrection indicates that we are not confined to the realm of our own possibilities. While Christ's death was a complete death with all the symptoms of death, his resurrection was not merely the elimination of death at one specific point for a specific time. After his resurrection Christ never died again. Consequently, his resurrection is different from a resuscitation.[25] The Easter event confirms Christ's authority for our own life. Since he could defeat his own death and replace it with a new possibility of life, he can also open for us a new option for the future. Christ's resurrection is the indication and the beginning of the total transformation of the world. Paul illustrates this with the example of grain (1 Cor. 15). When grain is sown it disappears, and anyone looking only at the surface of the earth would think that the grain had died. But actually, the grain is being transformed and soon will result in new wheat. Similarly, Christ did not return to our world and resume his life as one of us in our environment. He died and was buried. When he appeared again for a short while, he was a different being and no longer limited by the restrictions of space and time.

In his resurrected state Christ was no longer confined to our earthly limitations. He had overcome space and time. As the disciples witnessed, he penetrated walls, appeared among them, and then disappeared again from their midst. He was no longer a transitory being who was part of and subject to the history of our universe. He was exempt from and beyond our perishable state. Similarly, when we shall be received into this new life, all the ambiguities of this world will be left behind. We shall no longer need to ponder about a "yes" or a "no" or about good and evil. In the future the immediate confrontation with God will release us from these anxieties, because his immediate presence will suffice to let us find the answer. Through the Fall the whole creation lapsed into a polar dichotomy experienced as finitude, limitation, and transitoriness. Through the new creation, which was initiated in Christ's resurrection and will be completed in his final coming, our world will be lifted up into the supra-polar state of God. All limitations will cease and we will enjoy the immediate presence of God.

Heim presents a critical analysis of our present situation with its intrinsic arbitrariness. If we resort to this world only, he claims, we ultimately have to choose between fatalistic nihilism or positivistic ideologies. Only the redemptive act of God can lead beyond this basic alternative and provide our outlook on life with a foundation beyond ourselves. It makes life meaningful and leads to a fulfillment in the future eschaton. Of course, Heim died more than twenty years ago, and, since he was always concerned with the contemporary situation, some details of his analysis are dated. If a theological approach wants to be relevant, it always runs the risk of becoming soon obsolete, like the six o'clock news. But his overall concept is as modern as ever, since Christ's future-providing revelation has not changed. Without Christ the future is unattractive and shallow in the long run; it leaves us with a taste similar to stale beer.

3. Ecological considerations

Karl Heim and Teilhard de Chardin clearly perceived the finitude of our existence. But they did not yet notice that we are already experiencing our global finitude in increasingly painful ways. It seems as if we have taken the future in our own hands and, as a consequence, are being crushed by the onrushing future without the possibility of escape. Unless we want to engage in wishful thinking, any consideration of the future, whether of ultimate or penultimate duration, must also include a careful assessment of our ecological possibilities.

a. World come of age or an aging world?

In discussing here the vast field of ecology, we will consider it strictly within the context of eschatology. Most people are convinced that we must make drastic and immediate decisions concerning our own future and that of our environment in order to survive. With rapid technological expansion the possibilities for good and evil have increased to such a Promethean dimension that none of us can escape the implications of the decision-making process involved in technological progress. Book titles such as *The Second Genesis* or *Come, Let Us Play God,* indicate of what dimension such decisions will be.[26] But the content of such publications generally fails to point beyond the sphere of immanent experience.[27] The myth that humanity has reached maturity and, with sufficient determination, can solve its problems without resorting to God's guidance seems widely accepted. Yet we cannot avoid the impression that each time we thought we had solved a problem a new and bigger one emerged. Our solutions have largely been patchwork.

Langdon Gilkey aptly reminds us that the myth "of man come of age through an increase in his knowledge is not merely an inaccurate myth theologically. Even more, it is a dangerous myth in applied science." [28] Where we have become our own ultimate measure in the decision-making process, the development and use of technology do not emerge as our true servants but contribute to our bondage. They are used for the purpose of exerting technocratic tyranny (in socialist countries) or of stimulating our sinful and greedy impulses, i.e., the profit motive, national pride, and national or class paranoia (in Western capitalism). [29]

The assumption that we are autonomous contributes more to the aging process of the world than it indicates that we have freed ourselves and become mature. As a consequence we face mutual exploitation, misuse of the environment, and depletion of our natural resources. Mistreatment of the ecosphere is not limited to one nation; it is global because it is a human phenomenon; it occurs in the East as well as in the West and the Third World. Coupled with our rapid and gigantic technological progress it has taken on such huge dimensions that we cannot escape the thought that we might involuntarily bring the eschaton upon ourselves and our environment within the foreseeable future.

The eschatological dimension of ecology cannot be overstated. We must get used to the idea that our environmental exploitation has presently taken on apocalyptic dimensions. Let us illustrate this with three examples: [30]

(1) *Greenhouse Effect.* Through our rapidly increasing consumption of carbon-base fuels (coal, oil, gas) we release such a great amount of carbon dioxide into the earth's atmosphere that nature will no longer be able to balance this by absorbing carbon dioxide into the oceans or by using it up in plants and releasing the corresponding amount of oxygen. The dilemma is compounded by our encroachment on the world's forests, partly for agricultural reasons and partly for use of firewood and lumber. Roughly half of the earth's forests have disappeared since 1950 and the bulk of the destruction has been in the tropical zones. For instance, since 1950 Guatemala has lost 65 percent of its forests and El Salvador a staggering 93 percent. Thus not only immense water storage areas but also a vast exchange basin for absorbing carbon dioxide and releasing oxygen are rapidly disappearing.

Carbon dioxide, being relatively heavy, could easily perform the same function in our atmosphere as glass roofs do in greenhouses. They let the sun's rays permeate but prevent the resulting heat from escaping. Of all the carbon dioxide produced by combustion, one-third remains in the atmosphere. If the current rate of carbon dioxide deposition in the atmosphere continues, the amount of artificially caused carbon dioxide remaining in the atmosphere will double every 23 years. This would lead to an increase in atmospheric carbon dioxide of two percent per decade. In a climate typical of the midlatitudes that increase would lead to a warming of 0.2° C within 50 years.[31]

Though this alone may not account for too much climatic change, we must also consider the thermal pollution through utilization of energy to get the full picture. If the present rate of increase in energy consumption is maintained, we will have to increase energy production twenty-five fold in about 80 years. This artificial energy input into the atmosphere would be sufficient to start melting the polar ice. Consequently, the sea level would rise by 300 to 400 feet. The resultant worldwide flood is not difficult to visualize when we remember that most of Holland is already below sea level and preserved through dikes, and that most of the East Coast and the Gulf Coast, including Florida, is below the 400-foot mark.

However, experts claim that, similar to a sun roof, urban and agricultural atmospheric pollutants such as dust, sulfates, nitrates, and hydrocarbons tend to lower the earth's temperature. It is estimated that on the average about 31 percent of the earth's surface is now covered with a low cloud cover. Increasing this percentage to only 36 would drop the temperature about 4° C—a decrease very close to that required for the return of an ice age.[32] Which pollution will win in the end? Will we drown or freeze? Or should we continue to obscure the sky in trying to establish a balance of one form of pollution with another?

(2) *Pleonexia.* The next phenomenon is pleonexia, or the naturalistic attitude of accumulating an ever-growing and ever-changing amount of disposable material goods.[33] Apart from the ensuing identity problems, this creates an increasing strain on our natural resources. The steeply rising demand on energy supply not only has led to temporary shortages of gas and electric power but will lead in the foreseeable future to the depletion of our natural and global carbon-based fuel resources. It is estimated that 80 percent of our national resources of crude oil and natural gas will have been produced within the next 30 to 40 years (this estimate does not include Alaska).[34] Even increased imports would not provide much relief because the world's crude-oil and natural-gas production

would last only 10 to 20 years longer to reach the 80 percent mark. Even if we would expand our energy supply through rapid expansion of our present nuclear power plants, which operate by using uranium 238, we would run into a serious uranium shortage impending within 25 years.[35]

More promising seems the breeder type of reactor which also uses uranium 238 and thorium 232. But research and development of large reactors based on breeding of fissionable material is still seriously questioned because of the highly toxic plutonium 239 which is obtained in the process. In the more distant future nuclear fusion under controlled conditions may be a possibility of extending our energy resources. Approximately 25 years of intensive research in this field have brought steady progress, and it seems feasible that in another two or three decades we can simulate reactions that are normally going on only in stars, such as fusion of hydrogen into helium, or, rather, the fusion of deuterium and tritium into helium. Yet we should not forget that from a thermodynamic viewpoint nuclear plants are even less efficient than steam plants since they must reject nearly 75 percent of their energy as waste heat.[36] Thus nuclear reactors must be considered as a pre-eminent source of thermal pollution.

With regard to our energy supplies, we seem to be able to switch within the near future from one type if it faces depletion to another. But things are different when we look at other natural resources. In estimating the apparent lifetime of known recoverable reserves of 18 crucial mineral commodities—such as coal, iron, copper, and aluminum—at currently minable grades and existing rates of consumption, we notice that only eight on a world-wide scale and three on a national United States scale will last beyond the year 2000.[37] Of course, this does not take into consideration the increase in consumption or, on the other hand, new reserves that might be found or the introduction of recycling processes. Many ore deposits are being rapidly depleted, and the search for ores, such as manganese nodules, on the bottom of the sea only shows the immediacy of our dilemma. A mineral cornucopia beneath the seas exists only in a hyperbole.[38] The ocean basins beyond the continental margin are not easily accessible for seeking mineral resources. While we can expect the oceans to alleviate impending shortages of some minerals, they will not provide us with inexhaustible resources.

(3) *Overpopulation.* The last example we will mention is overpopulation.[39] Through our emphasis on extending medical aid in order to prolong life and to enable procreation, we have disturbed the natural equi-

librium between birth and death. Our earth can sustain only a limited number of living beings. Regardless of new agricultural methods or housing plans, our ecosphere is able to support at the most six to eight billion people. Beyond this number, problems of pollution, nutrition, and depletion of natural resources increase so vastly that only catastrophes can result. The tragic fact is that, taking present age structures and life expectancies of our world population into account, we can be certain that by about the turn of the century we will have reached this limit, regardless of how rigidly family planning is accepted and practiced.[40] From there on, zero population growth is the only way to survive. But it is shortsighted to blame only underdeveloped countries, where population is truly exploding, for putting us in such a precarious situation. To esti-, mate the impact of population growth on the environment we must also consider relative living standards. Thus one American child is fifty times more burdensome on the environment than is one child from India.[41] This shows what increased responsibility accompanies an increased standard of living.

It is now already impossible to bring the rest of the world up to American standards. For instance, if the world's food supply would be distributed at the present American dietary level, it would feed only about one-third of the human race. While over two billion of the world's population are seriously poor and experience food and water shortages, there are another 1.2 billion people who are destitute. They are the miserable of the earth, and their short lives are filled with deprivation, disease, grief and uncertainty. In stark contrast to these there exists an exclusive luxury club of nearly 400 million people, half of them Americans, who enjoy a rich and steadily more abundant diet as well as a high standard of living.[42] Not the children of the poor but the children of the affluent are the worst polluters and make the highest demands on the earth's resources. The poor, if left alone, would control themselves through famine, disease, and other factors which shorten their life expectancy. Yet drastic cutbacks in foreign aid to underdeveloped countries not only would be inhuman but would not solve the problem because it is we, the rich nations, who are no longer self-supporting.

The growth of multinational corporations indicates that the highly industrialized nations are not self-sufficient. They depend on cheap labor in developing countries, such as South Korea or Singapore, on cattle ranches in Latin America, and on timber from equatorial Africa. The supply for other natural resources, such as natural gas, oil, and ores, can also no longer be met domestically. It must come from other lands and must be found along other shores. Almost like parasites we are eating away other nations' resources. Thus controlling the poor is not the problem, but controlling the rich. And in terms of the world's population most Americans, even many of those who are on welfare, are among the rich. If our present rate of "progress" and procreation continues, the limit of what our ecosphere can endure will be reached within less than 40 years.

b. The eschatological context of ecology

These examples show that we live in an apocalyptic age in which many of us sense that the end is threateningly close at hand. Immediate and drastic steps must be taken to avoid a global catastrophe. Most alert people agree on this premise. But when it comes to guidelines, goals, and limitations of such measures, there is a great deal of disagreement. Some feel that we should leave everything up to the technocrats, because they know best what measures can be taken, while others protest, saying that the dominance of technocrats is already in part the cause of our present dilemma.[43] Some feel that a dictatorial regime could best enforce any necessary measures, while others rightly observe that the prospect of a dictatorship does not always include just beneficial features.[44] Finally, some say that individualism has always been the American way to solve problems.

But others object that our present dilemma is too complex for an individualistic approach. Looking for the direction in which steps must be taken, we again face several mutually exclusive possibilities.[45] We could go in the direction of an aesthetic approach and try to look for beauty and dignity as the values to be preserved. Or we could pursue the utilitarian route and say that it only matters how we can best use the available resources. Of course, the conservationists would object here, saying that it also matters to what degree we can preserve the naturalness of our environment. When we come to the limitations of the steps taken, again we face the dilemma of a multiple choice: Do we want a community of robots who do exactly what is best, or do we want, within certain limits, an approach of free enterprise with all its possibilities of failure and disobedience?

Confronted with these conflicting claims of what to do in our precarious situation, it is well to remember that we live in an apocalyptic age. Since an apocalyptic age is an age in which we presume to know what course world history will take and conclude that the *end* of history is close at hand, hope in an apocalyptic age can only come from perceiving apocalyptic thinking in the broader context of eschatology. This would mean that as we are confronted with our possible future doom and with a multitude of proposals on how to escape this doom a reliable directive for action can only come from the Judeo-Christian tradition out of which this apocalyptic prospect originated. In this context we must consider the anticipatory aspect of eschatology.

The Christian understanding of the anticipatory power of eschatology gives us both the incentive and the possibility for stopping the exploitation of our environment and for preventing our own self-destruction. The Christian gospel tells us that we already participate in a proleptic way in the new creation which was initiated in and with the resurrection of Jesus Christ. In this way the representatives of the Social Gospel Movement were right when they emphasized the this-worldly dimension of the kingdom of God. In the face of human depravity, this provided a positive evaluation of our abilities as caretakers of God's creation.

At this point we can agree only partially with the penetrating analysis of Lynn White, Jr.[46] White convincingly suggests that technology is a Western phenomenon. Even in our present post-Christian era our lives are still dominated by the faith in perpetual progress which was unknown to Greco-Roman antiquity or to the Orient. This faith is rooted in and is indefensible apart from Judeo-Christian teleology.[47] The Marxist movement, too, could not have developed without its Christian presuppositions. But when White labels Christianity as the most anthropocentric religion the world has seen he fails to convince us. We agree with him that the cause of our ecological crisis is our present anthropocentric attitude (that nature has no reason for existence save to serve us). But we have shown in our introductory chapter that this anthropocentricity is *not* a Christian axiom, as White believes.

On the contrary, it is the result of a process through which the theocentric world view of Judeo-Christian faith was turned into the anthropocentric world view of our present secular age. When humanity elevated itself into God's place, the source and direction of history became obscured, and "for the glory of God" was replaced by the glorification and deification of humanity. Since White finally proposes St. Francis as a patron saint for ecologists, we wonder if he is not suggesting an integration of our secular view of nature and progress into the context of a mystic religiosity. Yet what is necessary in the time of crisis is a reintegration of nature and progress into the Judeo-Christian tradition which made the desacralization of nature and the pursuit of progress both possible and meaningful.

Similar to White, Frederick Elder, in his stimulating book *Crisis in Eden,* distinguishes between an inclusionist and an exclusionist view of humanity and assigns each of them profound ethical implications.[48] The exclusionist view sees humanity over and against nature, and consequently carries forth a basic exploitative attitude toward nature. Elder notes that this anthropocentric view is represented by scholars such as Teilhard de Chardin, Harvey Cox, and Herbert Richardson. In contrast, the inclusionist view sees humanity within the context of nature and thus is much more open to a basic theocentrism which could eventually change our exploitative mentality. We agree with Elder's observation that an anthropocentric view of nature or life is in the long run no viable option. It must necessarily lead to exploitation and eventual destruction of both humanity and nature. But can we be fully included in the context of nature, except on strictly biological grounds? When paleoanthropology, for instance, distinguishes between humans and animals by the criterion that animals use tools whereas humans manufacture them *(homo faber),* then this indicates that we largely shape the world we live in, whereas animals are basically just inhabitants of a given environment. Consequently, we must also be distinguished from the rest of nature. Wolfhart Pannenberg argues convincingly that our openness to the world presupposes a relation to God.[49] In other words, it is precisely because we are not just part of nature that we can responsibly administer it (i.e., as God's administrators).

Since we are not just extensions of nature, we are able to come up with the tools and the knowledge of how to provide a better world. We are free to design and implement agrricultural reform and social and economic legislation, or even to redirect our understanding of basic family structures. Even the necessary reorientation of human progress, from accumulating more and more material goods at an ever increasing rate to the understanding of progress as a fulfillment of human abilities, lies within the possibilities of human reason. In their advocacy of social betterment some theologians, especially those who identify with the concerns of liberation theology, fail to perceive that these "reasonable" pursuits, while certainly concomitant with the proclamation of the Christian faith, are not synonymous with it.

When the church takes over service functions, such as instituting family planning centers or engineering schools in developing countries, then this social involvement is neither the prerogative of the Christian community nor should such activities be confined to Christian groups. Apart from being an expression of the corporate dimension of the Christian faith, these actions are primarily intended to incite other people to do the same and to remind the secular authorities that they do not serve the *whole* world (as they should), but only *part* of the world (at the expense of other parts).

The promise of a new creation foreshadowed in the resurrection of Jesus Christ can serve as a powerful stimulus to remind us that we are God's administrators in this world. Our task is not to exploit and abuse God's creation but to cherish and favor it. To accomplish this goal God has endowed us with reason, and he has given us his self-disclosure in Jesus Christ to remind us of this task. But in our bewildering and confusing time the main contribution of the Christian faith lies in another area, the proclamation of the future-directedness of eschatology.[50]

c. Future-directedness of eschatology

The fulfillment of the eschatological promise presented in the Judeo-Christian tradition enables us to envision the goals and limits of all human endeavors, including our involvement in the ecological crisis. The very fact that eschatology is essentially directed toward a God-provided eschaton shows us the limits of our possibilities. It shows us that, no matter what techniques we devise or how hard we try, our ecosphere has no eternal value in itself but is subjected to transitoriness. The resulting interim character of our present situation does not *necessitate* a deterioration of present conditions and a subsequent attitude of resignation.[51] On the contrary, the new creation has already started in Jesus Christ, and we are already invited to participate in this new creation in a proleptic way. Therefore the transitoriness of our present condition *can* also mean a transition toward the better.

Nevertheless, since our present situation is clearly marked as interim, we cannot expect perfection from our attempts. But it is realistic and indicative of responsibility to envision a state approaching perfection. Any attempt to transcend this limitation would result in the utopian venture of replacing the God-provided eschaton with an eschaton of our own making. But any eschaton imagined to result from our own actions or aspirations would in the long run only magnify the ecological problems, because the present ecological dilemma has resulted precisely from that basic denial of the Judeo-Christian eschatological context.

Besides showing us the limitations of our own possibilities, eschatology can also provide us with the goals for our ecological concern. Eugen Rosenstock-Huessy once said very appropriately, "Christianity is the founder and trustee of the future, the very process of finding and securing it, and without the Christian spirit there is no real future for man." [52] In building upon the Jewish tradition, and at the same time in a significant modification of it, the Christian faith knows about the first perfect human being, who made the transition from fragmentariness to completeness. Thus Christian faith is compelled to proclaim this transition as a possibility for all of us. [53]

In delineating our appropriate attitude during this present transitional stage we have to point to Jesus of Nazareth who has completed it. By imitating his way of life we discover that we should live as God-responsive and God-responsible beings within the matrix of our environment. This would rule out an understanding of progress either as an accumulation of material goods or as an emphasis on the quantity of life. It would also rule out a technocratic relinquishing of human responsiveness and responsibility on the one hand, and a neglect of this responsiveness and responsibility through carefree day-by-day living on the other hand. Instead, it would require the semi-detached, ascetic attitude toward civilization and an emphasis on the quality of life and on finding personal fulfillment in enjoying pleasure and providing it for others. [54]

Stimulated by the attempt to imitate Jesus, our goal would be to increase our responsiveness and responsibility to God within the environmental matrix. But, recognizing that the final realization of this goal can be attained only in the eschaton, ultimate and lasting hope can come only from the expectation of Jesus Christ and from the new creation that he initiated. The proper understanding of the interrelatedness between the imitation of Jesus and the expectation of Jesus Christ can lead us to an appropriate evaluation and a proper attitude toward our present ecological crisis. It shows us that we presently live in an apocalyptic age, and that there is reason for hope and not for despair.

NOTES

1. This issue has been set forth very convincingly by Philip Hefner, when he demands a theology beyond rhetoric and fantasy. As "fantasy" he understands the human tendency to dream dreams that cannot and will not ever become real, while "rhetoric"

denotes for him the tendency to describe the present and the future and to speak of our action in behalf of that future in terms that are so discontinuous with the experience of present reality that both future and action lose their credibility (Philip Hefner, "Die Konkretheit des Reiches Gottes als Problem für das christliche Leben," in *Christsein in einer pluralistischen Gesellschaft,* ed. by Hans Schulze and Hans Schwarz [Hamburg: Wittig, 1971] 323). Cf. also Philip Hefner, "The Relocation of the God-Question," *Zygon,* 5 (1970): 11, where he states that an increasing number of people, including "some Marxist dreamers of the future," are asking whether our hopes for the future are fantasies that may collapse through the fact that the survival of the human species is in doubt.

2. Cf. Ernst Benz, *Evolution and Christian Hope,* 212ff., who also alerts us to the fact that most of Teilhard's books were compiled and published posthumously.

3. Jean-Paul Sartre, *Being and Nothingness; An Essay on Phenomenological Ontology,* trans. and with an intr. by H. E. Barnes (New York: Philosophical Library, 1956) 476-481.

4. Martin Heidegger, *Being and Time,* trans. by J. Macquarrie and E. Robinson (London: SCM, 1962) 274-311.

5. Pierre Teilhard de Chardin, *The Future of Man,* trans. by N. Denny (New York: Harper and Row, 1964) 234f.

6. Ibid., 228ff.

7. Ibid., 265.

8. Ibid.

9. Ibid., 267.

10. Cf. ibid., 269, where Teilhard explains his view with the help of a diagram.

11. Ibid., 267.

12. Ibid.

13. So also Robert L. Faricy, *Teilhard de Chardin's Theology of the Christian in the World* (New York: Sheed and Ward, 1967) 210f.

14. Pierre Teilhard de Chardin, *The Divine Milieu: An Essay on the Interior Life* (New York: Harper & Row, 1960) 134.

15. Ibid., 135f.

16. Ibid.

17. Ibid., 137.

18. Ibid., 133f.

19. So Pierre Teilhard de Chardin, *Christianity and Evolution,* trans. by R. Hague (New York: Harcourt Brace Jovanovich, 1969) 80. For an evaluation of Teilhard cf. also Hans Schwarz, *Our Cosmic Journey* (Minneapolis: Augsburg, 1977) 116f. For a good introduction to Teilhard, cf. Philip Hefner, *The Promise of Teilhard; The Meaning of the Twentieth Century in Christian Perspective* (Philadelphia: Lippincott, 1970); and Henri de Lubac, *The Religion of Teilhard de Chardin,* trans. by R. Hague (New York: Desclee, 1967).

20. Cf. Sigurd Daecke, *Teilhard de Chardin und die evangelische Theologie; Die Weltlichkeit Gottes und die Weltlichkeit der Welt* (Göttingen: Vandenhoeck & Ruprecht, 1967) 223, who draws a very careful comparison between Teilhard de Chardin and Heim. For Heim's own thoughts cf. his works *Christian Faith and Natural Science,* trans. by N. H. Smith (London: SCM, 1953); *The Transformation of the Scientific World View,* trans. by W. A. Whitehouse (London: SCM, 1953); and especially *The World: Its Creation and Consummation; The End of the Present Age and the Future of the World in the Light of the Resurrection,* trans. by R. Smith (Philadelphia: Muhlenberg, 1962) 85-150.

21. Cf. the translated excerpt from Clausius' paper on entropy ("Über verschiedene für die Anwendung bequeme Formen der Hauptgleichungen der mechanischen Wärme-

theorie") in William F. Magie, ed., *A Source Book in Physics* (Cambridge, Mass.: Harvard University Press, 1965) 234ff. See also Adolf Grünbaum, "Time and Entropy," *American Scientist*, 43 (1955): 550-572.

22. George Gamow, *The Birth and Death of the Sun; Stellar Evolution and Subatomic Energy* (New York: Viking: 1946) 116-120.
23. Pierre Teilhard de Chardin, *The Vision of the Past*, trans. by J. M. Cohen (New York: Harper, 1966) 168ff. For a more extensive treatment of entropy cf. Hans Schwarz, *Our Cosmic Journey*, 44-47.
24. For the following cf. Karl Heim, *The World: Its Creation and Consummation*, 101-121.
25. Walter Künneth, *The Theology of the Resurrection*, trans. by J. W. Leitch (St. Louis, Mo.: Concordia, 1965) 72-80, therefore calls the resurrection of Jesus Christ appropriately the "primal miracle."
26. Albert Rosenfeld, *The Second Genesis; The Coming Control of Life* (Englewood Cliffs, N.J.: Prentice Hall, 1969); Leroy Augenstein, *Come, Let Us Play God* (New York: Harper & Row, 1969).
27. Cf. Augenstein, *Come, Let Us Play God*, 135-138, who affirms very strongly that our decisions must be based on fundamental values which are associated with the belief in a creator.
28. Langdon Gilkey, in his stimulating study *Religion and the Scientific Future; Reflections on Myth, Science, and Theology* (New York: Harper & Row, 1970) 95.
29. Ibid., 94.
30. For the following examples cf. the instructive essay by Bruce Wrightsman, "Man, Manager or Manipulator of the Earth," *Dialog*, 9 (1970): 213f. Cf. also the sourcebook compiled by Thomas R. Detwyler, *Man's Impact on Environment* (New York: McGraw-Hill, 1971). For the following cf. also Hans Schwarz, "The Eschatological Dimension of Ecology," *Zygon*, 9 (1974): 326ff.
31. Gordon J. F. MacDonald, "Pollution, Weather and Climate," in William W. Murdoch, ed., *Environment: Resources, Pollution & Society* (Stamford, Conn.: Sinauer Associates, 1971) 330f.
32. Ibid., 333f. Another possible cause for the melting of polar ice could be large oil spills in connection with off-shore drilling. Cf. Mihajlo Mesarovic and Eduard Prestel, eds., *Mankind at the Turning Point. The Second Report to the Club of Rome* (New York: Dutton, 1974) 149f.
33. With reference to these problems the term "pleonexia" seems to have been used first by V. A. Demant *(The Idea of a Natural Order: With an Essay on Modern Asceticism*, Facet Books [Philadelphia: Fortress Press, 1966] 39), who advocates a practical asceticism that witnesses to the truth of the maxim: Production is for humanity, not humanity for production. According to Demant, such asceticism would be a testimony to the old teaching "that the really satisfying life does not depend upon the number of commodities one can acquire, but upon the fruitful exercise of our inner powers" (39).
34. M. King Hubbert, "Energy Resources," in Murdoch, 102ff.
35. Ibid., 110ff.
36. Ferren MacIntyre and R. W. Holmes, "Ocean Pollution," in Murdoch, 250.
37. Preston Cloud in his sobering report, "Mineral Resources in Fact and Fancy," in Murdoch, 73.
38. Ibid., 85ff. So also Stephen E. Kesler, *Our Finite Mineral Resources* (New York: McGraw-Hill, 1976) 109. Other estimates are more optimistic. Cf. Herman Kahn, William Brown, and Leon Martel, *The Next 200 Years. A Scenario for America and the World* (New York: Morrow, 1976) 216, who are highly critical of the Second Report to the Club of Rome. While they do not take into consideration that not all resources can ever be economically used, they too admit that serious crises may evolve.

39. Most alert people are convinced that overpopulation lies at the root of our whole present ecological crisis. Cf. Frederick Elder, *Crisis in Eden: A Religious Study of Man and Environment* (Nashville: Abingdon, 1970) 108-109; and William E. Martin ("Simple Concepts of Complex Ecological Problems," *Zygon* 5 [1970]: 305) convincingly points out that the real problems are population growth and economic growth. Yet if the population declines as in some industrialized Western nations, we are also faced with immense difficulties in terms of socio-economic stability.

40. Cloud, "Mineral Resources" in Murdoch, 82.

41. Donald Imsland, *Celebrate the Earth* (Minneapolis: Augsburg, 1971) 74.

42. Cf. ibid., 75ff. See also the sobering report by Harrison Brown, *The Human Future Revisited: The World Predicament and Possible Solutions* (New York: Norton, 1978) esp. 79.

43. The power of the technocrats and of big business was first eloquently exposed as the cause of our environmental crisis by Rachel Carson in *Silent Spring* (Boston: Houghton Mifflin, 1962).

44. Cf. Hans Schwarz, "Theological Implications of Modern Biogenetics," *Zygon,* 5 (1970): 260.

45. Cf. Wrightsman, "Man, Manager or Manipulator of the Earth," 211.

46. Lynn White, Jr., "The Historical Roots of Our Ecological Crisis," first published in *Science,* 155 (1967): 1203-1207, reprinted in Thomas R. Detwyler, ed., *Man's Impact on Environment,* 27-35.

47. Ibid., 31f.

48. Cf. for the following Frederick Elder, *Crisis in Eden,* 19 and 160f.

49. Wolfhart Pannenberg, *What Is Man? Contemporary Anthropology in Theological Perspective,* trans. by D. A. Priebe (Philadelphia: Fortress, 1970) 12.

50. The eschatological dimension of ecology is very clearly pointed out by H. Paul Santmire in his book *Brother Earth; Nature, God, and Ecology in Time of Crisis* (New York: Nelson, 1970), when he talks about "the foretaste of the New Creation" (174ff.). He asserts that the overall matrix of the kingdom of God and his righteousness will allow us to have dominion without exploitation (191). No longer will either nature or civilization provide the ultimate norms for human life, either explicitly or implicitly. Both will be subordinated to the kingdom of God (182). But again we wonder what he means when he says that nature and civilization will be fellow citizens of the kingdom. Does he, similar to Elder, advocate an inclusionist view of humanity?

51. This does not mean that there will be less progress and a lesser spirit of progressiveness in the future. To conceive of the new era as a time of the "grand slowing down" (so Frederick Elder, "A Different 2001," *Lutheran Forum,* 4 [1970]: 10), seems to be misleading. A realistic wrestling with our ecological crisis will necessitate at least as much progress as we encounter now, though, of course, in an altogether different direction.

52. Eugen Rosenstock-Huessy, *The Christian Future; Or the Modern Mind Outrun,* with an intr. by H. Stahmer (New York: Harper Torchbook, 1966) 61.

53. Cf. ibid., 66.

54. Frederick Elder, *Crisis in Eden,* 145, has advocated this new asceticism very eloquently. However, he cautions that unlike medieval asceticism this would not involve a withdrawal from the world, but simply a new way of acting toward and with the world. The basic elements of this new asceticism are restraint, an emphasis on the quality of existence, and reverence for life. Different from Albert Schweitzer, Elder does not understand this reverence for life as mystic and religious dedication to life, but as "an appreciation for *any* expression of life, based on scientific, aesthetic, and religious considerations" (152).

5
Secular Varieties of Hope

WE HAVE SEEN THAT OUR PRESENT SITUATION is serious, perhaps more serious than any human situation ever before. But we have also seen that the seriousness of our present situation does not necessitate a speedy coming of the eschaton. Teilhard de Chardin has warned against the attempt to equate any global or sidereal disaster with the coming of the eschaton because such a disaster would affect only part of the world, not the total world, and would lead only to destruction, not to fulfillment in a new beginning.

In an attempt to consider our possibilities for the future, we cannot restrict our review simply to traditional Christian teachings. In an age often labeled post-Christian, in which society seems to be less and less informed by Christian values, we cannot ignore the many other spiritual movements that have developed through the years, either in indifference to the Christian faith or in direct antagonism to it. To assess their validity as they approach the future we must at least briefly describe and evaluate three major streams of thought: existentialism, Marxist Communism, and secular humanism.

1. The option of secular existentialism

For Søren Kierkegaard, the father of existentialism, life was a venture sustained by trust in a gracious God. Secular existentialism, however, having emancipated itself from the all-embracing assurance of God's grace, starts with the assumption that ultimate questions are beyond our grasp. Existence does not find its fulfillment in the eschaton but is basically defined as "being there" and "being in the world."

a. Life bounded by death (Martin Heidegger and Ernest Becker)

Martin Heidegger, one of the pioneers of modern secular existentialist thought, conceives of life as being in the world; it is a being-there and a being towards death. Temporality and death are constitutive factors of being-there. Since in our being-there we face death as the end of life, this final end of our possibilities causes anxiety as a basic phenomenon of life. Yet it would be foolish to flee from our being towards death or to cover up this characteristic feature of our being-there. In so doing we would live inauthentically and, turning anxiety into fear, would attempt to hide from ourselves. Heidegger instead opts for resoluteness and authentic existence. He claims that we must recognize anxiety as a basic state of mind and as being-there's essential state of Being-in-the-world.[1] Similarly, *"authentic* Being-towards-death can *not evade* its ownmost non-relational possibility, or *cover up* this possibility by thus fleeing from it, or *give a new explanation* for it to accord with the common sense of the 'they.' " [2] Since death is being-there's innermost possibility, "being towards this possibility discloses to Dasein [being-there] its *ownmost* potentiality-for-Being, in which its very Being is the issue." [3]

Heidegger describes existence as occurring strictly within this world. While he could substantiate his claim by a phenomenological survey that all being-there ultimately faces death, his secular premise notwithstanding, he goes beyond the verifiable and calls for authentic existence as the optimum and goal of human existence. Yet this goal can really no longer be grounded in the being-there, and therefore Heidegger leaves the impression that his appeal is arbitrary[4] and subject to revision.

In recent years Ernest Becker, in his award winning book, *The Denial of Death,* has pointed out with convincing clarity "that the fear of death is a universal." [5] Largely following the psychology of Sigmund Freud and combining it with the existential portrayal of humanity provided by Kierkegaard, Ernest Becker points out that "we are hopelessly absorbed with ourselves." [6] We hope and believe that the things we create in society are of lasting worth and meaning, that they outlive and outshine our death and decay.[7] Thus the urge to heroism is natural. But there is no escape from death. We are "doomed to live in an overwhelmingly tragic and demonic world." [8] We can drown our senses, but as soon as we awake we realize anew that we do not understand the purpose of creation and therefore the direction of life's expansion. "We only feel life straining in ourselves and see it thrashing others about as they devour each other." [9]

Similar to Heidegger, Becker is not content with our yearning to overcome death through heroic deeds. In his last book, posthumously pub-

lished, he argues that our "natural and inevitable urge to deny mortality
and achieve a heroic self-image are the root causes of human evil." [10] He
is not as optimistic as Heidegger, however, that we can introduce a
system by which we could live without causing painfulness and sorrow
for each other. Still, he also refuses to give up in despair. He closes his
book, hoping for "that minute measure of reason to balance destruction." [11] Such hope is certainly not grounded in empirical data. But
since the whole religious realm is explained by Becker as a device to
escape the reality of death and the dread of it,[12] he can no longer resort
to metaphysical powers. Neither will he give up living and hoping. This
hope without faith and against overwhelming odds is the trademark of
modern secular existentialism.

b. Humanity thrown upon itself (Jean-Paul Sartre and Albert Camus)

When we come to Jean-Paul Sartre, the French existentialist who radicalized Heidegger's philosophy, we are candidly confronted with a humanity that has lost its metaphysical reference point. Humanity is conceived of as an agent basically free of its destiny. But, in contrast to
Heidegger, Sartre can no longer understand human freedom as beneficial.
Humanity is condemned to be free.[13] We have no God, no truth, and
no values, in the traditional sense of these terms. This individualized
and non-directed world encounters us as a basically antagonistic world.[14]
Others are encountered as evil, desiring to infringe upon our freedom.

Sartre claims that existence precedes essence and that our essence is
what has been, or in short, our past. But there is no common essence
according to which we can act.[15] Rather each of us makes his/her essence
as we live our lives. Thus we must transcend the non-conscious level
of being-in-itself and rise to the conscious level of being-for-itself. At this
level we express lack of being, desire for being, and relation to being.
Yet by our option for being-for-itself we bring nothingness into the
world, since we now stand out from being and can judge other being
by knowing what it is not. Sartre emphasizes that we must be-for-our-
selves if we want to escape from bad faith.[16] This bad faith arises if we
oscillate between relying on the past and projecting ourselves toward
the future or, what is equally bad, if we attempt to synthesize both. It
is our destiny to venture toward the future without relying on the past
or on any pre-established norms.

It is a grim picture that Sartre has to offer us. We exist toward the future, solely relying on ourselves and in continuous conflict with others who, in a similar way, want to exist for themselves. But what should be our motivation to exist in this kind of solipsistic activism? One might find neither comfort nor assurance in such a world and opt for traditional values rather than to rely solely on oneself.

Sartre's compatriot, Albert Camus, attempted to move beyond an arbitrary existentialist position.[17] In his novel, *The Myth of Sisyphus* (1942), he describes the situation in which he found himself after having discovered that none of the speculative systems of the past can provide positive guidance for human life or guarantee the validity of our values.[18] Unlike Sartre, he at least poses the question of whether it makes sense to go on living, once the meaninglessness of human life has been fully recognized. Camus maintains that suicide cannot be regarded as an adequate response to the experience of absurdity that results from our discovery that we must live without the value-supporting "standards" and ideas of the past. Cutting through the tension-provoking polarity between the human being and the world by committing suicide would only be an admission of our incapacity. Camus finds us too proud of ourselves to seek this easy way out. Only by living in the face of our own absurdity can we achieve our full stature.

Camus realizes that our revolt against metaphysically guaranteed directives for conduct does not really improve the human predicament. Like Sartre, he portrays in his literary works the persisting injustice and cruelty committed by one human being against another. In his philosophical essay, *The Rebel* (1951), he concludes that it is precisely the revolt against metaphysics, against human conditions as such, that has led to 20th century totalitarianism.[19] Camus now rejects the metaphysical revolt and opts instead for an ethical revolt. He recognizes that the metaphysical revolt, while attempting to impose upon humanity a new world order, has resulted in the nightmare of unrestrained power struggle. Yet Camus still calls for nihilism as a cathartic device. While he now knows that it does not provide a principle for action, he is still convinced that it will clear the ground for new construction by disposing of any kind of mystification by which we might try to rid ourselves of our radical contingency and confer upon ourselves a cosmic status. But how should this clearance be filled with positive content? Even an essentially non-metaphysical and strongly moralistic humanism must derive its directives from somewhere; otherwise it would fall prey to what Camus rightly called "metaphysical" revolution.

In his last major work, *The Fall* (1956), Camus seems to imply that directives for ordering our lives cannot come from ourselves.[20] In this utterly pessimistic work Camus abandons political and social revolt. Evil is no longer understood as originating from the unjust social institutions in which we are doomed to exist; evil stems from the human heart. Then whence comes the incentive for life and living? In his short story, "The Growing Stone" (1957), Camus seems to give an answer to this all-decisive question.[21] When in the plot the French engineer D'Arrast substitutes for the exhausted mulatto ship cook and picks up the stone to fulfill the cook's vow, he does not carry that stone to the cathedral, the place where the cook had vowed he would deposit it. Instead D'Arrast carries the stone back to the little hut in which the man lives. In other words, Camus indicates that help for us can only come from human solidarity in taking upon ourselves each others' burdens. But for Camus such solidarity must serve a human purpose and not a metaphysical one.

We wonder, however, whether this alternative that Camus poses could and even should not be bridged by suggesting that one can serve the metaphysical purpose in fulfilling a human need. If we are strictly confined to ourselves and the world around us, how could we ever experience "a fresh beginning of life" that D'Arrast so vividly senses? Admitting the immense human depravity, secular existentialists opt for a heroic stand amid an antagonistic world. But they are unable sufficiently to explain what should give us the continuing courage to wage a losing battle, nor are they in a better position to elucidate how there could be a fresh beginning. In other words, secular existentialism provides us with an accurate assessment of the human situation without being able to lead us to a new future or even provide hope for the future.

2. The Marxist hope for utopia

When we briefly consider Marxism as another secular variety of hope we immediately notice that this movement is not riddled by existentialist pessimism but paints the future in bright and promising colors. The French Marxist Roger Garaudy, for instance, claims that Marxism is essentially humanistic. It does not start from negation but from affirmation; it affirms human autonomy and as a consequence it involves the rejection of every attempt to rob humanity of its creative power.[22] Hundreds of millions of people find in Marxist Communism their hope and meaning for life, and it certainly is the most powerful pseudoreligious movement the earth has ever seen. But to assess its true potential we must at least briefly survey its basic teachings.

a. A new world through revolution (Karl Marx and Ernst Bloch)

The fundamental goal of Marxism is to bring about a new world through revolution. Karl Marx stated this goal very precisely when he wrote: "The philosophers have only *interpreted* the world, in various ways; the point, however, is to *change* it."[23] Karl Marx and Friedrich Engels, the founders of the Marxist movement, were influenced by a variety of sources. Progressive industrialization and popularized Darwinism gave them their optimistic outlook; labor conditions in the early years of the Industrial Revolution showed them the plight of the working class; biblical criticism, especially of the Tübingen school, removed for them most of the supernaturalness of the Bible; and Bruno Bauer, a left-wing Hegelian and onetime close friend of Marx, gave them the idea that as a world religion Christianity was the product of the Greco-Roman world.[24]

This conception of Christianity, or religion as Marx and Engels usually call it, as the product of its environment was decisive for their thinking and was substantiated for them in Ludwig Feuerbach's claim that religion is a projection of our own desires which we in turn worship. But Marx felt that Feuerbach had only accomplished half of the task. It is not sufficient to label religion as the projection of our unfulfilled desires on the screen of the beyond; it is necessary to recognize that this projection is a "social product" which belongs to a particular form of society, modern capitalism.

Though the founders of Marxism admitted that early Christianity had notable points of resemblance with the modern working-class movement, being originally a movement of oppressed people, they faulted Christianity for refusing to accomplish social transformation in this world. Instead the Christians hoped for salvation from their plight in heaven, in eternal life after death, in the impending "millennium."[25] Thus Marx concluded contemptuously: "The social principles of Christianity preach cowardice, self-contempt, abasement, submission, dejection."[26] Since the proletariat needs courage, self-esteem, pride, and a sense of independence to attain its goal, it must do away with religion. "The criticism of religion ends with the teaching that *man is the highest essence for man,* hence with the categoric imperative to overthrow all relations in which man is a debased, enslaved, abandoned, despicable essence." [27]

Since the religious world is but the reflex of the real world, Marx demanded that we abandon the search "for a superman in the fantastic reality of heaven" where we can find nothing but the reflection of ourselves.[28] Marx therefore claimed that "the abolition of religion as the illusory happiness of the people is required for their *real* happiness." [29] As soon as religion as the general theory of this world is abolished—a theory which provides the justification for the exploitation of the working class and the consolation with a better future—we will abandon the fantastic heavenly reality and face our reality on earth.

When we remember the overwhelming other-worldliness of the Negro spirituals, who usually dared to claim for themselves only a better beyond and not a better earth, we can understand Marx's claim that "religion is the sigh of the oppressed creature." [30] But we cannot agree with his conclusion that therefore religion "is the *opium* of the people." [31] Religion has certainly been used for this purpose, but since the Judeo-Christian faith is by its very nature a forward-looking and world-transforming faith this could have never been its main intention. There is undoubtedly also some truth in the claim that religion is a tool of the capitalists to exploit the working class and to sanctify this exploitation with the comfort of a better hereafter. But it is a gross oversimplification to assert that religion is simply an interpretation of present conditions. Religion is just as decisively an anticipation of the "beyond" in earthly form. Engels may have sensed some of this when he conceded that "in the popular risings of the Christian West . . . a new . . . economic order . . . arises and the world progresses," while in the context of other religions, even when the uprisings "are victorious, they allow the old economic conditions to persist untouched. So the old situation remains unchanged and the collision recurs periodically." [32]

But the provision of a Marxist utopia does not simply hinge on the destruction of religion. Roger Garaudy, for instance, concedes that the future of humanity can be constructed neither by neglecting the hundreds of millions for whom religious beliefs provide meaning for life, death, and the history of our race, nor by neglecting the hundreds of millions who find that Communism gives a face to the hopes of the earth and a meaning to our history.[33] For Marxism, unlike existentialism, the meaning of life and history is not the creation of the individual hu-

man being but the work of people in the totality of their history. Yet
this meaning of life and history is not simply our own creation, as existentialism would claim. On the contrary, it already exists before us and
without us because the realities of the past must be taken into account
for the operation of our present initiatives. Nevertheless for Garaudy
this meaning of history "is still an open question, for the future still has
to be created even though its creation must start from the conditions
inherited from the past." [34]

The German Marxist Ernst Bloch betrays a similar optimism about
the future. Our journey moves irresistibly ahead toward "that secret
symbol" toward which our dark, seeking, difficult earth has moved since
the beginning of time.[35] In his monumental work, *Das Prinzip Hoffnung (The Principle of Hope)* Bloch shows that the principle of hope
is a universal characteristic of humanity. From the first cry of a helpless
baby, who wants to draw attention to its desires, to a tired old person,
who is waiting for eternal bliss, human existence is characterized by
hope and a movement to the future. Bloch is convinced that Marxism
will realize this future, because its motivation and goal is nothing but
the increase of humanness.[36] In its own way Marxism aims for the human goals of the revolutionary bourgeoisie and strives for the immanent
realization of religious transcendence.

Bloch even calls Marxism the quartermaster of the future because it
overcomes the antithesis of soberness and enthusiasm by letting both
cooperate toward "exact anticipation" and "concrete utopia." [37] Unlike
most abstract social utopia, the Marxist striving toward a better world
is not initiated to forget the world at hand, but to transform it in a dialectic and economic way. Marxism is not mere futurism; it takes the
fairy tale of the past seriously and *practices* the dream of a golden age.[38]
Like Marx, Bloch contends that the comforting aspect of the Marxist
world view lies not in contemplation but in guidelines for action.

For Bloch humanizing humanity is a calculable and reachable goal,
and the incomplete world can be brought to its conclusion.[39] Thus Bloch
advocates a militant optimism and, unlike Kant, does not need a purgatory to assure the perfection of humanity. His confidence is not based
on past experiences, since the essential is that which is not yet but which
strives for self-realization in the core of being and which expects its own
genesis. Since real, objective hope provides its own foundation for Bloch,
he seems to resort here to an Aristotelian first unmoved mover to endow

the future with a direction and a hidden goal which is the same for all of humanity. It is insignificant for Bloch whether one calls this goal eternal happiness, freedom, golden age, a land of milk and honey, or union with Christ in the resurrection. All these symbols and pictures illuminate hope and lead it to the ultimate goal which no one has yet reached and which will be our actual "home." Thus the true genesis is not in the beginning, but in the end.[40]

Bloch goes beyond the primitive projection hypothesis of Feuerbach and claims that this projection (i.e., the future), is certainly our god.[41] God is the utopian hypostasis of unknown humanity. When identity between our true humanness and our present condition is reached, we will occupy the place of God and religion will cease to exist. Consequently, Bloch has no reason to be hostile toward religion because it enlightens hope and gives it its direction. But the metaphysical dimension of religion is collapsed in the physical, since the future of the resurrected Christ and the future of God are the future of the hidden humanity and the hidden world. Bloch thus offers a meta-religion, transcending without being metaphysical and conceiving the metaphysical as our ultimate goal in the physical.[42] Eschatology under these presuppositions becomes a fiction,[43] and we end up with a new earthly kingdom without God.[44]

Bloch is certainly right and realistic when he points to the discrepancy between our actual existence and our selfhood, between the individual and the society, and between humanity and nature, which has to be overcome if we want to attain the ultimate identity we are striving for. But even if we concede to Bloch that achieving this identity is an attainable goal, we are still faced with the ultimate discrepancy between being and nothingness. Moltmann captures this deficiency very well when he states:

> All utopias of the kingdom of God or of man, all hopeful pictures of the happy life, all revolutions of the future, remain hanging in the air and bear within them the germ of boredom and decay—and for that reason also adopt a militant and extortionate attitude to life—as long as there is no certainty in face of death and no hope which carries love beyond death.[45]

It is one of the bizarre tragedies of history that Karl Marx and Ernst Bloch have emerged as the leading messianic prophets in modern history of truly Old Testament stature and yet by denouncing the God-inspired hope that made such messianic figures possible have denied their own origin and proclaimed a new world of their own desires.[46] Those who conceive of life as being unto death are perhaps much more realistic than those who claim that they have found a method to achieve human happiness.

b. The dawn of a new creation (Mao Tse-tung)?

While the Marxists so far reviewed hardly provide an empirical basis on which to judge whether their claims for hope are even partially justified, claims have repeatedly been made that a new humanity is appearing in China. Should this indicate at least a partial verification of the hope for a Marxist utopia?

According to Chairman Mao Tse-tung the transformation of the world has reached a historical moment in China of such great significance as has never been known in history: in China has occurred the complete removal of darkness from the world and the transformation into a new bright world.

Like most materialists, Mao regards spirit as secondary and subject to matter.[47] Yet, significantly, he does not go along with them in conceiving of the spirit as simply an extension of matter. Mao rejects idealism rather vehemently and affirms that "in the general development of history the material determines the mental, and the social being determines social consciousness." But then in dialectical fashion he asserts on the other hand that there is a "reaction of mental on material things, of social consciousness on social being and of the superstructure on the economic base." [48] Of course, this is not any kind of pressure to which the material basis reacts. Therefore, Mao claims, it is most important to utilize the insights into the objective laws of the world actively to transform this world.[49]

If we ask what the objectives of this transformation are even the so-called Red Catechism, the small red book of *Mao Tse-tung's Quotations,* does not give us definite clues. One objective is "to insure a better life for the several hundred million people of China and to build our economically and culturally backward country into a prosperous and powerful one with a high level of culture." [50] To achieve this end we must "have faith in the masses" and "faith in the Party." We must also abolish "the ruthless economic exploitation and political oppression of the peasants by the landlord class."

"A tremendous liberation of the productive forces" will be brought about through the change toward socialism.[51] Yet it is not only an economic change that Mao envisions. He feels a tremendous responsibility to educate the peasantry and allow them to participate in the evolutionary process. When Mao enumerates the virtues of a Communist we notice that he envisions more than just making China prosperous. We hear that

> at no time and in no circumstances should a Communist place his personal interests first; he should subordinate them to the interests of the nation and of the masses. Hence, selfishness, slacking, corruption, seeking the limelight, and so on, are most contemptible, while selflessness, working with all one's energy, wholehearted devotion to public duty, and quiet hard work will command respect.

Toward any person who has made a mistake in his work the attitude of a Communist "should be one of persuasion in order to help him to change and start afresh and not one of exclusion, unless he is incorrigible."

When we ask to what extent these visions have been realized we hear conflicting reports. On the one hand we are told that the people of China are moulding themselves and being moulded by internal forces derived from their messianic vision of a new society and a new world.[52] Mao's principles of equality, frugality, diligence, and hard work have made China prosperous and strong in an amazingly short time. Since we live, however, on a finite earth, in the long run there will be limits to growth even in China, and the creativity and prosperity of matter will encounter their most serious limitation. But we know that Mao wants more than prosperity; his goal is not just affluence but a reign of virtue.[53]

Yet we also hear that even the great proletarian Cultural Revolution of 1966, combined with years of political education before and after, could not do away with three subversive elements:

(1) the traditional family attitude in which the authority of the clan reigns supreme;

(2) the narrow mentality of the country people who still find deep satisfaction in the tales, myths, and customs of the past, and who are always more interested in their own survival than in that of others; and

(3) the bureaucracy that instead of showing a spirit of service and dedication still lapses back to the old Mandarin habit of superiority and autonomy.[54]

A comment at a regional conference attended by several leaders of a city is highly revealing: "We have got through the production barrier.

We are still rough old fellows whether we study or not." [55] Does this mean that Mao has overestimated the human potential as far as evolution towards a new being is concerned? When we consider Mao's premise that the history of humanity is one of continuous development from the realm of necessity to the realm of freedom,[56] we might find an answer to our question.

Mao assumes that human progression means freedom toward the good in a communal sense. He forgets, however, that freedom on a human basis is never just a communal action but also an individual action. It is exactly at this point that the conflicting and "subversive elements" become noticeable when their individual good conflicts with Mao's notion of the common good. The primal concern with human self-preservation simply does not allow for the completely unselfish human beings that Mao envisions as the perfect Communists. The attempt to secure one's own self-preservation can only be abandoned if one knows that one's preservation is guaranteed. But how can such knowledge be engendered by a philosophy that rejects any absolutes and in turn dictates as the common good an individual notion of good, namely Mao's way?

Mao's projection for the future contains more hope than the projection of a more traditional Marxism since he distinguishes between matter and spirit. But contrary to biblical insights, the spirit is not sufficiently understood as life-giving, but more as the emotive force within the life-process itself. Thus Mao's future is ultimately confronted with finitude and can only provide temporary relief. This has already become noticeable in a mundane way. Soon after Mao's death his successors opened China to the outside world and invited the industrialized Western nations to participate in the industrialization of China. This shows that in the long run even China cannot exist in isolation from the rest of the world and will therefore also share in the experience of finitude.

Though the history of Christianity, especially during the time of the Crusades and the Inquisition, is also drenched with blood, it would be unrealistic simply to ignore the obvious discrepancy between the bondage and slaughter of millions of people in Marxist countries and the claim of Marx and Engels to bring about true humanity and real happiness for the people. Yet it would be wrong for the Christian simply to ignore Marxism and the socio-political conditions that have made the hope that Marxism engenders in the minds of people so attractive.

Roger Garaudy is right when he claims that Marxism can sensitize Christians by enabling their faith "to be incarnate in historical reality and to become an effective force in the struggle to create the political and social conditions of the realization of the total man." [57] In his passionate book, *The Alternative Future: A Vision of Christian Marxism,* Garaudy confesses that after 37 years as a Party militant and 20 years as one of its leaders in France, he doubts "the very conception of this Party precisely in order to hold on to the hope that it brought to life." [58] He now realizes that hope for a tenable future can come neither from capitalism nor from Stalinist techno-bureaucracy, and neither from religion as the opium of the people nor from a positivistic atheism, but only from "a militant and creative faith to which the real is not only what is but includes all the future possibilities that appear impossible to the one who does not have the ability to hope." [59] He notes that we are not products of the environment, as materialists would have us believe; we are always open to new history.

In considering Jesus as our source of inspiration, Garaudy does not perceive him either as a revolutionary seeking to change structures or as a preacher of repentance intending solely to influence consciences. Rather he perceives him as the one who taught us in every action to look at its ultimate objectives. [60] Yet what would be the ultimate significance of our actions if we would end in death? Here the Marxist Garaudy emphasizes Christ's resurrection as the central point of history. "It is a creative act, an affirmation of the impossible through which history opens the future to all possibilities." [61] Faith in the resurrection, therefore, leads to freedom and participation in the act of creation. It is bewildering and strange that a Marxist would rediscover the necessity of faith and the resurrection for giving direction and meaning to social involvement and the pursuit of the future. Yet it also poses a challenge for us to question to what extent we ourselves enflesh our resurrection faith.

Being empowered by the new creation in which we participate through baptism, we Christians will become engaged in bringing about better socio-economic conditions and a better world. Yet, knowing about the eschatological promise, we cannot share in the Marxist utopian dream that we will bring about the new world. We know about the basic human alienation from God, and we know that a new social order created by human volition may bring about a better world to live in but cannot create a new and perfect humanity. This kind of creation out of nothingness is the privilege of God and not of humans. Thus, while we are engaged in building a more livable world, we must be critical of any endeavors to build a great or classless society.

3. The sobering of secular humanism

For a long time secular humanism, especially as exhibited in the West, advocated an unbridled optimism paired with technological and economic expansion. This tenacious tendency to believe in the power of human reason and the essential goodness of humanity as sufficient tools for coming to terms with the future is particularly well expressed in the *Humanist Manifestos I and II.*

a. Faith in human reason (Humanist Manifestos I and II)

In 1933, the same year that Adolf Hitler came to power in Germany, a group of 34 liberal humanists in the United States defined and enunciated the philosophical and religious principles that seemed to them to be fundamental. They drafted *Humanist Manifesto I,* which for its time was a radical document and portrayed a totally rationalistic approach to the world. Thesis 1 sets the tone when it declares: "Religious humanists regard the universe as self-existing and not created." [62] According to the *Manifesto* the nature of the universe depicted by modern science "makes unacceptable any supernatural or cosmic guarantees of human values." [63] Forty years later the *Humanist Manifesto II* is even more explicit when it states that "humans are responsible for what we are or will become. No deity will save us; we must save ourselves." [64] Thus we are told in 1933 that "man will learn to face the crises of life in terms of his knowledge of their naturalness and probability. Reasonable and manly attitudes will be fostered by education and supported by custom." [65] This faith in education and reason was expressed at the same time that Hitler was indoctrinating the Germans about the superiority of the Nordic race and the necessity of eliminating the Jews.

When the *Humanist Manifesto I* was updated in 1973 the drafters admitted in the preface that events since 1933 "make the earlier statement seem far too optimistic. Nazism has shown the depths of brutality of which humanity is capable. Other totalitarian regimes have suppressed human rights without ending poverty. Science has sometimes brought evil as well as good. Recent decades have shown that inhuman wars can be made in the name of peace." [66] Yet we are still assured that we are reasonable beings and have no need of religion since it would only divert people "with false hopes of heaven hereafter." [67] But the optimistic note still prevailing is now paired with caution when we are told that the future is filled with dangers and that "reason must be tempered by humility." [68] Still there is no doubt that "human life has meaning because we create and develop our futures." [69] Especially technology assumes salvific dimensions when we hear:

> Using technology wisely, we can control our environment, conquer poverty, markedly reduce disease, extend our lifespan, significantly modify our behavior, alter the course of human evolution and cultural development, unlock vast new powers, and provide humankind with unparalleled opportunity for achieving an abundant and meaningful life. [70]

It seems ironic that this faith in "achieving abundant life" was expressed on the eve of the first Arab oil embargo against the Western countries, an action that sent economic shock waves around the globe.

The drafters of this document, however, were not quite as convinced of their own optimistic predictions concerning the future as they might sound. This becomes noticeable especially in the closing comments on "humanity as a whole" when they interchange quite frequently indicative statements and imperative demands. So we are urged to use reason and compassion to produce the kind of world we want, a world in which peace, prosperity, freedom, and happiness are widely shared.

> Let us not abandon that vision in despair or cowardice. We are responsible for what we are or will be. Let us work together for a humane world by means commensurate with humane ends. Destructive ideological differences among communism, capitalism, socialism, conservatism, liberalism, and radicalism should be overcome. Let us call for an end to terror and hatred. We will survive and prosper only in a world of shared humane values. We can initiate new directions for humankind. [71]

While we certainly agree with the goals envisioned and may join secular humanists in pursuing them, we cannot but remain skeptical about their basis for attaining such goals and about their power to achieve them. Even if we disregarded our finitude, could we ever assume that there is a basis for hope if we trust in ourselves as the grantees of the future? While we cannot afford the luxury of despair, it is historically wrong to join with the *Humanist Manifestos* in blaming traditional religion for the stifling of human initiative. As we have seen, our enterprising and progressive spirit is intimately connected with the Judeo-Christian tradition. Yet precisely when this spirit has been left to itself, when reason becomes the sole court of appeal, it turns against humanity itself. From the French Revolution (1789) to the Russian Revolution (1917), with many revolutions in between and since then, all too often the achievement of humanistic revolutionary ends has been replaced with permanent terror. Thus the big unresolved question remains who should educate or at least guide the educators (or revolutionaries)? If there are no metaphysical values left we are thrown back to our own predilections, which quite often means our own selfishness.

Yet the deep-seated optimism about our own potential cannot be so easily discarded. Until very recently, and despite ethnic and class revolts in many countries and occasional brief shortages of energy and material resources, the overall picture in the West remained one of optimism. For instance, in a memorandum, "The Triple Revolution," addressed in 1964 to President Lyndon B. Johnson, the drafters (all advocates of socialist humanism) still declared: "The economy of abundance can sustain all citizens in comfort and economic security whether or not they engage in what is commonly reckoned as work." [72] Even if there was already doubt whether we were appropriately addressing the issues of the future, our resources were nevertheless seen as unlimited.

The German existentialist philosopher Karl Jaspers summed up this sentiment well when he claimed that we are always capable of doing more and other things than anyone expected. Our future is never sealed. But he dampened this optimism considerably when he wrote these words in the same essay on "Premises and Possibilities of a New Humanism":

> Civilizations have perished before. What is new today is that all of mankind is threatened, that the menace is more acute and more conscious, and that it does not only affect our lives and property but our very humanity. If we consider the ephemeral nature of all undertakings, our way of living under a stay of execution, we feel as though anything we might do would be senseless in the future. [73]

b. A Modest assessment of the future
(Alvin Toffler and Robert Heilbroner)

The ominous thunderclouds of the future have alerted even those who call it their business to map out the future. Alvin Toffler, in his book *Future Shock,* wanted to help us come to terms with the future. Analyzing the future he intended to make us cope more efficiently with both personal and social change as the future approaches ever more rapidly. But he was still convinced in his book that the threatening effects of the future could be harnessed.[74] In a more recent book, *The Eco-Spasm Report,* Toffler introduces a very different scenario. He has now realized that we are rapidly approaching the limits of technological expansion and that our technological civilization will break down and a wholly new civilization with different priorities will emerge.[75] The reports to the Club of Rome and many other assessments of the present and projections into the future have made us familiar with the paradigm of spaceship earth. On spaceship earth we are confronted with limited and exhaustible resources and can only insure a bearable future if we take drastic steps to achieve a basic reorientation of life-styles.

Others are less convinced that there are even enough resources to be shared regardless of which measures we implement. Therefore, they advocate the method of triage, dividing the human family into three groups:

(1) a first group will survive without needing outside help;

(2) a second will continue to live if immediate help is administered;

(3) a third is beyond hope for survival regardless of what we do.[76] Here we are provided with at least a semblance of hope, provided that we belong to the right group. A similar selective method is advocated by Garrett Hardin with his parable of a lifeboat ethic.[77] The lifeboat leading to human survival has a limited carrying capacity. Though it is not yet filled to the brim it cannot provide shelter for all the people attempting to get into it. Allowing any more people to get on board will potentially endanger the future of all who occupy it. Thus one reaches the conclusion to stay with the present occupants and concentrate on their survival. When we look at the increasing interdependence of humanity, especially in terms of energy supply, natural resources, and technological products, we wonder whether one can so easily distinguish between those occupying the lifeboat and those drowning outside. We could easily awaken to the dreadful realization that though we thought we were inside the boat we are actually the ones in the chilly waves fighting for survival.

The American economist Robert L. Heilbroner in his sobering book, *An Inquiry into the Human Prospect,* perhaps captures best the tremendous change that took place in the consciousness of secular humanism. He describes how our

sense of assurance and control has vanished, or is vanishing rapidly. We have become aware that rationality has its limits with regard to

the engineering of social change, and that these limits are much narrower than we had thought; that many economic and social problems
lie outside the scope of our accustomed instrumentalities of social
change; that growth does not bring about certain desired ends or arrest
certain undesired trends.[78]

Unlike many futurists, however, Heilbroner does not want to paint a
dark and threatening picture and then conclude with a final note of
optimism. Though he admits that much of the prospect he outlines is
deeply repugnant to our 20th century temper, as well as incompatible
with our most treasured privileges, we must have the courage to look
squarely at the dimensions of the onrushing predicament. We have become startlingly aware that the quality of life is already deteriorating, and
the question of whether worse impends must be answered in the affirmative. The industrial growth process, so central to our economic and social
life, will be forced to slow down, in all likelihood within a generation or
two, and will probably have to give way to a decline thereafter. Thus we
must shift away from energy and material intensive activities to service
intensive activities. If the myopic outlook that confines our vision to a
short-term future continues, Heilbroner contends, we will be confronted
with convulsive change, change forced upon us by external events rather
than by conscious choice, by catastrophe rather than by calculation. With
the full spectacle of the human prospect before us, the spirit quails and
the will falters.

Though Heilbroner has no intention of challenging us to moral awakening or social action on some unrealistic scale, he does "not intend to
condone, much less to urge, an attitude of passive resignation." [79] Our
present industrial society has no future and likely will be replaced by a
society that recovers some of the values of "primitive" cultures without
reverting to their level of ignorance and cruel anxiety. But the human
prospect is not an irrevocable death sentence. Though the risk of enor-
mous catastrophes exists, we are not headed toward an inevitable doomsday.[80] The challenges of the future will be overcome, if not by our fore-
sight, at least by the "saving" intervention of nature. Thus our future
will not be one of glory and brightness, but of survival.

In the crucial transitional years we shall need the Promethean spirit
that once provided the driving energy of modernity. Yet a Promethean
figure may despair of the future, recognizing that after so much effort
so little has been accomplished. Therefore Heilbroner also recalls from

Greek mythology the figure of Atlas, who in endless perseverance bore the weight of the heavens on his shoulders. If we want to rescue life, he contends, we must first preserve the will to live and rescue the future from the angry condemnation of the present. There the spirit of conquest and aspiration will not suffice; it must be supplanted by the spirit of perseverance. "If, within us, the spirit of Atlas falters, there perishes the determination to preserve humanity at all cost and any cost, forever." [81]

Heilbroner's diagnosis and perspective accurately portray contemporary secular human consciousness. He perceptively sees what possibilities the future has open for us, a future very much like the one Amos announced centuries ago when he pronounced the day of the Lord as impending (Amos 5:20). However, Heilbroner may have sensed that his prognostication about the future was too far-reaching. In a more recent publication he concludes on a much more modest, though no less somber, note when he says: "We can see more clearly than past generations . . . that in our time we will have to live through periods of wrenching change even if the system [of capitalism] survives. What comes thereafter is still a closed book." [82]

Our present situation makes us painfully aware that we are inextricably connected with the material basis that gave rise to humanity and has sustained it through the ages. It would therefore border on wishful thinking to expect that life's material basis could provide an avenue that would lead us out of finitude and eventual death. True hope can only come from something that provides the foundation of our lives and that can insure the sustenance of that foundation into the future.

NOTES

1. Martin Heidegger, *Being and Time*, 234.
2. Ibid., 304f.
3. Ibid., 307.
4. Laszlo Versényi, *Heidegger, Being, and Truth* (New Haven: Yale University, 1965) 184, rightly objects that Heidegger provides neither a practical process nor usable criteria for distinguishing between authentic and inauthentic possibilities of being.
5. Ernest Becker, *The Denial of Death* (New York: Free Press, 1973) ix.
6. Ibid., xi and 7.
7. Cf. ibid., 5.
8. Ibid., 281.
9. Ibid., 284.
10. Ernest Becker, *Escape from Evil* (New York: Free Press, 1975) xvii.

11. Ibid., 170.
12. Ernest Becker, *The Denial of Death*, 12.
13. Jean-Paul Sartre, *Being and Nothingness. An Essay on Phenomenological Ontology*, 485. Sartre's claim of support from Heidegger seems to be unwarranted at this point.
14. Jean-Paul Sartre, *No Exit*, in *No Exit and Three Other Plays*, trans. by L. Abel (New York: Knopf, 1949) 47.
15. Sartre, *Being and Nothingness*, 555f.
16. Ibid., 70.
17. For an excellent comparison between the "dramatic obsession with crisis" in Jean-Paul Sartre's writings and Camus' sober limitation to concrete experience cf. Germaine Brée, *Camus and Sartre. Crisis and Commitment* (New York: Delacorte, 1972).
18. Albert Camus, *The Myth of Sisyphus and Other Essays*, trans. by J. O'Brien (New York: Knopf, 1967).
19. Albert Camus, *The Rebel. An Essay on Man in Revolt*, foreword by Sir Herbert Read, trans. by A. Bower (New York: Knopf, 1961). Yet already at the conclusion of this book Camus mentions that "rebellion cannot exist without a strange form of love" (304), without, however, elaborating any further on the meaning of love.
20. Albert Camus, *The Fall*, trans. by J. O'Brien (New York: Knopf, 1960).
21. Albert Camus, "The Growing Stone," in *Exile and the Kingdom*, trans. by J. O'Brien (New York: Knopf, 1958).
22. Cf. Roger Garaudy, *Marxism in the Twentieth Century*, trans. by R. Hague (New York: Scribner, 1970) 107.
23. Karl Marx, "Theses on Feuerbach," in Karl Marx and Friedrich Engels, *On Religion*, 72.
24. Friedrich Engels, "On the History of Early Christianity," in *On Religion*, 324.
25. Ibid., 317.
26. Marx, "The Communism of the Paper *Rheinischer Beobachter*," in ibid., 84.
27. Marx, "Contribution to the Critique of Hegel's Philosophy of Right," in ibid., 50.
28. Ibid., 41.
29. Ibid., 42.
30. Ibid.
31. Ibid.
32. Friedrich Engels, "On the History of Early Christianity." Ibid., 317f. in a footnote.
33. Cf. Roger Garaudy, *From Anathema to Dialogue: A Marxist Challenge to the Christian Churches*, trans. by L. O'Neill (New York: Herder and Herder, 1966) 32.
34. Garaudy, *Marxism in the Twentieth Century*, 208f.
35. Ernst Bloch, *Thomas Müntzer als Theologe der Revolution* (1921) (Frankfurt am Main: Suhrkamp, 1969) 229.
36. Ernst Bloch, *Das Prinzip Hoffnung*, 3 vols. (Frankfurt am Main: Suhrkamp, 1969), 3: 1607.
37. Ibid., 1619.
38. Ibid., 1621.
39. Ibid., 1625.
40. Ibid., 1627f.
41. Jürgen Moltmann, "Hope and Confidence: A Conversation with Ernst Bloch," *Dialog* 7 (Winter 1968): 43.
42. Bloch, 1521f.
43. So Gerhard Sauter, *Zukunft und Verheissung; Das Problem der Zukunft in der gegenwärtigen theologischen und philosophischen Diskussion* (Zürich: Zwingli Verlag, 1965), 354.
44. Cf. the striking title of Alfred Jäger's investigation in Bloch's eschatology *Reich ohne Gott: Zur Eschatologie Ernst Blochs* (Zürich: EVZ-Verlag, 1969).

45. Moltmann, 49.
46. Cf. Karl Löwith, *Meaning in History*, 44.
47. Mao Tse-tung, "Dialectical Materialism" (March 1940), trans. by Dennis J. Doolin and Peter J. Golas in their article "On Contradiction in the Light of Mao Tse-tung's Essay on 'Dialectical Materialism,'" *The China Quarterly* (July-September 1964) 42. For a more extensive treatment of Mao Tse-tung in a slightly different context cf. Hans Schwarz, *Our Cosmic Journey*, 110-113.
48. *Mao Tse-tung's Quotations: The Red Guard's Handbook*, intr. by Steward Fraser (Nashville: International Center. George Peabody College for Teachers, 1967) 222.
49. Mao Tse-tung, "On Practice," in *Selected Works of Mao Tse-tung*, vol. 1 (Peking: Foreign Languages Press, 1967) 304.
50. For this and the following quotations see *Mao Tse-tung's Quotations*, 5; 3; 9.
51. For this paragraph cf. *Mao Tse-tung's Quotations*, 29f. and 187; for quotations see ibid., 26, 269, and 275. Very interestingly Jerome Ch'en, *Mao and the Chinese Revolution with Thirty-seven Poems by Mao Tse-tung*, trans. by M. Bullock and Jerome Ch'en (London: Oxford University, 1965) 6, points out the intense hatred "which is so essential a part of Mao's personality." Though it has been used toward liberating and educating China, it has also been directed against anybody who would disagree with Mao's way of bringing about his envisioned goal.
52. Cf. *Christian Faith and the Chinese Experience*. Workshop Reports from an Ecumenical Colloquium in Louvain, Belgium, September 9-14, 1974 (Lutheran World Federation/Pro Mundi Vita, 1974) 21. See also the very instructive papers of this Colloquium published in the same volume. Another important publication of the Lutheran World Federation/Pro Mundi Vita on China contains the papers of an ecumenical seminar held at Båstad, Sweden, January 29 to February 2, 1974, on *Theological Implications of the New China*. For information on the astounding accomplishments of the "New China" cf. *China. The Peasant Revolution*, ed. by Ray Wylie (London: World Student Christian Federation, 1972); and Maxwell S. Stewart, *China Revisited*. Public Affairs Pamphlet No. 505 (New York: Public Affairs Committee, 1974).
53. So rightly Leo Goodstadt, *China's Search for Plenty. The Economics of Mao Tse-tung* (New York: Weatherhill, 1973) 203. Jack Chen in his highly informative book, *Inside the Cultural Revolution* (New York: Macmillan, 1975) 439, even claims that now "China has resolutely rejected the way of superindustrialism, the 'affluent society.' China has wisely understood that conditions of life on our planet today call for a life-style of homely frugality and that to adopt such a life-style is not a denial of happiness but a wise caution in facing the future." If this statement is true, and some signs indicate it is, then not only young nations could learn from China, but highly developed ones too, in order to rethink their priorities and aspirations.
54. Cf. for the following ibid., 235ff. While he mentions that in private discussions Chinese Communists are insistent that the Cultural Revolution has corrected these phenomena, he claims that the many reports from all areas of the country indicate that heretical ideas continue. According to Goodstadt these conflicting stories imply that Mao's endeavors fall short of a total triumph. Chen, 436, admits that the main danger for China today comes from the emergence of a new class of bourgeois, the revisionists in leading positions in the state and inside the Party apparatus. One might wonder here whether a truly egalitarian society is not too much an eschatological goal to be *fully* realized in the present. Even a permanent revolution, of which the Cultural Revolution seemed to be part, can lead to the formation of an elitist group of revolutionaries.
55. Quoted in Goodstadt, *China's Search for Plenty*, 235, from a regional broadcast in mainland China (October 10, 1970).
56. *Mao Tse-tung's Quotations*, 203.
57. Garaudy, *From Anathema to Dialogue*, 112.

58. Roger Garaudy, *The Alternative Future: A Vision of Christian Marxism*, trans. by L. Mayhew (New York: Simon and Schuster, 1974) 177.
59. Ibid., 83.
60. Cf. ibid., 84.
61. Ibid., 85.
62. *Humanist Manifestos I and II* (Buffalo, NY: Prometheus Books, 1973) 8. For a good introduction of the problematic nature of the secular humanistic approach to the future cf. Ted Peters, *Futures—Human and Divine*, 134-149, where he also examines the *Humanist Manifestos I and II* (ibid., 137f.).
63. *Humanist Manifestos I and II*, 8.
64. Ibid., 16.
65. Ibid., 9.
66. Ibid., 13.
67. Ibid.
68. Ibid., 14 and 17.
69. Ibid., 17.
70. Ibid., 14.
71. Ibid., 23.
72. "The Triple Revolution," in *Socialist Humanism. An International Symposium*, ed. by Erich Fromm (Garden City, NY: Doubleday, 1965) 454.
73. Karl Jaspers, *Existentialism and Humanism. Three Essays*, ed. by Hanns E. Fischer, trans. by E. B. Ashton (New York: Moore, 1952) 83.
74. Cf. the concluding statement by Toffler, *Future Shock* (New York: Random House, 1970) 430, where he says: "For, by making imaginative use of change to channel change, we cannot only spare ourselves the trauma of future shock, we can reach out and humanize distant tomorrows."
75. Alvin Toffler, *The Eco-Spasm Report* (New York: Bantam, 1975) where he says on the cover: "What is happening is the breakdown of industrial civilization on the planet and the first fragmentary appearance of a wholly new civilization."
76. This idea was first vigorously advanced by William and Paul Paddock, *Famine—1975! America's Decision: Who Will Survive* (Boston: Little, Brown, 1967) esp. 205ff. When we read this proposal we are struck by the cold-blooded rationality of the argument.
77. Garrett Hardin, "Lifeboat Ethics. The Case Against Helping the Poor," *Psychology Today* 8 (September 1974); 38-43, 123-126. Cf. also Garrett Hardin, *Exploring New Ethics for Survival* (New York: Viking, 1972). For the discussion of the various aspects of a lifeboat ethics cf. the valuable contributions in the special issue of *Soundings. An Interdisciplinary Journal* 59 (Spring 1976): "World Famine and Lifeboat Ethics: Moral Dilemmas in the Formation of the Public Policy," ed. by George R. Lucas, Jr.
78. Robert L. Heilbroner, *An Inquiry into the Human Prospect* (New York: Norton, 1974) 17.
79. Ibid., 137.
80. Ibid., 138.
81. Ibid., 144. As a good response to Heilbroner's book cf. the papers in *Zygon* 10 (September 1975), resulting from a symposium on "The Human Prospect: Heilbroner's Challenge to Religion and Science (Washington, D.C., Oct. 23-24, 1974)."
82. Robert L. Heilbroner, *Beyond Boom and Crash* (New York: Norton, 1978) 89.

Part III

WHAT CAN
WE HOPE FOR?

AFTER OUR PRELIMINARY CONSIDERATIONS of a bewildering variety of views and issues in eschatology, we must now follow the biblical admonition to give account of the hope that is in us (1 Peter 3:15). It has become evident that, while we may be able to survive some of the thunder clouds that loom threatening on the horizon of history, lasting hope cannot come from within us. While we can always achieve temporary victories, ultimately death will stare us in the face. When we give account of the hope that is in us, we can only do so because it has been placed in us from beyond our time-bound world. Any tenable hope for the future thus cannot rest on us but must be affirmed by the God who created the world, does sustain it, and will eventually redeem it. If the temporary hopes grounded in life's material basis are subject to many differing interpretations, we need not wonder that we face a similar divergence when we approach hopes for the future based on God. Thus we must first consider some problematic approaches to eschatology. We shall then deal with the promised life beyond life, and finally we shall consider the prospect of a new creation, both in its present and its future aspects.

6
Blind Alleys
in Eschatology

WHEN WE MENTION HERE four blind alleys of eschatology [1] —setting a date, purgatory, universal homecoming, and millennialism—we do this with the understanding that these are the major circumventions of God's eschatological promise. They are rejected by most Protestant denominations and, with the exception of the second one, also by the Roman Catholic Church. In spite of their "off limits" character they always proved attractive for those who did not feel themselves strictly bound to the teachings of the main denominational bodies.

1. Setting a date

The first blind alley seems to be the oldest and was already popular at the time of Jesus. Following the apocalyptic tradition some of his followers were convinced that they could accurately predict the beginning of the eschaton and the parousia of the returning Christ. Jesus, however, always denied such a possibility, saying: "Of that day and hour no one knows, not even the angels of heaven, nor the Son, but the Father only" (Matt. 24:36), and "it is not for you to know times or seasons which the Father has fixed by his own authority" (Acts 1:7). The endeavor to predict the coming of the eschaton would deny the sovereignty of God, who has reserved for himself the detailed knowledge of the future. It would lead to security, since we could then calculate when to start preparing for the end, but it would also be a demonic and anti-Godly attempt to make our future secure, showing a total lack of understanding of what the eschaton implies.

The eschaton is not something for the coming of which we can start preparing from a certain period onward. The eschaton is the God-provided goal that will emerge at a certain God-provided point and toward which our whole life should be directed. The classic illustration of this is Jesus' parable of the five wise and the five foolish maidens (Matt. 25:1-13). Those who had directed their whole life toward the preparation for the coming kingdom were able to enter into it when it came. Those, however, who thought that they could start their preparation at a certain self-determined point were excluded. Thus the parable ends with the admonition: "Watch therefore, for you know neither the day nor the hour." [2]

Nevertheless the idea of being able to arrive at the date of the coming of the eschaton has remained amazingly attractive. Even Martin Luther, who often emphasizes the incalculability of this event, indulges in this speculation in a few instances. In his world chronological table he remarks that he is convinced that the world will come to its end before its sixth millennium is completed (in 2040 A.D.). [3] And in one of his table talks he concludes from the Book of Daniel that now (in 1538) it would take about another 20 years until the end will come. [4] Contrary to sectarian custom, however, he never endows these speculations with theological significance.

As the future both of the world and of personal life becomes more and more uncertain, the minds of many people in our secular society are increasingly deluded by fantasy and misguided by fear rather than comforted by biblical hope. Thus ignorance about the Christian message is paired with superstition, while responsibility and reasonable thought are often forsaken. In their attempt to counteract these tendencies some popular theologians pour oil on the flames of popular fears and hopes with books that closely resemble the apocalyptic literature produced during the darkest years of the Middle Ages. Especially Hal Lindsey's books, *The Late Great Planet Earth* (1970) which has sold over 10 million copies in ten years, and *The Liberation of Planet Earth* (1974), have had an immense impact on countless people. *The Late Great Planet Earth* has now even been made into a movie which is shown on cable TV throughout the U.S.

Hal Lindsey's publications are representative of many others that attempt to give the prophetic word of the Bible new credibility. Hal Lindsey is correct when he states that, in an effort to satisfy the concern and curiosity about the future, modern-day "prophets" are enjoying the greatest revival since the ancient days of Babylon. It should also concern us that in the United States alone 32 million people take astrology with some seriousness, and that 17 million experiment with esoteric religions that promise peace of mind and new insights. This means that more people take to astrology or to esoteric cults than those who claim to be Southern Baptists, Lutherans, or Methodists. Given this context, we appreciate the biblical realism underlying Lindsey's endeavor to point to the immediacy of the coming eschaton.

Though Lindsey does not settle on a specific date but calls for continuous preparedness, he is convinced "that according to all the signs, we are in the general time of His coming." [5] The end will climax in World War III with four principal power-blocs confronting each other. The Arab-African Confederacy headed by Egypt (King of the South) launches an invasion of Israel. Russia and her allies use this occasion to launch an invasion of the Middle East.[6] For a short while the Russian bloc will conquer the Middle East and set up command headquarters on Mt. Moriah or the Temple area in Jerusalem.[7] But then the ten-nation Revived Roman Empire of Europe (to which the United States may be aligned) will destroy Russia in Israel.[8] Thus "we have only two great spheres of power left to fight the final climactic battle of Armageddon: the combined forces of the Western civilization united under the leadership of the Roman Dictator and the vast hordes of the Orient probably united under the Red Chinese war machine." [9] In the movie, *The Late Great Planet Earth,* Hal Lindsey several times is shown overlooking the plain of Jezreel "which belts across the middle of the Holy Land, from the Mediterranean to the Jordan," [10] pointing out that this is the Armageddon where the final battle will take place. "As the battle of Armageddon reaches its awful climax, when it appears that all life will be destroyed on earth—in this very moment Jesus Christ will return and save man from self-extinction." [11]

Where does Hal Lindsey get this information, complete with detailed maps and diagrams? He points to the Bible, predominately to the Old Testament prophets, Isaiah, Jeremiah, Daniel, and Ezekiel, and also to the New Testament book of Revelation. He assures us that 70% of the biblical prophecies have come true and that the rest will find fulfillment in our lifetime. We certainly agree that ancient Israel received its courage to face the future from the fulfillment of certain Old Testament prophecies, and that the New Testament hope for the return of the Lord has proved to be a powerful stimulus for the Christian church to transform the world and to spread the good news of salvation. Yet we wonder about the appropriateness of Lindsey's highly imaginative but totally unhistorical approach to the biblical witnesses.

For two reasons it is unwarranted to take an Old Testament prediction or promise that has not yet been fulfilled and transpose it onto the contemporary scene with the claim that it will be fulfilled soon.

(1) The Old Testament predictions and promises were continuously being revised and expanded in their own time to include the new emerging historical situations, as we see paradigmatically in the promise of the Messiah. The mere progress of history necessitated a continuous reappropriation, even in instances where a promise or prediction had come to fulfillment. Thus a specific pinpointing of their fulfillment would contradict the progress of history through which God's working with Israel was understood in a continuously changing and expanding horizon.

(2) It was the deep conviction of the New Testament witnesses and of Jesus himself that *all* the Old Testament promises had found their fulfillment, and not just their continuation, in the Christ event. In him God's full self-disclosure had occurred (Heb. 1:1f.) and the first fruit of the new creation was reaped (2 Cor. 5:17). All further events are contingent upon the Christ event. To go back with Hal Lindsey to the Old Testament and look for signs and predictions that could be projected on the screen of the present or the future would not only turn the Bible into a jigsaw puzzle,[12] but would also relativize the Christ event as the culmination point of God's history with us. Christ would not be the answer to the Old Testament hopes and aspirations but a continuation of them. Thus the zeal for predicting the end instead of emphasizing the preparedness leads to an undermining of our trust in God and a circumvention of Christ and his efficacious work.

2. Purgatory

The concept of purgatory presupposes an intermediate state between death and resurrection and is an important part of Roman Catholic teaching. Thus we read in *The Catholic Catechism:* "There exists a purgatory in which the souls of the just who die with the stains of sin are cleansed by expiation before they are admitted to heaven." [13]

a. The biblical basis for the idea of a purgatory

Within the Judeo-Christian tradition the origin of the purgatory goes back into the intertestamental period. In the *Second Book of Maccabees* the religious practice of praying for the dead was first mentioned and sanctioned.[14] In their encounter with pagan religious cults, Jews and

Christians noticed that the worship of the dead played an important role. For instance, the Book of Jubilees (22:17) says: "They offer their sacrifices to the dead and they worship evil spirits, and they eat over the graves." However, Jews and Christians attempted to stay away from these pagan customs. Instead of praying *to* the dead, Jews and Christians prayed *for* the dead. Augustine expresses this very firmly when he states: "Any signs of veneration paid by pious people at the tombs of martyrs are mere tributes to their memory, not sacred ceremonies nor sacrifices offered to the dead, as to gods." [15]

In a similar way the Sifre to Deuteronomy states that the dead need atonement, i.e., the living can pray for them and atone for their sins committed on earth. Also the Pesikta Rabbati says: "Lest you say: when one has gone to Gehinnom there is no coming up (resurrection) for *him;* if, however, the living prayed for a dead person he is taken out of Gehinnom." [16] Many of the church fathers followed these thoughts. For instance, Tertullian in his *Treatise on Monogamy,* speaking about the widows, says: "She prays for his soul, and requested refreshments for him meanwhile, and fellowship (with him) in the first resurrection; and she offers (her sacrifice) on the anniversaries of his falling asleep." [17] And Augustine recalls in his Confessions that his mother Monica admonished him to remember her at the altar of the Lord, i.e., with intercessory prayers. [18]

When we try to find a scriptural basis for the concept of purgatory, where such atonement could take place, we are in trouble. The only source where purgatory is clearly mentioned (2 Maccabees 12:44f.) stems from the intertestamental period, while Matthew 5:25f., Matthew 12:32f., and 1 Corinthians 3:11-15, sources occasionally quoted by Roman Catholic theologians, are even less convincing. In immediate reaction to Luther's rejection of the idea of purgatory, the Roman Catholic Church affirmed that the idea of purgatory can be founded on biblical grounds, [19] but the Council of Trent was already more careful when it stated that purgatory is taught in conformity with the sacred writings (the Bible) and the ancient tradition of the Fathers. [20]

Modern Catholic theologians are even more hesitant in founding the idea of purgatory on biblical grounds. Ludwig Ott, for instance, says that the Holy Scripture teaches the existence of the cleansing fire indirectly, "by admitting the possibility of a purification in the other world." However, he has to concede that "the main proof for the existence of the cleansing fire lies in the testimony of the Fathers." [21] Karl Rahner is even more cautious when he states that the dogmatically defined doctrine of purgatory "is something different from a 'purifying fire.'"[22] But in his discussion of purgatory he does not mention a possible biblical basis even once.

b. Does Christ provide our total salvation?

Notwithstanding the narrow biblical basis, and in contrast to the Greek Orthodox Church, the Western church went beyond the Jewish custom of commemorative and intercessory prayer services. Though still referring to 2 Maccabees 12,[23] Augustine already named prayer, good works, giving of alms, and eucharistic sacrifice as means of intercession for the dead.[24] Gregory the Great, pope on the threshold of the dawning Middle Ages, popularized Augustine's thoughts. Unlike Augustine, he understood the eucharistic sacrifice not as a remembrance of Christ's suffering, but as a real repetition of Christ's sacrifice. Since some of the graver sins can be forgiven in purgatory, Pope Gregory the Great provided Christianity with an effective means to change the lot of the souls of the deceased. The eucharistic sacrifice was exceptionally efficacious, because it released the souls from purgatory.[25]

In the 11th and 12th centuries indulgences were introduced mainly with the idea of changing inconvenient church sanctions into more convenient ones, or of partially or even totally relinquishing them. Soon the idea emerged that indulgences could also be applied to the punishment in purgatory.[26] The church felt itself able to extend its power of absolution into purgatory. Through their excessive good deeds Christ and the saints had accumulated such a treasure of merits (*superabundantia meritorum Christi et Sanctorum*), which was to be administered by the church, that it could easily make up for the deficiences of those who suffered in purgatory. Thus we read in a 1518 decree of Pope Leo X: "The Roman Pope, as the successor of the keys of Peter and the representative of Christ on earth, can through the power of the keys . . . grant to those who are faithful Christians . . . in this life and in purgatory remission through the exceeding merits of Christ and the saints."[27] This can be done through actual remission or via intercession through indulgence. The possibility of indulgence is especially important for those who had not yet finished their preparation for death.

> (The Church) says and teaches that those who after baptism slip into sin must not be rebaptized, but by true penance attain forgiveness of their sins. Because if they die truly repentant in charity before they

have made satisfaction by worthy fruits of penance of (sins) committed and omitted, their souls are cleansed after death by purgatorical or purifying punishments. . . . And to relieve punishments of this kind, the offerings of the living faithful are of advantage to these, namely, the sacrifices of Masses, prayers, alms, and other duties of piety, which have customarily been performed by the faithful for the other faithful according to the regulations of the Church.[28]

The Synod of Florence (1439), the Council of Trent (1547-63), and the Roman Catechism of 1566 finalized the Roman Catholic understanding of purgatory.

When we remember that the Reformation started with a dispute over the practice of indulgences, it is no surprise that the reformers and the Protestant churches reject the idea of purgatory as a place or state where the living could still extend some influence and where the dead could make up for past deficiencies. John Calvin, describing the abuses and futility of indulgences and of purgatory, calls the idea of purgatory a revelation of Satan which can only be sustained through ignorant distortions or some scriptural passages.[29]

In his Ninety-Five Theses of 1517 Martin Luther reacts very strongly against the abuses of indulgences and declares in the opening thesis that according to Christ's teachings the whole life of the faithful should be a life of repentance. Still, being a faithful son of his church, he felt certain that "the Pope neither would or could forgive any punishments, except those, which were imposed through the judgment of the canon law or through himself." [30] And the following year, in his explanation of the Ninety-Five Theses, he still affirms: "I am most certain that there is a purgatory." [31]

Due to the lack of a scriptural basis and the misuses connected with purgatory Luther became more and more sceptical about its reality and in 1530 wrote his *Rejection of Purgatory*.[32] In his *Smalcald Articles* of 1536 we finally read in his statements about the misuses of the Roman Catholic Mass:

Consequently purgatory and all the pomp, services, and business transactions associated with it are to be regarded as nothing else than illusions of the devil, for purgatory, too, is contrary to the fundamental article that Christ alone, and not the work of a man, can help souls. Besides, nothing has been commanded or enjoined upon us with reference to the dead.[33]

With these remarks Luther pointed out an important reason why the idea of purgatory had gained such momentum. The idea of purgatory emerges when there is uncertainty whether God's justification of us sinners, as offered to those who accept Christ as their Lord, really extinguishes all punishment of sins and make us presentable to God. Once an uncertainty emerges, we want to make sure that we and our loved ones are safe from punishment. Thus the Roman Catholic Church distinguished between temporal punishment (in purgatory) and eternal punishment (after the last judgment). Only rare and deadly sins fall under the category of eternal punishment, while all others can be forgiven.

Another necessary ingredient of the idea of purgatory is the assumption that some or all people can influence our destiny beyond death. The popularized slogan of Johann Tetzel, indulgence-seller and contemporary of Martin Luther: "As soon as the coin in the coffer rings, the soul from purgatory springs," [34] certainly does not present accepted Roman Catholic doctrine. Indulgence and attribution of good deeds is thought possible only through intercession and not by such mechanical means. [35] But even the idea of intercession for the deceased considers the afterlife as similar to this life, [36] a thought almost constantly rejected in the New Testament.

Looking at the New Testament, we can neither assume that justification is uncertain or partial, nor that the afterlife is similar to life here on earth. We read in the Gospel of John: "He who hears my word and believes him who sent me, has eternal life; he does not come into judgment" (John 5:24), and Paul expressed the same conviction: "Therefore, if any one is in Christ, he is a new creation; the old has passed away, behold, the new has come" (2 Cor. 5:17). The coming of the eschaton and the coming of death are not something one can prepare for from a certain point onward; they are factors that determine the attitude of our whole life. In the same way the consequence is not open-ended or ambiguous, but definite. [37] Any thought of extending our influence on the destiny of those beyond death would do away with the radicality of death and its difference from life here on earth and anything beyond this life. Jesus says that "in the resurrection they neither marry nor are given in marriage" (Matt. 22:30), and the parable of the rich man and Lazarus shows such an abyss between the life here and the beyond that the rich man's plea for communication with his brothers on earth remains unheard (Luke 16:19-31). Both incidents illustrate the New Testament emphasis on the basic difference between our life here and the beyond.

The New Testament writers are also very hesitant to make any assertions concerning the whereabouts of the dead. This is in striking contrast to medieval scholastic thinking that divided the realm beyond death into five receptacles: (1) heaven for the saints; (2) purgatory for the average Christian; (3) limbo of the fathers, where the Old Testament patriarchs rested until Christ decended to them and led them to heaven; (4) limbo of the infants for the children who died unbaptized; and (5) hell for Satan and his followers. This concept of purgatory also seems to run contrary to the main eschatological outlook of New Testament.

There have also been attempts on the Protestant side to assert a purgatory-like state after death. Friedrich Schleiermacher occasionally implied a future development of the individual human being beyond death. He wondered what happened when death intervened "in some individual case before foreordination has fulfilled itself." [38] He concluded that even if foreordination to blessedness has not been fulfilled during one's lifetime, one will still be "taken up into living fellowship with Christ." Our life on earth needs a further development. Its brevity seems to indicate that it is only a "preparatory and introductory first stage." [39]

In popular piety purgatory is mainly conceived of as a state of punishment, but contemporary Roman Catholic reflection comes closer to Schleiermacher's thinking. Progressive Roman Catholic scholars admit that popular preaching has done a great disservice at times to the notion of purgatory by presenting it as a vast torture chamber where God exercises his vengeance upon the souls imprisoned there.[40] They in turn understand purgatory as a state of cleansing suffering where purification and growth take place. They are also hesitant to speculate about the destiny of unbelievers. Their concern is much more of existential nature and is directed toward the faithful. Thus purgatory is seen as the transition from our life here on earth to the final joy of the beatific vision of the essence of God. This, of course, changes the aspect of purgatory. It is not so much a "fire" of torment as a "fire" of joy, and it can even be called "blessed purgatory." "Purgatory is a time of maturing," [41] and, since the suffering involved in the expiating process cannot be compared with the torments of this life, these souls who are waiting for God are already better off than we here on earth. They are happy at being saved, though unhappy at being held back from the full light of the beatific vision.[42]

The concept of our spiritual growth beyond death expresses the right conviction that God's grace does not cease to work when we are dead. Unless we admit, however, that God would simply manipulate our growth, similar to a puppeteer bringing about the movements of his puppets, such growth would require our response to God's activity. But how could we conceive of our response if we just existed as bodiless souls? Apart from this obvious difficulty, the biblical witnesses do not conceive of death as just a transitional stage with a subsequent continuance similar to our life here on earth, but as a rupture and a dimensional borderline beyond which there is something entirely different from what we face here on earth.

Moreover, from the idea of a spiritual growth beyond death it is only a small step to metempsychosis, the migration of the soul, and to reincarnation, ideas prevalent in many Far Eastern religions. This is shown, for instance, by Rudolf Steiner (1861-1925), the founder of anthroposophism, who was deeply influenced by Roman Catholic liturgy, Indian theosophy, and Darwinian evolutionism, and who brought the concepts of metempsychosis and illumination of the soul to a unique symbiosis.

Karl Rahner here raises the interesting question

> whether in the Catholic notion of "interval," which seems so obsolete at first, there could not be a starting point for coming to terms in a better and more positive way with a doctrine of the "transmutation of souls" or of "reincarnation," which is so widespread in eastern cultures and is regarded there as something to be taken for granted.[43]

Indeed, the concepts of purgatory, transmutation of souls, and reincarnation can express the desire that human destiny will come to an ultimate fulfillment. Yet Rahner himself notes that "in Catholic theology the question is not yet settled with regard to the sense in which and the degree to which temporal categories can still be applied there." The Roman Catholic Church was indeed wise when it refrained from dogmatic statements concerning that which expresses with temporal or spatial categories things after death. It therefore avoided patterning them too much according to the way we experience things in this life. The big question, however, is whether it is legitimate and helpful to speak with Rahner of an interval in a person's destiny between death and the corporate fulfillment of this person as a whole. If there is no "void" (purgatory) after death, but a final destiny in terms of acceptance or rejection, then neither the doctrine of purgatory nor the notion of a process of maturation "after" death for the whole person is warranted.

In this context Ladislaus Boros advocates the fascinating hypothesis of a final decision at the moment of death, thus decisively modifying the traditional concepts of purgatory and death. Boros agrees that the church has only gradually developed the doctrine of purgatory. Though the scriptural basis of purgatory may be obscure, the fact and the essential nature of purgatory are of such quality that it must be called a "truth of revelation." [44] With his hypothesis of a final decision, however, Boros seems to view purgatory as the "point" of intersection between life and death. Purgatory is no longer conceived of as a process of purification that can be measured similar to the days and years we live here on earth. According to Boros "purgatory would be the passage, which we effect in our final decision, through the purifying fire of divine love. The encounter with Christ would be our purgatory." [45]

Of course, this hypothesis of a final decision also does away with the idea of a limbo for the children who died unbaptized, since in death they are able to make a decision for or against Christ and thus have the possibility of reaching the same status as all believers. [46] I must confess that this kind of reasoning almost coincides with my own approach (cf. "Universal homecoming or 'Christ's descent into hell?'"). Boros replaces an untenable concept of purgatory with the idea of a confrontation with Christ in death. Yet is it still necessary to reserve for this occurrence the term "purgatory"? It seems that what leads Boros to retain the term is not only a concession to tradition but also his view of death as something positive and liberating. For instance, he calls death *"man's first completely personal act"* and, *"therefore, by reason of its very being, the place above all others for the awakening of consciousness, for freedom, for the encounter with God, for the final decision about eternal destiny."* [47]

It is certainly scripturally well-founded to conceive of death as the point at which we will see God face to face and where the final decision about our eternal destiny will be made. Yet Boros would hardly find scriptural support when he calls death *"a sacramental situation"* [48] and when he looks upon death "as a 'basic sacrament,' mysteriously present in the other sacraments and inwardly supporting them at the same time as it transcends them." [49] Though we agree with Boros that death can and must also be understood as implying God's grace, we cannot escape the notion that the Bible looks upon death primarily as something negative and as implying God's punishment. While sympathizing with many facets of Boros' approach, for reasons that we shall develop later (cf. Chapter 7), we cannot agree with his optimistic view of death. Since his optimistic view of death is so overpowering we also wonder whether he does not finally opt for a universal homecoming.[50] This idea, however, is another blind alley of eschatological thinking, and we shall consider it next.

3. Universal homecoming

When we investigate the idea of a universal homecoming of all humanity to God it is again difficult to find a sound biblical basis. The Greek term for this idea *(apokatastasis panton)* occurs only once in the New Testament, in Acts 3:21, when Peter addresses the Jewish people, saying that heaven must receive Jesus "until the time for establishing all that God spoke by the mouth of his holy prophets from of old." Of course, it is evident that Peter refers here to the fulfillment of the Old Testament promises and not to a universal homecoming. Other passages in the New Testament, such as 1 Corinthians 15:22, where Paul says that as in Adam all die so "in Christ shall all be made alive," and where the all-inclusiveness of Christ's redemptive act is emphasized, seem to provide a sounder basis for the idea of a universal homecoming. In consulting some prominent representatives of this idea we will soon notice, however, that they are not much interested in founding this idea on biblical grounds.

a. Origen, Friedrich Schleiermacher, and Paul Tillich

The origin of the idea of a universal homecoming is very obscure. In Parsiism the dualism between the good god Ormuzd and the evil god Ahriman is resolved in a final monism. All people have the chance of eventual purification, and after the destruction of Ahriman and his demons even hell will be purified. And Plato, one of the founders of Western philosophy, holds that the human soul can return from Hades, the place of the "underworld," and be reincarnated. Then, after death, the migration starts again, because the human soul is like water. First, it comes down from heaven, then it ascends into heaven, and again it must go down to earth in eternal change.[51] This cyclic view of history coincides with the astrology of antiquity where the term *apokatastasis* stands for the return of the stellar bodies to their initial starting point.

Origen, one of the most brilliant and provocative theologians of the early church, advocates exactly such a cyclic view of history when he states:

> For the end is always like the beginning; as therefore there is one end of all things, so we must understand that there is one beginning of all things, and as there is one end of many things, so from one beginning arise many differences and varieties, which in their turn are restored, through God's goodness, through their subjection to Christ and their unity with the Holy Spirit, to one end, which is like the beginning.[52]

Origen believes that in his goodness God through Christ will restore the entire creation—even his enemies will be conquered and subdued.[53] By the instruction of angelic and higher powers and by the use of one's free will everyone will be renewed and restored, having undergone various movements of progress.[54] In the end there will be a complete destruction of the body, "for wherever bodies are, corruption follows immediately" and the end of all things will be incorporeal.[55]

> If then the end is renewed after the pattern of the origin and the issue of things made to resemble their beginning and that condition restored which rational nature once enjoyed when it had no need to eat of the tree of the knowledge of good and evil, so that all consciousness of evil has departed and given place to what is sincere and pure and he alone who is the one good God becomes all things to the soul and he himself is all things not in some few or in many things but in all things, when there is nowhere any death, nowhere any sting of death, nowhere any evil at all, then truly God will be all in all.[56]

Even the devil himself will not be excluded from the final spiritual unity with God. This return to the beginning is not, however, understood as final goal or fulfillment, because it always includes the possibility of a new fall and new salvational cycles.[57]

The constant scriptural references in Origen's discourse should not be overlooked (cf. Ps. 110:1; 1 Cor. 15:25, 27f.; John 17:22 f.; and others). It must also be mentioned that Origen proposed his ideas only for discussion and not as dogmatic statements.[58] Nevertheless, in his line of thought he seems to miss the intention of the biblical references he quotes. He is more influenced by Platonic philosophy than by the eschatological outlook of the New Testament. Even so, his thoughts proved to be so stimulating for adventurous minds that the church found it necessary to condemn him twice, first at a local synod in 543, where some of his statements were considered heretical, and more summarily at the fifth Ecumenical Council in Constantinople in 553.[59] Even the Presbyter Rufinus, to whom we owe the Latin translation of Origen's book *On First Principles* from the Greek, made certain adjustments in his translation to make Origen's thoughts, especially on the topic of universal homecoming, more acceptable to the Western mind.

The idea of universal homecoming always attracted speculative minds, and even the Augsburg Confession found it necessary to take a stand against some sectarian groups who maintained that the condemned and the devil will not suffer eternal punishment.[60] Due to the influence they exerted, we must mention at least two of the more recent representatives of this idea, Friedrich Schleiermacher and Paul Tillich.

We have noticed earlier that Schleiermacher advocated a kind of purgatory. This idea is necessary within his theological system in order to assert the universal homecoming of all humanity. Schleiermacher presupposes a unity of God and the world.

> The kingdom of grace or of the Son is absolutely one in origin with the kingdom of omniscient omnipotence, or of the Father: and since the whole government of the world is, like the world itself, eternal in God, nothing happens in the kingdom of grace without divine fore-ordination.[61]

He concludes rightly that God's grace is constantly at work, and that New Testament passages, such as Acts 2:41 and 13:48, certainly do not indicate that those who did not believe at one time could not possibly become believers at some later date. There are always some in whom the initiation of blessedness in Christ has not yet been attained. But those who appear to us to be passed over by God's foreordination to blessedness are not outside all divine activity and all divine decree. They are "objects of the same divine activity that gathered the Church together, and are embraced along with us all under the same divine foreordination.[62] As for Teilhard de Chardin, the church becomes the world and God's saving grace the spiritual development of humanity.

Schleiermacher asserts that, if there were a twofold outcome (blessedness and damnation) after the last judgment, the church would be incomplete. Furthermore, sympathy for the condemned would impair the happiness of the saved.[63] Divine foreordination will thus prevent the final victory of evil over even one part of the human race. Schleier-macher concludes:

> From whichever side we view it, then, there are great difficulties in thinking that the finite issue of redemption is such that some thereby obtain the highest bliss, while others (on the ordinary view, indeed, the majority of human race) are lost in irrevocable misery. We ought not to retain such an idea without decisive testimony to the fact that it was to this that Christ Himself looked forward; and such testimony is wholly lacking. Hence we ought at least to admit the equal rights of the milder view, of which likewise there are traces in Scripture; the view, namely, that through the power of redemption there will one day be a universal restoration of all souls.[64]

In spite of his strong criticism of the Roman Catholic doctrine of purgatory, Paul Tillich sympathizes with it too, since it is a "power-ful expression of belief in the unity of individual and universal destiny in Eternal Life." [65] Like Schleiermacher, he also rejects the idea of double predestination in which God has selected only a few for eternal bliss. God would thus become a demon, "contradicting the God who creates the world for the sake of fulfillment of all created potentialities." [66] Ac-cording to Tillich the idea of a twofold eternal destiny contradicts the idea of God's continuous creation of the finite as something "very good." "Everything as created is rooted in the eternal ground of being. In this respect non-being cannot prevail against it." [67] We find here a similar unity of God (the ground of being) and the world as we found in Schleiermacher. Similar to Schleiermacher, Tillich also feels that the condemnation of one person would impair the state of bliss of the other, because "his essence and that of the other cannot be absolutely sep-arated." [68]

Tillich realizes very well that the fear is not unfounded that "the teaching of *apokatastasis* would destroy the seriousness of religious and ethical decisions." [69] Still, he finds several reasons why a twofold outcome of life would be impossible. For instance, there are often distorted forms of human life where physical, biological, psychological, or sociological conditions make it impossible to reach a fulfillment of the essential goal of life even to a small degree, as in case of premature death or mental illness. Furthermore, the total being, including both conscious and un-conscious sides, of every individual is largely determined by the social conditions which one is influenced by upon entering existence.[70] There are uncounted millions who never had a chance to be exposed to the proclamation of the salvific message of Christ. Finally, there is the ambiguity of life itself. Even a saint remains a sinner and needs forgiveness. And if a sinner rejects forgiveness, "his rejection of it remains ambiguous," because even if we are pushed into despair it is the divine spirit who works in us.[71]

Tillich proposes the term "essentialization" to describe a solution that maintains a seriousness of one's life decision and still secures a universal homecoming. Essentialization means "a creative synthesis of a being's essential nature with what it has made of it in its temporal existence." [72] Insofar as the negative has maintained possession of this existence, it is excluded from life eternal, but insofar as the essential has conquered the existential distortion it will be lifted up into life eternal. The conceptual symbol of essentialization according to Tillich "emphasizes the despair of having wasted one's potentialities yet also assures the elevation of the positive within existence (even in the most unfulfilled life) into eternity." [73] This would mean that we are not accepted or rejected in our entirety. Part of us will participate in eternal life and part will be excluded from it. The decisive factor for participation is to what extent essentialization has taken place in our existence.

b. Universal homecoming or "Christ's descent into hell?"

When we look at the New Testament we notice that the tenor there is one not of universal homecoming but of a twofold outcome of human history (acceptance and rejection). Jesus' parables, of which the wise and foolish maidens (Matt. 25:1-12) or the rich man and Lazarus (Luke 16:19-31) are good examples, confront us with the prospect of a definite and irrevocable final judgment of rejection or acceptance. And a remark such as is found in Mark 9:43, "If your hand causes you to sin, cut it off; it is better for you to enter life maimed than with two hands to go to hell, to the unquenchable fire," again demands from us a decision having ultimate consequences. Even Paul, when he emphasizes salvation as the universal intention for all people, does not tone down Jesus' call for a decision; he just expands it.

A universalistic message would contradict the New Testament's clear insistence that our response to the gospel determines for us the outcome of the final judgment. God is not a puppeteer, and he takes us seriously as individual beings even if we deny him. God grants us the privilege of choosing our own destiny. A twofold outcome of the last judgment would not impair God's authority: God, who already rules over the saved and the condemned, will be revealed in the new world as the victor over hell and all anti-Godly powers. This is the deepest meaning of God being all in all. Consequently, we must conclude that God invites everybody to attain the final goal, but that there is also a "too late."

However, it should make us wonder that even for a conservative theologian like Walter Künneth the idea of *apokatastasis* "represents an ultimate consequence of the doctrine of the aeons, and as such a theological necessity." [74] Similarly, Paul Althaus states that until eternity commences faith is always on the way from the fear of a possible twofold outcome to a prayerful hoping for a universal homecoming. Dogmatics, he says, can neither take a stand for or against *apokatastasis* nor for or against a twofold outcome. Althaus concludes that only those can hope for a universal homecoming who are prayerfully on the way from the fear of a twofold outcome for themselves and for others to the faithfulness of God. [75]

We can receive guidance in this matter from the church as it once struggled with a similar issue, namely the question whether those who had lived before Christ and therefore could not respond to him while he preached among the people of Israel would be eternally lost. This issue was even more bothersome since everyone among the members of the first Christian community had loved ones who had not explicitly accepted Christ during their lifetime. In part, the results of their deliberations found their way into Scripture (cf. 1 Cor. 7:14 and 1 Cor. 15:29) [76] and in a very significant way into the Apostles' Creed when it states that "he [Jesus Christ] descended into hell."

The phrase "he descended into hell," or as it is now more adequately translated "he went to the dead," is one of the latest statements which was incorporated into the Apostles' Creed. Though the descent into the realm of the dead is nowhere explicitly mentioned in the New Testament, it is presupposed or at least implied at several places. [77] For instance, Matthew 12:40 indicates a passive stay in that realm, whereas other passages point to Christ's actions in this realm. Passages such as Revelation 1:18 ("I died, and behold I am alive for evermore, and I have the keys of Death and of Hades") show Jesus Christ as the one who has won the victory over the powers of the realm of the dead. At other places, in the context of Christ's death and resurrection, the redemption of some or all of the dead is mentioned (Matt. 27:51-53). And finally, there are some places where this descent is understood as the proclamation to some or all who are in the realm of the dead ("he went and preached to the spirits in prison," 1 Peter 3:19).

The neutral sojourn in the realm of the dead proved not very interesting for theological development.[78] His victorious entry into the realm of the dead, on the other hand, is vividly expressed by Luther. Following the tradition, Luther connected this entry with the liberation of the Old Testament patriarchs from the limbo of the fathers and with their transition to heaven.[79] That Jesus must have been active in the realm of the dead during the three days following his death on Good Friday is concluded from the idea that the divinity of Christ cannot just rest for three days and lie in the tomb.[80]

The church acted wisely when it never dogmatically decided that only some people could have benefitted from Christ's descent, i.e., the Old Testament patriarchs.[81] Some church fathers even thought that Jesus Christ redeemed all the dead, except perhaps for some very bad persons, (so Melito, Marcion, and Ephraem), and others thought that those who had died before the great flood were saved too (so the Alexandrian theologians and Origen). It is interesting to note that the Presbyter Rufinus of Aquileia in Northern Italy, who lived for a long time in the East and who translated the works of Origen, mentions a creed being used in his home town around 370 that already contained the phrase of Christ's descent which was subsequently introduced into the Apostles' Creed.[82]

But what does this mean? Is Christ's descent into hell an illegitimate speculation based on uncertain New Testament passages which we should confine to their literal meaning, that on Good Friday Christ went to the dead, as everyone else does when they die? Theologians, whether in the early church or in more recent times, who reflected on this phrase and on the biblical passages which it interprets did not just speculate on the whereabouts of Christ's divinity during his death. They were much more concerned that those who were geographically or temporally disadvantaged and therefore unable to live their life in conformity with Christ during their time on earth might be confronted with his offer of salvation in some other form. They found a possibility for such an offer beyond death in Christ's descent to the dead.

The church confessed then and still confesses today that one can be saved only by the compassion shown to us in Christ. While the church maintained that the response to the existential encounter with Christ had ultimate significance, it did not feel that it was its task to assert that everyone else who did not have a similar chance during life would have to suffer eternal consequences, the loss of eternal bliss. On the contrary, the church affirmed its hope that, without circumventing the salvific power of Christ, there was a possibility that those could be saved too who had not encountered Christ during their lifetime on earth. Yet the church never dared to declare that everyone will therefore eventually be saved, nor did it feel it was its task to define how someone could be saved through the descent.

Our reflection today must show a similar restraint. While we fervently hope and pray that all of humanity will be saved, we cannot take for granted that it will indeed be so or outline a way in which God will reach this goal. But we know that anybody will only be saved for Christ's sake. Contemplating the destiny of millions of people who have died since Christ's sojourn on earth without ever having known about him, or having known about him in such a distorted way that no appropriate response to him was possible, would it be unscriptural to conclude that these people might encounter a similar chance?

We agree with Prenter that the only criterion for the shape of our life beyond death is our relationship with Jesus Christ and the reconciliation with God which he offers.[83] We cannot quite agree with those who say that the principle of God's all-inclusive power and goodness necessitates or guarantees a universal homecoming, while the fear of a twofold outcome serves only as an ethical stimulus. We know that we are confronted with Christ's call for a decision; we know that the response to this call determines our life here and beyond; we know that we must confront as many as possible with this call. But with regard to the final destiny of those whom we cannot reach or who do not respond positively (as far as we can ever tell), we should not make their final destiny into a dogmatic issue [84] but should rest content with Luther's pastoral advice: "If you want to pray for your father's or your mother's soul, you may do so at home in your room, and that once or twice, and afterwards let it be with that."[85]

4. Millennialism or Chiliasm

The idea of millennialism or chiliasm has gained renewed interest within the last few years, especially in connection with the increasing popular attention to biblical prophecy. As the close of the second Christian millennium rapidly approaches, we may even witness a further intensity of millennial aspirations. To some extent millennialism is a universalized this-worldly replica of purgatory, opting for a final purge in connection with the coming of the kingdom. Millennialism, coming from the Latin "one thousand years," or chiliasm, meaning the same in Greek, usually stands for the expectation of a period of visible reign of the believers before the immediate coming of the end of the world. The origin of this idea is as complex as its meaning.

a. Origin and growth of millennialism

The idea of millennialism is mentioned only once in the New Testament (Rev. 20:1-15), where it says that the martyrs will be resurrected at the first resurrection and Satan will be bound on this occasion for a thousand years so that the martyrs can reign with Christ during this period. Other passages which are sometimes quoted to sustain the idea of millennialism do not mention the thousand years (cf. 1 Cor. 15:23-28) and provide ambiguous support for the idea. Its origin, however, seems to lie outside the New Testament in Jewish apocalyptic. As we remember, there were two main trends of apocalyptic expectation, a national expectation, which hoped for a messianic kingdom with the Jewish people ruling together with the Messiah over the non-believers after a final war, and a universal expectation, which hoped for the salvation of the faithful beyond the destruction and re-creation of the world. Though both ideas were often combined with each other and with non-Jewish eschatological thoughts, they were still different enough from each other that finally the national expectation emerged as a separate idea, signifying an interlude before the universal enthronement of the Messiah.

Prominent theologians of the early church, such as Irenaeus, Tertullian, and Hippolytus of Rome, favored the idea of millennialism. But the peak of its popularity came after Christianity had attained the status of an official state religion. Especially Eusebius of Caesarea in his history of the church interpreted the victory of the church during the reign of Constantine as the beginning of the "millennium."[86] This shows an essential part of this idea, a realistic hope in the future and at the same time the belief in a visible progress of the kingdom of God. The increasing culturalization of the church with its implications for good and bad rendered the idea of millennialism more and more meaningless in the Western church, whereas the East, apart from the followers of Origen, was never much fascinated by the idea. The material pleasures which it promised could not sufficiently attract the ascetic-minded Greek theologians.

b. Joachim of Fiore and the impact of an idea

From the end of the early church up to the present it was mostly sectarian groups that rejuvenated the idea of millennialism. Joachim of Fiore (c. 1135-1202), a Cistercian monk from Calabria, Italy, and founder of a community of hermits, was most influential.[87] Around A.D. 1000 chiliastic hopes were especially high because many followed the idea of Augustine and others that a millennium would elapse between Christ's first bodily appearance and his parousia.

In his commentary on the book of Revelation Joachim argued that a new third age was soon to appear. From an exact correspondence of the Old and the New Testament and from a claim of the equality of the persons in the Trinity he concluded that there would be three successive periods of revelation in which the three persons of the Trinity would be revealed. The first epoch was that of the revelation of the Father, characterized by law and fear. The second, the time from the coming of Christ up to 1260, was the period of the Son and was characterized by grace and faith. The third and final period was inaugurated by St. Benedict and is the period of the Spirit, dominated by love and spirit. The first period, resting on the Father, is an order of the married, the second, resting on the Son, is an order of the priests, and the third, resting on the Spirit, an order of the monks. Each of these periods overlaps somewhat with the next, and, through an accurate recapitulation of the former period on a higher level, one is able to make certain general predictions concerning the future. In the first period learning prevails; in the second, partly completed wisdom; but in the third, the fullness of knowledge.

Joachim thought of himself as still belonging to the second stage and he did not draw revolutionary conclusions from his historical and theological constructions. Though announcing the advent of a messianic leader, he did not even criticize the church of his time. Later followers of his were less patient. Especially the Franciscan Spirituals in the 13th and 14th centuries thought of themselves as leaders of the new order, with St. Francis as their new messianic head. Since knowledge of God could now be obtained immediately through contemplation, they rejected sacraments and preaching in this third age. They even rejected the clerical hierarchy, including the Pope; the scriptures and theology were replaced by the order of St. Francis as the essence of the gospel. When we hear that they also denounced the Emperor Frederick II as the anti-Christ, we are not surprised that their revolt did not last long and that church and state authorities persecuted them.

The fire once kindled, however, could not be so easily extinguished. Ernst Bloch calls Joachim the most influential social utopian of the Middle Ages because there were no class distinctions in the third age.[88] It was an age of monks, an age of universal monastic communism, a communism of consumption.[89] Bloch sees the fundamental principle of Joachimism in the fact that revelation is open-ended.[90] He appreciates the active fight of Joachimism against the social principles of a Christianity which since Paul had associated itself with the class-conscious society and consequently had to compromise its message a thousand times. This third period of history, as prophesied by Joachim, seems to emerge in the Soviet Union and, quite naturally, find its archfiend in the clerical domination of the second period. This clerical kingdom does not fully comprehend the third period, or if it does, it denounces it.[91]

These extrapolations show how much Bloch is interested in the anti-clerical and political-revolutionary implications of Joachim's thoughts.[92] In Marxist fashion Bloch also appreciates the relocation of the realm of light from the beyond into history, even if it was still thought of as the final state of history.[93] According to Bloch the relegation of our hopes to a better beyond must then cease too. Moreover, their attempt to date the projected kingdom of God made the sectarian revolutionaries employ their total energy, which for Bloch is a sign of the true sectarian.

For centuries Joachim's writings were propagated, and pamphlets were written in his spirit and under his name. Even Thomas Müntzer, the apocalyptic utopian and "new Daniel" who wanted to rigorously enforce God's will in this eschatological end-time, refers to Joachim.[94]. In a letter attached to his discourse *Von dem gedichteten Glauben* (Concerning the Invented Faith) he mentions Joachim's eternal gospel against which the "carnal scribes" extol themselves in mockery. Müntzer holds Joachim in high esteem, though he claims he relies not on Joachim but on the Word of God.[95] The Lutherans, however, rejected categorically any utopian ideas in the Augsburg Confession of 1530 where they stated: "Rejected, too, are certain Jewish opinions which are even now making an appearance and which teach that, before the resurrection of the dead, saints and godly men will possess a worldly kingdom and annihilate all the godless." [96]

Even with this rejection the fire of utopian dreams was not extinguished. Gotthold Lessing, one of the spiritual leaders of the enlightenment in Germany, shows a familiarity with a trinitarian periodization of history and refers to the third age as an age of "a new eternal gospel." [97] It is of much more far-reaching consequences that even Engels, Marx's collaborator in the Communist Manifesto, declares in 1842: "The self-consciousness of mankind, the new Grail, around whose throne the nations joyfully assemble, . . . that is our profession, that we become knights of this Grail, to put the sword around our waists and joyfully venture our life in the last holy war after which the thousand years empire of freedom will emerge." [98]

In the context of these secularized versions of millennialism we must also mention the idea of the kingdom of God in America, a country which is not called the New World just because it was discovered relatively late. And we must also mention the attempt in Germanic Europe to establish a thousand year *Reich* or a Third *Reich*. The messianic consciousness of this attempt can be seen in the fact that Adolf Hitler was called the Leader of this *Reich* and was greeted by millions with *Heil!* [99] It can only be considered as one of the bizarre tragedies of history that this "messianic" leader saw as one of his main goals to exterminate the same Jewish nation in whose midst these chiliastic ideas originated.

c. Millennialism—between realistic impatience and human fantasy

While secular versions of millennialism reflect largely a postmillennial view, namely our achievement of a golden age during a thousand-year reign, religious consciousness today is not quite as optimistic. In religious millennial circles a premillennial view of history usually prevails. Christ will physically return at the beginning of the thousand years. At a first resurrection some righteous will be raised to reign together with Christ. The temple in Jerusalem will be rebuilt and a general conversion of Jews and Gentiles will take place. Satan will be banished from this earth and everyone will enjoy a life in peace and harmony. At the end of the millennium Satan will be loosed for a while. Then everyone, righteous and unrighteous, will be raised, whereupon the Last Judgment will occur and a New World will dawn.

Among larger premillennial groups, we must mention here the Jehovah's Witnesses, who expect the establishment of a theocratic kingdom of God after the final battle at Armageddon. Charles Russell, their founder, established the year 1874 as the year of Christ's "invisible return" and designated the year 1914 "as the end of the Gentile times." [100] Though much less militant than the Jehovah's Witnesses, the Seventh-day Adventists expect a premillennial, personal, visible return of Christ at a time unknown but close at hand.[101] After the millennium, from the ruins of the old earth, a new earth will be created as the final place for the immortal saints.

Often millennial expectations are accompanied by withdrawal from the world. This can be seen best in utopian communities of this country such as the Shakers, who originated from a French Protestant sect and came via England to this country under the leadership of Ann Lee toward the latter half of the 18th century. Their high point was during the 1840s when they had founded over a dozen villages in eight states.[102] Another utopian community to be mentioned is the Oneida community of Oneida, New York. Its founder, John Humphrey Noyes, was converted to millennial beliefs at a protracted revival meeting in 1831.[103] This leads us to the last group of occasional millennialistic representatives, namely, the pietistic, fundamentalistic, and revivalistic groups. To demonstrate the necessity for conversion, they welcome chiliastic ideas.

Since such millennial ideas are again becoming increasingly popular, and since their characteristics are quite often confusing, we would like to follow the classifications used in the position paper, "Eschatology: The Doctrine of the Last Things," by the Presbyterian Church in the U.S., which in a very lucid way distinguishes between the four main types of millennialism:

1. Historic Premillennialism (Chiliasm)

Historic Premillennialism holds that Christ will return to the earth prior to the Last Day in order to exercise rule over the nations for a thousand years in the last stage of human history. It is pessimistic concerning the role and prospects of the Church in human history; therefore it posits another age, the millennium, between Christ's return and the Last Day, during which Christ rules in person over a theocratic kingdom to which all the nations of the world are subject.

Periods of great world upheaval and crisis have tended to spawn and multiply despair in society, and premillennial visions within Christianity.

2. Postmillennialism

Postmillennialism expects a future millennium or latter-day prosperity of the church prior to Christ's coming. It holds that the return of

Christ introduces, not a temporal kingdom but the eternal state. It does, however, expect a period before the return of Christ and the end of the age in which the Church will have fulfilled its task in the world.

The Reformed tradition, for the greater part of its history, has shown more affinity and support of the postmillennial perspective than for other interpretations. This is due largely to the Reformed emphasis upon the sovereignty of God, the belief that Christ is now Lord over all spheres of human life, and the conviction that the Christian community has been empowered by the Holy Spirit to call and work for the full promulgation of the Gospel and the transformation of culture and society to accord with the mind and will of Christ.

3. Amillennialism

Amillennialism holds that there will be no future golden age upon the earth for the Church. Whatever rule Christ exercises within history is in the spiritual sphere, in the souls of individuals, or in the life of the Church. It contains no vision of hope for its future prior to the Last Day when Christ returns to institute the eternal state and manifests His glorious Kingdom.

Optimistic amillennialism agrees with the above except that it holds the Church will *nearly* have finished its task.

Days of spiritual awakening and missionary advance have generally reinforced postmillennial and optimistic amillennial expectations.

4. Dispensational Premillennialism

Dispensationalism gives premillennialism a complete system. Human history is regarded as a series of ages (dispensations) in which man is tested with respect to some aspect revealed of God's will. In each case man fails, is judged by God, and then set on the trail under new covenant conditions. The seven ages are labeled: Innocence (in the Garden); Conscience (to the Flood); Human Government (from Babel); Promise (from Abraham); Law (from Moses); Grace (from Christ); Kingdom (the coming millennium). The age of Grace ends with the unseen coming of Christ *for* His Church (the Rapture), both the living, and by partial resurrection, the dead in Christ. A period of seven years ensues on earth marked by an international treaty of peace, including a protectorate of Israel. This seven years is "the time of Jacob's troubles" a leftover of the 70 times 7 years, or 490 years, promised as judgment captivity to Israel, but which lasted only 483 years. Midway, the Antichrist reveals himself, claiming to be the Messiah, and institutes a controlled world economy and hounds the Jews for their refusal to worship him. Christ appears *with* His Church and legions of angels to quell the Antichrist forces, bind Satan for a thousand years and establish the millennial kingdom under the reestablished throne of David on earth and by the Church out of the New Jerusalem hovering visibly in space above the earth. Following the millennium, man rejects the era of enforced peace and plenty by following the then-released Devil in an effort to conquer the Holy City. The uprising is crushed. The general resurrection then occurs, the Final Judgment, the renovation of Heaven and Earth, and the dawn of eternity.

This elaborate futurology has a number of strong appeals. First, it seems to accommodate affairs and events of the modern world to prophetic Scriptures, as other millennial theories have done in the past. Second, it places a benediction on the "world's mess" which only Christ can correct in visible power, eliminates social responsibility other than the Christian's duty in citizenship and provides joy in every sign of approaching calamity, for calamity demands Parousia. Third, it makes Divine Election absolute, and freedom of the human will is actually lost in the detailed chart of established future events.[104]

Especially dispensational premillennialism, with its concept of a rapture of the Christians, seems to attract the curious or frightened minds of many people. The term rapture has been used since the 19th century to express the idea that living Christians will be caught up from the earth to meet Jesus Christ in connection with his second coming. The term is derived from the Latin *rapere*, found in the expression "caught up" in the Latin translation of 1 Thessalonians 4:17. John F. Walvoord, President of Dallas Theological Seminary and editor of *Bibliotheca Sacra*, tells us in his book, *The Rapture Question*, that "if this is a literal, future event, it is a most important aspect of the hope of the church."[105] Since the Christians will be spared the final tribulations, "at the time of the rapture the saints meet Christ in the air, while at the second coming Christ returns to the Mount of Olives to meet the saints on earth."[106]

Yet the concept of a rapture is not as old as some of its advocates would like to think. It gained prominence in Great Britain with John Nelson Darby, a founder of the Plymouth Brethren, when in the 1830s he advocated a "secret rapture" of the faithful.[107] In this country it became popular through the Scofield Reference Bible, first published in 1909, in which the Presbyterian minister Cyrus Ingerson Scofield also advocated seven distinct periods of salvation, with the present time falling between the sixth and the seventh and therefore close to the impending end. A certain intellectual and theological respectability was further given to it in the seven-volume *Systematic Theology* (1948) of Lewis Sperry Chafer, founder and first president of Dallas Theological Seminary; [108] the tradition has been carried on under his successor John F. Walvoord in the seminary's theological quarterly, *Bibliotheca Sacra*. Dispensational theology is also taught at many Bible colleges and institutes and is promulgated by certain publishing houses, such as Zondervan. But it gained its greatest popularity with a graduate of Dallas Theological Seminary whose writings are saturated with dispensational theology, Hal Lindsey.[109]

There are at least four notable varieties of the idea of rapture:

1. Pre-tribulationalism holds that the rapture takes place before the seventh week of Daniel (Dan. 9:27).
2. Mid-tribulationalism teaches that the rapture takes place in the middle of what Daniel calls the 70th week.
3. Post-tribulationalism postpones the rapture until the resurrection, since the first resurrection is not mentioned until Rev. 20:4f.
4. Partial-rapturism introduces the idea that there are both spiritual and carnal Christians and argues that only the spiritual are translated before the tribulation, while the carnal are left to be tested.

As the many and often conflicting ideas concerning rapture and millennialism indicate, these are highly controversial topics, even for "conservative" Christians in whose circles one or the other variety is advocated. We could simply discard these theories as "undue speculation over highly symbolic teachings." [110] Indeed, most of these speculations do not stand up to historically informed exegesis of the biblical texts, and, as we have seen with Hal Lindsey, they often rest on dangerous theological presuppositions.

Yet we notice that even Lutheran theologians such as Reinhold Frank and J. C. K. von Hoffmann of the Erlangen School, and Carl A. Auberlen, advocated millennial ideas.[111] Does this, however, change the shaky scriptural basis for these ideas? Many Christians are looking for a visible sign of the proleptic anticipation of the goal they hope for. It is also tempting for many to identify the results of their eschatological life attitude with the fulfillment they are promised to reach in the eschaton. But can we really expect Christ, who during his life on earth rejected vehemently all nationalistic and political messianic aspirations, to establish a transitory kingdom of God on earth as millennial thinking requires? Millennialism can be considered a concession to our own human impatience, since it shows a fervent yearning for a visible progress of God's redemptive action. But it is void of any significance for our salvation because it contradicts what Jesus stood for, a kingdom that is neither of nor in this world.

NOTES

1. Cf. Wolfgang Trillhaas, *Dogmatik* (Berlin: Töpelmann, 1962) 454ff., who describes and evaluates what he calls "the four eschatological heresies."
2. Cf. Joachim Jeremias, *The Parables of Jesus*, 51ff., who regards v. 13 as "one of those hortatory additions." In other words, this verse reflects the thinking of the first Christian community.
3. *D. Martin Luthers Werke. Kritische Gesamtausgabe* (Weimar, 1883-), LIII, 171 (This edition is hereafter referred to as WA, followed by the volume number in Roman numerals, and the page(s) and line(s) numbers in Arabic numerals; cf. WA [volume] XV, [page] 121, [lines] 10-14).
4. WA TR III, 645, 1ff. [*TR* stands for the table talks of Luther.]
5. Hal Lindsey with C. C. Carlson, *The Late Great Planet Earth* (Grand Rapids: Zondervan, 1970) 144.
6. Ibid., 153-54.
7. Ibid., 158 and 160.
8. Ibid., 161.
9. Ibid., 162.
10. Ibid., 164.
11. Ibid., 168.
12. Cf. the book by T. Boersma, *Is the Bible a Jigsaw Puzzle . . . An Evaluation of Hal Lindsey's Writings* (St. Catharines, Ontario; Paideia, 1978) 186, who rightly claims that Lindsey's views about the end times are too speculative.
13. John A. Hardon, *The Catholic Catechism. A Contemporary Catechism of the Catholic Church* (Garden City, N.J.: Doubleday, 1975) 273f.
14. Cf. for the following *The Second Book of Maccabees*, ed. with an intr. and commentary by Solomon Zeitlin, trans. by Sidney Tedesche (New York: Harper & Row, 1954) 84f.
15. Augustine, *The City of God* (8.27), vol. 14 of *The Fathers of the Church; A New Translation*, ed. by R. J. Deferrari (New York: Fathers of the Church, 1952) 75.
16. According to Zeitlin, *The Second Book of Maccabees*, 85.
17. Tertullian *On Monogamy* 10, vol. 4 of *The Anti-Nicene Fathers; Translations of the Writings of the Fathers down to A.D. 325*, ed. by A. Roberts and J. Donaldson (Grand Rapids: Eerdmans, 1951) 67.
18. Augustine *Confessions* 9.11, vol. 21 of *The Fathers of the Church; A New Translation*, 254.
19. "Errors of Martin Luther" No. 37, in Heinrich Denzinger, *The Sources of Catholic Dogma*, trans. by R. J. Deferrari (St. Louis: Herder, 1957) 242, (777). Since the translation by Deferrari is at times unreliable all references to and quotes from this source book have been compared with Denzinger's original text, *Enchiridion Symbolorum*, 34th ed. revised by Adolf Schönmetzer (Barcelona: Herder, 1967). Whenever necessary we have corrected the translation without notice. The numbers in parentheses, e.g. (777) refer to the *Enchiridion*.
20. "Decree Concerning Purgatory," in Denzinger, *Sources*, 298 (983).

21. Ludwig Ott, *Fundamentals of Catholic Dogma,* ed. by J. C. Bastible, trans. by P. Lynch (Cork, Ireland: Mercier, 1963), 483-484.
22. Karl Rahner, *Foundation of Christian Faith. An Introduction to the Idea of Christianity,* trans. by W. V. Dych (New York: Seabury, 1978) 442.
23. Cf. Augustine *The Care to Be Taken for the Dead* 1.3, in vol. 27 of *The Fathers of the Church; A New Translation,* 353.
24. Cf. Augustine *Faith, Hope and Charity* 29.110, in vol. 4 of *The Fathers of the Church; A New Translation,* 461f.
25. Cf. St. Gregory the Great *Dialogues* 4.57-62, vol. 39 of *The Fathers of the Church; A New Translation,* 266-275.
26. Cf. Reinhold Seeberg, *Text-Book of the History of Doctrines,* trans. by Ch. E. Hay (Grand Rapids: Baker 1958), 2:41ff. Cf. also the very instructive essay by Karl Rahner, "Remarks on the Theology of Indulgences," in *Theological Investigations,* vol. 2: *Man in the Church,* trans. by K.-H. Kruger (Baltimore: Helicon, 1963) 175-201. After a good historical and dogmatic review Rahner comes to the conclusion that indulgences should not be found only in textbooks but also in the practical life of the faithful (201).
27. *Lateran Council V (1512-1517),* in Denzinger, *Sources,* 239 (740a; my translation).
28. *Council of Lyons II (1274),* in Denzinger, *Sources,* 184 (464).
29. Cf. John Calvin, *Institutes of the Christian Religion* (3.5-6), ed. by John T. McNeill and trans. by F. L. Battles, vol. 20 of *The Library of Christian Classics* (Philadelphia: Westminster, 1960) 676.
30. Martin Luther, *Disputation on the Declaration of the Virtue of Indulgences,* in WA I, 233, 18f.
31. Martin Luther, *Resolutions on the Disputation about the Virtue of Indulgences,* in WA I, 555, 36.
32. Martin Luther, *Widerruf vom Fegfeuer,* in WA XXX/2, 360-390.
33. Martin Luther, *The Smalcald Articles,* in *The Book of Concord: The Confessions of the Evangelical Lutheran Church,* trans. and ed. by Theodore G. Tappert (Philadelphia: Muhlenberg, 1959) 295.
34. Roland H. Bainton, *Here I Stand* (New York: Abingdon, 1950) 78.
35. Rahner, "Remarks on the Theology of Indulgences," 200f., expresses this very clearly: "An indulgence is the sacramental of the remission of sin's temporal punishment before God, and this in conjunction with a jurisdictional remission of an (at least hypothetically) imposed ecclesiastical penance. Being a sacramental, it operates *ex opere operantis (orantis) Ecclesia,* and not *ex opera operato"* . . . "even although, for historical reasons, it is connected with a jurisdictional act of the Church which is concerned with the remission of an ecclesiastical penance and produces a sure effect in this regard." Rahner advances here a much more tenable position, not only by moving away from the jurisdictionally and mechanically misunderstood idea of relying on the Treasury of the Church (199), but in referring to the prayers of the church. Indulgence thus could be understood as relying on God's gracious response to the intercessory prayer of the church and of individuals. Yet talking about indulgence as a sacramental raises further questions.
36. This becomes very evident when Rahner, "The Life of the Dead," in *Theological Investigations,* trans. by K. Smyth (Baltimore: Helicon, 1966), vol. 4: *More Recent Writings,* 353, asserts that "the many dimensions of man do not all attain their perfection simultaneously and hence that there is a full ripening of the whole man 'after' death, as this basic decision penetrates the whole extent of his reality." Though our basic determination does not change, our life comes to maturity. As we shall see, a similar idea of human growth after death has also been advanced by Schleiermacher.

37. Of course, we do not want to imply that the Roman Catholic doctrine of purgatory advocates a basic open-endedness of ambiguity of human destiny after death. The basic structure of human destiny is already definitely decided upon as a result of this life. Yet the "details" are to be worked out, since we are still maturing, even beyond death.

38. Friedrich Schleiermacher, *The Christian Faith,* ed. by H. R. Mackintosh and J. S. Stewart (Edinburgh: T. & T. Clark, 1960) 549.

39. Ibid., 703.

40. Robert W. Gleason, *The World to Come* (New York: Sheed & Ward, 1958) 100.

41. Maurice and Louis Becqué, *Life After Death,* trans. by P. J. Hepburne-Scott, vol. 28 of *Twentieth Century Encyclopedia of Catholicism* (New York: Hawthorn, 1960) 111.

42. Ibid., 112.

43. For this and the following quotations see Karl Rahner, *Foundations of Christian Faith,* 442.

44. Cf. Ladislaus Boros, *The Mystery of Death* (New York: Herder and Herder, 1965) 129.

45. Ibid., 139 and n. 93.

46. Ibid., 109f.

47. Ibid., 84.

48. Ibid., 169.

49. Ibid., 165.

50. Though Boros never explicitly advocates a universal homecoming, his "salvific" view of death points in this direction.

51. Cf. Plato *Phaedrus* 247c ff., in *The Collected Dialogues of Plato Including the Letters,* ed. by Edith Hamilton and Hundington Cairns (New York: Bollingen Foundation, 1961) 494.

52. Origen, *On First Principles: Being Koetschau's Text of De Principiis,* trans. together with an intr. by G. W. Butterworth, intr. to the Torchbook ed. by Henri de Lubac (New York: Harper Torchbook, 1966) 53.

53. Ibid. 52.

54. Ibid., 57.

55. Ibid., 247.

56. Ibid., 248.

57. Ibid., 249f.

58. Ibid., 52. This assertion might, perhaps, reflect more the opinion of the translator (Rufinus) than that of Origen.

59. Heinrich Denzinger, *The Sources of Catholic Dogma,* 84 and 88 (403-411 and 433).

60. *The Augsburg Confession* (17), in *The Book of Concord,* 38.

61. Schleiermacher, *The Christian Faith,* 547.

62. Ibid., 548.

63. Ibid., 716.

64. Ibid., 722.

65. Paul Tillich, *Systematic Theology* (Chicago: University of Chicago Press, 1963), vol. 3: *Life and the Spirit, History and the Kingdom of God,* 418.

66. Ibid.

67. Ibid., 415.

68. Ibid., 409.

69. Ibid., 416.

70. Ibid., 408.

71. Ibid. Of course, we notice in Tillich's last example that his understanding of God as the all-embracing (monistic) power endangers the New Testament emphasis on the anti-Godly and not just non-Godly reality of evil.

72. Ibid., 401.
73. Ibid., 407.
74. Walter Künneth, *The Theology of the Resurrection*, 291.
75. Cf. Paul Althaus, *Die christliche Wahrheit: Lehrbuch der Dogmatik*, 6th ed. (Gütersloh: Gerd Mohn, 1959), 671.
76. To the issues of sanctification of the unbelieving partner in a "mixed marriage" and "vicarious baptism" cf. Hans Conzelmann, *A Commentary on the First Epistle to the Corinthians*, trans. by J. W. Leitch (Philadelphia: Fortress, 1975), in his comments on the passages cited.
77. This is also admitted by Werner Bieder in his careful study *Die Vorstellung von der Höllenfahrt Jesu Christi; Beitrag zur Entstehungsgeschichte der Vorstellung vom sog. Descensus ad inferos* (Zürich: Zwingli Verlag, 1949), though he says that the way in which the descent into hell is referred to in the Creed lacks scriptural foundation (129).
78. Bieder, 202, mentions correctly that two factors contributed decisively to the development of the idea of Christ's descent: the postmortal concern for the destiny of those who had died in Israel prior to the Christ event, and the missionary concern of introducing a victorious Christ to the Gentiles.
79. Cf. Hans Schwarz, "Luther's Understanding of Heaven and Hell," in *Interpreting Luther's Legacy*, ed. by Fred W. Meuser and Stanley D. Schneider (Minneapolis: Augsburg, 1969) 92f.
80. The issue whether Jesus had died according to his divinity and his humanity, or only according to his human form, was evidently not yet reflected on at that time. The development of the idea of Christ's descent was also furthered by influences from other religions and from Jewish apocalyptic literature (e.g. Enoch!). Cf. for the issue of outside influences, Bieder, 100ff., 203ff., and other places.
81. Cf. Ignatius *Letter to the Magnesians* 9:2, in vol. 4 of *The Apostolic Fathers; A New Translation and Commentary*, ed. by Robert M. Grant, (London: Nelson 1966) 63, who claims that the prophets were disciples in the spirit and were raised by Christ from the dead. Cf. also Melito of Sardis, *Homily on the Passion* (101f.), in *The Homily of the Passion by Melito Bishop of Sardis*, ed. by Campbell Bonner, vol. 12 of *Studies and Documents*, ed. by Kirsopp and Silva Lake (London: Christophers, 1940) 180.
82. Cf. Denzinger, *Enchiridium Symbolorum*, 23 (16); and cf. also J. N. D. Kelly, *Early Christian Creeds* (London: Longmans, Green, 1950) 378f.
83. Cf. Regin Prenter, *Creation and Redemption*, trans. by Th. I. Jensen (Philadelphia: Fortress, 1967) 573f.
84. So also Wolfgang Trillhaas, *Dogmatik*, 460, who observes that the problems involved in the doctrine of *apokatastasis* cannot be solved theoretically.
85. WA X/3, 409, 9ff.; and Althaus, *Die christliche Wahrheit*, 673, who quotes this passage from Luther.
86. Though Eusebius rejects the idea of millennialism as advocated by others (cf. Eusebius Pamphili *Ecclesiastical History* 3.28 and 3.39, vol. 19 of *The Fathers of the Church: A New Translation*, 185 and 205f.), he describes the new era under Constantine with the same "millennial" imagery though not using the actual term millennium (cf. *Ecclesiastical History* 10.4, vol. 29 of op. cit., esp. 260ff.).
87. For Joachim of Fiore cf. especially the excellent description and evaluation by Löwith, *Meaning in History*, 145ff., and Benz, *Evolution and Christian Hope*, 35ff.
88. Bloch, *Das Prinzip Hoffnung*, 2:590.
89. Ibid., 592.
90. Ibid., 597.
91. Ibid., 596.

92. Though Joachim's thoughts had an unmistakably revolutionary character (cf. Benz, 42), Gerhard Sauter rightly cautions us against Bloch's interpretation of Joachim. The anti-clerical and political-revolutionary impulses of Joachim were less direct than Bloch assumes. Cf. Sauter, *Zukunft und Verheissung*, 331.
93. Bloch, *Das Prinzip Hoffnung*, 2:592.
94. Cf. the extensive biography by Walter Elliger, *Thomas Müntzer. Leben und Werk*, 3rd ed. (Göttingen: Vandenhoeck & Ruprecht, 1976) 444f.
95. Cf. Letter of "Müntzer an den Schösser Hans Zeiss, Allstedt, 1523 Dez. 2," in Thomas Müntzer, *Schriften und Briefe: Kritische Gesamtausgabe*, ed. by Günther Franz in collaboration with Paul Kirn (Gütersloh: Mohn, 1968) 398. Cf. also Bloch, 593f. When Müntzer mentions here that he has read Joachim's Commentary on Jeremiah, then this is based on a misunderstanding. The Commentary on Jeremiah was a pseudo-Joachimite document, printed in Venice in 1516 (cf. Müntzer, 398 n. 6). This shows us what popularity Joachim enjoyed in the 16th century.
96. *The Augsburg Confession* (XVII), in *The Book of Concord*, 38f.
97. Gotthold Ephraim Lessing, *The Education of the Human Race* (86-89), in *Lessing's Theological Writings;* Selections trans. with an intr. by Henry Chadwick (Stanford: Stanford University Press, 1967) 96f. Though not mentioning Joachim explicitly, he refers to some of the enthusiasts of the 13th and 14th centuries, who, according to Lessing, have perhaps caught a glimpse of this "new eternal gospel," and only erred in predicting its arrival as so near to their own time.
98. Karl Marx and Friedrich Engels, *Historisch-Kritische Gesamtausgabe*, (Frankfurt am Main: Marx-Engels-Archiv, 1927, I/2) 225f.; quoted in Bloch, 598.
99. Cf. Löwith, 159. It seems strange that in describing Joachim and his idea of the Third *Reich*, Bloch passes over Hitler and his utopian dreams with silence. Should this indicate that Hitler's program cannot be integrated into a "principle of hope"?
100. Anthony A. Hoekema, *The Four Major Cults: Christian Science, Jehovah's Witnesses, Mormonism, Seventh-day Adventism* (Grand Rapids, Mich.: Eerdmans, 1963) 224f.
101. Ibid., 137.
102. Edward D. Andrews, *The People Called Shakers: A Search for the Perfect Society* (New York: Oxford University Press, 1953).
103. Robert A. Parker, *A Yankee Saint: John Humphrey Noyes and the Oneida Community* (New York: Putnam 1935) 17f.
104. *Eschatology: The Doctrine of the Last Things. Twelve Theses and a Position Paper Adopted by the 118th General Assembly for Guidance and Study in the Church* (Atlanta, Ga.: Presbyterian Church in the United States, 1978) 12f. Another helpful and concise summary and critique of millennial ideas is given by Ted Peters, *Futures —Human and Divine*, 28-36. An extensive and careful treatment of millennialism is also given by Anthony A. Hoekema, *The Bible and the Future* (Grand Rapids, Mich.: Eerdmans, 1979), esp. 173-238.
105. John F. Walvoord, *The Rapture Question* (Grand Rapids, Mich.: Zondervan, 1957) 8.
106. Ibid., 198.
107. Cf. the informed study by Harold H. Rowdon, *The Origin of the Brethren. 1825-1850* (London: Pickering & Inglis, 1967) 97.
108. Cf. Lewis Sperry Chafer, *Systematic Theology*, vol. 4: *Ecclesiology—Eschatology* (Dallas: Dallas Seminary Press, 1948) 374-378.
109. Cf. C. Vanderwaal, *Hal Lindsey and Biblical Prophecy* (St. Catharines, Ontario: Paideia, 1978) 26-47, who gives a good introduction to the problematic nature of dispensationalism and Hal Lindsey's connection with this doctrine.
110. So rightly Dale Moody, "Rapture," *Encyclopedia of Southern Baptists*, 2:1133.
111. Cf. Paul Althaus, in his still unsurpassed treatment of eschatology: *Die letzten Dinge: Lehrbuch der Eschatologie*, 7th ed. (Gütersloh: Bertelsmann, 1957) 303ff.

7
Death and Beyond

AS WE NOW VENTURE TO OUTLINE the positive side of what we can hope for, we must guard ourselves against two frequent temptations, undue restraint and a travelog eschatology. Undue restraint would be represented by a position which asserts that all we can say about life beyond death is that God who was good to me in life will also be good to me in death. Though this statement reflects part of the biblical message, it does not reflect biblical theology in its attempt to render the Christian hope in its entirety. At key points the New Testament talks about a hope which is enabled and characterized by terms such as resurrection, new creation, heaven and hell, parousia, and judgment. Regardless of how we interpret these terms we have to interpret them and cannot pass over them in silence and at the same time claim to be scriptural.

Yet, in interpreting these terms we cannot succumb to the temptation of a travelog eschatology. As far as we can reconstruct Jesus' proclamation, it was essentially a proclamation that enables us to reach the eschaton. But Jesus did not give us an eschatological timetable so that we are sure when the Son of man will return, nor did he paint the eschaton in daring and vivid colors, as for instance Mohammed did for his followers in the Koran. With the exception of the book of Revelation the New Testament shared this restraint with Jesus. This is in remarkable contrast to the exuberant speculation of the apocalyptic literature of the Old and New Testament period. The fact that the church did not accept a Book of Enoch or an Apocalypse of Paul into the biblical canon and that even someone like Luther had serious doubts about the right of the Revelation to be in the canon,[1] should caution us when we want to indulge in a travelog eschatology.

Nevertheless, we have to make assertions about the eschaton. To talk here only about symbols[2] would endanger the depth of these assertions

195

and would place them in the same category with such metaphoric terms as "the symbols of Christmas," or "the symbols of peace." We are inclined rather to follow a suggestion of Rudolf Bultmann in his noteworthy essay "What Does It Mean to Speak of God?"[3] There he asserts that to talk *about* God is a sinful and blasphemous attempt, since it presupposes that we are on equal ground with him. We can only talk about something which is on the same level as we are, such as another person, or an animal, or a beautiful scene. In making assertions concerning God we can only talk *from* God, i.e., in repeating what God has spoken to us. This reutterance of God's self-disclosure (in Jesus Christ), however, is not done in divine vocabulary (since we don't have any) but with our conceptual tools. Since God has come to us in the humanity of Jesus, we can talk from God as if he were one of us, though knowing that ultimately he is not. Bultmann concludes that even the attempt of talking *from God* is ultimately a (necessarily) sinful attempt.

Applying this to eschatology, neither the conceptual tools of the biblical witnesses nor our 20th century categories can adequately "describe" the eschaton. Our assertions, even if they are the most profound reflections on God's self-disclosure in Jesus Christ, are by necessity only inadequate approximations of what the eschaton is all about. These limitations, however, do not release us from the necessity of searching for the most appropriate approximations in our time. If we are not constantly reconceptualizing the biblical reflections on God's self-disclosure, we not only speak in ancient tongues, but we misrepresent God's word, which is a word for our time and a pointer to our future.

1. Death

In starting with the understanding of death, however, we are not yet faced with the dilemma of language. Death still pertains to this world, as the end of our life here on earth. The question that we face here more and more frequently is: "When does death set in?" or "What actually is death?" An answer to these questions is the more necessary because the "life" prolonging techniques of modern medicine sometimes make the length of a patient's life almost a matter of the relatives' or the patient's finances or of someone "pulling the plug."

a. The ambiguity of death

The verdict of clinical death is traditionally based on the following criteria: the absence of peripheral pulse and heart beat, the absence of respiration, the lack of eye reflex, and the presence of a bluish color that results from a lack of oxygen in the blood.[4] With our constantly increasing medical skills doctors can bring about and sustain the absence of these criteria even when the absence of these criteria could never be sustained by the patient himself. Does this mean that in certain cases they are keeping "alive" dead corpses? [5] To reach an adequate definition of death we have to get away from the merely biological (or technological?) side of death and start with a definition of life itself.

Life, as we experience it, is our active participation in the ongoing processes of our environment. Of course, this participation can vary extremely according to our possibilities, and it is expressed differently by a university professor in his best years than by a youngster with multiple sclerosis and an IQ of 70. Dying would then mean the decline of this participation. It is not confined to terminal illness but accompanies the whole aging process of the individual.[6] Death is then the irreversible cessation of this active participation. With such an understanding of death we would free ourselves from the strictly biological understanding and, at the same time, we could extend a helping hand to physicians. We could suggest to them that they might let our biological side rest too if they cannot regain for us this state of active participation.[7]

One can always debate at what point this loss of active participation occurs; this in turn opens the question of what active participation means. For instance, the famous Harvard definition of an irreversible coma, a state of profound unconsciousness that cannot be reversed, centers on the functioning of the brain. But it is stated at the outset that the first problem is to determine the characteristics of a permanently nonfunctioning brain.[8] Among the criteria listed are total unawareness and unresponsiveness to externally applied stimuli and inner need, no movements or breathing, no reflexes, and a flat electroencephalogram. If these criteria are met for a certain period of time we may conclude that a person is clinically dead.

If we had to wait until all of these criteria were met before we could pronounce someone dead, we might still inflict a dehumanizing treatment on the patients prior to their "death." Thus the issue of euthanasia, or "death with dignity," emerges as a consequence of both our increasing ability to determine the exact point of death and our medical advancements that allow us to interfere more and more with the process of dying. Two problems arise, however:

(1) There is no good death, as the term euthanasia (meaning "good death" in Greek) presupposes. Death is always ambiguous; it can be a release from suffering but is at the same time the loss of life.

(2) The idea of a natural death that is presupposed in the claim of "death with dignity" is a fiction as far as its biological and physiological aspects are concerned.[9]

All forms of biological death have a cause, and that cause is potentially susceptible to description and control, or at least to modification. It is agonizing to realize, but every case of death, along with the suffering that accompanies it, is the result of some human choice and therefore something for which we must assume responsibility.

While we cannot touch here upon all the ethical issues involved in euthanasia, we must mention at least two extreme positions that are not acceptable for us. If God is the giver of all life, we must treat life as a gift entrusted to our care. Therefore we cannot concede that it is proper to deliberately terminate life in case of terminal illness (i.e., active euthanasia), as suggested in the Voluntary Euthanasia Act of 1969, submitted for consideration in the British Parliament.[10] Such action would imply a disrespect for God's gift of life, a gift that we should treasure until it is taken away. Yet to hang on to life and preserve it at all costs shows a basic selfishness, since the measures needed to do that cannot be afforded to everyone. It also indicates the misunderstanding that this present life is all that there is to our existence. Thus we cannot opt for preserving life at all costs.

But with every meal we eat to sustain ourselves and with every pill we take to alleviate pain we prolong not only life but also the dying process. Life and death are too intricately connected to allow a simple answer as to the right point of letting life go. Legislation concerning euthanasia and "death with dignity" will be able to establish boundaries within which we must assume responsibility for life and death. Even a living will that asks that no heroic measures be taken (i.e. measures that do not promise reasonable benefits and cannot be administered without excessive cost, pain, and considerable inconvenience) in case of terminal illness, is unable to remove the ambiguity and the agony of making decisions about life and death. Yet our actions should always be guided by the knowledge that in all its forms life is a precious gift that we dare not corrupt either by the selfishness of unduly hanging on or by its willful abolition. Rather, life should be enhanced through growth and maturation.[11] When life has become totally dependent on others for sustenance, when it can no longer, even in the foreseeable future, contribute to the sustenance of others, e.g., through signs of joy or compassion, very likely life has run its course, and then we may also allow the body to come to rest.

If we do not restrict death to the cessation of life, we must also affirm that death is a necessary companion of life and its actual presupposition. Especially Karl Heim has pointed out with convincing clarity that life can only be sustained if someone or something else dies. There is a great chain of being in which one form of life depends on the other for growth and sustenance. For instance, humans eat meat and vegetables, cattle eat grass, and grass dissolves chemicals to survive, to live, and to grow. But death is even more central to life; it starts already with conception. The sperm dies after the egg has been fertilized and the egg cell in turn dies to permit the growth and division process of the cells. All cells are constantly being replaced by new ones and, by the time we die, even without artificial dentures or a wig, there is hardly anything original left. The biological phenomena of aging and decay are shared by the whole creation and we are no exception. Yet the whole life stream gives the impression that it wants to escape death. Charles Darwin, with his concept of the struggle for existence, seems to substantiate this observation, and the French philosopher Henri Bergson even spoke of an *élan vital,* an original life force, that pervades all nature. Small wonder that Teilhard de Chardin claimed in consequence that the stream of life will evolve further and further and cannot be stopped by the law of entropy.[12] But this evolutionary struggle is not a sign of victory over death; it is an attempt to escape from the all-pervading power of death.

Yet we are not just caught in the death-escaping, though death-determined process of life. We are the only living beings on our earth who have an actual death-awareness.[13] Knowing about death we live our lives, and knowing about death as the irrevocable, unconditioned, and ultimate end of our individual lives we face death. Our reflections, feelings, and actions are accompanied by our knowlege of death, whether we suppress it or enhance it. Knowing about our finality and limitation need not lead to pessimism; we can live a fulfilled and satisfied life and die at a good old age, full of years (Gen. 25:8). We can even long for an end of this struggle here on earth and be glad that this life need not be continued forever. Yet death can also strike in the middle of life, and an unfulfilled life can suddenly be terminated. Then we encounter death as bitterness, as an enemy we want to escape, though knowing that there is no ultimate escape.

The immense publicity that the first heart transplants received witnesses indirectly to our desire to prolong life and to escape from death. We encounter death as a contradiction to our human nature, because it destroys everything that pertains to us. Thus we want to memorialize ourselves in our children, through charities, or through products of our mind. And when an idealistic philosopher exclaims that: "It is impossible to conceive that Nature should annihilate a life which does not proceed from her;—the Nature which exists for me and not I for her," [14] he cannot convince us that he has found a remedy for death. He only helps us to confirm that the biological naturalness and necessity of death is something extremely unnatural; it is an "ought not."

The Swiss-born psychiatrist, Elisabeth Kübler-Ross, brings our death-denying attitude into focus when she proposes five discrete stages through which each dying person will go:[15]

(1) *Denial and isolation:* Denial, Kübler-Ross claims, is used by almost all patients. It functions as a buffer after the unexpected shocking news of terminal illness and allows the patients to collect themselves and, in time, mobilize other, less radical defenses. "Since in our unconscious mind we are all immortal, it is almost inconceivable for us to acknowledge that we too have to face death." [16] Thus we deny the news of impending death and withdraw from the world. Yet sooner or later another method of defense sets in.

(2) *Anger:* When "the first stage of denial cannot be maintained any longer, it is replaced by feelings of anger, rage, envy, and resentment." [17] Often the hospital personnel or the person's relatives are the targets of anger.

(3) *Bargaining:* This stage is again an attempt to postpone the inevitable death. One bargains with God or with the doctors in a vain attempt to be granted extension of one's life span.

(4) *Depression:* Finally, we come to the stage of depression. It sets in when we can no longer pretend that the symptoms of on-coming death will disappear, and when we become more and more incapacitated. Numbness and stoicism, anger and rage, are now replaced with a sense of great loss. What has been so dear to us on earth—our shapely figure, our travel plans, or our financial security —is now taken away from us. We realize that our this-worldly dreams will not come true. We are in the process of losing every-

thing and everyone we have. When we have passed through this stage, through denial, grief, and anger, we finally reach what Kübler-Ross describes as the fifth stage.

(5) *Acceptance:* Kübler-Ross cautions us that this should not be construed as a happy stage. "It is almost void of feelings. It is as if the pain had gone, the struggle is over, and there comes a time for 'the final rest before the long journey' as one patient phrased it." [18] It is a gradual weaning away from life with longer and longer periods of sleep, similar to a newborn child but in reverse order.

Not all of these stages are always clearly discernible, and some may be more pronounced than others or may be simply skipped. Kübler-Ross has also made her observations mainly with terminally-ill hospital patients, but not with accident victims who die a sudden death, or with people who simply die of "old age." But two items are most significant for us in Kübler-Ross' analysis: (1) When we look at the five stages she has listed, we notice that four out of the five stages deny our mortality. We seem to fight until the last moment. Kübler-Ross also notes how oblivious we are to death, and that when we have faced up to our finitude we live a different quality of life.[19] Much more startling, however, is another insight. (2) Kübler-Ross confesses: "Working with dying patients over many years has made me much more religious than I have ever been. . . . Before I started working with dying patients, I did not believe in a life after death. I now do believe in a life after death, beyond a shadow of a doubt." [20]

Elisabeth Kübler-Ross has observed many terminally ill people die and has attempted to describe the various stages these people go through. We should wonder why in a research preoccupied with death she does not give up the notion of life after death, but instead discovers it to have immense validity. We could surmise that a defense mechanism against admitting her own mortality has been operative, inducing in her the strong notion of life after death. But could her newly-found belief in life after death not also have resulted from the conclusion that this life, especially as it shows itself in its final stages, cannot be all that is to one's existence? At least we should be open to this possibility.

Moving from the biological ambiguity of death to an understanding of death in the context of the Judeo-Christian tradition, at first glance we do not get a very reassuring answer because death is conceived there as our way to the eschaton.

b. Death as our way to the eschaton

According to the biblical witnesses, death is not just something unnatural. It is primarily and first of all a constructive factor of God's creation and belongs to the fundamental orders of God.[21] This is nowhere
better expressed than in Psalm 90, where the Psalmist says: "The years of
our life are threescore and ten, or even by reason of strength fourscore;
yet their span is but toil and trouble; they are soon gone, and we fly
away" (Ps. 90:10). Death shows us our creatureliness, i.e., our distance
from and our dependence on God. He alone is immortal (1 Tim. 6:16),
while everyone and everything else is subjected to mortality. There is an
insurmountable, dimensional border between us finite beings and God's
infinity. Paul states this in a metaphorical way: " 'The first man Adam
became a living being;' the last Adam became a life-giving spirit" (1 Cor.
15:45).

At the very moment humanity emerged it received its life from God
and we became living beings. Only Christ, being true God, was not only
a living but a life-giving being. In knowing about the finitude of our
life and in knowing about death as our ultimate end, we know about
ourselves as human, as being created and not the creator. Realizing this
decisive difference between the creator and the created, there also emerges
fear before the creator, who cannot only give and protect life but can
also take it away. Even a king can cry to God that he may not take his
life away from him (Isa. 38:9-20).

Death gives each moment of our life its singularity; we cannot repeat
one act of our life. Unceasingly and unresistingly we are on our way
to the eschaton. Whether we want it or not, whether we realize it or not,
we exist truly eschatologically, since the potential presence of the eschaton at any moment of our life gives our life its peculiarity. Even love
has to be seen under this aspect of death, since love is essentially giving
away part of oneself to another person or persons. This means that we
irretrievably give away part of our life and die a little more each time
we extend our love. Thus love is sacrifice of our life. But it would be
totally wrong to understand this kind of voluntary sacrifice as a heroic
deed. Giving away life is only possible because we received it in the first
place.

Dying is primarily suffering; it is losing what we have received.
Though we naturally would rather keep what we have received and not
lose it, we know too that our life, because it is creaturely life, does not

contain a divine quality that could lead to a union with God. It is a sign of the goodness of creation that we are able to die and thus cease being dimensionally separated from our creator. Already Jesus reminded us that we can gain real life only in the eschatological fulfillment beyond this present life: "For whoever would save his life will lose it; and whoever loses his life for my sake and the gospel's will save it" (Mark 8:35).

Death does not just show us the dimensional difference between God and ourselves and our dependence on God's life-giving power. Death also discloses God's opposition to us sinful people. We encounter death not only as the inescapable end of our life but as God's "no" to the way we conduct our life, to our continuous sinful alienation from God. The singularity of every moment of our life is finalized in death, and our total life with all its omissions, failures, and commissions becomes irreversible. In death we are immediately confronted with God, who holds us responsible for our actions and makes us accountable for our doings. Death also shows us that our life is not of eternal value. God regards the way we live our life here on earth as unworthy to be preserved, and he rejects its anti-Godly character.

It would be shortsighted to conclude that biological death can be inferred from sin and fall, as if there had been a time when death did not prevail. But Western theologians from Augustine onward taught that humanity had once been in an integer or original state, where it had the possibility of not sinning and consequently of not dying.[22] Death, sorrow, and pain came into the world through human sinfulness.[23] Only those outside the confines of orthodox faith dared to assert that the first human couple would have died whether they had sinned or not.[24] Fortunately, most contemporary theologians refrain from speculations about a premortal original state of humanity.[25]

The idea of a pre-mortal state would bring us into deep conflict with the clear findings of paleontology which shows that biological death already prevailed for millions of years before humanity emerged. Furthermore, we would miss the essential task of theology, which is not to indulge in vague metaphysical speculations founded on a narrow biblical basis, but to interpret our present reality by relating it to God's will, a will to which our present situation witnesses. Thus when Paul stated that "the wages of sin is death" (Rom. 6:23), or that "sin came into the world through one man and death through sin, and so death spread to all men because all men sinned" (Rom. 5:12), he did not merely intend to talk about a single individual who lived long ago and whose sinful action had cosmic significance. He wanted to talk about the emergence of the age of death (not just in a biological way). This age has its head in Adam, who is the antitype to Christ, the head of the age of life, the new aeon.[26] Unlike animals, we no longer experience the fear of a merely biological death. Knowing about our sinfulness, our alienation from God, and our shortcomings, we encounter death as the final irreversible termination in which these distortions of life can no longer be patched up or concealed. Fear of death becomes fear of judgment, fear of this final inescapable confrontation with the God who is not only our creator but also our judge.

But judgment is not the final word of God. Luther, for instance, in following the biblical witnesses, talked about a threefold aspect of death.[27] There is first the biological death which entails the same result for humans as for a cow or an ox, namely natural decay of the physical body. Then there is the spiritual or eternal death of those who are condemned. This death normally coincides with the biological death and is for those who never accept God's grace. Finally, there is a kind of "death" where we actually overcome this spiritual or eternal death. This "death" takes place whenever we accept God as a gracious God. Since grace is also the good news, we wish to call this third aspect "death in the light of the gospel."

We have already mentioned that death can be seen under the aspect of grace, since it shows us that we are not forced to live our life here on earth forever. Being confronted with God's grace, we also notice that our life on earth is inexorably connected with sin. Thus death as the end of this life means the end of the possibility of sinning, the end of our shortcomings, and the end of our continuous estrangement from God. The gospel even indicates that this kind of death can already be anticipated proleptically before we encounter our biological death. Paul, for instance, emphasizes that in this life we should die to our sinful existence so that we can be resurrected with Christ. He even ventures to say that "we were buried therefore with him (Christ) by baptism into death, so that as Christ was raised from the dead by the glory of the Father, we too might walk in newness of life" (Rom. 6:4). Though this "baptismal death" initiates the process of dying, it never comes to an end in this life. We always deviate from our eschaton-directed life-style. Thus Luther pointed out in his *Small Catechism* that we must die daily according to our "old Adam" and be daily resurrected to newness of life.[28]

But death in the light of the gospel is not just anticipation of the escha-

tological fulfillment, as this "daily resurrection" might indicate. Anticipation as prolepsis always reminds us that there is still something to
come. Thus our daily dying points to a final fulfillment and perfection
beyond all anticipation. It also promises us that even biological death is
not a departure into nothingness but the removal of the dimensional
difference which separates us from the one who alone is immortal. We
can even venture to say that death is the precondition and the reverse
side of the resurrection. Therefore, death as judgment and condemnation
is not the final word of God, since God does not have "pleasure in the
death of the wicked, but that the wicked turn from his way and live"
(Ezek. 33:11). God wants our death only insofar as it leads to our final
fulfillment in the eschaton and to our real life.

Though not everybody admits that death is the reverse side of resurrection and the entrance to our fulfillment in the eschaton, most agree
that death is not the entrance to nothingness. Even those people who do
not claim to be religious usually affirm that death is not the ultimate
end of life. While the concepts of existence beyond death vary, it is
commonly accepted that we are not just mortal. Kübler-Ross, for instance,
concludes from her observation and research that there are only "very
few people who do not believe in some form of immortality." [29] There
is or must be some sort of immortality. But is such a belief tenable?

2. Immortality

Besides the fact that people express their desire for immortality through
cultural activities, through religious practice, and through the simple
assertion that death cannot be the end, there are three phenomena that
seem to substantiate the idea of immortality. Occultism and near-death
experiences seem to give the idea of immortality an experiential basis;
philosophy seems to provide for immortality a theoretical reference system; the biblical soul-body distinction seems to endow the idea of immortality with theological sanctification.

a. Immortality and occultism

Through the endeavors of the late Episcopal Bishop James A. Pike to
communicate with his deceased son, the idea of communication with the
beyond received new and wide-spread attention in the late 1960s. A
much older and classic example of the same type is found in the experiences of the Protestant Pastor John Frederic Oberlin (1740-1826) of

Alsace, France, who also was a pioneer of social involvement of the church. He claimed that he communicated with his deceased wife for 17 years until she informed him that she had to ascend to higher spheres. Even the Bible is free to admit this kind of occultism. King Saul in his despair over his future asked a medium at Endor to provide him with a chance to talk to Samuel, who had died a few years previously (1 Sam. 28). When Samuel appeared, Saul was able to recognize him, since he wore his usual gown and looked like an old man.

It is impossible to do away with the fact that human minds can extend themselves beyond the physical limitations of space, time, and matter.[30] Research in parapsychology has shown that, within certain limits, occult phenomena can no longer be doubted. But how should they be explained? When media are involved one can apply an animistic explanation and understand occult phenomena as resulting from subconscious powers of the media, or one can apply a spiritualistic explanation and understand occult phenomena as being caused by the activity of the souls of deceased people. Even if we concede the spiritualistic explanation of a communication from the beyond, what do we actually gain in our knowledge about the immortal state or soul? [31] The "spirits" tell us minute and exact details about events of long ago, and they tell us about family ties, but they are remarkably vague in their assertions concerning their own state. They do not allow us to get a glimpse of the beginning of the new state of existence; on the contrary, they dwell on irrelevant details of past events in this life.

The Bible concedes the possibility of establishing such a communication with the beyond, but with the same breath it rejects these practices as anti-Godly (Deut. 18:10ff.). It considers these practices as attempts to bypass God, who is the Lord on both sides of death. According to New Testament testimony our faith in the life beyond death is sustained not through our communication with the beyond, but through the one who was not consumed by death, Jesus Christ.

It is interesting to note that during the era of the enlightenment there was a great interest in the appearances of spirits and especially in Swedenborg's communications with the "spirits." The reason for this increased importance of spiritualism seems to be the fact that the Christian belief in life beyond death had become more and more uncertain in this rationally minded age.[32] Does the recent resurgence of spiritualism during this present second phase of the enlightenment indicate a similar decline in the Christian belief in life beyond death?

b. Immortality and near-death experiences

In recent years the idea of life after death has gained new attention through reports on dying patients who continue to have a conscious awareness of their environment after being pronounced clinically dead. If they make a comeback, totally against expectations of the medical personnel, they tell of experiences that are strikingly similar: "A floating out of their physical bodies, associated with a great sense of peace and wholeness. Most were aware of another person who helped them in their transition to another plane of existence. Most were greeted by loved ones who had died before them, or by a religious figure which was significant in their life and which coincided, naturally, with their own religious beliefs." [33]

The phenomena experienced in close encounters with death are not a current discovery. They are reported by Plato, especially in Book 10 of the *Republic*, in the *Tibetan Book of the Dead*, by the Venerable Bede in *A History of the English Church and People*, and by Sir Edward Burnett Tylor in *Primitive Culture*, to name a more recent writer.[34] Especially the American psychiatrist Raymond A. Moody, in his two seminal books, *Life after Life* (1976) and *Reflections on Life after Life* (1977), has systematically investigated reports on near-death experiences. He comes to the interesting conclusion that all these reports show a remarkable similarity, though none of them is precisely identical. People interviewed usually relate several of the following experiences:[35]

- Hearing their doctors or other spectators pronounce them dead;
- Extremely pleasant feelings and sensations during the early stages of their experiences;
- Unusual and often extremely unpleasant auditory sensations at or near death;
- The sensation of being pulled very rapidly through a dark space of some kind;
- Looking upon one's own physical body from a point outside of it and floating in a weightless spiritual body;
- Awareness of the presence of other spiritual beings in the vicinity;
- Glimpses of other beings who seemed to be "trapped" in an apparently most unfortunate state of being (i.e., limited consciousness, unable to surrender their attachments to the physical world, and apparently kept in that state until their problems are solved);
- Encounter with a bright light which at first is dim and rapidly gets

brighter until it reaches an unearthly brilliance and often is identified with Jesus Christ or an angel;

- Rapid panoramic review of one's life presented to the dying person
  by the light(-being);
- A flash of universal knowledge and insight into the nature of things;
- A vision of a city of light of some sorts; the approach to a border or
  limit of some kind;
- And the coming back into the physical body and to life and an initial
  regret about it.

Moody also relates that people report being saved from impending
death by a voice or light manifesting itself and rescuing them in a
"miraculous" way at the brink of death.[36] This means that these experiences are not just confined to instances in which persons have been somehow resuscitated after having been declared dead by a physician upon
the failure of initial resuscitation measures. They are also reported by
people who have simply been resuscitated once (e.g., after cardiac arrest),
or who have found themselves in a situation in which they could very
easily have been killed or have died, even though they have escaped
without injury.[37]

It is, of course, interesting to investigate whether those who were pronounced dead and subsequently regained consciousness had in fact been
dead. Moody contends that in many of these cases the testimony of physicians and the clinical records show that death, defined as the absence
of clinically detectable vital signs, had taken place.[38] Since all cases of
resuscitation involve a state of extreme clinical emergency, there was no
time to set up an electroencephalograph to measure brain wave activity.
And even an EEG reading does not always give the foolproof answer
to the issue of clinical death, since both overdoses of drugs which depress
the central nervous system and abnormally low body temperature can
also result in flat EEG tracings. Thus Moody concludes that these people
were clinically dead at least at the time when resuscitation was administered.

Since we have reports of near-death experiences from people who were
not resuscitated, the decisive issue is not whether people have returned
to life from death, but what kind of reality is reflected in their experiences. On a subjective level Moody reports that, although they were very
reticent to tell others about what had happened to them, the people who
had the experiences confessed that these phenomena had a profound im-

pact on their lives. They have become more reflective and more concerned with ultimate philosophical issues.[39] They have also acquired a different approach toward the physical life to which they returned. "Almost everyone has stressed the importance in this life of trying to cultivate love for others, a love of the unique and profound kind. . . . Many others have emphasized the importance of seeking knowledge."[40] But no one felt morally perfected or holier than others. Rather their vision "left them with new goals, new moral principles, and a renewed determination to try to live in accordance with them, but with no feeling of instantaneous salvation or of moral infallibility."[41] There was a new reverence for life and even those who had these experiences as the result of a suicide attempt mentioned that they would never consider trying suicide again.[42]

In attempting to evaluate that which is experienced in near-death phenomena, we must first note that Moody records his reports only from persons within the Judeo-Christian tradition.[43] Thus his working within a fairly homogeneous group of humanity may in part account for the similarity of the experiences (e.g., identification of the bright light with Christ or an angel). We must also note that Moody is not trying to prove that there is life after death, and that he is even convinced that *"within the context of science alone,* there may never be a proof of life after death."[44] He is concerned that these "near-death experiences not be perverted by using them as an excuse for a new cult," and he rightly mentions that they "are also similar in many respects to mystical and religious visions described by great seers in the past" (cf. Acts 7:54-58).[45]

In assessing these experiences Moody leaves open the possibility of conceiving of "near-death experiences either as intimations of immortality or merely as the result of terminal physiological events."[46] Thus we could conclude that in cases of extreme shock or anxiety, whether induced by oneself or by external circumstances, some or all of the described phenomenon can result. Such an explanation might account for these visions and experiences. But it would not answer the queries of physicians who reportedly "just can't understand how their patients could have described the things they did about the resuscitation efforts unless they really were hovering just below the ceiling."[47]

The difficulty in coming to terms with these phenomena may perhaps result from our conception of the mind or the psyche as too coextensive with the physical body. For instance, psychic research has amassed a plethora of data that seem to indicate that with certain people human knowledge can extend beyond the present in cases of precognition (the power of the mind to foretell certain events). It has also been attested many times that at the point of death loved ones "have said goodbye" to close relatives or friends in geographically distant regions by stopping a clock at the time of their death or by appearing in some kind of vision to these people.[48] In some cases the mind or the psyche evidently can extend itself far beyond the physical boundaries of the body. This could also be the case in near-death experiences.

We might even shed more light on these near-death experiences by considering the broader question. Sir John Eccles, Nobel laureate in medicine, has reminded us that the self-conscious mind effectively acts on the brain when we plan and carry out actions (voluntary movements) or when we try to recover a memory or solve a problem. He rightly claims: "There must be a partial independence of the self-conscious mind from the brain events with which it interacts." [49] Thus ultimately we are confronted with the issue of the origin and destiny of the self. Sir John ponders how "each of us as self-conscious being comes to exist as a unique self associated with a brain . . . [and] . . . what happens to the conscious self at brain death? . . . Is the self renewed in some other guise and existence? This is a problem beyond science, and scientists should refrain from giving definite negative answers." [50]

Perhaps we should not rule out the conclusion that occasionally (not all near-death encounters result in conscious experiences) and in highly unusual situations we obtain a glimpse of a larger whole of which we are part, whether the experiences be induced by the self or by external circumstances. Since each moment in our life is unique and non-repetitive, each near-death experience included, such experience cannot lead to the conclusion that we have finally proven our immortality. Rather it would make us appreciate more the transitory but precious and singular character of our present life, and it might also make us aware that our present existence is but a necessary prelude to a large entity—life eternal.

c. Immortality and philosophy

Another claim for immortality was brought forth by the founders of Western philosophy, by Plato and Aristotle. Many eminent theologians, such as Augustine, Thomas Aquinas, and John Calvin, accepted their body-soul dichotomy and taught the immortality of the soul. According to Plato the soul is invisible, immaterial, spiritual, and trans-earthly.[51] The demiurge, the creator of the world, created each human soul. This means that a human soul, though it is of the same being as the universal soul of the world, is not an emanation or part of this soul.[52] Humanity is a combination of body and soul.

Plato leaves no doubt that the soul is of prime importance. For the soul the body is only accidental, a vehicle it uses. The soul is the actual human being and the body is only a shadow. Plato even conceives of the body as the prison of the soul, as an evil which never permits the soul to attain the full measure of its intentions, namely to attain the truth.[53] But God will redeem the soul from its prison. Though Plato also talks about a soul of courage and a soul of desire, the soul in its actual sense is only the soul of reason or of spirit. Soul is not just spirit or consciousness; it is the principle of life.[54] The whole world is animated by the soul because, whether in humanity, or animals, or plants, wherever there is life, there is soul.

But why does Plato claim that the soul is immortal? According to Plato one reason for the immortality of the soul lies in its composition. Since the soul is invisible, immaterial, and indivisible, it cannot undergo change and be dissolved. It must be immortal. The other reason for its immortality lies in its content. The soul knows about the eternal ideas of truth, goodness, and beauty and longs to attain them. Since these ideas do not occur at any place within our world, they must be recollections of perceptions that the soul had prior to its present state, i.e., in its pre-existent state. If the soul is pre-existent, then the conclusion is unavoidable that it extends its existence also beyond death. Plato even assumes a cycle of rebirths and purifications until the soul attains union with the godly.

Aristotle largely follows Plato in his understanding of the soul.[55] In his early dialogues Aristotle advocates a Platonic dualism. Body and soul are only formally connected and act like two separate and hostile substances. Later Aristotle regards them as still independent but cooperative entities. And when he writes his *Physics* he conceives the soul as the energy of life that resides at a certain point in the body. Thus one can distinguish in all living beings between something that is moved (body) and something that causes the movements (soul). Finally in his treatise *On the Soul* he abandons this distinction and regards a person primarily as a unity. Body and soul are merged into a unity of substance in which body and soul pertain to the whole person.

In analogy to Plato, Aristotle also distinguishes between three souls, the soul which enables growth and procreation and which emerges in the realm of plants, the soul which enables sense-perception, desire, and movement and which emerges in the animal kingdom, and the soul of reason which is peculiar to humans and which makes one into a rational animal.[56] In spite of his own delineation of different "souls" he polemicizes against Plato that he does not emphasize enough the unity of the soul in a person.[57]

But Aristotle seems to be in a worse dilemma than Plato. Though emphasizing the one human soul "by or with which primarily we live, perceive, and think," [58] he asserts that the lower souls are passed on from father to child through procreation, while active reason enters from outside "through the door" and is of godly origin.[59] This means that the actual soul (soul of reason) is pre-existent and not created. Unlike the lower soul it does not cease to exist when the body dies but is immortal. Although Aristole asserted the immortality of this soul of reason, he did not attempt to prove it.

In his *Critique of Pure Reason* Immanuel Kant disproved the attempt to assert with certainty that there is something indivisible (e.g., a soul) in our world.[60] He also claimed that all our proofs can only pertain to the world of which we can conceive in the categories of space and time. Thus a proof of the existence of a soul is as impossible as a proof of the existence of God. Yet in his *Critique of Practical Reason* Kant claims the immortality of the soul as a postulate of pure practical reason.[61] We know, he asserts, that the fulfillment of the moral law is the highest good. Though we strive to fulfill it, we never come to an end of our endeavors in this life. This evident disproportion between the direction of our existence (attaining the highest good) and the actual content of our existence (not completely attaining the highest good) demands a solution. The solution can only come from an infinite life beyond our present existence so that through infinite progress we may realize the fulfillment of the moral law as the highest good. Kant, of course, knows very well that an immortal soul can only be theoretically demanded and cannot be proved in reality.

We should wonder why humanity's greatest philosophers proposed or attempted to prove the immortality of the person or the soul. Confronted with death throughout our life, we seem to feel that with death our existence cannot be completely over. There must be something beyond death. The idea of immortality shows the contradiction that we experience in our own existence and can rightly be regarded as an inborn idea of the human mind. But does not Christian faith itself hold the immortality of the human soul as one of its essential features?

d. Immortality and Christian faith

Toward the end of the 12th century the Arabic philosopher Averroes (1126-1198) introduced Aristotle's philosophy to Christian theologians. But the Roman Catholic Church soon took steps to ban the resulting Averroistic movement in Christian theology because Averroes had concluded from Aristotle's treatise *On the Soul* that the soul of reason, or of the spirit, is a single, universal, and active intellect in which all people participate during their lifetime. He believed that in death, however, this human participation ceases, so that only the one universal soul is left. According to Averroes this means that the immortality of neither the person nor the soul can be proved philosophically.

Conservative theologians, such as Thomas Aquinas *(De unitate intellectus contra Averroistas),* protested immediately. At the Fifth Lateran Council in 1513 the church officially condemned the "pernicious errors . . . concerning the nature of the rational soul, namely, that it is mortal, or one in all men." [62] This decision reflects the understanding of official Roman Catholic dogma, according to which each person is endowed with an immortal soul.

Once we assume that humanity gradually developed from pre-human forms, however, the claim of an immortal soul is very difficult to maintain. The Roman Catholic Church realized this too, and in 1950 Pope Pius XII tried to reconcile the theory of evolution with the doctrine of the immortality of the soul. He stated that

> The *magisterium* of the church does not forbid that the teaching of "evolution" be treated in accord with the present status of human disciplines and of theology, by investigations and disputations, by learned men in both fields; insofar, of course, as the inquiry is concerned with the origin of the human body arising from already existing and living matter;—the Catholic faith commands us to retain that the souls are created immediately by God.[63]

The Roman Catholic Church thus attempted to solve the difficulties caused by the theory of evolution by claiming that the human body is procreated in a natural way, while its eternal soul is infused immediately by God. *The Catholic Catechism* still teaches: "The fact of a direct creation of each individual soul belongs to the deposit of the Christian faith." [64] But the Roman Catholic Church is not alone in its emphasis on the immortality of the soul. Most Protestant hymns express the hope that after our life on earth our immortal soul will be united with God.

Even many of the leading Protestant theologians of the past, such as
Zwingli, Calvin, and, to some extent, Luther advocated the immortality
of the soul. But can this idea be maintained on biblical grounds?

When we consult a concordance of the Bible, we find the term "soul"
quite often. But the creation stories in the beginning of the Bible, where
we would expect mention of the human soul, are remarkably silent about
a creation or infusion of the human soul through divine intervention.
Genesis 1 simply states that "God created man in his own image" (1:27),
and in Genesis 2 we hear in more picturesque language that "the Lord
God formed man of dust from the ground, and breathed into his nostrils
the breath of life; and man became a living being" (2:7).[65]

The distinction is made not between body and soul but between body
and life. Or, in other words, God created the whole person according
to the body (from dust) and then gave this body life through his life-
giving breath. This can hardly substantiate the teaching that our "soul"
is created in an immediate way, while our body is created in a mediated
way. It also runs contrary to the Platonic idea that the body is a prison
of the soul. The divergence from Plato's conception becomes even more
evident when we remember that in early Israelite thinking a person
after death leads a shadowy, bodiless existence in sheol. One certainly
cannot call this existence a genuine life, since not even the praise of the
Lord is possible there. According to Plato, by contrast, it is precisely
apart from the body that the soul attains full development of its life.

When we consult the New Testament, however, the distinction between body and soul is quite common. This is not surprising, since the
New Testament writers use Greek terminology to express God's self-
disclosure. But these writers do not conceive of the soul as by nature
good and the body as by nature evil. Both belong together and both are
created by God. And together they can be influenced by flesh or by
spirit. If we live according to the flesh, we live in a sinful existence in
our totality of being as body and soul (Rom. 7:14). Paul can use the
terms "flesh" and "sin" almost synonymously as denoting demonic powers by whom we are enslaved.[66] If we live according to the spirit, we
live our existence as children of God in our total being, in body and
soul (Rom. 8:14). But neither the term "flesh" nor the term "spirit"
is *given with human existence as such.*" [67] We must conclude that the
analogy to Platonic ideas lies only in the words and not in their content.

Besides Platonic philosophy there is also Gnosticism which, in analogy
to a soul-body dualism, asserts that we possess a divine spark which is

contaminated in this life by the material body. Salvation is redemption from the material and mortal body and entrance into the divine fullness of light. Even Paul seems to be influenced by Gnostic ideas when he exclaims: "Wretched man that I am! Who will deliver me from this body of death?" (Rom. 7:24). But unlike Gnosticism, Paul is not expecting redemption from his mortal body. Rather he is confident that Christ will give life to our mortal bodies through his Spirit who dwells in us (Rom. 8:11).

Paul, and with him the whole New Testament, is not longing for the liberation of the self from the bodily prison, but for the resurrection of the body.[68] He has no hope that from our mortal nature something worthwhile and immortal will survive (there is nothing to survive), but he hopes and is sure that through the resurrection of the body our mortal nature will be transformed into immortality (1 Cor. 15:35-57).

It is also interesting in this context that Raymond Moody in his analysis of near-death experiences distinguishes between the physical body that is temporarily left and the spiritual body in which the person has his/her experiences.[69] Unlike Gnostic thought or Platonism the physical is not conceived of here as a prison or as being secondary. The image of a spiritual body implies that one is not faced with the experience of nothingness, but one encounters a continuation of existence on a different level. There is also no mention made that the continuation of existence is a (natural) result of the person having a spiritual body, a thought we might expect in the pursuit of a soul-body dualism. It is also clear that these near-death experiences do not yet reach the state of a resurrected existence, since they are temporary and are resolved in a continuation of life here on earth.

How incompatible the Greek idea of the immortality of the soul and the Christian belief in the resurrection are is demonstrated by Paul's own missionary activity.[70] When Paul preached for the first time in Athens, laughter erupted when he spoke of the resurrection (Acts 17:32). And in his letters to the congregation in Corinth, he had to devote a whole chapter (1 Cor. 15) to the Christian belief in the resurrection, since many (Christians) of this congregation claimed that there was no need for this belief. Even around A.D. 150 Justin Martyr mentions people "who say that there is no resurrection of the dead, and that their souls, when they die, are taken to heaven." [71]

Even today the idea of immortality of the soul is "one of the greatest misunderstandings of Christianity." [72] Death is the end of this life in its totality; nothing and nobody will survive. Many Roman Catholic scholars fully agree with this insight. Karl Rahner, for instance, says that there is no rectilinear continuation of our empirical reality beyond death. "In this regard death puts an end to the *whole* man." [73] Though we sense our immortality, only God's word reveals to us "the *actuality of eternity*." [74] When the Roman Catholic Church proposes the doctrine of immortality of the soul, then this is a "truth of faith and not just a philosophical tenet." [75] According to Rahner the assertion of immortality is directed to both, the *whole* reality and meaning of a person as this individual depends on the creative and life-giving power of God, and what the philosopher as such may call soul in contrast to body, with a destiny which one may try to trace after death. [76]

Consequently immortality can denote (1) immortality in the philosophical sense, and (2), a gift of God which means that God continues his relationship with us beyond our biological death. Joseph E. Kokjohn stated this very well when he said that the human desire for immortality is a hope for some, a wish for others; "immortality is a promise, not a premise." [77] *The Catholic Catechism,* for instance, does not even use the term "immortal soul," but instead talks appropriately about the immortality of the glorified body as "coming from the divine strength." [78]

Roman Catholic scholars are not unanimous on the idea of a gift-immortality, and some claim "that every man is destined and capacitated for life after death by his very nature, in virtue of a naturally immortal soul that is an essential principle of every man." [79] The reason for this kind of argument is found in the very idea of a gift-immortality. Why, it is argued, should the wicked obtain the gift of immortality if they were so bad that they are to be punished after death anyhow? Would it not be much more logical to assume a continuance of existence that is finally determined as eternal bliss or eternal woe? While we cannot find fault with this kind of logic, we wonder about the implications of the argument.

(1) Death denotes a demarcation between this life and the hereafter, a demarcation so radical that it could hardly sustain the idea of a continuance, unless we talk about a "shadowy existence" in analogy to the existence in sheol. But the Old Testament writers never talked about continuance, realizing that sheol allowed for no life in the real sense.

(2) The very notion of a new creation and a resurrection, so central to the New Testament, is so different from our life here that it

would contradict the idea of a continuance through and beyond death.

Yet, we might ask, why should we assume a new creation or resurrection of those who are rejected? Again the New Testament seems to enlighten us when we hear that the dead will come forth, "those who have done good, to the resurrection of life, and those who have done evil, to the resurrection of judgment" (John 5:29). This indictates that the resurrection is not an independent (benevolent) state but a transition that ensues in two different kinds of eternal destinies. Since immortality as a gift of God is so easily confused with an innate immortality of the soul and thus with a non-biblical soul-body dichotomy, most leading figures in contemporary Protestant theology reject the idea of immortality.[80]

But a theologian like Regin Prenter notes that the usual polemics against the immortality of the soul are often very superficial.[81] Contrary to its original valid Christian meaning immortality is often polemically construed as a denial of the Christian hope in the resurrection. Karl Barth, for instance, mentions the idea of immortality of the soul only once in his *Church Dogmatics* and calls it a "typical thought inspired by fear."[82] Emil Brunner is more discerning when he rejects only the Platonist understanding of immortality of the soul but accepts the genuinely "Christian Biblical and Christological concept of immortality" which we have "only in God's creative Word."[83] Paul Tillich seems to go one step further, when he observes that of the two terms Christianity uses for the individual participation in eternal life only "resurrection" is biblical, while "immortality" dates back to the Platonic doctrine of the immortality of the soul.[84]

Tillich still concedes that, notwithstanding the inherent dualistic dangers, the term immortality can be used, not as expressing a continuation of temporal life after death, but as denoting "a quality which transcends temporality." In this way even the term "immortality of the soul" can be used as implying the power of universal essentialization. Though Tillich's symbolic understanding of immortality should be acceptable to Roman Catholic scholars, we wonder if they would also agree with his preference for Aristotle's ontological interpretation of Plato's teaching on immortality. Participation in a world-soul as life eternal not only seems relatively unattractive as the final goal of our individual lives but is also non-biblical.

Since the many misunderstandings caused by the term "immortality" necessitate that we treat it with extreme care we do not want to discard its valid theological significance. Thus we do not advocate that death is the dissolution of the person or that we plunge into a state of blissful void once we die. If that were so, death would provide the escape from this life and its consequences, and if one wanted to escape those consequences one could simply commit suicide. However, nobody can escape from God and from his sustaining hand, because he is on both sides of death. God's relationship with us in this life is sustained and finalized in and through death. Thus death can result in eternal death as eternal damnation, or it can result in eternal life as eternal joy. This does not mean that death *is* already eternal damnation or eternal life, but it entails it. Death, in other words, is the reverse side of resurrection.

3. Resurrection

Since we are not endowed with divine qualities that could make us hope for a gradual purification of an immortal soul, our only hope in ultimate fulfillment is beyond death, in the resurrection from the dead. This hope of the resurrection from the dead is inseparably based on the certitude of Jesus Christ's resurrection.

a. Decisive character of Christ's resurrection

The first Christian community was absolutely certain that Jesus was resurrected from the dead. Contemporary theology from the conservative wing to the extreme liberal is united on this basic insight. But as soon as we attempt to explain this observation and ask, for instance, what the statement means that "Jesus Christ was resurrected from the dead," there are many diverse opinions.

We cannot agree with those who claim that the statement "Jesus Christ was resurrected from the dead" has no meaning for us today.[85] It was precisely the resurrection of Jesus Christ which provided the focal point of the first Christian community and which kept the Christian faith alive until today. But it is impossible for us simply to resort to the resurrection of Christ in order to remove the ambiguity of the cross. Rudolf Bultmann has made this point unmistakably clear. The fact of the resurrection of Christ does not lend itself to a strictly empirical proof as would the historical fact of the crucifixion. The resurrection is an inference drawn from other facts which can always be arranged to allow for differing interpretations.[86] Thus Albert Schweitzer could try to explain the resurrection as a psychological phenomenon that occurred within the disciples.[87] Though we have seen that such an immanent explanation has trouble explaining sufficiently how the Christian faith spread as rapidly and durably as it did, we notice that even Paul in his best attempt "to prove the fact" of the resurrection could at most refer to the faith of others and to the Scriptures (documents of faith). But it is an overstatement to claim that "cross and resurrection form a single, indivisible cosmic event." [88] We agree with Bultmann that we cannot resort to the one event to prove the importance of the other. There is, however, a decisive difference between the events of Good Friday and those of Easter Sunday. God acted very differently at these two occasions.

It is also questionable whether one can call the resurrection of Jesus Christ a means of interpreting the historical Jesus.[89] It is true that only in the light of the resurrection did the Christian community arrive at the interpretation of Jesus contained in the New Testament. The origin of the New Testament cannot be explained without the "happening" which the Christian community called the resurrection of Jesus Christ.[90] But the first Christians were not interested in ancestor worship. They did not just gather to remember that something unique had happened with Jesus. The resurrection is both the basis for the present and the provision of the future. This is especially expressed in the title *kyrios* (Lord), which was conferred on Jesus Christ by the post-Easter Christian community. The term *kyrios* was used, for example, in talking about the Emperor in the official Roman state cult. It was also used in talking about pagan gods, and it served in the Septuagint to render the Hebrew name Yahweh into Greek. In the hymn in Philippians 2:5-11 which describes the whole salvific mission of Jesus, the term *kyrios* indicates the end of Jesus' earthly career and implies equality with God: Every knee shall bow and he shall be proclaimed *kyrios*. This new status does not threaten the sovereignty of God but is granted to glorify God.[91]

Of course, this new status is unthinkable without Jesus' resurrection. In one of the oldest creedal statements in the New Testament (Rom. 10:9) the confession of Jesus as the Lord runs parallel to faith in his resurrection from the dead, and both have salvific character. This equality with God implies cosmic lordship as well as lordship over individual Christians. We remember, for instance, that it was decisive for Paul's call and for his missionary activity that Jesus Christ was Lord; this means designated Son of God *in power* through his resurrection (Rom.

1:4). Of course, Jesus did not become some super-human mediator between God and us through his resurrection. At times Paul does not even distinguish between Jesus Christ and God. The term *kyrios* signifies the way in which God deals with the world; it expresses his rule over the world. All of the powers and "lords" are derived and secondary, but Jesus Christ's lordship is unconditioned and all-pervading.

The fact that Jesus became Lord through his resurrection means also that he, the hidden Messiah, became the revealed Messiah. In other words, the term "Christ the Lord" expresses that the one who was Jesus of Nazareth was not just a human being, but God himself. Thus he is not a fact of the past, but, as Christ the Lord, he is the decisive factor who provides the present and the future.

b. Creative newness of Christ's resurrection

The character of newness implied in the resurrection is already indicated in the affirmation that Jesus became Christ and Lord, and that as the hidden Messiah he was disclosed as the revealed Messiah. But the character of newness becomes especially evident when we consider the resurrection of Christ in the context of God's creative activity. The Bible suggests in many places that God's salvific activity must be seen in analogy to God's creative activity in the beginning. For instance Second Isaiah, the book that proclaims salvation as offered through the sacrifice of the servant of Yahweh, connects the creation in the beginning very intimately with salvation as the goal of history (cf. Isa. 42:5; 44:6; 45:8).[92] And in its opening sentences the Gospel of John sees the coming of Christ in the perspective of the creation in the beginning. Also Paul points out a clear correspondence between the appearance of the first Adam and the appearance of Christ as the last Adam (Rom. 5).

It would be erroneous to interpret this perspective of creation as if the resurrection were to open for us the opportunity to return to an ideal state of the past. Such an interpretation would force us into the cyclic view of history represented by most religions and philosophies: after a new beginning the wheel of world history would move on to a new revolution. But the opposite direction is indicated by Paul when he says: "For in him all things were created, in heaven and on earth, visible and invisible, whether thrones or dominions or principalities or authorities —all things were created through him and for him" (Col. 1:16). This means that everything is created toward Christ. When Paul calls him the first-born of creation (Col. 1:15) he wants to emphasize that Christ, being equal to God, does not stand only at the beginning of creation. Through his resurrection Christ is also the goal toward which creation moves.[93] Clearly, such an understanding cannot condone a static view of creation: the world was once created, then came the Fall and distorted this good and perfect creation, then came Christ and enabled its restoration, and finally the parousia will come when the creation will be restored to its original beauty. The "very good" which God pronounced over his creation does not mean unsurpassable. Here lies the fallacy of understanding our world as the best possible one.[94]

Our present world, of course, is good, but it could be better. To deny this is to belittle the facts of evil and death. To understand Christ as the goal toward which creation moves also requires a radical reorientation concerning the Fall of humanity and our sinful state. The Fall of humanity can no longer be viewed as a jump from a God-provided basis to some kind of lower level, i.e., a state of constant sinfulness. The Fall is the initial denial of the Christ line which extends from the original creation to its final fulfillment. Each of our sinful acts is a reaffirmation of this initial denial and thus a rejection of God's plan for us and a rejection of his redemptive act in Christ (cf. Heb. 1:1ff.).

God is continually with his creation, even in its alienated or fallen state. Nothing is farther away from the biblical understanding than a deistic God far beyond who watches in a detached manner the predetermined course the universe takes. Even immediately following the Fall God does not withdraw from the first humans in his wrath, but, in an act of compassion, he provides them with necessary clothing (Gen. 3:21). And the church's desire to find in the words of the curse a primal gospel (Gen. 3:15), or the endeavor of a gospel writer to trace the ancestry of Jesus back to Adam and finally to God himself, witness to the fact that God's acting in the beginning and his acting in Jesus Christ are seen as a unity. Paul attests this too in pointing to Christ as the anti-type of Adam. Through Christ in antithetic manner law is superseded by grace, sin by justification, and death by life.[95]

Death is not superseded by life to restore the original state; for the resurrected Christ death is no longer even a possibility. In a similar way grace is not the opposite of law and justification, or the reverse of sinfulness. Jesus Christ's resurrection does not indicate the fulfillment of a restorative process that had started with the Old Testament covenant community. His resurrection is rather the first point of a *new* creation, a creation in perfection. Could it be just accidental that Paul in his letter to the Romans progresses from declaring Christ as the new Adam (Chapter 5), to our participation in the new creation through baptism (Chapter 6), to the tension within us as being citizens of a new world yet still living in the old one (Chapter 7), to the implications for the whole creation of God's creative act in Christ's resurrection (Chapter 8)?

God's creative act in Christ's resurrection goes beyond this present creation. It witnesses to the new creation which replaces this present creation at one specific point. (This is where the question of the empty tomb becomes important, not as a proof for the historicity of the resurrection of Jesus Christ, but as an indication that this present creation has no permanence, that it will be replaced by and transformed into something new. Not even the first Christian community used the story of the empty tomb as a proof of Christ's resurrection [cf. Matt. 27:62—28:15, esp. 28:15]). This inauguration of the new creation inspires in us the hope of being incorporated in it.

c. Christ's resurrection as the presupposition of our own resurrection

From the preceding it should be clear that the Christian belief in the resurrection does not just result from a gradual development of the idea of resurrection in the Judeo-Christian faith. The Christian belief in the resurrection is basically Christ-centered. The *idea* of the resurrection from the dead was a matter of fact for both Jesus and the first Christian community.[96] But the resurrection of Jesus does not just verify the validity of the apocalyptic idea of resurrection. For instance, Paul in 1 Corinthians 15 does not refer to the common agreement on the idea of a resurrection when he advocates the resurrection. Rather he refers to and explains the Christian tradition concerning *Christ's* resurrection. This means that Christ is not only the first of the resurrected, as could be expected according to apocalyptic thinking, but he is at the same time the presupposition of our own resurrection.[97]

Paul drives this point home very clearly: "If Christ has not been raised, then our preaching is in vain and your faith is in vain" (1 Cor. 15:14). The resurrection of Jesus Christ cannot be isolated from the rest of world history and refuted as irrelevant. It is the presupposition of the Christian existence as a community of people who participate proleptically in the newness of life, and it is the foundation of Christian hope in the final realization of this new life.

Nevertheless, the full implications of Christ's resurrection are only disclosed to us when we consider it in the context of apocalyptic hopes. Only in relation to the apocalyptic view of history, with its conviction of a resurrection at the end of time, can the resurrection of Jesus Christ be understood as an anticipation of this end.[98] Even the very fact that the disciples could recognize their once familiar leader in their post-Easter experiences, in something entirely different from the possibilities of this life, and that they called the reality behind these experiences resurrection, can only satisfactorily be explained from an understanding of apocalyptic hopes. Otherwise it would have been interpreted as an encounter with a spirit or a phantom (cf. Luke 24:37).

In the context of apocalyptic hopes and expectations the disciples realized that God had verified the authority that Jesus had claimed already in his earthly life. They also realized that in the destiny of Jesus as the Lord the end had already occurred in proleptic anticipation, and God had already disclosed himself in fullness in Jesus as the Lord. In other words, through the resurrection of Jesus Christ the apocalyptic *idea* of a common resurrection is modified to the Christian *hope* in the resurrection, because of Christ and because of his resurrection. Thus the New Testament proclaims Jesus not only as "the first to rise from the dead" (Acts 26:23), "the beginning, the first-born from the dead" (Col. 1:18), but also as the one in whom we shall be united "in a resurrection like his" that we too "might walk in newness of life" (Rom. 6:4f.). And we trust in God who "raised the Lord and will also raise us up by his power" (1 Cor. 6:14). Apocalyptic ideas provide the background material for a full understanding of the implications of Christ's resurrection; still our hope in a resurrection is not based on these ideas but depends solely on Christ's resurrection.

d. Resurrection of the body

The hope for our resurrection is expressed in the Apostles' Creed with the phrase that we believe "in the resurrection of the body." Though the question already arises here as to what kind of body this will be, the issue gets more confusing when we notice that in the original Greek and Latin texts the word for body actually denotes flesh *(sarx* or *caro)*. Of course, in a biblicistic manner we could claim that the Creed contradicts the Bible where Paul states: "Flesh and blood cannot inherit the kingdom of God, nor does the perishable inherit the imperishable" (1 Cor. 15:50).

If we would conceive of our resurrection in analogy to a strictly bio-

logical revivification, similar to what the biblical witnesses tell us about
the young man in the village of Nain (Luke 7:15) and about Lazarus
(John 11:44), we would also encounter many other objections.[99] First,
we would have to fight for the elements of our own bodies, perhaps
coming to find out that we would have to share them with others, since
through natural decay and our intake of food products we might easily
incorporate elements in our bodies which once belonged to other people.
Second, to receive a body in analogy to our own present body would
actually mean continuation of the limitations and tensions to which we
now are subjected. Third, our resurrection would stand in an odd contrast to Christ's resurrection, for he was resurrected as and into a new
creation with different possibilities than those he possessed before. When
the early church decided to include the belief in the resurrection of the
"flesh" into the Creed it did not intend to create these problems. Rather
it was trying to protect itself against the idea that the resurrection is
only a docetic, spiritualistic resurrection in Greek or Gnostic fashion. Not
the soul or some other divine spark in us lives on in eternity, but we
ourselves are resurrected. Such a resurrection is expressed as a bodily
resurrection.

In popular Greek *sarx* did not just mean flesh, but it could also mean
body. A bodily existence was thus conceived of as a real one in contrast
to an existence encountered in a dream or in art.[100] Here lies for us
today the importance of the belief in the resurrection of the body. Resurrection is not a paranormal occurrence in analogy to occult phenomena
or to hallucinations; it is a reality that involves our whole being. But
what does "a reality that involves our whole being" mean? First of all,
it means that death is not our final destiny. The resurrection which takes
place at the parousia of the Lord includes everybody, with no exceptions.
Even after we are dead everything is not over. This is true for those
who are accepted into the immediacy of God and for those who are
banned from it.

It is simply too easy to say that the eternal judgment coincides with
physical death and that those who are excluded from eternal joy will
not be resurrected.[101] There is no escape from God since God, who is not
confined to this life, is on both sides of death. Otherwise the last judgment would simply be God's acceptance of everybody (who is resurrected). Such a belief, of course, would run counter to the emphasis on
the final separation of humanity (cf. the Parables of the Kingdom, esp.
Matt. 13). We must also affirm that this universal resurrection will be a

resurrection in personal identity or a resurrection that "involves the whole being." If the one who is resurrected would not be the one who died previously, redemption and damnation would be meaningless. It would involve our existence only as much as does the news that someone we do not know has just inherited a million dollars. But resurrection means that for me, as one who is bound to die, God will provide a future above and beyond death. Just as we cannot say that part of my ego will go in this direction and part in the other, we cannot say that only part of me will be resurrected.

The question whether there will be different stages of resurrection seems almost speculative. The seriousness of the decision we have to make in being confronted with the gospel and the seriousness of the final judgment would suggest that all will be resurrected to an immortal state, since their future will be never-ending. Apocalyptic ideas that the dead will first be resurrected in an unchanged way (so that they can be recognized), and that those who will be condemned and those who will be accepted will then be changed the way they deserve (2 Apoc. Bar. 50f.) seem to lie beyond the scope of the New Testament. When Paul, for instance, suggested that the dead will be raised imperishable, and we will be changed (1 Cor. 15:52b), he expected that he would still be alive when Christ would return, whereupon he together with other Christians would be transformed to participate in the new creation. Furthermore, even in mentioning the dead, he seemed to talk only about deceased Christians and not about the dead in general.[102] If we would suggest first a universal resurrection, then a final judgment, and then the respective transformation of accepted and rejected, we would be talking in terms of a sequential progression and introduce the concept of time which is simply no longer applicable to anything beyond death.

Of much more importance is the question of what we can look forward to when we hope and believe in the resurrection of the body. To conclude from passages such as "in the resurrection they neither marry nor are given in marriage, but are like angels in heaven" (Matt. 22:30) that the state of the resurrection is an asexual state is a gross misconception and indicates the desire for a travelog eschatology. Such imagery indicates the same thing Paul points out when he says that the mortal cannot inherit the immortal, nor the perishable inherit the imperishable. Resurrection does not indicate a continuation of our present life, not even on a different level. Our whole life, including the anti-Godly desires it succumbs to, must perish. This "otherness" of the resurrection makes it so difficult even to talk about it. Even Paul talks about the resurrection by negating our present conditions. Perishable-imperishable, dishonor-glory, physical-spiritual, mortal-immortal, are some of the antitheses he uses (1 Cor. 15:42-54). These antitheses explain why resurrection is "a reality that involves the whole being." Nothing is exempt from this fundamental change.

Yet if this change is so decisive, if we no longer live in dishonor, if we are no longer limited by the physical world, if we are no longer confronted with death, if we no longer age, and if we are no longer distinguished by certain sexual behavior patterns, is not the "I" who will be resurrected so different from the "I" who died that we shall face a tremendous identity crisis? We would immensely underestimate the radicality of the resurrection if we held the idea that the resurrection does not imply a radical change in identity and personality. After all, we are looking forward to a *new* creation. Even now our personality undergoes steady changes when we advance from childhood to adolescence, to maturity, and to old age and senility. Sometimes these changes cause considerable identity crises. But each time we remain the same person. So we need not be afraid that we would miss ourselves when we are received into God's new world.

e. "Between" death and resurrection

Realizing that death terminates our individual lives and that resurrection is our destination beyond death, the question emerges what happens "between" death and resurrection. We have been forced to discard the idea of purgatory, and we have found the idea of a continuance of life through an immortal soul to be highly questionable. We observe, however, that not everybody dies at the same time, and that death does not coincide with the universal resurrection we hope for. What is our destiny "between" our death and the common resurrection of which we will be part? Or do we face an individual resurrection?

Already Paul encountered this uncertainty when people asked concerning those who had already died. Paul did not comfort these people in their anxiety by elaborating on the ideas of immortality, reincarnation, or purgatory, ideas which were certainly known to them. He tried to point out to them that there is no preferred state. It does not matter whether we are still alive at the return of the Lord, or whether we have been dead a long time. Our destiny will lie in our confrontation with the returning Lord (1 Thess. 4:15; 1 Cor. 15:25). For us too it is neither necessary nor legitimate to speculate on an intermediate state between death and resurrection. This becomes especially evident when we consider that time is only a this-worldly entity.[103]

Time as a this-worldly entity: Already Augustine emphasizes that time is an indication of transitoriness and is inextricably connected with this world. Time always needs something to pass by, because only through changes in objects can there be time. Thus it is pointless to talk in a literal way about "the time before the creation" of this world. God created this temporal world, and through the transitoriness of this world we are able to observe time.[104] In a similar manner Luther asserts that in the beginning there was nothing except God, no time, no objects, and no space.[105] And in his picturesque and drastic manner he tells those curious questioners who want to know what God did "before" he created the earth that he was sitting behind a shrub, cutting off good-sized rods for spanking those who ask these stupid questions.

Concerning God, Luther asserts, one has to do away with time. Only for us is there time and hour, whereas for God everything occurs in the eternal now. This means that God is co-temporal to all possible and actual time constellations. He who created the world and with it time and transitoriness is not subject to change but equipresent in each possible and actual change. In other words, past, present, and future are equally present before God. Time is an order of God for his creation (cf. Ps. 102:25-27 and Heb. 1:10-12). Thus we are always experiencing certain successions of time and cannot accomplish things properly unless it is the right time to do them. Since we are time-bound, we are not in command of time but subject to it.[106]

Immanuel Kant in his *Critique of Pure Reason* stresses the person-centeredness of time so much that he declared it to be an anthropological phenomenon. Like space, time is not an "empty box" into which our observation places certain objects, but time and space are for us necessary conceptual tools with which we perceive these objects. Kant clearly recognizes that time and space are not independent entities but are only existent in relating certain objects to each other.

Finally, Albert Einstein in his *Special Theory of Relativity* (1905) came to the scientific conclusion that space and time are related not only to each other but also to matter. Each of these three entities necessitates the others, and all three depend on the observer. Einstein was unable to assert with Kant that time and space are just conceptual tools.

More like Augustine he affirmed that time does not make sense apart from something by which it can flow. But he also showed, much like Kant had suggested, that time, space, and matter are not independent entities. How space, time and matter appear always depends on the correlating system, i.e., the standpoint of the observer.[107] Thus time can stand almost still or disappear rapidly, and matter and space can shrink or increase accordingly. In affirming the inseparable unity of time, space, and matter, Einstein validly showed that time, as the indicator of transitoriness, can only be conceived of in the context of space and matter. This means that time is an inadequate category to describe anything beyond this material and space-bound world. When we talk about the state "between" death and resurrection and do not just talk about the biological decay of the physical body, then the category of time as denoting transitoriness is inadequate. Rather we must talk about the end or fulfillment of time or about eternity.

The eternity of God as fulfillment of time: In talking about eternity we have to refrain from equating eternity with infinity, especially in its scientific sense. When used theologically, eternity denotes the dimension of God, and in talking about it we encounter the same difficulties as in talking about God. In the Bible, for instance, eternity is often conceived of anthropomorphically as never-ending time.[108] Even for us sophisticated people of the 20th century it is difficult to envison eternity other than as "endless time." Yet when the Bible talks about the eternity of God it is also aware that this is not the same as time stretched out to such an extent that it does not have boundaries.[109]

Eternity is generally understood as belonging to God in contrast to the time of our world, which is limited by the creation in the beginning and by the end. In Greek philosophy, however, eternity is usually understood as timelessness, a state where there is no day, no month, no year. Especially Plato in his *Timaeus* thinks of eternity as an ideal state, of which time is only a faint copy.[110] The Bible knows about the infinite qualitative difference between time and God's eternity too, since it knows that creation and its creator are fundamentally different. But it does not disassociate God's eternity from time. To envision the eternity of God as some kind of nirvana, where time is overcome and dissolved, would be impossible for biblical thinking. Not even the Greek position of a static relationship between time and eternity would be sufficient. Ranke's well-known claim that each moment is equidistant from eternity is closer to a platonic time-eternity dichotomy than to the biblical religion. The Bible proclaims not an eternal God up there but a living God who gives time its direction.

In the Christian understanding time is on its way from creation via redemption to perfection. Cullmann has rightly called Christ the midpoint of time, since he is God's visible sign pointing out the direction in which this time-bound world moves. This is especially important in coming from a physical understanding of time. According to science time is bound to matter; it is not directed by itself but receives its direction only from the correlating system of the observer. What happens, however, if we as observers have nothing absolute by which to orient ourselves, except the scientific doomsday version of an eventual rundown of our universe?[111] Here Christ provides us with a point of orientation beyond the confines of our physical world.

Dialectic theology, initiated by Kierkegaard's insistence on the qualitative difference between God and humanity and modified by Moltmann's christocentric future-directedness of history, has enabled us to rediscover the lost direction of our time-bound world. If time is on its way toward perfection, we can envision eternity neither as endless, infinite time nor as the end of time in the sense of continuous rest or quiescence. Eternity is rather the fulfillment of time in perfection. This means that all the life-impairing effects of time will be overcome. Transition, suffering, decay, and death are all inextricably connected with temporality and change.[112]

When time has been completed and perfected through the redeeming power of God, these life-impairing characteristics will have been overcome. Of course, such completion and perfection of time is not due to the fact that there is eternity, but due to the fact that there is God. Eternity is an empty term unless it is designated as belonging to God. Only God, who is a God not of the dead but of the living, who is a God who wants not the death of the wicked but that the wicked be saved and live—only because there is such a God can we hope for the perfection of time and for eternity.

It is important to know that, especially in the later parts of the Old Testament, the eternity of God is not asserted to show that God is of old, but to demonstrate his power to bring about salvation. "The Lord is the everlasting God, the Creator of the ends of the earth. He does not faint or grow weary, his understanding is unsearchable . . . they who wait for the Lord shall renew their strength" (Isa. 40:28, 31).[113] The one who created the world provides its direction and completion since he is eternal. His eternal being extends beyond the time of the world. He is from eternity to eternity and the Psalmist confesses to him: "The heavens are thine, the earth also is thine; the world and all that is in it, thou hast founded them" (Ps. 89:11). He was before the world was created, and when heaven and earth will have disappeared he still is. "Of old thou didst lay the foundation of the earth, and the heavens are the work of thy hands. They will perish, but thou dost endure; . . . thou art the same, and thy years have no end" (Ps. 102:25ff.).

It is not by chance that the writer of the Letter to the Hebrews quotes these verses and transfers them to Jesus (Heb. 1:10ff.). Already John confesses of Jesus Christ that he was "before the foundation of the world" (John 17:24). Jesus Christ is co-eternal with God, he is before and after the aeons of the world. Only because he is co-eternal with God can he give time its direction and signify through his first coming the turning point between this aeon and the coming aeon. In Jesus' coming and especially in his resurrection the future has already started. Christians therefore are no longer just waiting for the future, but they live in anticipation of the future, since in Christ all possible future occurred already in proleptic anticipation.[114]

Eternity as the sphere of God (and of Christ) thus endows time with meaning and direction. In pointing to the fulfillment of time, eternity does not indicate a final monotony,[115] but active, unrestrained, and unlimited participation in the new world in full harmony with the living God. But we have not yet addressed the question of when this fulfillment will be reached, whether at death or some "time" after.

Death as finality and transition: The Bible does not seem to give us a clear answer to the question of when the fulfillment is reached. At times death seems to be depicted as leading to a final state and at other times as leading to a transitory state. In the New Testament the dead are referred to as those who are asleep or as those who have fallen asleep (1 Cor. 15:20; Luke 8:52; 2 Peter 3:4). They will sleep until judgment day, and then they will be resurrected. This would imply that they have not reached the final goal, heaven or hell, but are still waiting for it.

There are other passages in the New Testament, however, that indicate that with death some kind of finality is already reached. For instance, when Jesus tells the parable of the rich man and Lazarus he mentions that both found their (preliminary) destinations, Abraham's bosom and

Hades, immediately after they died (Luke 16:19-31). And Jesus also promised the one criminal on the cross: "Today you will be with me in Paradise" (Luke 23:43).

In the Gospel of John we can almost notice an attempt to bridge the obvious dichotomy between transition and finality. We hear Jesus say: "Truly, truly, I say to you, the hour is coming, and now is, when the dead will hear the voice of the Son of God, and those who hear will live" and then, almost in the same breath, the comment is made "For the hour is coming when all who are in the tombs will hear his voice and come forth, those who have done good, to the resurrection of life, and those who have done evil, to the resurrection of judgment" (John 5:25, 28f.).

The writers of the New Testament knew very well that the response to the confrontation with Jesus and his message determined the final outcome of our lives, acceptance or rejection by God. They also were realistic enough not to indulge in the speculation that those who lived their lives in accordance with the incarnate word of God would at one point leave this life and immediately enter into a kind of visible heaven. They knew that at the end of this earthly life everyone had to die. Thus when they assumed that at death one fell into a sleep, we should not simply see this as an attempt to reconcile Jesus' decisive message of the immediacy of the eschaton with the idea of a sleep of the dead.[116] They rather tried to maintain both finality and transition. They encountered in Jesus Christ God's final word and action, which allowed them already to participate proleptically in the new creation, and they observed in death a cessation of this proleptic participation which pointed to something beyond death. Whether finality or transition, one thing was clear to them: there is no vacuum after death.

Luther went along similar lines as the New Testament.[117] He was convinced that an intermediate state after death could not be a neutral state but would already presuppose our being accepted or rejected by God. Yet it would be a final state, since it would still anticipate the fulfillment and perfection of the resurrection. Often Luther "described" this state as a deep sleep without dreams, without any consciousness and feelings. He confessed that he often had tried to observe himself when he fell asleep. But he never succeeded. He remembered that he was awake, and then, suddenly, he woke up again. So, it is with death: "In a similar way as one does not know how it happens that one falls asleep, and suddenly morning approaches when one awakes, so we will suddenly be resurrected at the Last Day, not knowing how we have come into death and through death." [118] And on another occasion he says: "We shall sleep until he comes and knocks at the tomb and says: 'Dr. Martin, get up!' Then in one moment, I will get up and I will rejoice with him in eternity." [119]

Actually, he confesses, we don't know much about this state between death and resurrection. Perhaps those who will be rejected will already suffer, and perhaps those who will be accepted will have a foretaste of the eternal joy they are waiting for and will listen to God's discourses with his angels. Endowed with a sound and natural curiosity, Luther would, of course, have liked to find out where and how we exist between death and resurrection. But he realized that in staying as close as possible to God's self-disclosure as reflected by the biblical witnesses there is not much we can say about this state.

Through this restraint Luther modified decisively the tradition out of which he came. The church, for instance, had rejected the notion, once adopted in some sermons by Pope John XXII, that the human soul sleeps after death and does not enjoy the beatific vision until judgment day. In an edict of 1336, Benedict XII, the successor to John XXII, declared that the soul of the just already enjoys the beatific vision.[120] This face-to-face vision of the divine essence and the resulting enjoyment exist continuously "and will continue even up to the last judgment and from then even unto eternity." The souls of those, however, "who depart in actual mortal sin immediately after death descend to hell where they are tortured by infernal punishments, and that nevertheless on the day of judgment all men with their bodies will make themselves ready to render an account of their own deeds before the tribunal of Christ."

It would surely be one-sided to absolutize a passage such as Revelation 6:9 and conclude that the souls of the deceased who were faithful will remain under the altar of God until judgment day and are not yet allowed to see God face-to-face. But is the other view not just as one-sided in assuming that we can define our destiny between death and resurrection as beatific vision or infernal punishment? This notion would make the final judgment into a reaffirmation of what had happened already in death so that no destinies will be changed. Furthermore, the New Testament is much more reluctant to settle for a definite either-or of what happens to us between death and resurrection. This obvious disparity within the New Testament itself reflects the difficulty we encounter when we attempt to "define" this state between death and resurrection.

Contemporary Roman Catholic theologians are more open at this point. They are aware that the dogmatic definitions of the church rightly wanted to safeguard the insight that death is the final end only of this life but not of human life altogether. Since the church refrained from defining how to talk about what results from death, various conceptualizations are available to us. Michael Schmaus, for instance, suggests two options: (1) The more traditional option of the immortality of a spiritual soul which will continue to exist. He concedes that this option tends to devaluate the significance of the resurrection. (2) The other option, that he favors, concludes that at death humanity enters into completion, and therefore a change to a new life occurs in death. Of course, he notes that this concept then faces the issue of reconciling many individual "resurrections" (at death) with the final universal resurrection.[121]

But is it even necessary to assume a distinction or even tension between an individual resurrection and the final universal resurrection? First, we remember that our hope is not a hope for a state between death and resurrection; we hope and believe in "the resurrection of the body and life everlasting."[122] Second, we realize that death is not only the border of this life but the border of time. Beyond death there is no diminishing, aging, or increasing; there is only God's eternal presence. Of course, we see people encountering their own individual death at different points in time and we know that the last judgment, which provides the end of all possible and actual time, does not coincide with these different points in time. Otherwise there would be an individualized last judgment, occurring at many different points, whenever someone departs from this life.

As people cross the borderline of time at different points, it is legitimate to use New Testament imagery and say that the dead "sleep" until judgment day. But we also know that in God all the different points of time coincide. For God there is no sooner or later, not even a too late. In God's eternal presence there is no distinction between past, present, and future. This distinction exists only for us as time-bound creatures, not for the creator. When through death we cross the borderline of time we encounter God's eternal presence. We are then co-eternal not only with God but also with all human creatures. Regardless of when we cross this line we will appear on the "other side" at the "same moment" as everyone else. Thus the confrontation with God in death will result in the eternal judgment. This is not to be understood as an individualized act, because together with everyone else we will encounter God's eternal presence.

As anything between death and resurrection is beyond space and time, we can only talk about the "transitory state" in approximations. When we call it a state of "bodiless sleep" this shows very drastically the limits of our conceptual tools. A "bodiless sleep" is an obvious contradiction, since we cannot conceive of sleep without thinking about a body. Yet for the sake of expressing that death and resurrection are not the same, and in attempting to relate our present experiences to the future we hope for, we have to resort to such inadequate, though necessary concepts.

NOTES

1. The only way Luther could justify the Revelation of John's place in the canon was to interpret it as witnessing to the history of the church (cf. Paul Althaus, *The Theology of Martin Luther*, 84f.).
2. When Paul Tillich, *Systematic Theology*, 3:401, 411, 414, refers to the ultimate judgment, to immortality, and to the resurrection as symbols, we know, of course, that this means more than mere symbolism. Yet we wonder if the very term "symbol" does not endanger the reality for which these concepts stand.
3. Rudolf Bultmann, "What Does It Mean to Speak of God?" (1925), in *Faith and Understanding*, 1:53-65. But we cannot follow Bultmann when he suggests that if we will speak of God, we must evidently speak of ourselves (p. 55), since with this statement Bultmann seems to abandon his valid theocentric approach in favor of an anthropocentric one.
4. Cf. Elisabeth Kübler-Ross in *Encyclopaedia Britannica*, 15th ed., s.v. "Death." For similar definitions cf. Harmon L. Smith, *Ethics and the New Medicine* (Nashville: Abingdon, 1970) 128f.
5. Leroy Augenstein, *Come, Let Us Play God*, 44, 48ff., illustrates this point very shockingly. Cf. also Smith, *Ethics and the New Medicine*, 133ff.
6. Thornton Wilder's graveyard scene in *Our Town* is to some extent a good illustration of this definition.
7. We agree here fully with what Smith, *Ethics and the New Medicine*, 166f., calls indirect or passive euthanasia.
8. Ad Hoc Committee of the Harvard Medical School to Examine the Definition of Brain Death, "A Definition of Irreversible Coma," in Robert F. Weir, ed., *Ethical Issues in Death and Dying* (New York: Columbia University, 1977) 83.
9. So rightly Robert M. Veatch, *Death, Dying, and the Biological Revolution. Our Last Quest for Responsibility* (New Haven: Yale University, 1976) 302.
10. Cf. Arthur J. Dyck, "An Alternative to the Ethics of Euthanasia," in Weir, 281f.
11. Elisabeth Kübler-Ross, *Death. The Final Stage of Growth* (Englewood Cliffs, N.J.: Prentice-Hall, 1975) 166, rightly talks about death and its acceptance as the final stage of growth in this life.
12. Pierre Teilhard de Chardin, *The Phenomenon of Man*, 289.
13. This is very clearly expressed by Theodosius Dobzhansky, *The Biology of Ultimate Concern* (New York: New American Library, 1967) 68ff.
14. Johann Gottlieb Fichte, *The Vocation of Man*, trans. by W. Smith, with biographical intr. by E. Ritchie (La Salle, Ill.: Open Court, 1940) 175.
15. For the following distinction cf. the extensive description by Elisabeth Kübler-Ross, *On Death and Dying* (New York: Macmillan, 1969) 38-137.
16. Ibid., 42.

17. Ibid., 49.
18. Ibid., 113.
19. So rightly Elisabeth Kübler-Ross, *Questions and Answers on Death and Dying* (New York: Macmillan, 1974) 4.
20. Ibid., 166f.
21. For the following cf. Paul Althaus, *Die letzten Dinge*, 83ff.; and "Tod IV: Dogmatisch," in *Religion in Geschichte und Gegenwart*, 3rd ed., 6:9 14ff.
22. Augustine *On Rebuke and Grace* 33, in *A Select Library of the Nicene, and Post-Nicene Fathers of the Christian Church*, ed. by Philip Schaff (Grand Rapids, Mich.: Eerdmans, 1956), vol. 5: *Saint Augustine Anti-Pelagian Writings*, 484f.
23. So W. Rohnert, *Die Dogmatik der evangelisch-lutherischen Kirche* (Braunschweig: Wollermann, 1902) 198. Francis Pieper, *Christian Dogmatics* (St. Louis: Concordia, 1950), 1:551ff., even ponders whether original sin caused immediate death or only started the process of dying which results in the complete separation of body and soul. Cf. also Chr. Ernst Luthart, *Kompendium der Dogmatik*, new edition by Robert Jelke (Leipzig: Dörffling & Franke, 1937) 215.
24. Mari Mercatoris, *Commonitorium de Coelestio* (II), in vol. 48 of J.-P. Migne, *Patrologiae Cursus Completus: Series Latina Prior*, 83ff.
25. Althaus, *Die letzten Dinge*, 85.
26. Anders Nygren, *Commentary on Romans*, trans. by C. C. Rasmussen (Philadelphia: Muhlenberg, 1949) 206ff.
27. For the following cf. Luther in his *Lectures on Romans;* commentary on Rom. 6:3 in WA LVI, 322, 11-20 ("There is a twofold death, namely a natural or temporal death and an eternal" . . . "The eternal death is two-fold. The one is good and even very good, since it is the death from sin . . ."); and WA LVI, 323, 5f.; 327, 13f.; cf. also WA XXXVI, 246, 11-17; WA XXXI/1, 153, 34ff.
28. Cf. Martin Luther, *Small Catechism* (The Sacrament of Holy Baptism) in *The Book of Concord*, 349.
29. Kübler-Ross, *Questions and Answers on Death and Dying*, 159.
30. Cf. Howard C. Wilkinson, "Parapsychology and Religion," in *Parapsychology Today*, ed. by J. B. Rhine and Robert Brier (New York: Citadel, 1968) 223ff.; and G. N. M. Tyrrell, *Science and Psychical Pheonomena: Apparitions* (New Hyde Park, N.Y.: University Books, 1961).
31. After careful considerations of what we can say about survival beyond death and after claiming that we know details about the hereafter, Hornell Hart, *The Enigma of Survival: The Case for and Against an After Life* (London: Rider, 1959) arrives at the conclusion that human personality does survive bodily death (p. 263), and that the accounts of the astral world, though agreeing in many fundamentals, vary considerably (p. 244).
32. Althaus, *Die letzten Dinge*, 96 n. 2, draws this convincing conclusion.
33. So Elisabeth Kübler-Ross in her foreword to Raymond A. Moody, *Life after Life. The Investigation of a Phenomenon—Survival of Bodily Death* (Harrisburg, Pa.: Stackpole Books, 1976) 7. Moody also mentions that when Kübler-Ross was reviewing this book she remarked that she had collected hundreds of reports of this kind. So Raymond A. Moody, *Reflections on Life after Life* (Harrisburg, Pa.: Stackpole Books, 1977) 13.
34. Cf. the extensive quotations in Moody, *Life after Life*, 82-85, and *Reflections on Life after Life*, 67-74.
35. Cf. the numerous reports to each of these experiences in Moody, *Life after Life*, 26-62, and *Reflections on Life after Life*, 18-30.
36. Cf. Moody, *Reflections on Life after Life*, 30-34.
37. Cf. ibid., 113-116.

38. For the following cf. Moody, *Life after Life*, 101ff. Moody, however, admits that the definition of "death" is by no means settled. That may be one of the reasons why, very appropriately, he uses the term "near-death experiences."
39. Cf. for the following ibid., 65ff.
40. Ibid., 67.
41. Ibid., 67f.
42. Moody, *Reflections on Life after Life*, 48.
43. Ibid., 79.
44. Cf. Moody, *Life after Life*, 10, and see *Reflections on Life after Life*, 128.
45. See Moody, *Reflections on Life after Life*, 103 and 90.
46. Ibid., 78.
47. Ibid., 101.
48. Cf. Ian Stevenson, *Telepathic Impressions. A Review and Report of Thirty-five New Cases* (Charlottesville: University of Virginia, 1970), who presents many different and well-attested cases of precognition and visionary appearances. He also helped Moody with refining his methodology in obtaining and analyzing the reports.
49. John C. Eccles, in his noteworthy essay "The Brain-Mind Problem as a Frontier of Science," in *The Future of Science. 1975 Nobel Conference*, ed. by Timothy C. L. Robinson (New York: Wiley, 1977) 87.
50. Ibid., 88.
51. Plato *Phaedo 79*, in *The Collected Dialogues of Plato*, 62f.
52. Plato *Timaeus* 41f., in ibid., 1170f.
53. Cf. Plato *Phaedo* 66f, in ibid., 49; and Plato *Laws* 12.959, in ibid., 1503, where he affirms that the soul is "utterly superior to body" and that the body is "no more than a shadow which keeps us company."
54. Plato *Phaedrus* 245, in ibid., 492f.
55. For the following cf. Johannes Hirschberger, *Geschichte der Philosophie* (Basel: Herder, 1960), vol. 1: *Altertum und Mittelalter*, 211.
56. Cf. Frederick Copleston, *A History of Philosophy* (Westminster, Md.: Newman, 1960), vol. 1: *Greece and Rome*, 328.
57. Aristotle *On the Soul* 414a.22ff., in *The Basic Works of Aristotle*, ed. with an intr. by Richard McKeon (New York: Random, 1941) 559.
58. Aristotle *On the Soul* 414a.14, in ibid., 559.
59. Aristotle *De Generatione Animalium* 2.3.736b.20-30, in *The Works of Aristotle*, ed. by J. A. Smith and W. D. Ross; trans. by Arthur Platt (Oxford: Clarendon, 1949), 5:736b.
60. Cf. Kant's second antinomy of pure reason and the conclusions he draws from these antinomies.
61. Cf. Immanuel Kant, *Critique of Practical Reason* (5.121), in Immanuel Kant, *Critique of Practical Reason and Other Writings in Moral Philosophy*, trans. and ed. with an intr. by Lewis W. Beck (Chicago: University of Chicago Press, 1949) 225f.
62. *The Human Soul (Against the Neo-Aristotelians)*, in Denzinger, *The Sources of Catholic Dogma*, 237 (738).
63. Encyclical *Humani Generis*, in *Enchiridion Symbolorum*, 779 (3896), or Anne Fremantle, *The Papal Encyclicals in Their Historical Context*, with an intr. by G. Weigel (New York: New American Library, 1963) 297f.
64. John A. Hardon, *The Catholic Catechism*, 106.
65. Cf. Gerhard von Rad, *Genesis*, 75, who calls this verse a *locus classicus* of Old Testament anthropology.
66. Rudolf Bultmann, *Theology of the New Testament*, 1:244f.
67. Oscar Cullmann, *Immortality of the Soul or Resurrection of the Dead? The Witness of the New Testament* (London: Epworth, 1958) 33.

68. Cf. Bultmann, 1:202, who shows convincingly that, according to Paul, Christians do not desire to be unclothed, like the Gnostics, but desire to be further clothed and yearn for the heavenly garment.

69. Cf. Moody, *Life after Life*, 38.

70. Cf. for the following Cullmann, 59, where he quotes Justin Martyr (cf. n. 71).

71. Justin *Dialogue with Trypho* (80), in *The Ante-Nicene Fathers: Translations of the Writings of the Fathers down to A.D. 325*, 1:239.

72. Cullmann, 15.

73. Karl Rahner, "The Life of the Dead," in *Theological Investigations*, 4:347.

74. Ibid., 351.

75. Ibid., 352.

76. Ibid.

77. Joseph E. Kokjohn, "A Hell of a Question," in *Commonweal* 93 (1971): 370.

78. Cf. John A. Hardon, *The Catholic Catechism*, 265f.

79. Edmund J. Fortmann, *Everlasting Life After Death* (New York: Alba, 1976) 42, advocates very vigorously this idea.

80. An excellent survey and evaluation from the Roman Catholic side is provided by the study by Ansgar Ahlbrecht, *Tod und Unsterblichkeit in der evangelischen Theologie der Gegenwart* (Paderborn: Bonifacius-Druckerei, 1964).

81. Regin Prenter, *Creation and Redemption*, 576 n. 171.

82. Karl Barth, *Church Dogmatics* trans. by A. T. Mackay, et al. (Edinburgh: T. & T. Clark, 1961), vol. 3: *The Doctrine of Creation*, Part 4, 590. Cf. also Walter Künneth, *The Theology of the Resurrection*, 37ff., who understands the resurrection as the antithesis to the idea of life and immortality. Cf. also Werner Elert, *Der christliche Glaube: Grundlinien der lutherischen Dogmatik* (Hamburg: Furche, 1956) 508, who claims that all ideas of immortality are shattered by the fact of bodily death.

83. Emil Brunner, *Dogmatics*, trans. by D. Cairns in collab. with T. H. L. Parker (Philadelphia: Westminster, 1962), vol. 3: *The Christian Doctrine of the Church, Faith, and the Consummation*, 383f., and 390f.

84. Paul Tillich, *Systematic Theology*, 3:409ff.

85. William Hamilton, *The New Essence of Christianity* (New York: Association, 1966) 116, does not want to put the resurrection in one line with ascension and exaltation, assertions that according to him do not have any precise meaning today. However, he mentions the resurrection only as an afterthought, and then only in the context of humiliation and suffering, since the risen Lord still bears the marks of his suffering. This seems to run contrary to the New Testament affirmations, where the resurrection is conceived of as a part of Christ's kingly office, which is, according to Hamilton's evaluation, without precise meaning for us today.

86. Cf. George Eldon Ladd, *I Believe in the Resurrection of Jesus* (Grand Rapids, Mich.: Eerdmans, 1975) 21. Ladd carefully marks out the limits of historical knowledge and comes to the conclusion that: "Although it was an event in history, Jesus' resurrection had no antecedent historical cause—a sequence which the historian assumes" (ibid., 125), and, we might add, attempts to establish if necessary even by hypothetical means.

87. Albert Schweitzer, *The Quest of the Historical Jesus*, 284f., and 345f.; cf. also Richard R. Niebuhr, *Resurrection and Historical Reason: a Study of Theological Method* (New York: Scribner, 1957) 11.

88. Rudolf Bultmann, "New Testament and Mythology," 39. Even Bultmann admits that the resurrection of Jesus is often used as a miraculous proof in the New Testament.

89. Cf. Willi Marxsen, *The Resurrection of Jesus of Nazareth*, trans. by M. Kohl (Philadelphia: Fortress, 1970) 138ff., and Marxsen, "The Resurrection of Jesus as a Historical and Theological Problem," trans. by D. M. Barton, in *The Significance of the*

Message of the Resurrection for Faith in Jesus Christ, ed. with an intr. by C. F. D. Moule (London: SCM, 1968) 48ff. Cf. also the valid criticism of Marxsen's position by Bas van Iersel, "The Resurrection of Jesus—Information or Interpretation?" in *Immortality and Resurrection*, ed. by Pierre Benoit and Roland Murphy, vol. 60 of *Concilium* (New York: Herder & Herder, 1970) 65ff., who maintains that the resurrection is both interpretation and information.

90. Referring to Augustine's *Confessions*, Richard R. Niebuhr, *Resurrection and Historical Reason*, 67, gives an excellent analogy to the influence of the resurrection on the formation of the New Testament. In his *Confessions* Augustine reflects on his entire life from the perspective of his conversion experience.

91. For the following cf. Werner Foerster, "kyrios," in *Theological Dictionary of the New Testament*, 3:1089.

92. Cf. also Werner Foerster, "ktizo," in *Theological Dictionary of the New Testament*, 3:1012f.

93. This has been pointed out especially clearly by Walter Künneth, *The Theology of the Resurrection*, 161ff.

94. Cf. Gottfried Wilhelm Leibniz, *The Monadology and Other Philosophical Writings*, trans. with an intr. and notes by Robert Latta (London: Oxford University Press, 1951) 270f., where he states that if we could sufficiently understand the order of the universe, we would find out that it exceeds all the desires of the wisest men, and "that it is impossible to make it better than it is."

95. Cf. Otto Michel, *Der Brief an die Römer* (Göttingen: Vandenhoeck & Ruprecht, 1957) 121, in his explanation of Rom. 5:12-21.

96. So Hans Conzelmann, *A Commentary on the First Epistle to the Corinthians*, trans. by J. W. Leitch (Philadelphia: Fortress, 1975) 261, in his explanation of 1 Cor. 15:11.

97. Ibid., 249, in his explanation of 1 Cor. 15:1-11, where he mentions that Paul emphasizes unmistakably that our belief in the resurrection is founded in the Christ event.

98. Cf. for the following Wolfhart Pannenberg, *Revelation as History*, 146; and his *Jesus —God and Man*, 81f.

99. Pannenberg, *Jesus—God and Man*, 77, rightly asserts that these stories speak only of a *temporary* return of a dead person into *this* life.

100. Eduard Schweizer, "sarx," in *Theological Dictionary of the New Testament*, 7:100f.

101. Joseph E. Kokjohn, "A Hell of a Question," in *Commonweal* 93:370, seems to imply this when he suggests that the unjust person's moral catastrophe is one of nonexistence, not only the isolation from other people and God but the utter alienation from all forms of life.

102. Cf. Conzelmann, 289ff., in his exegesis of 1 Cor. 15:50-58.

103. This has been elaborated very clearly by Pierre Benoit, "Resurrection: At the End of Time or Immediately after Death?" in *Immortality and Resurrection*, ed. by Benoit and Murphy, esp. 112ff. He affirms that we are already here united in the Holy Spirit with the body of the risen Lord to a union that will not be interrupted by death. Thus there is no continuance through an immortal soul, but through the already initiated union with Christ. The "between" death and consummation is relativized by the fact that our time is of different nature than the time of the "future" or "new" or "higher" world.

104. Cf. Augustine *De Genesi; Contra Manichaeos Libri Duo* 2.3 in J.-P. Migne, *Patrologiae Cursus Completus: Series Latina*, 34:174f., where he says: "God also made the times: therefore before he made the times, there were no times. And we cannot say that there was any time prior to God having made something."

105. WA XXIV, 24, 8f.

106. WA XX, 58, 24-31; cf. also the excellent treatment of Luther's idea of appointed time *(Stündelein)* by Gustav Wingren, *Luther—On Vocation,* trans. by C. C. Rasmussen (Philadelphia: Muhlenberg, 1957) 213-234.

107. Cf. Werner Heisenberg, *Physics and Philosophy: The Revolution in Modern Science* (New York: Harper 1958) 114ff., who gives a very good description of Einstein's theory and its implications.

108. Cf. Cullmann, *Christ and Time,* 63, who, however claims that eternity can and must be expressed "in terms of endless time." We wonder if this is really the only way to talk adequately about eternity.

109. In the earlier writings of the Old Testament, however, the eternity of God is described with the metaphor "Everlasting God" (Gen. 21:33), which implies a conception of time extending forward and backward without end (cf. Gerhard von Rad, *Genesis,* 232, in his exegesis of Gen. 21:33).

110. Plato *Timaeus* 37d, in *The Collected Dialogues of Plato,* 1167; cf. also Cullmann, *Christ and Time,* 61f.; and Hermann Sasse, "aion," in *Theological Dictionary of the New Testament,* 1:197f., who refers to Plato's *Timaeus.*

111. The relevance of such a christocentric world view in an age dominated by science has been demonstrated very eloquently by Teilhard de Chardin. However, by taking the incarnation of Christ as the focal point, instead of the cross and resurrection, he arrives at an evolutionary type of eschatology.

112. This has been pointed out especially well by Karl Heim in his book *The World: Its Creation and Consummation.*

113. Hermann Sasse, "aion," in *Theological Dictionary of the New Testament,* 1:201.

114. Cf. Cullmann, *Christ and Time,* pp. 81ff.; cf. also the emphasis on the proleptic aspect of the Christ event by Pannenberg in *Revelation as History,* 139ff.

115. Cullmann, *Christ and Time,* 66f.

116. Cf. Bultmann, *The Gospel of John,* 257, in his exegesis of John 5:24-28, where he seems to imply this idea.

117. Cf. Althaus, *Die letzten Dinge,* 146f.

118. WA XVII/2, 235, 17-20.

119. WA XXXVII, 151, 8ff.

120. For the following cf. "The Beatific Vision of God and the Last Days," in Heinrich Denzinger, *The Sources of Catholic Dogma,* 197f. (530-531).

121. Cf. Michael Schmaus, *Der Glaube der Kirche,* 2 vols. (Munich: Hueber, 1969-70), 2:744ff. and 773ff.

122. For the following cf. Althaus, 158f.

8
The New
World to Come

FOR A LONG TIME the new world to come has been regarded as proper subject matter for eschatological inquiry. Yet by the same token

eschatology has often been regarded as the most questionable and speculative of all Christian doctrines since it deals with that which is completely inaccessible to man's observation and experience, namely, the future—not the immediate future about which some reasonable prognostications can be made, but the final future, beyond death, the end of history.[1]

We have seen that we are not alone with our belief in the new world to come. Most religions envision a final end of all history when our present world will come to a close and a new world will appear. Within the Christian sphere of influence these hopes have often been intensified, and sizeable human communities have believed at one time or another that they lived in a time close to the end of the world. Mass conversions, fervent religious exercises, and exodus into virgin land to await the coming Lord, were the immediately visible signs of such feverish expectations. But today, due to our non-religious secular education and to our secular, rationalistically analyzing mass media, such attitudes are now restricted to a few hard-core members. To us it seems almost inconceivable that someone like Martin Luther could once interpret floods, wars, and comets as signs of the impending end of this world. In our technological age we are confronted with an ever increasing number of people who have given up the hope for God's new creation altogether. They have given up the idea of an intervention from "beyond," and they attempt to tailor the planet which they inhabit according to their own ends.[2]

Beyond resignation and futurist activism: Many of these people who have decided to give up the hope for a new world might even consider themselves Christians. But others have thought through the consequences of such a decision and have realized that without hope for an actual transformation of our world into God's kingdom faith is empty and meaningless, or simply a fraud.

Already Friedrich Nietzsche proclaimed nihilism as the alternative to Christianity. Under the impact of our technological domination of the world and in response to the collapse of the earth-centered pre-Copernican world view Nietzsche's madman exclaims: "God is dead. God remains dead. And we have killed him. How shall we, the murderers of all murderers, comfort ourselves?" And then he asks: "Whither are we moving now?" . . . "Are we not plunging continually? Backward, sideward, forward, in all directions?" . . . "Are we not straying as through an infinite nothing? Do we not feel the breath of empty space? Has it not become colder?" [3] Like few before him Nietzsche felt what it meant to live as an atheist in post-Christian fashion.

While in other religious environments atheism does not amount to much, since there are always many other directive and mysterious forces, it is different with Christianity. Christian faith knows only of one divine force, who is the creator, sustainer, and redeemer of everything. Everything else is secular and not divine or sacred. Even the "sanctuary" is only so called because people agree to worship together at this place, not because it is a divine place by its own quality. But once this one God is denied, nothing divine is left. This means that there is no point of orientation, and time is bereft of its origin and destination. Of course, one can claim that time is elapsing from a predictable future into a knowable past, but this simple process of growth and aging no longer endows life with meaning. Whether we adopt biological standards in saying that life always seeks self-expression, or anthropocentric standards in suggesting that everything must ultimately serve us, or any other standards, they are arbitrary and without firm foundation. What life is for, nobody knows.

Faced with a continuously onrushing future that allows no escape, we could simply tighten our belts and flex our muscles to make it on our own. Yet exactly this practical atheism, followed by many both within the Christian tradition and outside it, seems to be encountering increasingly larger obstacles. As soon as one problem is solved, at least two greater ones seem to emerge. Our faith in harnessing the future has become more and more uncertain. Even if we concentrate on survival instead of conquest and mastery, we ultimately have to face the question, survival for what?

Confronted with our finite nature and our many compounding problems we are apt to conclude that we come into life through accident, drag through life in weakness, and vanish from life in resignation. But our present situation, with its threats of overpopulation, world hunger, scarcity of resources, and nuclear over-kill, is so precarious that we cannot afford the luxury of despair. Yet any activism resulting from an assessment of our situation would only prolong our agony, since sooner or later we have to admit the finitude and futility of all our actions. If there is a meaningful future at all, it must come not by our own strength but by provision "from above." Thus we find it impossible to dispense with the eschatological expectations of the Christian faith and still maintain a meaningful hope in the future. "And yet we must also recognize that these are simply *hopes* not yet realized, hopes with a foundation outside themselves." [4] This means we have to avoid two extremes: We cannot so concentrate on the hereafter and the transitory character of earthly things that we undervalue the importance of this life; nor can we so ignore the terminal character of death that we canonize the goods of this world and distract believers from the pursuit of holiness.[5]

1. Keeping the hope alive

Christians do not just sit around and hope. Taking their name from Jesus Christ, they recall God's visitation to his people, and they look forward to the final revelation of God's glory. Situated between memory and hope, they are allowed to anticipate proleptically the new world to come. In this context the church plays a vital role, as the symbol of the future in which the eschatological hope is kept alive, as the semblance of the whole people of God, and as the anticipation of the heavenly city.

a. The church as the reminder of God's future

In our present world the church is an erratic block, continuously in danger of becoming a stumbling block. The church does not fit into a world that assumes that the course of its history is predictable, being determined by humanity's own efforts and the resources available. The church knows and confesses that "did we in our own strength confide, our striving would be losing." In a secular and self-relying culture it gives witness to a future provided not by humanity but by God.

The symbol of the future: The involvement of the church in the affairs of the world, in the struggle for justice, human rights, and access to the necessities of life, serves a dual purpose. On the one hand the church does serve those who are in need. Yet, being aware that all of its efforts are at best patchwork, Band-Aids on the wounds of a hurting world, the church also witnesses with its actions to a world that will be without anguish and suffering. Similar to the miracles of its Lord which were both help for people in need and signs of a new creation, the church is the symbol of God's future. This eschatological symbol of the new creation becomes visible not just in social involvement, but in every activity of the church. Each time our sins are forgiven, we are reminded of the love of God that will one day find its completion. Each time we celebrate the Lord's Supper, we are reminded of the celestial banquet.

The two-fold phrase in the words of the institution of the Lord's Supper: "This do in remembrance of me" does not just imply that we should remember Christ's sacrifice. It also means that God should remember the sacrifice of his Son and speed up the coming and completion of the kingdom. At every celebration of the eucharist when the community prays for the coming of the Lord, it proclaims the beginning of the time of salvation, and it anticipates the blessed hour of the parousia.[6] The community reminds itself and God that it will celebrate the eucharist until Christ returns and the eschatological promises are fulfilled.

That the Christian community understands itself as the symbol of the future, a future that has already commenced, is again emphasized in the Lord's Prayer.[7] As a constituent part of the early church's communion liturgy, the Lord's Prayer belonged to that part of the service in which only those who were baptized were permitted to participate.[8] Both petitions, "hallowed be your name, your kingdom come" are in content closely related to the expectant cry "Come, Lord Jesus!" (Rev. 22:20).[9] They yearn for the hour in which God's profaned and misused name will be glorified and the reign of his kingdom will be revealed. In a world enslaved by the rule of evil, a world of distress and conflict, they look forward to the revelation of God's glory.

These petitions are not wishful prayers but are filled with confidence. In the face of the world surrounding and encroaching upon the church, the Christian community takes God's promise seriously. It addresses him with the utter confidence of "Our Father." Remembering who taught them this prayer they are absolutely certain that God will redeem his promises as he spoke by the prophet Ezekiel: "I will vindicate the holiness of my great name, which has been profaned among the nations, and which you have profaned among them; and the nations will know that I am the Lord, says the Lord God, when through you I vindicate my holiness before their eyes" (Ezek. 36:23).

Other phrases in the Lord's Prayer witness similarly to this yearning for and expectation of the eschaton. For instance, in the petition for bread and forgiveness the church asks that God might grant them already today and in this place the bread of life and the blotting out of sins. Like a beacon of hope in the darkness of this world, the church prays amid failure, apostasy, and denial, that God's kingly rule over the lives of his people might be realized. Though still symbols of the future, the bread of life and the endless mercy of God are already present now in the eucharist, a symbol of God's almighty glory and the coming of his kingdom.

Considering baptism in this context, we recognize that the prevalent practice of infant baptism would be utterly ridiculous if we were to regard baptism simply as incorporation into the visible, institutional church. The notion of dying and rising with Christ or of being incorporated into his body envisions more than institutional membership. It even means more than being converted to Christ and becoming a confessing Christian. When Paul insists that as new creatures we should walk in newness of life (Rom. 6), he makes two points:

> 1. We are still in a state of transition from this aeon to the future aeon. The world, though unable to hold us completely, still ensnares us. Luther was therefore right when he called for a drowning of the old Adam through daily repentance.[10]
>
> 2. Yet we must recognize a second moment. The Christian existence is a dynamic existence and not a static one. Together with the whole creation we are yearning and longing for the revelation of the sons of God and for the manifestation of the kingdom (Rom. 8:19ff.).

Dying and rising with Christ therefore can only instill hope if it implies a breaking out of the natural cycle of birth and death from which this image is borrowed. It must point to a time when death will no longer score a victory and when we can forever walk in newness of life. Similarly, becoming part of the body of Christ can only evoke hope when there is one point at which the separation from Christ through our sinful alienation is forever overcome. In other words, baptism remains an empty shell unless verified through the coming of the kingdom. Yet at the same time baptism today still is a sign and symbol of that future verification, and it is administered in trust and hope. Similarly, the same is true for the eucharist. It is intrinsically eschatological, foreshadowing and hoping for the final celestial banquet when we will be allowed to enjoy Christ's presence forever.

It has become clear that the church in its actions, in its liturgical celebrations, and in its prayer life is a symbol of the future, in part foreshadowing the things to come, and in part patiently but intensely hoping and trusting for their ultimate verification. Yet the church would deny its own foundation if it would attempt to bring about the realization of this future through its own actions. The power and the encouragement for both its anticipation and its expectation are derived from its experience of Christ. Through the presence of Christ and the power of the Spirit the church realizes that the life and destiny of Jesus the Christ are the prime examples of its own life and destiny. Knowing about his death and resurrection, it acknowledges that ultimately all history will serve to make his kingdom triumph. We can be confident that God "will vindicate his people, and have compassion on his servants" (Ps. 135:14), so that the hope he inspired in and through them will not be in vain.

The whole people of God: Intrinsic to these hopes is the commission to make disciples of all nations (Matt. 28:20). The hopes for the common destiny of humanity include the hope for the unity of the whole church, the unity of church and synagogue, and the unity of all people under the dominion of God. The church must be the vivid and living reminder that God wants all people to be saved. Its reason for being is to represent Christ in this world and to bring the Gospel of Christ to the world. If the church wants to be the reminder of the future, it dare not leave humanity as it is, in its dispersion, antagonism, and self-destruction. Its faithful proclamation of the Gospel tradition must challenge every status quo, whether of Muslim or of Buddhist persuasion, whether Marxist or capitalist. Yet the acknowledgement and proclamation of Christ as Lord of the whole world will not simply bring Christ to the world; it would also have to ask how Christ is "present and operative in the faith of the individual non-Christian." [11]

There is a positive point of contact, however hidden, in every religious expression, something worthy of cultivation, augmentation, and enlargement. At the same time we dare not close our eyes to that which is wrong and misapprehended, and which needs true supplanting and conversion. But since the church is not identical with Christ, it too stands under both affirmation and judgment. Only the Lord himself and his Gospel constitute the criterion for what is good and true and what is wrong and misconceived. The dialogue with people from all religious backgrounds will bring us closer together, since it will place all of us under the judging and liberating word of our Lord.

Though we do hope that his word will make a difference in this world, creating increasing solidarity among all people, we dare not assume prematurely that all people will eventually listen to him. Even our most sincere proclamation of the Gospel in word and deed, through words of grace and acts of mercy, can never assume a universal homecoming of all people as a fait accompli. The realization of our common destiny as the whole people of God can only be a most daring eschatological hope and the content of fervent prayers. Still, sharing Christ even at the most remote places of the earth is a reminder that in one way or another, whether with everyone's consent or without, the Christ will one day be acknowledged as Lord by all creation so that God may be everything to everyone (1 Cor. 15:28).

It would be totally irresponsible for the church to bring the Gospel to non-Christians, calling for solidarity and joint listening to the Lord of the world, without being utterly disturbed about its own divided house. The division into different churches and denominations is not just the fault of others. It is always also our own fault. While we realize more and more that the church must be Greek to the Greeks and Jewish to the Jews, the necessary cultural distinctiveness and diversity do not justify our present divisions. Though immense progress has been made toward representing the whole people of God in the World Council of Churches, various world federations of confessional families, national councils, and bilateral talks on all levels, institutional inertia and our sinful pride of being holier than others seem to be the greatest obstacles to actual unity.

Every day we discover anew how much we actually share in common. Thus in many cases division into different denominations and churches seems anachronistic and sinful. But the sentiment for institutional self-preservation looms high even in ecumenically-minded circles. Nevertheless, in the last 50 years approximately 60 church unions have taken place, resulting in churches such as the Church of South India or the United Church of Christ in the U.S.A., and in about 30 countries negotiations towards union are being conducted. The Salamanea Consultation (1973) of the Faith and Order Commission put our dilemma, our task, and our hope very succinctly: *Jesus Christ founded one Church. Today we live in diverse churches divided from one another. Yet our vision of the future is that we shall once again live as brothers and sisters in one undivided Church.*[12]

A divided church is an offense to its Lord and the Gospel, and therefore an impediment to mission. Divided Christendom is not only a reminder of our sinfulness and of the task still ahead. It is also a reminder of the eschatological future, when our human divisiveness will be overcome and no longer intrude on the manifestation of the whole people of God. Intermediate steps toward union are not necessarily designed to result in one super-church. But involvement in joint mission projects, shared worship, public declaration of our common intention on all levels, united theological education, training of laity, Christian education and literary work, and joint evaluation of priorities and use of funds are all signs of repentance of a past that was often characterized by unholy crusades against other members of the body of Christ and by competing against each other in the name of our Lord. Our joint witness to the world is that the power of God's Spirit is at work in his people and that they are willing to anticipate something of the great celestial banquet when all will share the same table and the same food.

The vision of the whole people of God would be incomplete without envisioning the union between church and synagogue, between Jew and Gentile (cf. Rom. 11:12-26). It should make us wonder why a people without a homeland for nearly 2,000 years, a people who suffered the most cruel and systematic persecution ever inflicted, a people dispersed throughout the world—that such a people did not abandon their faith in God and in the promised Messiah. This people have now finally obtained a homeland, disputed and embattled though it may be. The Jewish people are both an enigma and a source of inspiration and hope. They remind us that God may lead his people through the valleys of shadow and death, but he will not abandon them forever. He sustains, calls, and nourishes them.

But the Jewish people are more than a symbol of survival. They are a symbol of insight. As the sculpture of the blindfolded synagogue on medieval churches shows, the Jewish people may have been tolerated, but they were never really accepted as equals by Christians. Yet this did not prevent them from perceiving all of humanity "as the descendants of one father and the creatures of one Creator" and similarly cherishing "the complementary vision of a reunited mankind under God at the end of time." [13] If in the light of its own history, Israel has not renounced the hope for a reunited humanity under God, how can the church ever dare to give up its hope for the visible union of the whole people of God? Moreover, the Christian community knows that the ethnic restrictions of the old covenant no longer hold and that the new covenant should include all people. The church will not want to take the great commission lightly to go into all the world, to proclaim the good news, and to baptize those who follow Christ.

But the Jewish people remind us that it also is our task to keep ourselves holy and to sanctify God's name among all people. We would renounce our eschatological hope if we would just aim at winning victories for our Lord. We must remind ourselves and others that the victory has already been won and that our Lord's compassion has been more powerful than our achievements. Thus Israel's hope for a reunited humanity can serve as a timely reminder that the wholeness of God's people does not depend on us. While it should be furthered by our own actions, it does not depend on them. We must trust that God's promises will not return empty.

The anticipation of the heavenly city: A theology of glory is not a proper topic in today's distressed world. Even the Roman Catholic Church, with which the notion of a theology of glory has often been associated, is rediscovering the role of servanthood and suffering. But persecution and suffering are not the signs of the true church either.[14] God distributes suffering and pain indiscriminately among believers and unbelievers, among Christians and non-Christians. If the church is the living organism which connects the historical acts of God, through which he overcame our self-centered sinfulness, with the future acts of the establishment of the new Jerusalem, then it would be anachronistic to contemplate only suffering and pain. Festivity and celebration provide moments in a troubled world when we look forward to a time of eternal sabbath, of continuous joy and rejoicing.

Remembering Christ as both crucified and resurrected, we celebrate our liberation and freedom as children of God, even while knowing that we are still entangled in this world. The church would betray its own source of strength and hope if it would see its function exhausted in rendering assistance to a world in need. The church also serves as a beacon of hope by demonstrating the Christ-won freedom in its own life and by manifesting its rejoicing in that freedom.[15] A theology of glory need not be a betrayal of the Gospel tradition if it means glorying in what God has done in and through the church, what God is doing, and what God will do. Anticipation of the heavenly glory both as a reminder of God's past acts and as a looking forward and hoping for the eschatological perfection is as important for the church as remembering that it still lives in a valley of death and injustice.

When we focus here on the proleptic anticipation of the heavenly city, we must remember that the "ultimate hope in the lordship of Christ and the coming kingdom of God cannot be divorced from, or identified with, our historical hopes for freedom, justice, equality and peace." [16] The anticipation of the heavenly city cannot mean that we accomplish now what is promised to us as an eschatological, i.e., heavenly, reality. The church is an interim institution between Pentecost and parousia, waiting and hoping for replacement by the heavenly community of all the saints. Any utopian attempt to bring about in totality that by and towards which the church lives would destroy the condition that makes its future-directed existence possible. For instance, it is one of the strange paradoxes of Marxism that it lives and strives for the establishment of a classless society in anticipation of the heavenly community. But by refusing to admit that these attempts and programs are only provisional, Marxism destroys that which engendered and encouraged its hopes, the God-provided eschatological perfection. Moreover, since in a secular society perfection must be attained in this world, utopian systems by necessity behave intolerantly and dictatorially, diminishing the ideal vision they stand for.

The anticipation of the heavenly city is not a human accomplishment, but a divine gift. Community is not something we accomplish; we discover it as something given. We do not attempt to fulfill a dream or a utopian vision but live according to the presence of God through his Spirit. The theocentric structure of the Christian community reminds us of God, our ultimate allegiance and authority. All dreams and visions are destroyed by the cross of Christ, the vivid reminder that we still live under the realities of this world. Dietrich Bonhoeffer reminded us that "God hates visionary dreaming; it makes the dreamer proud and pretentious." [17] Living under the new life means to live under the work of forgiveness, the source of new life, and God's word which meets us through other Christians.

The anticipation of the heavenly city is not just a spiritual reality but something enfleshed in everyday life. Bonhoeffer rightly observed that "a purely spiritual relationship is not only dangerous but also an altogether abnormal thing." [18] The enfleshment of the anticipation of the heavenly city has perhaps been captured best in the monastic ideal. Monastic groups are usually formed to strengthen the spiritual life of their members. The monastic ideal, however, also informs their daily lives and transforms the surroundings in which they live and work through education, buildings and art, and community projects of charity. Similarly, their Protestant counterparts, such as the Oxford group of the Lutheran Pastor Frank Buchman or the Moravians under Count Zinzendorf, had a profound impact on their own members and on the communities in which they lived and worked.

The same influence can emerge from the local worshiping community. The Christian faith is not a Sunday morning affair. It lays claim on the total lives of its members and has an impact on the community in which a congregation is located. As anticipation of the heavenly city on the local level, the church cannot but become a visible reality, a beacon of hope, a bastion of a new humanity in a fallen and hurting world. The vision of the church is always larger than the local church. As J. Robert Nelson pointed out, "the primary task of the church in history is to be the bearer of that reconciling work in every generation." [19] Foreshadowing the heavenly city which is not torn by rivalry, strife, or injustice, the church not only manifests these signs on a global scale, but by erecting them it also serves as a powerful stimulus for sensitizing the whole of humanity. Without the presence of the church, the present would grow colder and more merciless.

It is unfortunate that the expectation of the heavenly future has rarely been sufficiently emphasized in the life of the church. Quite often it fell to sectarian groups to remind the church of the necessity and centrality of an eschatological Gospel from which we derive our vision and power. In this century theology has recaptured the significance of an eschatological vision. Yet the rediscovery of the so-called last things still remains to be completed. Perhaps the church rightly feels threatened by the vision of the seer in the book of Revelation when he says:

> I saw no temple in the city, for its temple is the Lord God the Almighty and the Lamb. And the city has no need of sun or moon to shine upon it, for the glory of God is its light, and its lamp is the Lamb. By its light shall the nations walk; and the kings of the earth shall bring their glory into it, and its gates shall never be shut by day—and there shall be no night there (21:22-25).

In the midst of a cruel, unjust, and divided earth, such eschatological harmony among people and nations seems unreal. We also feel too solidly grounded in our own achievements on this earth to abandon them in favor of the complete dominion of God in a heavenly city. Some staunch church members and ecclesiastical administrators may also become uneasy with the vision of the city in which the presence of God will replace all temples. How dearly we love the church structures and ecclesiastical empires we erect and safeguard!

But the church does a disservice to its members and to the world when it neglects to remind us in time of trouble and turmoil of the eschatological future that God will establish in the midst of his people. Such a message, proclaimed with vigor and confident hope, will not induce a relinquishing of our responsibility and become a heavenly escape valve as Karl Marx predicted. On the contrary, it will encourage us to take the parable of the faithful steward seriously (Matt. 25:21), because we know that our Lord and the Lord of all the world is coming. Only when we become oblivious to the coming of our Lord will we be tempted to shed our responsibility and set ourselves up as masters and oppressors (Luke 12:45), even in the name of freedom and liberation. When the church keeps alive the hope in God's future, it will instill hope, courage, and a sense of direction of a confused world. It will remain and become a beacon and a rallying point for the future, a stumbling block for some and a reminder for many others that the gates of hell shall not prevail (cf. Matt. 16:18).

b. Proleptic anticipation and the signs of the end

Quite often present and future are perceived as so radically disjunctive that neither one has any bearing on the other. Thus either otherworldly retreat or this-worldly activism results. But the very fact that we call ourselves Christians, followers of Jesus Christ, indicates that we embrace both the present by following Jesus and the future by expecting the return of Christ. The bridge between present and future is not only seen in Jesus Christ as our present Lord, but in individual Christians as well, as they mold themselves and are being molded through that presence.

It is therefore no surprise that Bultmann, in his research with the Gospel of John, has pointed to the *now* as the decisive eschatological moment in which our decision between life and death is made.[20] The last things are already anticipated in our present confrontation with the word of God. Through Jesus' whole life and destiny the decisive question was posed to the Jewish people, asking them whether they wanted to live in conformity with God or to reject him. We hear Jesus say: "He who hears my word and believes him who sent me, has eternal life; he does not come into judgment, but has passed from death into life" (John 5:24), or "He who does not believe is condemned already" (John 3:18). These would be difficult words to explain as a projection of human desires as Feuerbach thought. The present is decisive time; it determines our future, not by way of complementing, but as consolidation and clarification.

This emphasis on the now as the anticipatory moment of the end is not restricted to John. Paul devotes almost a whole chapter (Rom. 6) to clarifying that we are now dying and rising with Christ, and he declares that "now is the acceptable time; behold, now is the day of salvation" (2 Cor. 6:2). This is not an attempt to comfort us with the hope for a better "hereafter." And already Jesus, referring to his actions, tells his inquirers: "But if it is by the finger of God that I cast out demons, then the kingdom of God has come upon you" (Luke 11:20; Matt. 12:28). Especially this remark, which was elicited by people who asked Jesus in whose name he performed his actions, shows that anticipation of the end does not make the end demonstrable. Eternity in time is only possible in disguise. Even the evident results of the encounter of the divine with our earthly sphere are subject to contrary interpretations. Although this holds true for Jesus himself as well as for the life and actions of Christians, it does not exempt Christians from anticipating the end.

If Christians would refrain from anticipation, that would modify not only their present but also their future existence. This means that the present decision and the present attitude do not eliminate the final judgment but determine it. Thus the present is the decisive time for Christians, because the whole future is at stake. Of course, it would be a gross misunderstanding to conceive of the present activity of a Christian as works-righteousness and the final judgment as the big "awards day." Any anticipation of the end, whether in a positive or a negative way, is only possible because Christ has already anticipated the end of his resurrection—and we are invited to share in this anticipation. Our attitude can only be an attitude of response and not of initiative. Though Marxists are right in pointing out that, contrary to our own intentions, we have often not responded well enough to our eschatological situation, they have gone to the other extreme of exclusively emphasizing the human initiative.

Christians are creative because they accept and anticipate the new world which will come by the provision of God.[21] No matter how much we emphasize the anticipatory character of eschatology, it is only proleptic anticipation and not the end itself. If it were otherwise, there would be no anticipation possible and we would understand our activities exclusively as the creative high point of evolution. But the anticipatory character of our activities is enabled by and points to the future fulfillment. Throughout the New Testament the now as the anticipated end points to and enables the future fulfillment and vice versa.[22] This becomes especially evident in the so-called signs of the end.

There are several major apocalyptic passages in the gospels (Matt. 24; Mark 13; Luke 21) that indicate the signs of the end: emergence of false prophets, climactic wars, catastrophes in nature, famines, persecution of the Christians, and the proclamation of the gospel to all people (Mark 13:10). The Gospel of John, which does not contain any long apocalyptic passages, is complemented by the book of Revelation, where the signs of the end are especially dealt with in Chapters 6, 8, 13, and 16. Since many of these signs had already occurred when they were written down (cf. destruction of Jerusalem; Luke 21:20, 24), they are a theological evaluation of history in the light of the expected end and not a calendar according to which one can calculate when the end will come. Sentences such as "This generation will not pass away before all these things take place," with the following interpretation: "Heaven and earth will pass away, but my word will not pass away" (Mark 13:30f.), show that the evangelists did not want to enhance an apocalyptic fever in which people were convinced that they knew the course of world history, including its end.

The evangelists rather returned to Jesus' own message, which culminated in the demand for immediate readiness. We hear Jesus say: "What I say to you I say to all: Watch" (Mark 13:37), and "For as the lightning comes from the east and shines as far as the west, so will be the coming of the Son of man" (Matt. 24:27), and we hear him telling the parable of the five wise and the five foolish maidens (Matt. 25:1-13). Even Paul asserts: "The day of the Lord will come like a thief in the night" (1 Thess. 5:2). These passages, and many more, convey the demand for immediate readiness. To interpret them as an indication of an immediate expectation of the end by Jesus or the first Christian community, an expectation which proved to be wrong, seems to miss the point.[23]

Immediate readiness, similar to the decisive character of the now, does not necessarily express belief in the near return of the Lord, but it shows that our present attitude determines for us the outcome of the future, the eschaton. The watchword of the Middle Ages *memento mori* (be aware of your death) thus was closer to the New Testament than the traditional belief in the final end of history. *Memento mori* does not just remind us that we never know when we will die, but that death will make our present life attitude irreversible. This is why we are called to respond to the demand for immediate readiness with a life attitude of preparing anticipation and not with a once-in-our-lifetime decision. That the demand for immediate readiness stands next to and is interspersed with indications of the end should also tell us that, no matter how carefully we interpret history, the coming of the end will be a total surprise; it will be absolutely unexpected. The consequence for Christians is that they will live their lives in active anticipation, as if each moment would be their last. Anthony A. Hoekema, in his extensive treatment of the signs of the end, rightly reminds us: "When they occur, we are not to become fearful, but accept them as the birthpangs of a better world." [24]

There is one sign of the end, however, which deserves special attention, the concept of the anti-Christ.[25] The imagery which is incorporated in the concept of the anti-Christ is partly of Jewish origin. For instance, in Daniel 9:27 we hear that someone, perhaps Antiochus IV Epiphanes, will come on the "wing of abominations" and will make desolate the holy place (the temple). In the New Testament it is said that in the last days "false Christs and false prophets will arise and show signs and wonders, to lead astray" (Mark 13:22). Paul warns of the "son of perdition, who opposes and exalts himself against every so-called god or object of worship, so that he takes his seat in the temple of God, proclaiming himself to be God" (2 Thess. 2:3f.). In the First Letter of John we hear that in the last hour the anti-Christ is coming; therefore we know that it is the last hour (1 John 2:18), and a few verses further on we hear that the anti-Christ denies the Father and the Son (1 John 2:22). In the Second Letter we read of the many deceivers who have gone out into the world, "men who will not acknowledge the coming of Jesus Christ in the flesh; such a one is the deceiver and the anti-Christ" (2 John 7). Finally, in the book of Revelation the anti-Christian power is understood as being represented in the Roman state with its cult of the emperor

(Rev. 13:1-10), and the anti-Christ also signifies the false prophets who advocate this cult (Rev. 13:11-18).

This diversity of the concept of the anti-Christ shows us that the New Testament has no clear "doctrine" of the anti-Christ. The anti-Christ comes in disguise and power and will mislead many; he looks like a lamb, but talks like a dragon; he wants to dethrone God and put himself in God's place. Sometimes there is just one anti-Christ, at other times there are many. Sometimes the anti-Christ comes from within the Christian community, for instance when he denies the incarnation of God in Jesus Christ; sometimes he comes from outside.

The church accepted the idea of the anti-Christ and used it widely. For the early church the Roman emperors, especially Nero and Domitian, who persecuted the Christians, were called the anti-Christ. In the Middle Ages, during the papal schism, usually the counter-pope was declared the anti-Christ, and he in turn called the original pope the anti-Christ. The Franciscan Spirituals, who had followed the millennial ideas of Joachim of Fiore were also quick to declare the pope as anti-Christ, simply because he denied their claim for poverty. Later, the forerunners of the Reformation, John Hus and John Wyclif, sometimes extended the idea of the anti-Christ to the whole Catholic Church.

Luther was at first very reluctant to use the term anti-Christ.[26] However, under the impact of Laurentius Valla's discovery that the papacy had illegally usurped its supremacy over worldly authorities with the forgery of the Donation of Constantine, Luther came to the conclusion that the papacy must be the anti-Christ. The papacy, not an individual pope, is the anti-Christ because it puts its own authority above that of the word of God. With this conviction Luther, of course, regretted that the Augsburg Confession made no mention of the anti-Christ. Though in contemporary history many dictators, such as Stalin or Hitler, have been labeled as anti-Christ, the question for us is what we shall do with this concept. Shall we simply recognize its frequent and manifold use and then go on to more important business?

Without disregarding all diversity in the use of this concept, three features seem to be consistent and noteworthy:

(1) Whereas in dualistic Parsiism, which undoubtedly influenced the emergence of the concept of the anti-Christ, there is a gradual disappearance of the anti-Godly powers, the Christian faith is aware of the threatening presence of the anti-Christ up to the final consummation

of the world. This shows the conviction that humanity does not gradually work itself up to the kingdom of God, with God sanctifying these human endeavors by recognizing the goal of their work as his kingdom. The alienation from God and the usurpation of anti-Godly sovereignty seem to increase instead of decrease.

(2) The anti-Christ is not a possibility of the future, but a reality of the present. The conviction that the anti-Christ is already here emphasizes that we must constantly be on alert. There is no neutral ground on which to stand and wait. Either we are engaged in active preparation, or we fall prey to the anti-Christ who will lead us to a different activism.

(3) The activities of the anti-Christ do not result in events whose theological significance has to be shown; they already *have* theological significance. The anti-Christ, be it from within or from outside the Christian community, attempts to dethrone God and assume God's throne. Belief in technology and progress instead of faith in God, belief in essential human goodness instead of faith in the love of God, hope for the Christianization of all people instead of hope for the coming of the kingdom of God, are only a few alternatives that show us the anti-Godly tendency of the anti-Christ. Yet, realizing the seriousness of the *many* faces of the anti-Christ, we know that this figure too is subject to temporality, and the last judgment will terminate all anti-Godly endeavors.

2. Last judgment and the love of God

a. Consummation of the world

In considering the concepts of time and eternity we have noticed that any kind of last judgment as a universal judgment demands the consummation or at least transformation of the categories of time, space, and matter, or of the world as we know it. This is also the conviction of the New Testament. "Immediately after the tribulation of those days the sun will be darkened, and the moon will not give its light, and the stars will fall from heaven, and the powers of the heavens will be shaken; then will appear the sign of the Son of man in heaven, and then all tribes of the earth will mourn, and they will see the Son of man coming from the clouds of heaven with power and great glory" (Matt. 24:29f.). And the Second Letter of Peter tells us in even greater detail: "But the day of the Lord will come like a thief, and then the heavens will pass away with a loud noise, and the elements will be dissolved with fire, and the earth and the works that are upon it will be burned up" (2 Peter 3:10).

Inquisitive spirits have always tried to investigate how such a consummation could be possible, and modern scientific insights have paved the road for many speculations. For instance, the possible collision of our earth with other planets or planetoids would certainly darken the sun and the moon for us and might perhaps lead to the extinction of life on earth. A cosmic nuclear reaction could also dissolve the elements with fire, and if militarists would employ all our presently available "over-kill" they could even usher in the eschaton at their own wish. Also the looming prospect of a global pollution of life could lead to the end of life here on earth. But Teilhard de Chardin already observed that such a sidereal disaster would affect only part of the universe and not the total universe. Even the final heat death through an equilibrium of all energy levels, to which Karl Heim alluded, would not lead to the consummation of this world, but only to the end of life within it. At best, science can tell us that our universe does not contain any eternal life force. It cannot, however, show us that or how our universe will be consumed. Science, by its very nature is bound to work within the categories of space, time, and matter, and this means with the universe we live in. But consummation of the world does not just affect existence in the universe; it affects the very existence of the universe.

According to the New Testament, the consummation of the world is not primarily destruction. It is rather the universal incorporation into the creative and transforming act of Christ's resurrection. No one has expressed this more clearly than Paul in his Letter to the Romans, where he writes that "the creation waits with eager longing for the revealing of the sons of God," that it will be "set free from its bondage to decay," and that we ourselves wait for adoption as God's children, "the redemption of our bodies." This is no vague or uncertain hope, because "he who raised Jesus Christ from the dead will give life to your mortal bodies also" (Rom. 8:11, 19-23).

Salvation in the eschaton pertains to our whole being, to the whole cosmos, and to the whole creation. It is a salvation described as redemption from transitoriness.[27] When our adoption as sons and daughters, which we have received in baptism, is made manifest, then we shall be not merely in anticipation but in reality, no longer subjected to transitoriness. Consummation of the world is perfection and completion. It is completion of time[28] and perfection of our limiting forms of space, time, and matter.

A foretaste of this new world, as far as it pertains to us, has already been given to us in the witnesses of those who encountered the resurrected Christ.[29] The biblical witnesses tell us that the risen Lord was no longer limited in time, space, and matter. The material and spatial bounds of a closed room or of hunger could no longer confine him. But, of course, he could appear in a room and he could eat. In a similar way, he was no longer bound to the transitoriness of time, yet he could appear sooner, or later, or now. Perfection of the forms of this world also means the elimination of the anti-Godly distortion of this world, of sin, destruction, and death. Again this is shown in the resurrected Christ who is beyond the possibility of sinning and beyond the possibility of dying.

Whenever we talk about the new world to come we must mention Christ and his resurrection because "all things were created through him and for him" (Col. 1:16). There is no other goal of creation than Jesus, who as the Messiah enabled this creation to move toward this goal.[30] The consummation is then the disclosure of the new world which was enabled by and has started in the resurrection of Jesus Christ. Martin Luther, in his unique and picturesque language, has expressed the point of the consummation very well when he says:

> This world serves for God only as a preparation and a scaffolding for the other world. As a rich lord must have a lot of scaffolding for his house, but then tears the scaffolding down as soon as the house is finished, . . . so God has made the whole world as a preparation for the other life, where finally everything will proceed according to the power and will of God.[31]

b. Final judgment

The final judgment is a difficult subject to mention because everybody wants to be saved but only a few are willing to accept judgment as its prerequisite. H. Richard Niebuhr's famous phrase about 19th century American liberalism: "A God without wrath brought men without sin into a kingdom without judgment through the ministrations of a Christ without a cross," [32] is a vivid description of humanity in general. We desire heaven, but we do not want to accept that the only way to heaven is through judgment. But the New Testament in all its witnesses makes it unmistakably clear that the only way to the new world to come is through judgment, and that the consummation of the world does not mean final evolution but implies the parousia of the Lord and the final judgment.

"For the Son of man is to come with his angels in the glory of his Father, and then he will repay every man for what he has done" (Matt. 16:27). "When the Son of man comes in his glory, and all the angels with him, then he will sit on his glorious throne. Before him will be gathered all the nations, and he will separate them one from another as a shepherd separates the sheep from the goats" (Matt. 25:31f.). "For the Lord himself will descend from heaven with a cry of command, with the archangel's call, and with the sound of the trumpet of God" (1 Thess. 4:16). "We must all appear before the judgment seat of Christ, so that each one may receive good or evil, according to what he has done in the body" (2 Cor. 5:10). "And I saw the dead, great and small, standing before the throne, and books were opened. Also another book was opened, which is the book of life. And the dead were judged by what was written in the books, by what they had done" (Rev. 20:12). The imagery of these quotes from the New Testament, which could easily be multiplied, betrays Old Testament and Jewish apocalyptic influences. The language is that of a past age and need not necessarily be reiterated, but the tendency of these passages is crystal clear: there is a final judgment.

Often this final judgment has been conceived as the great awards day. This is especially evident in the chiliastic hopes of a 1000-year rule over and at the expense of others. Yet, the final judgment is not a judgment of our own merits, but of our response to God's grace which he has extended to us in Jesus Christ. We are not awarded a certificate of loyalty simply because we happened to be on the right side at the right time. Such cheap grace would neglect our wrongdoings. Voltaire was not right when he mocked: "God will forgive, because it is his job." Paul caught the seriousness of the final judgment much more appropriately when he cautioned: "For whatever a man sows, that he will also reap" (Gal. 6:7). Our Lord will take into consideration each of our individual situations and judge to what extent we have attempted to respond to the promise he offers and to the exemplary life-style he has shown us.

The judgment is not an occasion when everybody will be measured by the same standards, it is rather a judgment according to one's possibilities. "Everyone to whom much is given, of him will much be required; and of him to whom men commit much they will demand the more" (Luke 12:48). This does not mean that we should take it easy; we are called to measure up to the possibilities of our own response and not to some ambiguous standards we might adopt. Since this judgment will concur with the parousia of the Lord, it becomes evident that Christ will be the judge. In judging us in the name of God and as God, this judgment is irrevocable, final, and binding. There is no higher court of appeal possible.

Since Christ the Savior is also the judge, the judgment in all its seriousness has a comforting aspect. By confronting us with himself and his gospel, Christ has shown us the direction of our life, and through his dying and resurrection he has enabled us to pursue this direction of our life, to live in conformity and toward conformity with God. The first Christian community, who preserved for us all the dreadful apocalyptic imagery of the final judgment, was not scared by the prospect of this judgment. It knew that it was the necessary "entrance gate" to the new world to come. Thus *marana tha* ("our Lord, come!") was a familiar word in the first Christian community (cf. 1 Cor. 16:22),[33] and the book of Revelation closes in a similar way with "Amen. Come, Lord Jesus!" (Rev. 20:20). Martin Luther recaptured this New Testament confidence in the face of the judgment when, contrary to the mood of the Middle Ages, he did not conceive of this day as a day of wrath, but as a day of the glory of God, a day he was looking forward to when he said in many of his letters: "Come, dear, last day." [34]

But is not such an ultimate, universal judgment day as obsolete as the apocalyptic imagery in which its coming is expressed? Are we not finally indulging in a travelog eschatology? Our answer must be no, because human destiny aims at participation in God's eternity.[35] If we were to realize this determination, then we would live at each moment in accordance with the eternity of God at which we are aiming. But we are self-centered, and instead of living each moment in the light of eternity we live mainly in the light of ourselves or of transitoriness. When we die, we are unable to continue our self-centered life; our temporal life ceases and only the eternity of God is left, into which we are received. Thus death becomes the boundary line that we cross as we enter into the eternity of God.

Death also finalizes and completes our participation in the eternity of God. Our earthly life, which is only known to us partially as long as we live it, will become known in totality. Nevertheless, it will become known in totality not for itself but in confrontation with the "blueprint" of its eternal destination. Then its fragmentariness will become visible and irreversible, and the discrepancy between the possibility and the actuality of our earthly life will be what we experience as God's final judgment, a judgment which, in anticipation, we have already long ago pronounced upon ourselves in our earthly life. Only those who are already in this life connected with eternity in time, with Jesus Christ, have the assurance that this discrepancy will be overcome, because Jesus Christ, though human, never allowed this discrepancy to develop in his life, in his death, and beyond death. Consequently, through alignment with him, death will result in resurrection not only to judgment, but to eternal life.

c. Paradox between justice and love of God

The option for a universal homecoming becomes at no time more urgent than when we are confronted with the final judgment and realize that not everybody will be saved. But Jesus, and with him the New Testament witnesses, are convinced of a twofold outcome of this final judgment.[36] "The gate is wide and the way is easy, that leads to destruction, and those who enter by it are many. For the gate is narrow and the way is hard, that leads to life, and those who find it are few" (Matt. 7:13f.), we hear Jesus say. And we read the same in the Gospel of John, only actualized in the now: "He who believes in the Son has eternal life; he who does not obey the Son, shall not see life, but the wrath of God rests upon him" (John 3:36). And the book of Revelation expresses in typical apocalyptic fashion: "And the smoke of their torment goes up for ever and ever; and they have no rest, day or night" (Rev. 14:11).

To make the issue more confusing, the New Testament also contains many assertions that God wants all people to be saved. Paul, for instance, in wrestling with the destiny of Israel, expresses the conviction that "God has consigned all men to disobedience, that he may have mercy upon all" (Rom. 11:32). The goal of the cosmos and of all saving history is universal salvation, a goal which embraces the destiny of all individuals, Jews, and pagans alike.[37] In a similar way, to quote just one more reference, we hear that God our Savior "desires all men to be saved and to come to the knowledge of the truth" (1 Tim. 2:4). All this boils down to a final paradox that states on the one hand that God's love wants all to be saved and declares on the other hand that God's justice requires all the disobedient to be punished.

Of course, we could attempt to solve the evident paradox by asserting that God's justice is only preliminary, and justice and love are related to each other like law and gospel. God threatens with his justice in order that we might flee to his love.[38] But this evidently anthropomorphic construct of a pedagogic God, who punishes only in order to save (cf. Schleiermacher!), does not take into account that the judgment is disclosure and finalization of our life attitude and not a transition to the universal love of God. If our life attitude runs counter to the love God extends, the result is a dichotomy that cannot be bridged through evolution or amelioration.

Another attempt to solve the paradox between God's justice and love, though only a half-hearted one, is to assert that the condemned will be annihilated and thus all (who are left) will be saved.[39] But how can there be an annihilation of anybody if there is no escape from God, since God is everywhere, even in death and beyond death? The solution must rather be sought in what we mean when we talk about the justice and love of God. Do we really mean that we *describe* God with these terms, or do they not rather *disclose* certain aspects of God *for us?* We must remember that God's self-disclosure to us can only be expressed in human language, and this means with necessarily anthropomorphic and inadequate conceptual tools.[40] Thus we can rightly conclude that God is beyond justice and love, just as he is beyond being a person when we call him a personal God.

We must remember too that we are confronted with God's decision-demanding word that says: Repent and follow me. As we accept God's offer to direct our lives according to his eternal purpose, a universal homecoming will be meaningless for our salvation, since we will be saved according to the promise of his redemptive word. Ultimately, the idea of a universal homecoming can emerge only as a speculation about the final destiny of others. Even in our most sincere concern for them we have to acknowledge the ultimate hiddenness of God, a God who is beyond justice and love, and we can only hope that his never-ending grace will ultimately prevail.

3. The new world

When we finally attempt to make assertions about the new world it seems next to impossible to say something meaningful here without indulging in speculations. Yet .Jesus and the New Testament invite us to put our trust in something concrete, something we can already to some degree anticipate in our present life. We also remember that the goal of history and humanity has already started with Jesus' coming. These two facts, the New Testament's own insistence on a "concrete" future and the anticipatory aspect of this future, seem to provide enough room for positive assertions about the new world.

a. Disclosure of the kingdom of God

When Jesus entered our scene, it was announced: "The time is fulfilled, and the kingdom of God is at hand; repent, and believe in the gospel" (Mark 1:15). The kingdom of God or the new world to come has already started with Christ's coming. But the kingdom also has a future, and admission into it demands a decision, because "not every one who says to me, 'Lord, Lord,' shall enter the kingdom of heaven" (Matt. 7:21).

All the parables of the kingdom seem to indicate that at one point it will become evident who has entered the kingdom of God and who has not, or in other words, good and evil will be separated (cf. Matt. 13:30, 49ff.). Jesus even had to hold back enthusiastic disciples who demanded that, since the decision about entrance must be made now, the evidence of entrance or non-entrance must also be disclosed. But Jesus rejected any attempts to build a pure "Christian community" here on earth by pointing to the future dimension of such a perfection: "Let both grow together until the harvest; and at harvest time I will tell the reapers, Gather the weeds first and bind them into bundles to be burned, but gather the wheat into my barn" (Matt. 13:30). This future dimension will find its fulfillment with the final judgment. Then the already existing invisible separation will become visible and irreversible. The kingdom of God, or the new world which will be disclosed, is described with the term heaven, while the term hell denotes exclusion from the new world.

b. Heaven and hell

To talk about heaven or hell as the final stages of the human destiny seems, at first glance, a re-mythologization of eschatology. In most religions heaven is understood as the location of the gods, while hell is usually associated with the devil, with demons, and other figments of a world of fantasy. When looking at the New Testament we discover, however, that the term heaven is used at least as frequently, and not just primarily in the gospels, as the term kingdom of God. At some places the terms are even merged to a "kingdom of heaven" (cf. Matt. 3:2; 5:3; and others).

Already Luther mocked at the idea of picturing hell as built of wood or bricks so that it would have gates, windows, locks, and bars as does a house here on earth. And, of course, Christ did not destroy hell with a flag of cloth in his hands.[41] For Luther "hell means that death is accompanied by the feeling that the punishment is, at once, unchangeable and eternal. Here the soul is captured and surrounded so that it cannot think anything else except that it is to be eternally damned."[42] In a similar way Luther mocked at the "Schwärmer" who understood God's dwelling place in heaven in a local way. Because the visible heaven or sky is constantly moving, Luther concludes that this would mean that God cannot sit still for one moment. It is, however, absurd to understand God's realm in a local way so that one thinks of God as sitting on high, somewhat like a stork in its nest. But Luther was also aware that the Bible in its pre-Copernican world view often uses the terms hell and heaven in a local way.

Already in the Old Testament the term heaven is not just used in a cosmological topography, but also in a theological understanding in which heaven denotes the dimension of the source of salvation, namely God and his power.[43] In rabbinic literature heaven can even become a paraphrase for God.[44] The differentiation between a cosmological and a theological understanding of heaven is intensified in the New Testament. Theologically speaking, heaven can be the dimension of God, the source of salvation, and the integrating focus for the present and future blessings of salvation in the new aeon.[45] That such a theological understanding of heaven demands a transcendence of the prevalent three-story world-view of the Bible is indicated in such passages as the exclamation of Solomon: "Behold, heaven and the highest heaven cannot contain thee; how much less this house which I have built!" (1 Kings 8:27) and the assertion of Paul: "He who descended is he who also ascended far above all the heavens, that he might fill all things" (Eph. 4:10).

Although in the earlier parts of the Old Testament sheol or "hell" is understood indiscriminately as the shadowy existence of all who have died (cf. Ps. 89:48), it is at the same time the dimension of alienation from God in death. In post-exilic times, perhaps through the influence of Parsiism, sheol is conceived as a temporary dwelling place and as different for the righteous than for the godless.[46] Gehenna, the New Testament word for hell, already presupposes resurrection and final judgment.[47] The whole person with body and soul will be tormented in Gehenna, "where their worm does not die, and the fire is not quenched" (Mark 9:48). While hell does not just originate in the eschaton (Matt. 25:41), it is only after the resurrection and judgment that it will be disclosed as the realm of eternal torment. In apocalyptic thinking Gehenna was still associated with the Hinnom valley near Jerusalem, where once King Ahaz and King Manasseh had brought sacrifice to foreign gods. This kind of localization was abandoned in the New Testament. In contrast to apocalyptic, the New Testament usually did not paint the torments of hell in drastic colors, and when it did, it did so to awaken the conscience of the listeners (cf. Matt. 10:28).

When we now attempt to draw a final conclusion, we realize that hell and heaven receive their peculiarities neither from any cosmological localities, nor from any imageries that are associated with them, but only from their respective relationship with God. Only in the world of fantasy is hell the domain of the devil. But according to the biblical witnesses even the anti-Godly powers are under God's control.[48]

In talking about hell, we talk about something we do not know. The allusions of the New Testament such as: "nether gloom of darkness" (2 Peter 2:17), "outer darkness," "weeping and gnashing of teeth" (Matt. 22:13), and "eternal fire" (Matt. 25:41), describe hell in terms of pain, despair, and loneliness. In so doing these words are taken from present negative experiences and attempt to transcend them. These negative experiences express the reaction to the disclosure and finalization of the discrepancy between one's eternal destiny and one's realization of this destiny. They express the anguish of knowing what one has missed without the possibility of ever reaching it. They witness to a state of extreme despair without the hope of reversing it. It becomes clear that such an anguish and despair will not just result from a local separation from God. It will be a dimensional separation from God and from the accepted. Yet God and the destiny of the accepted will be somehow present as a curse.

Since Christians do not confess faith in hell, but in "resurrection of the body and life everlasting," hell is of no ultimate concern to us. It serves for us only as an admonition to reach our eternal destiny. In talking about life everlasting or about heaven, we have to agree with Luther's fitting remark: "As little as children know in their mother's womb about their birth, so little do we know about life everlasting." [49] When we read about our habitation in the new Jerusalem, a city of gold, similar to pure

glass, with walls of precious stones, and with twelve gates, each made
of one pearl (Rev. 21), then this apocalyptic imagery resembles so much
a world of fantasy that it looks more like an attraction in Disneyland
than the eternal goal of our lives. Even the much more restrained assertion that once we have reached our final goal, we will see God "face to
face" (1 Cor. 13:12) sounds unreal. And the promise that God will dwell
with the elect "and they shall be his people and God himself will be with
them; he will wipe away every tear from their eyes, and death shall be
no more, neither shall there be mourning nor crying nor pain any more,
for the former things have passed away" (Rev. 21:3f.), and that God
will be "everything to every one" (1 Cor. 15:28) looks like wishful thinking.

Union with God, abolition of anguish and sorrow, and permanent
beauty and perfection seem so unreal to our life of alienation, pain and
suffering, transition and change that we are about to discard these hopes
as utopian dreams. We would be right in so doing if Jesus Christ had
not shown us through his death and resurrection that this fulfillment is
attainable. Because of Jesus Christ and because of the promise that is
contained for us in the Christ event, the hope for a final realization of
such a destiny is a realistic hope. It shows us that our immanent and
perpetual yearning for self-transcendence, for deification, for elimination
of death, and for progress toward perfection is not a utopian dream but
will find its fulfillment in life everlasting. But it also poses the all-decisive question: Do we understand our attempt to fulfill our inborn
yearning through pursuit of technological progress and peace for all
people in Marxist or Western materialistic fashion as ends in themselves,
thus excluding ourselves from any true fulfillment that is not provided
by us? Or do we understand our endeavors here on earth as proleptic
anticipation of that which "God has prepared for those who love him"
(1 Cor. 2:9), and consequently hope for a God-provided true fulfillment?

"Only he who is certain of his future can relax and turn to today's
business."[50] It is necessary to check our life-attitude and once again put
our trust alone in Jesus who is "the pioneer and perfecter of our faith"
(Heb. 12:2).

We have concluded the survey of our way to the future. We have seen
how the understanding of eschatology has developed, and what views and
factors we must consider if we want to talk meaningfully about eschatology. Confronted with life and its possibilities for the future, we have

also noticed that we can choose among the three basic attitudes of despairing resignation, futurist activism, and proleptic anticipation.

Despairing resignation is perhaps the least viable option. Once we give up wrestling with the future, we no longer participate meaningfully in it and can offer no solution for the course it should take. Since our future is not absolutely predetermined, it needs our contribution. We cannot afford the luxury of despair. Yet so many do drop out of the future-directed stream of life and dull their minds with drugs and medications of all sorts. This should make us wonder whether we are still meaningfully pursuing the future or whether we have turned it into a dehumanizing monster from which many of our younger generation want to escape.

Considering *futurist activism* as the next possibility, we become aware that for a growing number futurist activism in the classical Western materialistic fashion seems no longer attractive. It has been tarnished by doubt in the possibilities of technological expansion and by the growing awareness of its undesirable side effects. Many voices are raised these days warning that we cannot live by the increase of the gross national product alone. We also need a vision by which to live. Here Marxist Communism claims to have the solution. Though as materialistically oriented as the West, it still dreams of a new world. And, endowed with a deeper messianic consciousness than any other philosophy, it attempts to create a classless society through worldwide revolution. Though the fact should not be overlooked that Marxism has enthralled the masses primarily in countries much less technologically advanced than Western industrial countries, its missionary influence is felt throughout the world. It has overcome the narrow Western materialistic understanding of progress as a goal to be pursued for its own sake. In Marxist Communism progress is directed toward the betterment of the human community. But Marxist Communism shows a decisive lack in its understanding of humanity. Contrary to Marxist ideology, we are not just an extension of matter. People are not only interested in the future of society, but in the ultimate future of their personal existence and of the world in which they live.

Here the Christian view of the future as *proleptic anticipation* seems to provide the most viable option. Knowing that the future has already begun in the resurrection of Jesus Christ, it dares to anticipate proleptically this future along the avenue which the Christ-event provides. This process of active anticipation strives for a better humanity, a more just society, and a more worldly world to live in. But since it is only anticipation, Christian faith is realistic enough to take into account our intrinsic alienation from God as the source of all wisdom and all good things. Thus we must reject the illusion that we could ever create a good humanity, a just society, or a new world. Ultimate perfection and removal of death as the dimensional border between our world and the new world to come will be brought about through God's gracious action, undeserved by us. Unfortunately, the right understanding and true expectation that the new world will be brought about through God's own activity has often been used as an excuse to take the Christian attitude of active anticipation less seriously. To indicate that such neglect can surely impede the credibility of the Christian message, I close this postscript with a little story:[51] In a dialog with an agnostic Jew, held in the presence of persons who were contemplating Christianity, I asked him what he looked for in Christians. He was well acquainted with all the relevant Christians, the born-again Christians, and the secular Christians. But he said: "I wish they would try to speak of and live with their own great teachings. If I could believe these, I would. Since they claim to, I would like to see how different the world would look if incarnation, crucifixion, and resurrection were taken seriously." And what a difference it would make.

NOTES

1. Gordon D. Kaufman, *Systematic Theology: A Historicist Perspective* (New York: Scribner, 1968) 314.
2. Cf. Emanuel Hirsch, *Geschichte der neueren evangelischen Theologie*, 5 vols. (Gütersloh: Bertelsmann, 1949-54), 5:626, who mentions in the concluding remarks of his magnificent work that in our historical epoch the thoughts and dreams of humanity go above all in the direction of tailoring the planet which it inhabits according to its own ends.
3. Friedrich Nietzsche, *The Gay Science*, in *The Portable Nietzsche*, sel. and trans. with an intr., pref., and notes, by Walter Kaufmann (New York: Viking, 1960) 95.
4. Kaufman, *Systematic Theology*, 325.
5. So rightly, John A. Hardon, *The Catholic Catechism*, 257. As a good treatment of the content of Christian hope cf. *Eschatology. The Doctrine of the Last Things.* Twelve Theses and a Position Paper Adopted by the 118th General Assembly for Guidance and Study (Presbyterian Church in the U.S.) 19-25 (Eschatology in Biblical Perspective; Implications for Individual and Church; and Principles of Faith Related to Eschatology); and the refreshing booklet by Stephen Travis, *The Jesus Hope* (Downers Grove, Ill.: InterVarsity, 1976).
6. So Joachim Jeremias, *The Eucharistic Words of Jesus*, trans. by N. Perrin, 3rd ed. (Philadelphia: Fortress, 1977) 254.

7. Raymond E. Brown, "The Pater Noster as an Eschatological Prayer" in *New Testament Essays* (Milwaukee: Bruce, 1965) 253, rightly comments "how coherently the eschatological viewpoint binds together the petitions into one picture."

8. Cf. Joachim Jeremias, *The Lord's Prayer*, Facet Books, trans. by J. Reumann (Philadelphia: Fortress, 1969) 2.

9. So ibid., 22.

10. Martin Luther, *The Small Catechism*, in *The Book of Concord. The Confessions of the Evangelical Lutheran Church*, trans. and ed. by Th. G. Tappert (Philadelphia: Fortress, 1959) 349.

11. So rightly Karl Rahner, *Foundations of Christian Faith*, 315, who, however, still seems to underestimate the necessity of proclaiming Christ to the non-Christians.

12. As reported in "Ecumenical Chronicle: Unity of the Church—Next Steps," in *The Ecumenical Review* 26 (April, 1974): 293.

13. So Moshe Greenberg, "Mankind, Israel and the Nations in the Hebraic Heritage," in *No Man Is Alien. Essays on the Unity of Mankind*, ed. by J. Robert Nelson (Leiden: Brill, 1971) 35.

14. So rightly Paul Althaus, *Die Christliche Wahrheit. Lehrbuch der Dogmatik* (Gütersloh: Mohn, 1959) 503.

15. Cf. Jürgen Moltmann, *Theology of Play*, trans. by R. Ulrich (New York: Harper, 1972) 71f.; and Jürgen Moltmann, *The Church in the Power of the Spirit*, 300f. Unfortunately Moltmann did not balance sufficiently in his ecclesiology the strong call for involvement with the need for rejoicing and festivity.

16. "A Common Account of Hope," Statement on Hope approved and adopted by the Commission on Faith and Order of the World Council of Churches at its meeting in Bangalore in August 1978, reprinted in *The Ecumenical Review* 31 (January 1979):5-12; quotation 7. Nevertheless, the statement focuses very much on the socio-political dimension of the this-worldly aspect of hope.

17. Dietrich Bonhoeffer, *Life Together*, trans. by J. W. Doberstein (New York: Harper, 1954) 27.

18. Ibid., 38.

19. J. Robert Nelson, "Signs of Mankind's Solidarity," in *No Man Is Alien*, 14.

20. Bultmann, "The Eschatology of the Gospel of John" (1928), in *Faith and Understanding*, 1:175.

21. Cf. Moltmann, "Die Revolution der Freiheit," in *Perspektiven der Theologie: Gesammelte Aufsätze* (Munich: Kaiser, 1968) 210, in his discussion of Marxist anthropology.

22. Cf. Gustav Stählin, "nun," in *Theological Dictionary of the New Testament*, 4:1118ff., where he mentions that the thought of a twofold fulfillment runs through the whole New Testament.

23. At this point it is difficult for us to agree with the otherwise excellent presentation of Paul Althaus, *Die letzten Dinge*, 273f., who states on the one hand that the expectation of the impending eschaton was not fulfilled and who claims on the other hand that the end is in essence near and is at each point a threatening possibility. This spiritualist interpretation seems to neglect the progressiveness of history and comes close to a dualism of time and eternity.

It is certainly true that there were people in the first Christian community and at many other points in the history of the Christian church, who expected the immediate return of the Lord. It is also true that Jesus unmistakably emphasized the nearness of the eschaton or, in other words, mentioned more than once that the end is close at hand. Yet he also consistently rejected any attempts to date the "point" at which the eschaton might come. This reservation would be unexplainable if he had expected the coming of the eschaton in connection with his death or with his resurrection, or after 30 or 40 years (destruction of Jerusalem). Should Jesus not rather have meant: the hour of fulfillment has begun, the kingdom of God is manifesting itself already here and now, the final end will come soon; therefore, make use of the time as long as you can? But Jesus refused to limit God's sovereignty by imparting to us an eschatological timetable (cf. the excellent treatment of the issues involved by Joachim Jeremias, *New Testament Theology*, Part 1, 131-141).

24. Anthony A. Hoekema, *The Bible and the Future*, 129-163, quotation on 163. He also reminds us that all of the signs of the end are present throughout the history of the church. While we agree with him as to their continuous presence, there is a building up of their intensity as the apocalyptic passages indicate.

25. For the concept of the anti-Christ, cf. Regin Prenter, *Creation and Redemption*, 555f.; and Paul Althaus, *Die letzten Dinge*, 282-297.

26. Cf. for the following Ulrich Asendorf, *Eschatologie bei Luther* (Göttingen: Vandenhoeck & Ruprecht, 1967) 173ff.

27. Otto Michel, *Der Brief an die Römer*, 171.

28. Walter Künneth, *The Theology of the Resurrection*, 285f. The term "consummation" which is used to translate the German *Vollendung* does not render the full meaning of this term.

29. Karl Heim, *Jesus the World's Perfecter: The Atonement and the Renewal of the World*, trans. by D. H. van Daalen (Philadelphia: Muhlenberg, 1961) 166ff.

30. Cf. Eduard Lohse, *A Commentary on the Epistles to the Colossians and to Philemon*, trans. by W. R. Poehlmann and R. J. Karris (Philadelphia: Fortress, 1975) 52, in his exegesis of Col. 1:16.

31. WA TR II, 627, 29-628, 4.

32. H. Richard Niebuhr, *The Kingdom of God in America*, 193.

33. Hans Conzelmann, *A Commentary on the First Epistle to the Corinthians*, 301, claims in his exegesis of 1 Cor. 16:22, that it must be left open whether this phrase invokes God's participation in the eucharist or his parousia. Since the eucharist must be regarded as an eschatological meal the phrase in either way points to the coming eschaton.

34. Cf. Althaus, *The Theology of Martin Luther*, 420f., in his excellent treatment of Luther's interpretation of eschatology.

35. For the following cf. the profound thoughts of Wolfhart Pannenberg, *What Is Man?*, 76-81.

36. Joachim Jeremias, *New Testament Theology*, Part 1, 131, in exegeting Matt. 22:14, mentions that the invitation is unlimited, but the number is small of those who follow it and are being saved.

37. Cf. Michel, 253, in his exegesis of Rom. 11:32.

38. This misunderstanding seems to be implied in Emil Brunner's otherwise excellent book *Eternal Hope*, 182ff.

39. This idea is, for instance, advanced by Joseph E. Kokjohn, "A Hell of a Question," in *Commonweal* 93 (January 15, 1971): 369. Maurice Carrez, "With What Body Do the Dead Rise Again?" in *Immortality and Resurrection*, ed. by Benoit and Murphy, 101, is closer to the truth when he suggests that resurrection implies the entering into the fulness of life with a transformed body. While *all* will appear before the Lord on the day of judgment, there is only one resurrection, namely to eternal life.

But we must ask here, how can we meaningfully speak of a judgment of all if we do not speak of a resurrection for all? Of course, resurrection to a "newness of life" and a subsequent damnation (of this newness) seems to be an obvious contradiction. The question, however, is, whether resurrection must be understood this way. Albrecht Oepke, "anhistēmi," in *Theological Dictionary of the New Testament*, 1:371, claims rightly that the predominant view of the New Testament is that of a twofold resurrection.

40. Karl Rahner, "The Hermeneutics of Eschatological Assertions," in *Theological Investigations*, 4:344f., points out very convincingly that each term conveys its own particular imagery, and that no new assertion *adequately* renders the real content of the assertion which it attempts to translate and interpret. This means that any new interpretation is not a better one that replaces the old, but it is a new and necessary attempt in our search for a more contemporary and adequate approximation in expressing God's relationship to us and to our final destiny.
41. WA XXXVII, 65, 33. Cf. for Luther's understanding of heaven and hell Hans Schwarz, "Luther's Understanding of Heaven and Hell," 83-94.
42. WA V, 497, 16-19 *(Studies in Psalms)*.
43. Cf. Gerhard von Rad, "ouranos, B. Old Testament," in *Theological Dictionary of the New Testament*, 5:502-509.
44. Cf. Helmut Traub, "ouranos, C. The Septuagint and Judaism," in ibid., 512. The term "kingdom of heaven," frequently used in the Gospel according to Matthew, reminds us of this usage.
45. Ibid., 532.
46. Joachim Jeremias, "hades," in *Theological Dictionary of the New Testament*, 1:147.
47. Cf. for the following Joachim Jeremias, "geenna," in ibid., 657f.
48. A dramatic dualism occasionally introduced by biblical writers to emphasize the threatening power of evil, cannot challenge their basic monotheistic outlook.
49. WA TR III, 276, 26f.
50. Pannenberg, *What Is Man?*, 44 (my translation).
51. Adopted from the stimulating book by Martin E. Marty, *The Search for a Usable Future* (New York: Harper & Row, 1969) 144f.

Bibliography

(For further bibliographic information, particularly of a more specialized nature, please consult the footnotes.)

1. Introductory Material:

Allison, Henry E. *Lessing and the Enlightenment.* Ann Arbor: University of Michigan Press, 1966.

Althaus, Paul. *Die letzten Dinge: Lehrbuch der Eschatologie.* 7th ed. Gütersloh: Carl Bertelsmann, 1957.

Ariès, Philippe. *Western Attitudes Toward Death: From the Middle Ages to the Present.* Translated by Patricia M. Ranum. Baltimore: Johns Hopkins University Press, 1974.

Baillie, John. *The Belief in Progress.* New York: Scribner's, 1951.

Bainton, Roland Herbert. *Yesterday, Today, and What Next? Reflections on History and Hope.* Minneapolis: Augsburg, 1978.

Benz, Ernst. *Evolution and Christian Hope: Man's Concept of the Future from the Early Fathers to Teilhard de Chardin.* Translated by H. G. Frank. Garden City, N.Y.: Doubleday, Anchor Books, 1968.

Brunner, Emil. *Eternal Hope.* Translated by H. Knight. London: Lutterworth, 1954.

Collingwood, R. G. *The Idea of History.* London: Oxford University Press, 1957.

Dumont, Richard G., and Foss, Dennis C. *The American View of Death: Acceptance or Denial?* Cambridge, Mass.: Schenkman, 1972; distributed by General Learning Press, Morristown, N.J.

Eliade, Mircea. *Death, Afterlife, and Eschatology: A Thematic Source Book of the History of Religions,* Part 3 of *From Primitives to Zen.* New York: Harper & Row, 1974.

Gilkey, Langdon. *Naming the Whirlwind: The Renewal of God-Language.* Indianapolis: Bobbs-Merrill, 1969.

——. *Reaping the Whirlwind: A Christian Interpretation of History.* New York: Seabury, 1976.

Ginsberg, Morris. *Essays in Sociology and Social Philosophy.* Vol. 3: *Evolution and Progress.* New York: Macmillan, 1961.

Jaspers, Karl. *Origin and Goal of History.* Translated by M. Bullock. New Haven: Yale University Press, 1953.

Kant, Immanuel. "What Is Enlightenment?" *Foundations of the Metaphysics of Morals and What Is Enlightenment?* Translated with an Introduction by L. W. Beck. Indianapolis: Bobbs-Merrill, 1959. Pp. 85-92.

Löwith, Karl. *Meaning in History.* Chicago: University of Chicago Press, Phoenix Books, 1957.

Marty, Martin E. *The Search for a Usable Future.* New York: Harper & Row, 1969.

Mitford, Jessica. *The American Way of Death.* New York: Simon and Schuster, 1963.
Moltmann, Jürgen. *The Future of Hope.* New York: Herder & Herder, 1971.
———. *Theology of Hope: On the Ground and the Implications of a Christian Eschatology.* Translated by J. W. Leitch. New York: Harper & Row, 1967.
Niebuhr, H. Richard. *The Kingdom of God in America.* New York: Harper and Row, Harper Torchbooks, 1959.
Skrade, Carl. *God and the Grotesque.* Philadelphia: Westminster, 1974.
Stannard, David E. *The Puritan Way of Death: A Study in Religion, Culture and Social Change.* New York: Oxford University Press, 1977.
Toynbee, Arnold. *Civilization on Trial.* London: Oxford University Press, 1953.
Troeltsch, Ernst. *Protestantism and Progress: A Historical Study of the Relation of Protestantism to the Modern World.* Translated by W. Montgomery. Boston: Beacon, 1958.
Weber, Max. *The Protestant Ethic and the Spirit of Capitalism.* Translated by T. Parsons, with a Foreword by R. H. Tawney, London: George Allen & Unwin, 1948.

2. Old Testament and Related Areas:

Bentzen, Aage. *King and Messiah.* London: Lutterworth, 1955.
Eichrodt, Walther. *Theology of the Old Testament.* Translated by J. A. Baker. 2 vols. Philadelphia: Westminster, 1961-67.
Engnell, Ivan. *Critical Essays on the Old Testament.* Translated and edited by J. T. Willis with the collaboration of Helmer Ringgren. London: SPCK, 1970.
———. *Studies in Divine Kingship in the Ancient Near East.* Oxford: Blackwell, 1967.
Hooke, S. H., ed. *Myth and Ritual: Essays on the Myth and Ritual of the Hebrews in Relation to the Culture Pattern of the Ancient Near East.* London: Oxford University Press, 1933.
———, ed. *Myth, Ritual, and Kingship: Essays on the Theory and Practice of Kingship in the Ancient Near East and in Israel.* Oxford: Clarendon, 1958.
Jackson, A. V. Williams. *Zoroastrian Studies: The Iranian Religion and Various Monographs.* New York: AMS, 1965.
Jacob, Edmond. *Theology of the Old Testament.* Translated by A. W. Heathcote and Philip J. Allcock. London: Hodder & Stoughton, 1958.
Kraus, Hans-Joachim. *Worship in Israel: A Cultic History of the Old Testament.* Translated by G. Buswell. Richmond, Va.: John Knox, 1966.
Köhler, Ludwig. *Old Testament Theology.* Translated by A. S. Todd. Philadelphia: Westminster, 1957.
Mowinckel, Sigmund. *The Psalms in Israel's Worship.* Translated by D. R. Ap-Thomas. 2 vols. New York: Abingdon, 1962.
Nickelsburg, George W. E. *Resurrection, Immortality, and Eternal Life in Intertestamental Judaism.* Cambridge: Harvard University Press, 1972.
Nötscher, Friedrich. *Altorientalischer und alttestamentlicher Auferstehungsglauben.* Postscript by Josef Scharbert. Darmstadt: Wissenschaftliche Buchgesellschaft, 1970.
Rad, Gerhard von. *Genesis: A Commentary.* Translated by J. H. Marks. Philadelphia: Westminster, 1961.
———. *Old Testament Theology.* Vol. 1: *The Theology of Israel's Historical Traditions.* Translated by D. M. G. Stalker. Edinburgh: Oliver & Boyd, 1962.
———. *Old Testament Theology.* Vol. 2: *The Theology of Israel's Prophetic Traditions.* Translated by D. M. G. Stalker. New York: Harper & Row, 1965.
———. "The Theological Problem of the Old Testament Doctrine of Creation" (1936). *The Problem of the Hexateuch and Other Essays.* Translated by E. W. Trueman Dicken. Edinburgh: Oliver & Boyd, 1966. Pp. 131-43.

Rowley, H. H. *The Relevance of Apocalyptic: A Study of Jewish and Christian Apoca-lypses from Daniel to the Revelation.* New York: Harper & Brothers, 1955.
Russell, D. S. *The Method and Message of Jewish Apocalyptic: 200 BC-AD 100.* London: SCM, 1964.
Vriezen, Th. C. *An Outline of Old Testament Theology.* Newton, Mass.: Bradford, 1958.
————. "Prophecy and Eschatology." *Supplements to Vetus Testamentum.* Vol. 1: *Con-gress Volume, Copenhagen 1953.* Leiden: Brill, 1953. Pp. 199-229.
Westermann, Claus. *Beginning and End in the Bible.* Translated by Keith Crim. Phila-delphia: Fortress, Facet Books, 1972.
————. *The Praise of God in the Psalms.* Translated by Keith Crim. Richmond, Va.: John Knox, 1965.
Wolff, Hans Walter. *Anthropology of the Old Testament.* Translated by Margaret Kohl. Philadelphia: Fortress, 1974.
Zaehner, R. C. *The Dawn and Twilight of Zoroastrianism.* London: Weidenfeld and Nicol-son, 1961.
Zimmerli, Walther. *Man and His Hope in the Old Testament.* Studies in Biblical Theology, 2nd series, no. 20. Naperville, Ill.: Allenson, 1971.

3. New Testament:

Beasley-Murray, G. R. *A Commentary on Mark Thirteen.* London: Macmillan, 1957.
————. *Jesus and the Future: An Examination of the Criticism of the Eschatological Dis-course, Mark 13, with Special Reference to the Little Apocalypse Theory.* London: Mac-millan, 1954.
Bornkamm, Günther. *Jesus of Nazareth.* Translated by I. and F. McLuskey together with James M. Robinson. London: Hodder and Stoughton, 1960.
————. *Paul.* Translated by D. M. G. Stalker. New York: Harper & Row, 1971.
Brandon, S. G. F. *Jesus and the Zealots: A Study of the Political Factor in Primitive Christianity.* New York: Scribner's, 1969.
Brown, Raymond Edward. *The Virginal Conception and Bodily Resurrection of Jesus.* New York: Paulist, 1973.
Bultmann, Rudolf. *Faith and Understanding.* Vol. 1. Edited with an Introduction by R. W. Funk. Translated by L. P. Smith. London: SCM, 1969. The following essays con-tained in this volume are especially important for our topic:
"The Eschatology of the Gospel of John" (1928), pp. 165-83.
"The Christology of the New Testament," pp. 262-85.
"What Does It Mean to Speak of God?" (1925), pp. 53-65.
"On the Question of Christology" (1927), pp. 116-44.
"The Significance of the Historical Jesus for the Theology of Paul" (1929), pp. 220-46.
————. *The Gospel of John: A Commentary.* Translated by G. R. Beasley-Murray et al. Philadelphia: Westminster, 1971.
————. "History and Eschatology in the New Testament." *New Testament Studies* 1 (1954-55): 5-16.
————. *Jesus Christ and Mythology.* New York: Scribner's, 1958.
————. "New Testament and Mythology." *Kerygma and Myth: A Theological Debate.* Vol. 1. Edited by Hans Werner Bartsch. Translated by Reginald H. Fuller. London, SPCK, 1953. Pp. 1-44.
————. *The Presence of Eternity: History and Eschatology.* New York: Harper & Brothers, 1957.
————. *Theology of the New Testament.* Translated by K. Grobel. 2 vols. New York: Scribner's, 1951-55.

Conzelmann, Hans. *An Outline of the Theology of the New Testament.* Translated by J. Bowden. New York: Harper & Row, 1969.

———. *The Theology of St. Luke.* Translated by G. Buswell. London: Faber & Faber, 1960.

Cullmann, Oscar. *Christ and Time: The Primitive Christian Conception of Time and History.* Translated by Floyd V. Filson. London: SCM, 1962.

———. *The Christology of the New Testament.* Rev. ed. Translated by S. C. Guthrie and Charles A. M. Hall. Philadelphia: Westminster, 1963.

———. *Jesus and the Revolutionaries.* Translated by G. Putnam. New York: Harper & Row, 1970.

———. *Salvation in History.* Translated by S. G. Sowers *et al.* London: SCM, 1967.

Dibelius, Martin. *Paul.* Edited and completed by W. G. Kümmel. Translated by F. Clarke. Philadelphia: Westminster, 1953.

Dodd, C. H. *The Coming of Christ: Four Broadcast Addresses for the Season of Advent.* Cambridge: Cambridge University Press, 1954.

———. *The Epistle of Paul to the Romans.* New York: Harper & Brothers, 1932.

———. *The Founder of Christianity.* New York: Macmillan, 1970.

———. *The Interpretation of the Fourth Gospel.* Cambridge: Cambridge University Press, 1958.

———. *The Parables of the Kingdom.* New York: Scribner's, 1961.

Ellis, Edward Earle. *Eschatology in Luke.* Philadelphia: Fortress, Facet Books, 1972.

Evans, Christopher Francis. *Resurrection and the New Testament.* Studies in Biblical Theology, 2nd series, no. 12. Naperville, Ill.: Allenson, 1970.

Fridrichsen, Anton. *The Apostle and His Message.* Uppsala Universitets Årsskrift 1947:3. Uppsala: Lundequistska Bokhandeln, 1947.

Fuchs, Ernst. "The Quest of the Historical Jesus" (1956). *Studies of the Historical Jesus.* Translated by A. Scobie. Naperville, Ill.: Allenson, 1964. Pp. 11-31.

Fuller, Reginald Horace. *The Formation of the Resurrection Narratives.* New York: Macmillan, 1971.

Goguel, Maurice. *Jesus and the Origins of Christianity.* Vol. 2: *The Life of Jesus.* Translated by O. Wyon. New York: Harper & Row, Harper Torchbooks, 1960.

Hahn, Ferdinand. *The Titles of Jesus in Christology: Their History in Early Christianity.* Translated by H. Knight and G. Ogg. London: Lutterworth, 1969.

Hiers, Richard H. *The Historical Jesus and the Kingdom of God: Present and Future in the Message and Ministry of Jesus.* Gainesville: University of Florida Press, 1973.

Jeremias, Joachim. *The Parables of Jesus.* Translated by S. H. Hooke. New York: Scribner's, 1963.

Kümmel, Werner Georg. *Promise and Fulfilment: The Eschatological Message of Jesus.* Translated by D. M. Barton. Naperville, Ill.: Allenson, 1957.

Macquarrie, John. *The Scope of Demythologization: Bultmann and His Critics.* New York: Harper & Row, Harper Torchbooks, 1966.

Manson, T. W. *The Teaching of Jesus: Studies of Its Form and Content.* Cambridge: Cambridge University Press, 1948.

Moule, C. F. D. *The Birth of the New Testament.* New York: Harper & Row, 1962.

Perrin, Norman. *Rediscovering the Teaching of Jesus.* New York: Harper & Row, 1967.

———. *The Resurrection According to Matthew, Mark, and Luke.* Philadelphia: Fortress, 1977.

Robinson, James M. *A New Quest of the Historical Jesus.* Naperville, Ill.: Allenson, 1959.

Robinson, John A. T. *In the End, God.* New York: Harper & Row, 1968.

———. *Jesus and His Coming: The Emergence of a Doctrine.* London: SCM, 1957.

Rohde, Joachim. *Rediscovering the Teaching of the Evangelists.* Translated by D. M. Barton. London: SCM, 1968.

Schweitzer, Albert. *The Kingdom of God and Primitive Christianity.* Edited with an Intro-
duction by Ulrich Neuenschwander. Translated by L. A. Garrad. London: Black, 1968.
————. *The Mystery of the Kingdom of God: The Secret of Jesus' Messiahship and Passion.*
Translated with an Introduction by W. Lowrie. New York: Macmillan, 1950.
————. *The Quest of the Historical Jesus: A Critical Study of Its Progress from Reimarus
to Wrede.* With a Preface by F. C. Burkitt. Translated from the first German edition by
W. Montgomery. New York: Macmillan, 1966.
Stauffer, Ethelbert. *Jesus and His Story.* Translated by Richard and Clara Winston. New
York: Knopf, 1960.
————. *New Testament Theology.* Translated by J. Marsh. New York: Macmillan, 1959.
Taylor, Vincent. *The Gospel According to St. Mark.* London: Macmillan, 1957.
————. *The Names of Jesus.* New York: St. Martin's Press, 1953.
Tödt, Heinz Eduard. *The Son of Man in the Synoptic Tradition.* Translated   by D. M.
Barton. London: SCM, 1965.
Wilckens, Ulrich. *Resurrection: Biblical Testimony to the Resurrection: An Historical Ex-
amination and Explanation.* Translated by A. M. Stewart. Atlanta: John Knox, 1978.
Wilder, Amos N. *Eschatology and Ethics in the Teaching of Jesus.* Rev. ed. New York:
Harper & Brothers, 1950.
————. "Kerygma, Eschatology, and Social Ethics." *The Background of the New Testa-
ment and Its Eschatology.* Edited by W. D. Davies and D. Daube. Cambridge: Cambridge
University Press, 1956. Pp. 509-36.
————. *Otherworldliness and the New Testament.* New York: Harper & Brothers, 1954.
Williams, Sam K. *Jesus' Death as Saving Event: The Background and Origin of a Concept.*
Cambridge, Mass.: Harvard Theological Review, 1975; distributed by Scholars Press,
Missoula, Montana.

4. Present Discussion of Eschatology:

Alves, Ruben A. *A Theology of Human Hope.* New York: Corpus, 1971.
Assmann, Hugo. *Theology for a Nomad Church.* Translated by Paul Burns. Maryknoll,
N.Y.: Orbis, 1976.
Beardslee, William A. *A House for Hope: A Study in Process and Biblical Thought.* Phila-
delphia: Westminster, 1972.
Berkouwer, Gerrit Cornelis. *The Return of Christ.* Grand Rapids, Mich.: Eerdmans, 1972.
Braaten, Carl E. *Christ and Counter-Christ: Apocalyptic Themes in Theology and Culture.*
Philadelphia: Fortress, 1972.
————. *Eschatology and Ethics: Essays on the Theology and Ethics of the Kingdom of
God.* Minneapolis: Augsburg, 1974.
————. *The Future of God: The Revolutionary Dynamics of Hope.* New York: Harper &
Row, 1969.
————. "God and the Idea of the Future." *Dialog* 7 (Autumn 1968): 252-58.
————. "Toward a Theology of Hope." *Theology Today* 24 (July 1967): 208-26.
Buri, Fritz. *How Can We Still Speak Responsibly of God?* Translated by Charles D. Hard-
wick. Philadelphia: Fortress, 1968.
————. *Christian Faith in Our Time.* Translated by E. A. Kent. New York: Macmillan,
1966.
————. *Theology of Existence.* Translated by H. H. Oliver and G. Onder. Greenwood,
S.C.: Attic, 1965.
Capps, Walter H. *Hope Against Hope: From Moltmann to Merton in One Theological
Decade.* Philadelphia: Fortress, 1976.

————. *Time Invades the Cathedral: Tension in the School of Hope,* Philadelphia: Fortress, 1972.

Cone, James H. *God of the Oppressed.* New York: Seabury, 1975.

Elert, Werner. *Last Things.* Translated by Martin Bertram. Edited by Rudolph F. Norden. St. Louis: Concordia, 1974.

Ellul, Jacques. *Hope in Time of Abandonment.* Translated by C. Edward Hopkin. New York: Seabury, 1973.

Goulet, Denis. *A New Moral Order: Studies in Development Ethics and Liberation Theology.* Maryknoll, N.Y.: Orbis, 1974.

Gutiérrez, Gustavo. *A Theology of Liberation: History, Politics, and Salvation.* Translated and edited by Sister Caridad Inda and John Eagleson. Maryknoll, N.Y.: Orbis, 1973.

Herzog, Frederick. *Liberation Theology: Liberation in the Light of the Fourth Gospel.* New York: Seabury, 1977.

————. *The Theology of the Liberating Word.* Nashville: Abingdon, 1971.

————, ed. *The Future of Hope: Theology as Eschatology by Jürgen Moltmann with Harvey Cox and Others.* New York: Herder & Herder, 1970.

Macquarrie, John. *Christian Hope.* New York: Seabury, 1978.

Meeks, M. Douglas. *Origins of the Theology of Hope.* Foreword by Jürgen Moltmann. Philadelphia: Fortress, 1974.

Metz, Johannes Baptist. *Theology of the World.* Translated by W. Glen-Doepel. New York: Herder & Herder, 1969.

Miguez Bonino, José. *Doing Theology in a Revolutionary Situation.* Philadelphia: Fortress, 1975.

Moltmann, Jürgen. *The Experiment Hope.* Edited and translated with a Foreword by M. Douglas Meeks. Philadelphia: Fortress, 1975.

Mozley, E. N. *The Theology of Albert Schweitzer for Christian Inquirers.* With an Epilogue by Albert Schweitzer. London: Black, 1950.

Pannenberg, Wolfhart. *Basic Questions in Theology: Collected Essays.* Vol. 1. Translated by G. H. Kehm. Philadelphia: Fortress, 1970.

————. "Dogmatic Theses on the Doctrine of Revelation." *Revelation as History.* Edited by Wolfhart Pannenberg. Translated by D. Granskou. New York: Macmillan, 1968. Pp. 123-58.

Pittenger, William Norman. *"The Last Things" in a Process Perspective.* London: Epworth, 1970.

Reuther, Rosemary Radford. *The Radical Kingdom. The Western Experience of Messianic Hope.* New York: Harper & Row, 1970.

Schweitzer, Albert. *The Philosophy of Civilization.* Translated by C. T. Campion. New York: Macmillan, 1949.

Segundo, Juan Luis. *Liberation of Theology.* Translated by John Drury. Maryknoll, N.Y.: Orbis, 1976.

Shaull, Richard. "Christian Faith as Scandal in a Technocratic World." *New Theology No. 6.* Edited by Martin E. Marty and Dean G. Peerman. New York: Macmillan, 1969. Pp. 123-34.

————. "Does Religion Demand Social Change?" *Theology Today* 26 (April 1969):5-13.

————. *Encounter with Revolution.* New York: Association, 1955.

————. "Revolutionary Change in Theological Perspective." *Christian Social Ethics in a Changing World: An Ecumenical Theological Inquiry.* Edited by John C. Bennett. New York: Association, 1966. Pp. 23-43.

————. "Theology and the Transformation of Society." *Theology Today* 25 (April 1968): 23-36.

Sherman, Franklin, ed. *Christian Hope and the Future of Humanity.* Minneapolis: Augsburg, 1969.

Werner, Martin. *The Formation of the Christian Dogma: An Historical Study of Its Problem*. Translated with an Introduction by S. G. F. Brandon. New York: Harper and Brothers, 1957.

Woodyard, David O. *Beyond Cynicism: The Practice of Hope*. Philadelphia: Westminster, 1972.

5. Eschatology, Science, and Secular Varieties of Hope:

Augenstein, Leroy. *Come, Let Us Play God*. New York: Harper & Row, 1969.

Barnette, Henlee H. *The Church and the Ecological Crisis*. Grand Rapids: Eerdmans, 1972.

Becker, Ernest. *The Denial of Death*. New York: Free, 1973.

————. *Escape from Evil*. New York: Free, 1975.

Bloch, Ernst. *Das Prinzip Hoffnung*. 3 vols. Frankfurt am Main: Suhrkamp, 1969.

Camus, Albert. *The Fall*. Translated by J. O'Brien. New York: Knopf, 1960.

————. "The Growing Stone." *Exile and the Kingdom*. Translated by J. O'Brien. New York: Knopf, 1958.

————. *The Myth of Sisyphus and Other Essays*. Translated by J. O'Brien. New York: Knopf, 1967.

————. *The Rebel: An Essay on Man in Revolt*. Foreword by Sir Herbert Read. Translated by A. Bower. New York: Knopf, 1961.

Carson, Rachel. *Silent Spring*. Boston: Houghton Mifflin, 1962.

Cobb, John B. *Is It Too Late? A Theology of Ecology*. Beverly Hills, California: Bruce, 1972.

Cousins, Ewert H., ed. *Hope and the Future of Man*. Philadelphia: Fortress, 1972.

Demant, V. A. *The Idea of a Natural Order: With an Essay on Modern Asceticism*. Philadelphia: Fortress, Facet Books, 1966.

Detwyler, Thomas R., ed. *Man's Impact on Environment*. New York: McGraw-Hill, 1971.

Dobzhansky, Theodosius. *The Biology of Ultimate Concern*. New York: New American Library, 1967.

Elder, Frederick. *Crisis in Eden: A Religious Study of Man and Environment*. Nashville: Abingdon, 1970.

Falk, Richard A. *This Endangered Planet: Prospects and Proposals for Human Survival*. New York: Random House, 1971.

Ferkiss, Victor C. *The Future of Technological Civilization*. New York: Braziller, 1974.

Garaudy, Roger. *From Anathema to Dialogue: A Marxist Challenge to the Christian Churches*. Translated by L. O'Neill. New York: Herder and Herder, 1966.

Gilkey, Langdon. *Religion and the Scientific Future: Reflections on Myth, Science, and Theology*. New York: Harper & Row, 1970.

Gill, David M. *From Here to Where? Technology, Faith and the Future of Man*. Geneva: World Council of Churches, 1970.

Hefner, Philip. *The Promise of Teilhard. The Meaning of the Twentieth Century in Christian Perspective*. Philadelphia: Lippincott, 1970.

Heidegger, Martin. *Being and Time*. Translated by John Macquarrie and Edward Robinson. New York: Harper & Row, 1962.

Heilbroner, Robert L. *An Inquiry into the Human Prospect*. New York: Norton, 1974.

————. *Beyond Boom and Crash*. New York: Norton, 1978.

Heim, Karl. *Christian Faith and Natural Science*. Translated by N. H. Smith. London: SCM, 1953.

————. *The Transformation of the Scientific World View*. Translated by W. A. Whitehouse. London: SCM, 1953.

————. *The World: Its Creation and Consummation: The End of the Present Age and the*

Future of the World in the Light of the Resurrection. Translated by R. Smith. Philadelphia: Muhlenberg, 1962.

Heisenberg, Werner. *Physics and Philosophy: The Revolution in Modern Science.* New York: Harper & Brothers, 1958.

Humanist Manifestos I and II. Buffalo, N.Y.: Prometheus, 1973.

Klotz, John William. *Ecology Crisis: God's Creation and Man's Pollution.* St. Louis: Concordia, 1971.

Lorenz, Konrad. *Civilized Man's Eight Deadly Sins.* Translated by Marjorie Kerr Wilson. New York: Harcourt Brace Jovanovich, 1974.

Lubac, Henri de. *The Religion of Teilhard de Chardin.* Translated by R. Hague. New York: Desclee, 1967.

Lutz, Paul E., and Santmire, H. Paul. *Ecological Renewal.* Philadelphia: Fortress, Confrontation Books, 1972.

Mao Tse-tung. *Mao Tse-tung's Quotations: The Red Guard's Handbook.* Introduction by Steward Fraser. Nashville: International Center, George Peabody College for Teachers, 1967.

Marx, Karl, and Engels, Friedrich. *On Religion.* Introduction by Reinhold Niebuhr. New York: Schocken, 1964. The following excerpts and translations are especially important for our topic:

   Marx, *Capital: Book I* (Extracts), pp. 135-41.

   ———, "Contribution to the Critique of Hegel's Philosophy of Right" (Introduction), pp. 41-58.

   ———. "The Communism of the Paper *Rheinischer Beobachter*" (Extract), pp. 82-87.

   ———, *Theses on Feuerbach,* pp. 69-72.

   Engels, "On the History of Early Christianity," pp. 316-47.

Meadows, Donella H., *et al. The Limits to Growth: A Report for the Club of Rome's Project on the Predicament of Mankind.* New York: Universe, 1972.

Mesarovic, Mihajlo D., and Pestel, Eduard. *Mankind at the Turning Point: The Second Report to the Club of Rome.* New York: Dutton, 1974.

Moltmann, Jürgen. "Hope and Confidence: A Conversation with Ernst Bloch." *Dialog* 7 (Winter 1968): 42-55.

———. *Hope and Planning.* Translated by M. Clarkson. New York: Harper & Row, 1971.

Oestreicher, Paul, ed. *The Christian-Marxist Dialogue: An International Symposium.* London: Macmillan, 1969.

Pannenberg, Wolfhart. *What Is Man? Contemporary Anthropology in Theological Perspective.* Translated by D. A. Priebe. Philadelphia: Fortress, 1970.

Peters, Ted. *Futures: Human and Divine.* Atlanta: John Knox, 1978.

Raines, John C., and Dean, Thomas, eds. *Marxism and Radical Religion: Essays Toward a Revolutionary Humanism.* Philadelphia: Temple University Press, 1970.

Rosenfeld, Albert. *The Second Genesis: The Coming Control of Life.* Engelwood Cliffs, N.J.: Prentice-Hall, 1969.

Rosenstock-Huessy, Eugen. *The Christian Future: Or the Modern Mind Outrun.* Introduction by H. Stahmer. New York: Harper & Row, Harper Torchbooks, 1966.

Santmire, H. Paul. *Brother Earth: Nature, God, and Ecology in Time of Crisis.* New York: Nelson, 1970.

Sartre, Jean-Paul. *Being and Nothingness: An Essay on Phenomenological Ontology.* Translated with an Introduction by H. E. Barnes. New York: Philosophical Library, 1956.

Sherrell, Richard E. *Ecology: Crisis and New Vision.* Richmond, Va.: John Knox, 1971.

Slusser, Dorothy Mallett, and Slusser, Gerald H. *Technology: The God That Failed.* Philadelphia: Westminster, 1971.

Teilhard de Chardin, Pierre. *The Divine Milieu: An Essay on the Interior Life.* New York: Harper & Row, 1960.

————. *The Future of Man.* Translated by N. Denny. New York: Harper & Row, 1964.

————. *Hymn of the Universe.* New York: Harper & Row, 1965.

————. *The Phenomenon of Man.* Translated by B. Wall with an Introduction by J. Huxley. New York: Harper & Row, 1959.

White, Lynn, Jr. "The Historical Roots of Our Ecological Crisis." *Man's Impact on Environment,* Edited by Thomas R. Detwyler. New York: McGraw-Hill, 1971. Pp. 27-35.

6. Blind Alleys in Eschatology:

Althaus, Paul. *The Theology of Martin Luther.* Translated by R. C. Schultz. Philadelphia: Fortress, 1966.

Andrews, Edward D. *The People Called Shakers: A Search for the Perfect Society.* New York: Oxford University Press, 1953.

Barkun, Michael. *Disaster and the Millennium.* New Haven: Yale University Press, 1974.

Erickson, Millard J. *Contemporary Options in Eschatology: A Study of the Millennium.* Grand Rapids: Baker, 1977.

Hoekema, Anthony A. *The Bible and the Future.* Grand Rapids: Eerdmans, 1979.

————. *The Four Major Cults: Christian Science, Jehovah's Witnesses, Mormonism, Seventh-day Adventism.* Grand Rapids: Eerdmans, 1963.

Ladd, George Eldon. *The Blessed Hope.* Grand Rapids: Eerdmans, 1956.

Lindsey, Hal, with Carlson, C. C. *The Late Great Planet Earth.* Grand Rapids: Zondervan, 1970.

Ott, Ludwig. *Fundamentals of Catholic Dogma.* Edited by J. C. Bastible. Translated by P. Lynch. Cork, Ireland: Mercier, 1963.

Parker, Robert A. *A Yankee Saint: John Humphrey Noyes and the Oneida Community.* New York: Putnam's, 1935.

Plueger, Aaron Luther. *Things to Come for Planet Earth: What the Bible Says About the Last Times.* St. Louis: Concordia, 1977.

Prenter, Regin. *Creation and Redemption.* Translated by Thomas I. Jensen. Philadelphia: Fortress, 1967.

Saarnivaara, Uuras. *Armageddon, Before and After: Biblical End-Time Prophecies and Their Fulfillment in Our Time.* Minneapolis: Osterhus, n.d.

Schleiermacher, Friedrich. *The Christian Faith.* Edited by H. R. Mackintosh and J. S. Stewart. Edinburgh: T. & T. Clark, 1960.

Seeberg, Reinhold. *Text-Book of the History of Doctrines.* Translated by Charles E. Hay. 2 vols. Grand Rapids: Baker, 1958.

Tillich, Paul. *Systematic Theology.* Vol. 3: *Life and the Spirit, History and the Kingdom of God.* Chicago: University of Chicago Press, 1963.

Torrance, T. F. *Kingdom and Church: A Study in the Theology of the Reformation.* Edinburgh: Oliver and Boyd, 1956.

Walvoord, John F. *The Rapture Question.* Grand Rapids: Zondervan, 1957.

Wilkerson, David R., Kuhlman, Kathryn, *et al. Jesus Christ Solid Rock: The Return of Christ.* Grand Rapids: Zondervan, 1973.

7. Death, Immortality, and Resurrection:

Aldwinckle, Russell Foster. *Death in the Secular City: A Study of the Notion of Life After Death in Contemporary Theology and Philosophy.* London: George Allen and Unwin, 1972.

Aristotle, *The Basic Works of Aristotle.* Edited with an Introduction by Richard McKeon. New York: Random House, 1941.

Badham, Paul. *Christian Beliefs About Life After Death.* New York: Barnes & Noble, Library of Philosophy and Religion, 1976.

Barth, Karl. *Church Dogmatics.* Vol. 3/4: *The Doctrine of Creation.* Translated by A. T. Mackay et al. Edinburgh: T. & T. Clark, 1961.

Barth, Markus, and Fletcher, Verne H. *Acquittal by Resurrection.* New York: Holt, Rinehart, and Winston, 1964.

Beard, Paul. *Survival of Death: For and Against.* London: Hodder & Stoughton, 1966.

Benoit, Pierre, and Murphy, Roland Edmund, eds. *Immortality and Resurrection.* Vol. 60 of *Concilium.* New York: Herder & Herder, 1970.

Boros, Ladislaus. *The Mystery of Death.* New York: Seabury, 1973.

Brunner, Emil. *Dogmatics.* Vol. 3: *The Christian Doctrine of the Church, Faith, and the Consummation.* Translated by D. Cairns in collaboration with T. H. L. Parker. Philadelphia: Westminster, 1962.

Cargas, Henry J., and White, Ann, eds. *Death and Hope.* New York: Corpus, 1971.

Congdon, Howard K. *The Pursuit of Death.* Nashville: Abingdon, 1977.

Copleston, Frederick. *A History of Philosophy.* Vol. 1: *Greece and Rome.* Westminster, Md.: Newman, 1960.

Corell, Alf. *Consummatum Est: Eschatology and Church in the Gospel of St. John.* London: SPCK, 1958.

Cullmann, Oscar. *Immortality of the Soul or Resurrection of the Dead? The Witness of the New Testament.* London: Epworth, 1958.

Doss, Richard W. *The Last Enemy: A Christian Understanding of Death.* New York: Harper & Row, 1974.

Fortman, Edmund J. *Everlasting Life After Death.* New York: Alba, 1976.

Fremantle, Anne. *The Papal Encyclicals in Their Historical Context.* Introduction by G. Weigel. New York: New American Library, Mentor-Omega Books, 1963.

Gatch, Milton McC. *Death: Meaning and Mortality in Christian Thought and Contemporary Culture.* New York: Seabury, 1969.

Greinacher, Norbert, and Müller, Alois, eds. *The Experience of Dying.* Vol. 94 of *Concilium.* New York: Herder & Herder, 1974.

Hardon, John A. *The Catholic Catechism.* Garden City, N.Y.: Doubleday, 1975.

Hart, Hornell. *The Enigma of Survival: The Case for and Against an After Life.* London: Rider, 1959.

Jackson, Charles O., ed. *Passing: The Vision of Death in America.* Contributions in Family Studies, no. 2. Westport, Conn.: Greenwood, 1977.

Jüngel, Eberhard. *Death: The Riddle and the Mystery.* Translated by Iain and Ute Nicol. Philadelphia: Westminster, 1975.

Kant, Immanuel. *Critique of Practical Reason and Other Writings in Moral Philosophy.* Translated and edited with an Introduction by Lewis W. Beck. Chicago: University of Chicago Press, 1949.

Kübler-Ross, Elisabeth, ed. *Death: The Final Stage of Growth.* Engelwood Cliffs, N.J.: Prentice-Hall, 1975.

———. *On Death and Dying.* New York: Macmillan, 1969.

———. *Questions and Answers on Death and Dying.* New York: Macmillan, 1974.

Künneth, Walter. *The Theology of the Resurrection.* Translated by J. W. Leitch. St. Louis: Concordia, 1965.

Ladd, George Eldon. *I Believe in the Resurrection of Jesus.* Grand Rapids: Eerdmans, 1975.

Leibniz, Gottfried Wilhelm. *The Monadology and Other Philosophical Writings.* Translated with an Introduction and Notes by Robert Latta. London: Oxford University Press, 1951.

Mack, Arien, ed. *Death in American Experience*. New York: Schocken, 1973.

Maguire, Daniel C. *Death by Choice*. Garden City, N.Y.: Doubleday, 1974.

Marxsen, Willi. *The Resurrection of Jesus of Nazareth*. Translated by M. Kohl. Philadelphia: Fortress, 1970.

Matson, Archie. *The Waiting World: Or, What Happens at Death*. New York: Harper & Row, 1975.

Moody, Raymond A., Jr. *Life After Life*. Harrisburg, Pa.: Stackpole, 1976.

————. *Reflections on Life After Life*. Harrisburg: Stackpole, 1977.

Niebuhr, Richard R. *Resurrection and Historical Reason: A Study of Theological Method*. New York: Scribner's, 1957.

Nygren, Anders. *Commentary on Romans*. Translated by C. C. Rasmussen. Philadelphia: Muhlenberg, 1949.

Osis, Kārlis, and Haraldsson, Erlendur. *At the Hour of Death*. Introduction by Elisabeth Kübler-Ross. New York: Avon, 1977.

Penelhum, Terence, ed. *Immortality*. Belmont, California: Wadsworth, Basic Problems in Philosophy Series, 1973.

Pieper, Francis. *Christian Dogmatics*. Vol. 1. St. Louis: Concordia, 1950.

Pieper, Josef. *Death and Immortality*. New York: Herder & Herder, 1969.

Plato. *The Collected Dialogues of Plato Including the Letters*. Edited by Edith Hamilton and Hundington Cairns. New York: Bollingen, 1961.

Rahner, Karl. *Foundations of Christian Faith*. New York: Seabury, 1978.

————. *Theological Investigations*. Vol. 2: *Man in the Church*. Translated by K.-H. Kruger. Baltimore: Helicon, 1963. The following essays contained in this volume are especially important for our topic:

"Remarks on the Theology of Indulgences," pp. 175-201.

"The Resurrection of the Body," pp. 203-16.

————. *Theological Investigations*. Vol. 4: *More Recent Writings*. Translated by K. Smyth. Baltimore: Helicon, 1966. The following essays contained in this volume are especially important for our topic:

"The Hermeneutics of Eschatological Assertions," pp. 323-46.

"The Life of the Dead," pp. 347-54.

————. *On the Theology of Death*. New York: Herder & Herder, 1965.

Reichenbach, Bruce R. *Is Man the Phoenix? A Study of Immortality*. Grand Rapids: Eerdmans, 1977.

Reynolds, Frank E., and Waugh, Earle H., eds. *Religious Encounters with Death: Insights from the History and Anthropology of Religion*. University Park: Pennsylvania State University Press, 1977.

Rhine, J. B., and Brier, Robert, eds. *Parapsychology Today*. New York: Citadel, 1968.

Schwarz, Hans. "Luther's Understanding of Heaven and Hell." *Interpreting Luther's Legacy*. Edited by Fred W. Meuser and Stanley D. Schneider. Minneapolis: Augsburg, 1969. Pp. 83-94.

Shibles, Warren A. *Death: An Interdisciplinary Analysis*. Whitewater, Wis.: Language, 1974.

Smith, Harmon L. *Ethics and the New Medicine*. Nashville: Abingdon, 1970.

Swihart, Philip J. *The Edge of Death*. Downers Grove, Ill.: InterVarsity, 1978.

Taylor, Michael J., ed. *The Mystery of Suffering and Death*. Staten Island, N.Y.: Alba, 1973.

Torrance, Thomas Forsyth. *Space, Time, and Resurrection*. Grand Rapids: Eerdmans, 1976.

Tyrrell, G. N. M. *Science and Psychical Phenomena: Apparitions*. New Hyde Park, N.Y.: University, 1961.

Veatch, Robert M. *Death, Dying, and the Biological Revolution: Our Last Quest for Responsibility*. New Haven: Yale University Press, 1976.

Wingren, Gustav. *Luther on Vocation*. Translated by C. C. Rasmussen. Philadelphia: Muhlenberg, 1957.

8. The New World to Come:

Edwards, David Lawrence. *The Last Things Now*. London: SCM, 1969.

Fackre, Gabriel J. *The Rainbow Sign: Christian Futurity*. Grand Rapids: Eerdmans, 1969.

Heim, Karl. *Jesus the World's Perfector: The Atonement and the Renewal of the World*. Translated by D. H. von Daalen. Philadelphia: Muhlenberg, 1961.

Kaufman, Gordon D. *Systematic Theology: A Historicist Perspective*. New York: Scribner's, 1968.

Kik, Jacob Marcellus. *The Eschatology of Victory*. Introduction by Rousas John Rushdoony. Nutley, N.J.: Presbyterian and Reformed Publishing Company, 1971.

Ladd, George Eldon. *The Last Things: An Eschatology for Laymen*. Grand Rapids: Eerdmans, 1978.

——. *The Presence of the Future: The Eschatology of Biblical Realism*. Grand Rapids: Eerdmans, 1974.

Moody, Dale. *The Hope of Glory*. Grand Rapids: Eerdmans, 1964.

Nietzsche, Friedrich. *The Gay Science. The Portable Nietzsche*. Selected and translated with an Introduction, Preface, and Notes by Walter Kaufman. New York: Viking, 1960.

Pannenberg, Wolfhart. *Theology and the Kingdom of God*. Philadelphia: Westminster, 1969.

Papin, Joseph, ed. *The Eschaton: A Community of Love*. Villanova, PA: Villanova University Press, 1971.

Smedes, Lewis B. *All Things Made New: A Theology of Man's Union with Christ*. Grand Rapids: Eerdmans, 1970.

Travis, Stephen. *The Jesus Hope*. Downers Grove, Ill.: InterVarsity Press, 1976.

Wainwright, Geoffrey. *Eucharist and Eschatology*. London: Epworth, 1971.

Index of Names

Index of Subjects

Index of Biblical References